AN INTRODUCTION TO

SUSTAINABLE

DEVELOPMENT

AN INTRODUCTION TO

SUSTAINABLE

DEVELOPMENT

PETER P. ROGERS • KAZI F. JALAL • JOHN A. BOYD

Published by
Glen Educational Foundation, Inc.

publishing for a sustainable future

First published by Earthscan in the UK and USA in 2008
Reprinted 2008

ISBN: 978-1-84407-520-1   (paperback)
       978-1-84407-521-8   (hardback)

Preliminary production work by Island Publishing House, Inc., Philippines
Editing by Stephen J. Banta, David Sheniak, and Anita Feleo
Formatting by Segundo P. dela Cruz Jr., Zenaida S. Antonio, and Dyosa Marie S. Antonio
Information technology by Joseph Reyes and Roberto S. Anselmo
Design and layout by Felix Mago Miguel
Layout Assistant: Susan Lascano-Dungan
Final typesetting by JS Typesetting Ltd, Porthcawl, Mid Glamorgan
Printed and bound in the UK by MPG Books Ltd, Bodmin, Cornwall
Cover design by Susanne Harris

Materials sourced from the Asian Development Bank are reproduced with its permission. For more information on development in Asia and the Pacific, see www.adb.org.
Materials were also sourced from the United Nations System, including the World Bank. Some pictures were provided by Asian Development Bank (Chapters 1, 2, 4, 5, 6, 7, 8, 9, 10, 11, 12. and 15) and Felix Mago Miguel (Chapters 3, 13, and 14).

For a full list of publications please contact:

Earthscan
Dunstan House
14a St Cross Street
London, EC1N 8XA, UK
Tel: +44 (0)20 7841 1930
Fax: +44 (0)20 7242 1474
Email: earthinfo@earthscan.co.uk
Web: **www.earthscan.co.uk**

22883 Quicksilver Drive, Sterling, VA 20166-2012, USA

Earthscan publishes in association with the International Institute for Environment and Development

A catalogue record for this book is available from the British Library

Library of Congress Cataloging-in-Publication Data

Rogers, Peter P., 1937-
        An introduction to sustainable development / Peter P. Rogers, Kazi F. Jalal, John A. Boyd.
           p. cm.
        Includes bibliographical references and index.
        ISBN-13: 978-1-84407-521-8 (hbk.)
        ISBN-13: 978-1-84407-520-1 (pbk.)
    1. Sustainable development. 2. Environmental policy. I. Jalal, Kazi F. II. Boyd, John A., 1942- III. Title.
        HC79.E5R63134 2007
        338.9'27—dc22

                                                                                    2007039463

CONTENTS

FOREWORD

The concept of sustainable development has been evolving for more than 30 years. The 1972 United Nations (UN) Conference on the Human Environment in Stockholm, Sweden, contributed to this evolution by emphasizing that protection of the human environment is a crucial element in the development agenda. As a result of that conference, the United Nations Environment Programme Secretariat was established to promote international environmental cooperation. On the national front, countries throughout the world began to set up or improve their respective environmental institutions. Earlier, in 1970, the United States had already established the Environmental Protection Agency for a cleaner, healthier country.

In 1987, the World Commission on Environment and Development, chaired by then Prime Minister of Norway Gro Harlem Brundtland, issued a report entitled *Our Common Future*. Also known as the Brundtland Report, this landmark document suggests that creating separately existing environmental institutions is not enough because environmental issues are an integral part of all development policies. They are crucial to economic considerations and sector policies and should be integrated as part of energy decisions, social issues, and other aspects of development work.

The next milestone in the evolution of sustainable development occurred at the 1992 UN Conference of Environment and Development in Rio de Janeiro, also known as the Earth Summit. Its major contribution was to give equal importance to the environment and development. It endorsed Agenda 21, both a think piece and a program of action governing human activities with an impact on the environment. It also endorsed the Rio Declaration on Environment and Development, and the Statement of Forest Principles.

Most importantly, the Earth Summit helped finalize the UN Climate Change Convention and the Biodiversity Convention, both signed by a great number of heads of state. The UN Climate Change Convention and the recently ratified Kyoto Protocol have made significant contributions to the evolution of sustainable development. Article 4 of the UN Climate Change Convention provides that "the Parties [to that Convention] have the right to, and should, promote development." The Kyoto Protocol's Clean Development Mechanism is designed in part to assist participating developing countries "in achieving sustainable development."

At the 2002 World Summit on Sustainable Development held in Johannesburg, South Africa, heads of state and world leaders committed to implement Agenda 21. They also decided to carry out a plethora of partnerships to promote sustainable development. These endeavors in our common cause have made sustainable development a part of everybody's vocabulary and agenda. Once of concern only to environmental specialists, sustainable development has become a concept that concerns everyone.

Since the phrase "sustainable development" gained prominence after the 1987 publication of *Our Common Future*, it has been defined in many ways, as described in the first chapter of this book. When did the concept of sustainable development reach the academic world? In the 1960s, a broadly conceived concept of sustainable development was unheard of in the halls of academe. By the 1980s, courses dealing with environmental impacts of industrial activities, especially problems arising from air pollution and toxic waste, were introduced into the curriculum.

During the same decade, the idea of conservation was gathering momentum. People were becoming more aware of the value of wildlife—of birds, of fish and other marine species, of plants and forests. As the importance of looking at all aspects of natural life gained wider appreciation, environmental programs were broadened to include natural resources management.

Taking conservation a step further, while looking at the plants, water, and air, people began to ask what place they themselves have in the environment. Should not people also be a part of the environmental picture? People observed that many of the poor were becoming poorer. Some of them were suffering from destroyed forests or declining stocks of fish. Still others were becoming poorer as a consequence of being resettled to facilitate development projects. A great many people were adversely affected by pollution. Should not environmental concerns also encompass social concerns? As a consequence, not only have studies in environmental and social fields begun to dovetail, but the study of environmental economics has emerged with clearer definition. In like manner, environmental law, environmental journalism, and other related disciplines have developed.

From my perspective at the Asian Development Bank (ADB), where we deal with investments, we have to be realistic. If ADB is to loan more than $6 billion in a year, such loans have to make sense. Otherwise, there will be no takers.

It is the same with sustainable development. The concept has to be adapted to the real world so that it makes sense to finance ministers, economists, entrepreneurs, environmentalists, anthropologists, investors, traders, and other development people. In this way everyone who is concerned will make investments as well as produce, consume and participate in creating what is needed in a sustainable manner.

In the 1980s, ADB established an Office of the Environment. By the 1990s, ADB had an Office of Environment and Social Development headed by Kazi Jalal, and I worked for him as manager of the Environment Division. In 2002, ADB established the Department of Regional and Sustainable Department, which I headed until last year. My work experience has taught me a few lessons.

First, every development project and program must be economically and financially viable. This is why economic and financial considerations are integral factors in making sustainable development decisions.

Second, every development project and program must be environmentally sound. We cannot have projects or programs with unacceptable impacts on our environment, because such impacts can overwhelm the benefits of any development.

Third, we have to take into account social issues. People and the environment are part of every development program and project. Clearly, people and the environment do not exist apart from each other. Any significant change introduced into the environment will likely change people's lives, including those of women, indigenous peoples, and the youth of the world. Also of key importance are how to achieve and maintain good governance and sustainable institutions. If a program or project is not governed properly, or if concerned institutions provide insufficient support, any related development program or project will not be sustainable.

In sum, sustainable development has many aspects, including economic and financial, environmental and ecological, as well as social.

I recommend this book because it deals with all of these aspects. The authors designed it to help the reader to learn the key ideas and tools of sustainable development. Accordingly, they present a holistic concept of sustainable development.

This book can help us learn better, more sustainable ways of producing, consuming, investing and otherwise participating in projects and programs in both the developing and the developed world. In this way we can contribute to the achievement of the Millennium Development Goals and respond affirmatively to the call in Our Common Future for "a new development path" for "sustained human progress not just in a few places for a few years, but for the entire planet into the distant future."

Bindu N. Lohani
Vice President, Finance and Administration
Asian Development Bank
Metro Manila, Philippines
11 July 2007

PREFACE

This book is based in part on lectures and materials used in a course on sustainable development at the Harvard Extension School. It is designed to introduce students and others to basic definitions, challenges, and perspectives arising under the heading of sustainable development. The book, in its draft form, was used as the textbook for the courses in the fall of 2004 and 2005.

Sustainable development is a broad, interdisciplinary concept that could be analyzed at a length greater than many who are seeking a basic introduction might wish. This book does not attempt a comprehensive review of all contributions to sustainable development, but does deal with all three dimensions—environmental, economic, and social—of sustainable development. Of necessity this introductory book is selective in dealing with the issues and perspectives presented.

The book introduces the concept and practice of sustainable development and presents some of its key challenges including poverty reduction. It deals with consumption, production, and distribution as the principal determinants of sustainable development. The focus is on a new production revolution (both industrial and agricultural) which aims at minimizing the current problems of unsustainable production systems.

Selected issues on the environment that influence sustainable development have been presented. These include environmental management policies and tools; the environmental impacts of infrastructures; environmental indicators; and environmental legislation and institutions related to development.

An understanding of the economics of sustainability and natural resources accounting are essential for promoting sustainable development. Accordingly, the book deals with the evolution of economic thinking on the environment; the issue of policy and market failures with several examples; the concepts of welfare, externalities and valuation, and how they affect development decisions.

On the social dimensions of sustainable development, the book presents a strategy to reduce poverty based on sound economic growth, distributional effectiveness, and population planning. It also deals with selected social issues affecting sustainable development including the participation of all categories of stakeholders in a development project; and the principles and practices of involuntary resettlement, gender mainstreaming, and social exclusion.

The final chapter deals primarily with the coming crisis, conflict, and need for compromise. The Epilogue also recognizes that we all need to work together to achieve sustainable development. This includes nongovernment organizations, social entrepreneurs, and corporations. Clearly, individuals at the grassroots levels and local and regional level organizations will play salient roles in the achievement of sustainable development.

We recognize that many of the topics in the book could, in their own right, be the subject of an introductory book. Even a subtopic in the chapter on Social Dimensions such as the relationship between indigenous peoples and sustainable development would be worthy of an analysis longer than that offered in an introductory book. In an effort not to overwhelm readers seeking an introduction to sustainable development, we have tried to limit the discussion of each such topic or subtopic to basic information, issues, and descriptions. We trust that the reader will forgive us for the lack of completeness in dealing with some of these topics.

This book was initially prepared with assistance from Island Publishing House, Inc., in Manila, Philippines. The present version is a revision of that book. We have tried to be clear, concise, and complete. Nevertheless, we recognize that in numerous areas the book needs further refinement and that many of the materials may need to be updated and perhaps expanded to take into account recent events. We invite readers to bring to our attention ways in which we can improve the book.

Grants from the GLEN Foundation, a not-for-profit Philippine corporation, supported production of this book. GLEN stands for Governance, Law and Environment Network. The GLEN Foundation is contributing to various projects designed to create a more sustainable future.

Despite its shortcomings, we hope that readers will find that this book leads to a better understanding of the concept of sustainable development, the policy choices presented to each of us to achieve sustainable development, and the opportunity to achieve human well-being in a way that was not discussed before. Let us keep in mind what Albert Einstein once stated: "The world we have created today as a result of our thinking thus far has problems that cannot be solved by thinking the way we thought when we created them." (Nattrass and Altomare, 1999, Chapter 2, p. 2.)

Peter P. Rogers
Kazi F. Jalal
John A. Boyd
Cambridge, Massachusetts
11 July 2007

ACKNOWLEDGEMENTS

There are many contributors to the intellectual life of this book; the most important being John A. Dixon, Kristalina Georgieva, and Warren Evans, at the time all senior staff of the World Bank, who gave guest lectures in our course on Sustainable Development on economics, environmental management, and sustainable development as practiced by their own institution. Dixon was particularly helpful when we were drafting Chapters 9, 10, and 11, as were Georgieva and Evans in informing Chapter 12.

In addition to these early contributors, the list of contributors to this book has grown to include many others located in Metro Manila, Philippines, where the initial pilot edition was published, as well as elsewhere. In preparing the text, the technical editor, John Boyd, was assisted by: Stephen J. Banta, David Sheniak, and Anita Feleo. Formatting was done by Segundo P. dela Cruz Jr., Zenaida S. Antonio, and Dyosa Marie S. Antonio. Information technology work was handled by Joseph Reyes and Roberto S. Anselmo. Felix Mago Miguel designed the layout of the book with the assistance of Susan Lascano-Dungan, all of The Philippines.

Additional thanks are due to Raul Pangalangan, Dean of the School of Law of the University of the Philippines, and Professor Kheng-Lian Koh of the Faculty of Law of the National University of Singapore for their comments on Chapter 7. Thanks as well are extended to Professor John Malcolm Dowling; Piya Abeygunawardena; Anne Sweetser; Eugenia McGill; Francoise Burhenne Guillman, Senior Counsel of the Center for Environmental Law of the International Union for the Conservation of Nature; and Amber Pant, Professor of Law, Tribhuvan University for reading and commenting on various chapters.

An initial pilot edition by Island Publishing House, Inc., was used as the text in the Extension School in the fall of 2004 and 2005. The present book incorporates feedback from that course and from reviewers. About 300 students from locations spanning the globe have taken the courses over the last six years and we gratefully acknowledge their comments and suggestions; their questions and term papers helped us to sharpen the presentation.

The authors greatly appreciate assistance provided by Professor Jack Spengler of the Harvard School of Public Health and Len Evanchick of the Harvard Extension School in encouraging us to write this book. We are also grateful for the assistance and support of Mary Higgins, Assistant Dean of Continuing Education at the Extension School of Harvard University.

Our graduate students and teaching assistants; Molly Kile, Scott Kennedy, Junenette Peters, Amy Zota, Casey Brown, and Linda Liang, were very helpful in bringing the book to fruition. Grateful thanks are also extended to assistant librarian Nelia R. Balagapo of the ADB Law Library and Larisa Duponte, staff assistant in the Division of Engineering and Applied Sciences at Harvard University.

We are especially thankful to Molly Kile and Scott Kennedy for their assistance in teaching the courses and redrafting portions of the text. Molly Kile completed her doctorate in 2006 and is now a member of the teaching faculty for the course, Scott Kennedy is now an Assistant Professor at the Malaysian University of Technology, and Junenette Peters and Casey Brown now hold academic positions at Harvard School of Public Health and the Earth Institute at Columbia University, respectively. Finally, a special thanks is due Margaret Owens who seized the moment, made the index, edited the revised texts, checked the references, and made a timely production of this edition possible.

Cambridge, Massachusetts
11 July, 2007

AUTHORS AND CONTRIBUTORS

Dr. Peter P. Rogers is Gordon McKay Professor of Environmental Engineering and Professor of City Planning, Harvard University.

Dr. Kazi F. Jalal is a Lecturer at Harvard's Extension School, and was the Chief of the Office of Environment and Social Development of the Asian Development Bank and the Director of the Division of Industry, Human Settlements and Environment of UN/ESCAP.

John A. Boyd was a guest lecturer in the 2002, 2004, 2005, and 2006 Harvard Extension School course on sustainable development. Formerly he was a lawyer for the U.S. Department of State and the Asian Development Bank. He also was Principal Sector Specialist (Sustainable Development) for ADB.

Dr. John A. Dixon, was a guest lecturer in the 2002 Harvard Extension School course on sustainable development, and formerly an environmental economist at the World Bank.

Dr. Kristalina Georgieva was Director of the Environment Department in the Environmentally and Socially Sustainable Development Vice Presidency and Chair of the Environment Sector Board of the World Bank when she was a guest lecturer in the 2002 Harvard Extension School course on sustainable development.

J. Warren Evans was the Director of the World Bank's Department of Environment in 2004 and 2005 when he was a guest lecturer. Previously he was Director of the Environment and Social Safeguard Division within the Regional and Sustainable Development Department of ADB.

Dr. Scott Kennedy was a Support Teaching Staff for the 2002 Harvard Extension School course on sustainable development.

Dr. Molly Kile is a Research Associate at the Harvard School of Public Health and has been a Support Teaching Staff of the Harvard Extension School course on sustainable development since 2002.

ABBREVIATIONS AND ACRONYMS

ADB	Asian Development Bank
BCA	benefit-cost analysis
BMI	body mass index
BOD	biochemical oxygen demand
CEQ	Council on Environmental Quality
CFC	chlorofluorocarbon
CO	carbon monoxide
CO_2	carbon dioxide
COR	cost of remediation
CPI	consumer price index
DDT	dichlorodiphenyltrichloroethane
DFI	development finance institution
DFID	Department for International Development, United Kingdom
DNA	deoxyribonucleic acid
EIA	environmental impact assessment
EIRR	economic internal rate of return
EIS	environmental impact study
EPA	Environmental Protection Agency, United States
ESCAP	United Nations Economic and Social Commission for Asia and the Pacific
EU	European Union
FAO	Food and Agricultural Organization
FIRR	financial internal rate of return
GDP	gross domestic product
GE	genetically engineered (in relation to crops)
GEF	Global Environmental Facility
GM	genetically modified (in relation to crops)
GNP	gross national product
GPI	genuine progress indicator
HDI	human development index
HIID	Harvard Institute for International Development
IADB	Inter-American Development Bank
IBRD	International Bank for Reconstruction and Development
ICJ	International Court of Justice
IEE	initial environmental examination
ILO	International Labour Organization
IMF	International Monetary Fund
IP(s)	indigenous people(s)
IRRI	International Rice Research Institute
IUCN	World Conservation Union
Lao PDR	Lao People's Democratic Republic
MBDOE	million barrels daily oil equivalent

MDB	multilateral development bank
MDG	Millennium Development Goal
MEA	multilateral environmental agreement
MFI	multilateral financing institution
MIQR	modified interquartile range
NAAQS	National Ambient Air Quality Standard
NEPA	National Environmental Policy Act
NGO	nongovernment organization
NPK	nitrogen, phosphorus, and potassium
O_3	ozone
ODA	overseas development assistance
OECD	Organisation for Economic Co-operation and Development
OPEC	Organization of Petroleum Exporting Countries
PCF	Prototype Carbon Fund
PPP	purchasing power parity
PRC	People's Republic of China
PSI	pollution standard index
RSA	rapid social assessment
SDE	social development elasticity
SDI	social development indicator
SDS	social design study
SEA	strategic environmental assessment
SO_2	sulfur dioxide
SUV	sports utility vehicle
TSP	total suspended particulates
UK	United Kingdom
UN	United Nations
UNCED	United Nations Conference on Environment and Development
UNCHE	United Nations Conference on the Human Environment
UNDP	United Nations Development Programme
UNEP	United Nations Environment Programme
UNFPA	United Nations Population Fund (Fonds des Nations Unis pour la population)
US	United States
USAID	United States Agency for International Development
WB	World Bank
WCED	World Commission on Environment and Development
WEO	World Environment Organization
WHO	World Health Organization
WSSD	World Summit on Sustainable Development
WTO	World Trade Organization
WWF	World Wildlife Fund (for Nature)
ha	hectare
kg	kilogram
mg	milligram

FROM MALTHUS TO SUSTAINABLE DEVELOPMENT

W hat do we mean by sustainability? First, we will talk about some ideas surrounding the issue articulated by various thinkers. Since a discussion of sustainability can cover a time span between now and kingdom come, we will keep our discussion within a realistic time frame. We will deal with the challenges of sustainable development, including environmental policy management and some social dimensions. And we will utilize some environmental economics, because economics is quite important in understanding some of the potentials and problems when we talk about sustainability and development.

SOME INTELLECTUAL UNDERPINNINGS
(AND A DISCLAIMER)

In 1798, Thomas Malthus, an economist and a country pastor in England, wrote *An Essay on the Principle of Population*, revised in 1803 as *An Essay on the Principle of Population; or, a View of its past and present Effects on Human Happiness; with an Inquiry into our Prospects respecting the Removal or Mitigation of the Evils which it occasions*. He believed that population was held in check by *"misery, vice, and moral restraint."* Malthus maintained that *"... population, when unchecked, increased in a geometrical ratio, and subsistence for man in an arithmetical ratio."*

The debate about Malthusian limits has raged over the centuries, with many critics asking how it became possible to have a six-fold increase in global population (from one to six billion) since 1798 and still be able to more or less feed the population. As recently as 1973 a renewed burst of Malthusianism was published by the Club of Rome in a book entitled *Limits to Growth*, by Donella Meadows et al. (1972). Most if not all of the Club of Rome's predictions for the next 30 years, from 1973 to 2003, were not borne out. Another leading Malthusian, Lester Brown, has over the years regaled us with many jeremiads of gloom and doom predicting dire consequences within the next few years, which never seem to be quite fulfilled, but which are plausible based upon projecting trends. An expert on crop production, Brown set up the prolific World Watch Institute in 1974, which has provided much-appreciated summaries of the global use of natural resources and the environment, usually accompanied by warnings of imminent collapse. Brown's annual *State of the World* series and the associated working papers have been important steps in the development of the concepts on sustainability. Despite their tone of immediate collapse, the Malthusians provided a useful reminder to society and governments that continued profligate consumption could sooner or later get us into trouble.

In addition to the well-founded evidence that we had, indeed, not run out of resources as the Malthus hypothesis predicted, there arose a school of thought referred to as the *cornucopians*. The group dismisses Malthus and sees instead an ever-increasing human population enjoying ever more benefits from the planet. In contrast to Malthus, Ester Boserup (1981) believed *"necessity is the mother of invention,"* and asserted that the increase in population pressure acts as an incentive to developing new technology and producing more food. Her analysis concluded that population growth naturally leads to development, at which point population pressures would decline. Writers such as Julian Simon (1981) and Wilfred Beckerman (2003) also disagreed with Malthus. Simon saw a future limited only by human ingenuity, not by mundane issues such as food and energy consumption; Beckerman sees the future as not resource limited, but limited by humans' inability to get the economic institutions right. Even as long ago as 1848 Karl Marx saw ever-expanding consumption possibilities, based surprisingly upon the enterprise of the capitalists in promoting globalization. (This was pointed out by the major cornucopian, Herman Khan (1976), in his book, *The Next Two Hundred Years*.)

More recently there has been a series of important books promoting more nuanced views of the Malthus/Cornucopian debate. Bjørn Lomborg's *The Skeptical Environmentalist: Measuring the Real State of the World* in 2001 and Jared Diamond's 2005 *Collapse: How Societies Choose to Fail or Succeed* both in their own ways look carefully at ecosystems from a historical perspective and draw mixed conclusions with, in some cases, dire consequences for societies that misbehave environmentally and adaptive survival strategies in others. Both see social and political adaptability as the major difference between catastrophe and survival.

Despite more than a generation since the resurgence of Malthusian ideas, we still do not have a consensus as to how seriously impaired the world ecosystems are, or the potential for continued development for the growing population. The United Nations (UN) and its resource agencies, UNDP, UNESCO, UNFPA, WHO, WMO, UNIDO, and the global multinational funding agencies such as the World Bank, the Inter-American Development Bank, the Asian Development Bank, the African Development Bank, and the European Bank for Reconstruction and Development all report with reasonable frequency upon the status of the environment and the ecosystems in their areas of interest. The news from the agencies is typically mixed. The good news is that we can feed more than 6.5 billion people with enough food to keep them functioning each day of the year. The bad news is that we appear to be seriously compromising our life support systems to accomplish this.

This was borne out in a special series on the "State of the Planet" in November 2003 in *Science*. The authors looked selectively at air, fresh water, fisheries, food and soil, energy, biodiversity (including human species), and climate change. As the editor of the series, H. Jesse Smith (2003), said:

> This collection of articles is offered in the spirit of "forewarned is forearmed," not "the sky is falling." Whether we find ourselves forearmed or under the fallen sky depends upon what we choose to do about these issues over the next generation.

Who then is to be believed and what, if anything, should be done? The irony of the debate is that Malthus wrote his original essay to counteract what he thought to be dangerous ideas about human perfectibility being propounded at that time. Nowadays most Malthusians coat their recommendations and aspirations in terms of human perfectibility. (Gus Speth's 2004 book, *Red Sky at Night*, is an example of this hortatory style.) The debate still swirls around us. What should we attempt to do? Our goal is to avoid the major intellectual perils on both sides of the coin. We must look coldly and soberly on what we know and have experienced and what is predictable in the short run and then settle on the continuum between the two sides of the issue. Intuition, if nothing else, tells us that Malthus makes sense in the long run: we just cannot keep on expanding and using resources, because something will be exhausted in the end. But in the short run, we can rely on human ingenuity to get us through the next 30 or 50 years. After that, all bets are off. Our definition, therefore, of sustainability is time-bound to a couple of human generations. Along with the journal *Science*, we believe this is the most scientifically supportable position to take.

WHY SUSTAINABILITY?

Sustainability is the term chosen to bridge the gulf between development and environment. Originally it came from forestry, fisheries, and groundwater, which dealt with quantities such as "maximum sustainable cut," "maximum sustainable yield," and "maximum sustainable pumping rate." How many trees can we cut and still have forest growth? How many fish can we take and still have a fishery functioning at the end of the time period? How much ground water can we draw and still have a viable aquifer at the end of the pumping period? Even when these "maximums" are observed, the ecosystem itself is not necessarily sustainable, as these are just the components of the overall ecosystem. Furthermore, sustainability can often be achieved in the short run, but not necessarily in the long run.

The attempt now is to apply the concept of all aspects of development simultaneously. The problem is, we experience difficulties in defining sustainable development precisely or even defining it operationally.

The major discussion initiating sustainable development is found in the report of the World Commission on Environment and Development (WCED), a body created by the UN General Assembly in 1983. This Commission was headed by Gro Brundtland, then prime minister of Norway and later head of the World Health Organization. The Commission's 1987 report, often referred to as the Brundtland Commission Report, defined "sustainable development" as development that "meets the needs of the present without compromising the ability of future generations to meet their own needs."

How is sustainable development to be achieved? This question harkens back to the sustainable fishery concept. What is a sustainable fishery? Should we ask what number of whales is sustainable? Many think that having more whales is probably better than having fewer whales. And we do not really need to eat whale meat. We have domesticated animals that we could use for that purpose.

Robert Repetto focuses his discussion of sustainable development on "... increasing long-term wealth and well-being." In his 1986 book, *World Enough and Time*, Repetto wrote that "the core idea of sustainability is that current decisions should not impair the prospects for maintaining or improving future living standards. This implies that our economic systems should be managed so that we can live off the dividends of our resources." By "resources" Repetto includes natural and otherwise, considering both as an endowment fund. As he was connected at the time with the World Bank, it is understandable that Repetto's definition relies heavily on economic concepts.

Herman E. Daly, who was also with the World Bank, suggested an ethical concept. In 1987 he talked about requiring an "increase in moral knowledge or ethical capital for mankind."

John C.V. Pezzey, another former World Bank official, listed (Rogers et al. (1997) p. 44) 72 definitions of sustainable development, commencing as long ago as 1972. Mohan Munasinghe (1993) drew the "...distinction between 'survivability,' which requires welfare to be above a threshold in all periods, and 'sustainability,' which requires welfare to be non-decreasing in all time periods." Pezzey suggests that *survivability* means that you are always above some threshold at all points in time, whereas *sustainability* takes a sort of millennial view that things are getting better all the time in a monotonic way. Our sense of this definition is that survivability is what we may have in our future rather than sustainability.

In 1993, Mohan Munasinghe discussed (Rogers et al. (1997) p. 44) three approaches to sustainable development:

- economic – maximizing income while maintaining a constant or increasing stock of capital;
- ecological – maintaining resilience and robustness of biological and physical systems; and
- social-cultural – maintaining stability of social and cultural systems.

Munasinghe, an economist from the World Bank, offers a somewhat precise definition for his economic approach to sustainable development. However, his discussion of ecological approaches that maintain resilience and robustness of biological and physical systems does not tell us what resilience and robustness mean in biological systems. We have some notions of that, but we do not have good operational definitions. And then in the social-cultural domain, he calls for maintaining stability of social and cultural systems. While this is desirable, he is not clear; besides, how can one actually calculate such stability? We are left to wonder.

NINE WAYS TO ACHIEVE SUSTAINABILITY

In the 1997 book entitled *Measuring Environmental Quality in Asia*, by Peter P. Rogers, Kazi F. Jalal, et al., indicators for environmental development are discussed. Nine ways to achieve sustainability are described (Box 1-1).

Box 1-1. Nine Ways to Achieve Sustainability

- Leave everything in the pristine state, or return it to its pristine state.
- Develop so as to not overwhelm the carrying capacity of the system.
- Sustainability will take care of itself as economic growth proceeds (Kuznets).
- Polluter and victim can arrive at an efficient solution by themselves (Coase).
- Let the markets take care of it.
- Internalize the externalities.
- Let the national economic accounting systems reflect defensive expenditures.
- Reinvest rents for nonrenewable resources (weak and strong sustainability).
- Leave future generations the options or the capacity to be as well off as we are.

First, leave everything in a pristine state, or return it to its pristine state. While that sounds nice, it is not going to happen. Nobody is going to do that, not when people are living, because it would involve a tremendous amount of pain and anguish.

Second, develop so as not to overwhelm the carrying capacity of the system. Again, what is the carrying capacity of the globe? Does anybody want to hazard a guess in terms of the number of people that might constitute the carrying capacity of the globe? The current global population is estimated at 6.3 billion. Is the carrying capacity of the world 6.3 billion people? If the standard of living to be achieved is the equivalent of current United States (US) standards, the carrying capacity is probably about 1 billion, based on our indicators. A carrying capacity of 6.3 billion people is possible at some greatly reduced standard of living below the US standard, but certainly not at the US standard. Carrying capacity is a difficult concept to define. And if we decided that we have exceeded our carrying capacity, what should we do about it? That is another complex question.

Third, sustainability will take care of itself as economic growth proceeds. This is sort of a cornucopian view and it is attributed to the economist Simon Kuznets, (ADB, *Emerging Asia* (1997), pp. 213-215), though he was already dead when the idea was attributed to him, so he could not complain about it. Basically his followers pointed out that as per capita income rises, people tend to take better care of the environment. When you are very poor, you are concerned about surviving and getting along at any cost. As you obtain more and more income, you can achieve environmental sustainability through the production of superior goods and services because you would then start to divert income to such purposes as air quality.

Consider the US in the 1960s, when the income per capita rose to about $6,000. Americans started to spend a lot of money on reducing the levels of air and water pollution. Despite current reports of gloom and doom in the newspapers, the ambient air quality in the US has greatly improved over what it was in the 1960s. That does not mean that it is perfect, but the US peaked on the parabolic curve relating environmental damage with per capita income, as Kuznets followers suggested (see Figure 1-1). The figure also suggests some arguments based upon property rights and ecological thresholds as to why and how the Kuznets hypothesis might work.

The implication of Kuznets' thinking is to develop as quickly as possible. We see this hypothesis at work in the People's Republic of China (PRC): develop quickly, as rapidly as possible, and the environment will take care of itself. However, those who have been to the PRC or India notice that the environment is not doing very well right now under this particular hypothesis, because the proponents would say, we will just wait a while, when the per capita income gets up to about $6,000, and then things will start to improve. The current per capita income in the PRC and India is probably about $3,000 to $4,000, so they have got quite a way to go before that would be possible. Meanwhile, we can expect a continuously deteriorating environment.

Fourth, Ronald Coase suggested that the polluter and the victim can arrive at an efficient solution by themselves. Under the Coase theorem (discussed in more detail in Chapter 10), everyone should get together and decide on an efficient level of pollution and on an efficient level of degradation of

Figure 1-1. Causes of Environmental Degradation

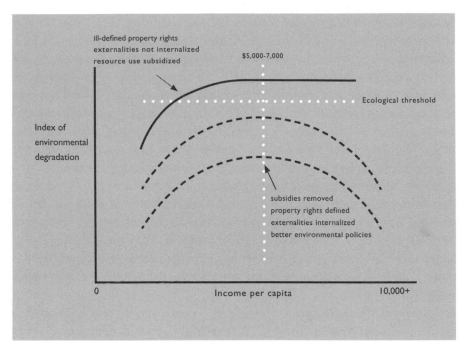

Source: Modified from T. Panayotou, ADB, *Emerging Asia* (1997), p. 213

the environment. Coase won a Nobel Prize in economics mainly for this particular theorem, which seems to work fairly well in small-scale situations. However, it is hard to imagine it working with a large number of people, because the transaction costs could be very high.

Fifth, let the markets take care of it. This is another economic solution. If one prices pollution and permits trading of pollution rights along with similar market operations, then sustainability can be achieved. Many people believe in this solution.

Sixth, internalize the externalities, which would provide an elegant solution. According to the 1997 Asian Development Bank (ADB) *Guidelines for the Economic Analysis of Projects* (1997), an "externality" is defined in part as the

> [e]ffects of an economic activity not included in the project statement from the point of view of the main project participants, and therefore not included in the financial costs and revenues that accrue to them. Externalities represent part of the difference between private costs and benefits, and social costs and benefits.

To internalize an externality, the ADB publication continues, "[e]xternalities should be quantified and valued, and included in the project statement for economic analysis." Of course it is a good thing to internalize the externalities, because people will then see in fact the real cost of activities, such as driving automobiles, and realize the damage caused by such activities. When we think of the cost of running an automobile, we think of the cost of gasoline at about $3 a gallon. But if we think about the environmental damage arising from the use of automobiles, it is equivalent to another $3 per gallon. Those of us who drive automobiles are taking a free ride on the environment for the equivalent of about $3 a gallon. We do not internalize these costs. If we were to internalize those externalities, then fewer people would use automobiles, or they would be driving much more fuel-efficient types of automobiles.

Seventh, perhaps we could have the national economic accounting system reflect defensive expenditures. This suggests that we worry about making sure that when we do our accounting, we do it correctly from the point of view of resource accounting. Most people probably do not realize that a good way of increasing gross domestic product (GDP) is to have lots of pollution and lots of sewage treatment plants, because GDP measures expenditures for all goods and services. This is why building more prisons with more prisoners is good for GDP; the same holds with building more schools. However, far more money is spent per prisoner than per student. But then more prisons means that GDP increases. Is this a real measure of what we want in terms of sustainability? Since prison expenditures are defensive expenditures, perhaps we should reflect such expenditures in some other way.

Eighth, reinvest the rents from nonrenewable resources (sometimes referred to as the Hartwick Rule, which is discussed more in Chapter 10.) Under this hypothesis, if we are using petroleum resources, then we should take the revenues resulting from such resources and invest them in some other way of dealing with the environment, for example, improving mobility, if use of gasoline is the issue. Some of the big oil companies are now using the profits from the oil to invest in a renewable resource such as solar technologies.

Ninth, leave future generations the options or the capacity to be as well off as we are, which comes from Robert Solow (1991). We are not quite sure how to do that. We keep on doing more of the same, although it is a truism, certainly in the western, industrialized nations, that generally each generation is better off than the last one. We are better off than our parents were, and so on. But whether we can continue with this progression, and how we can actually ensure it, is not obvious.

Sir John Hicks, an early twentieth-century English economist, defined income as "the maximum value that a person can consume in a period of time and still expect to be as well off at the end of the period as he was at the beginning." This has been redefined in the context of sustainable development as "sustainable social net product," which is a measure of a sustainable national income (see Box 1-2). Thus for a nation, sustainable social net product is the net national product (net national product equals GNP minus consumption of fixed capital) minus defensive expenditures to protect the environment minus the depreciation of natural capital. This means that we cannot chop down all the trees in the forest and count them as income, but that we can only use the amount of trees that are going to grow during the time period of such use.

Box 1-2. Sustainable Social Net Product

Sustainable social net product is based on Sir John Richard Hick's definition of income (i.e., maximum value that a person can consume in a period of time and still expect to be as well off at the end of the period as he was at the beginning) as net national product minus defensive expenditures minus the depreciation of natural capital:

$$SSNP = NNP - DE - DNC$$

Source: Daly (1996)

That is a prudent definition, and one would hope that we would all behave that way. However, it seems that a great deal of current behavior does not conform to this line of thinking. When the net national product is measured without taking into account defensive expenditures and depreciation of natural capital, we tend to overestimate how well we are doing (this is discussed more in Chapter 11). In *Measuring Environmental Quality in Asia* (Rogers et al., 1997), measures of environmental quality are developed, including a cost of repair approach, which emphasizes measurement of defensive expenditures. This suggests that if we have damaged the environment, we should be concerned with what it would cost to repair it, which means what it would cost to get it back into the condition in which we would like to have it.

Savings is the key to sustainability. The formula in Box 1-3 is also a sentence, which in English says, savings, as a percentage of GDP, should be greater or equal to the sum of the depreciation of human knowledge plus the depreciation of human-made capital plus the depreciation of natural capital.

Box 1-3. Savings: Key to Sustainability

A simple rule for sustainability would be:

$$\frac{S}{y} \geq \frac{\delta_H K_H}{y} + \frac{\delta_M K_M}{y} + \frac{\delta_N K_N}{y}$$

Savings as Percentage of GDP		Depreciation of Human Knowledge		Depreciation of Human-made Capital		Depreciation of Natural Capital
$\geq$		+		+		

Human Capital (H), Man-made Capital (M), and Natural Capital (N).
Weak sustainability requires: Sum of all forms of capital constant or increasing over time
Strong sustainability requires: Each is constant or increasing over time

Source: Modified from Pearce and Atkinson in Rogers et al. (1997), p. 52

Weak sustainability requires that the sum of all capital be constant or increasing over time. In other words, it implies the possibility of substitutions among human-made capital, human knowledge, and natural capital. Strong sustainability requires that each of these three types of capital be increasing over time. Most of the literature basically thinks in terms of weak sustainability, meaning that we can substitute between natural capital, human-made capital, and human knowledge, but there are many counter-examples to this assumption. For example, how can we substitute human-made capital for an extinct species such as the dodo bird?

ECONOMICS AS THE DISMAL SCIENCE

Why is economics considered the dismal science? It is because of the relationship of decreasing returns to scale, posited by Malthus and the English economist David Ricardo, among geometric population growth, the arithmetic depletion of resources, and the expansion to ever-declining quality of resources. Both did not paint a very pretty picture of what was going to happen to the world, and so economics earned the appellation, "the dismal science," and they are considered its fathers.

Boxes 1-4 and 1-5 are often referred to as the "rule of seventy." It is a useful trick to help remember the time taken for a number to double when the number is constantly increasing at a certain percent. If a number, such as the number of people in a population, is increasing at r percent per year, then after one year the number will equal the original number times one plus r, or $(1.0 + r)$, percent, which is the rate of growth. After two years, the number of people in the population equals the original population times one plus r squared, or $(1.0 + r)^2$, because we are compounding the increase in the number. After t years, the total population is equal to the original population multiplied by $(1.0 + r)$ to the power of t $(1.0 + r)^t$.

The formula also applies to calculating increases in the value of money invested at R percent per annum. Such calculations may be more interesting to most laypersons as they indicate how much money can be made by a particular investment over a period of time. If we use exponentials we can do these computations quickly. For instance, the time taken for a number to double is shown in Box 1-4 as $0.6931/r$. This means that the doubling time is close to $70/r$ where R is expressed in percentage terms.

Box 1-4. Geometric Growth: The Foundations of the Dismal Science

If the growth rate of a population is r percent per annum, an initial population of N_0 becomes N_1 after one year, or

$$N_1 = N_0 (1+r)$$

and after two years,

$$N_2 = N_1 (1+r) = N_0 (1+r)^2$$

and after t years,

$$N_t = N_0 (1+r)^t$$

So for a population of 100 persons growing at a rate of 2% per annum, after 1 year the population will be 102 persons. After 2 years the population will be 104.02.

The same holds true for money invested at r percent per annum.

Continuous compounding can be expressed as

$$N_t = N_0 e^{rt}$$

This is a very useful form to compute. For instance, the time taken for N_0 to double is

$$N_t / N_0 = 2$$

or

$$2 = e^{rt}$$
$$\ln 2 = rt$$
$$t = (\ln 2)/r = 0.6931/r$$

For r as a percentage the doubling time is close to 70/r.

For example, for an interest rate of 10%, the doubling time will be 7 years; $^{70}/_{10}= 7$.

POPULATION, RESOURCES, ENVIRONMENT, AND SUSTAINABILITY

The above calculations can often be done in one's head. This is a useful trick and a useful tool to calculate rough values for investment returns, world population trends, north-south distribution rates, and the like.

Table 1-1 shows that it took all of previous history until the 1800s before the earth had a population of one billion. The next billion was reached in 1930, or 130 years later. The next billion

Table 1-1. World Population

Number of Years to Add Each Billion

	Year	Years to Add
First billion reached	1800	all of human history
Second	1930	130
Third	1960	30
Fourth	1975	15
Fifth	1987	12
	Projected	
Sixth	1998	11
Seventh	2009	11
Eighth	2020	11
Ninth	2033	13
Tenth	2046	13
Eleventh	2066	20
Twelfth	about 2100	34

Source: Population Reference Bureau (1991), United Nations and World Bank estimates for the projections

Figure 1-2. World Population Trend and North-South Distribution

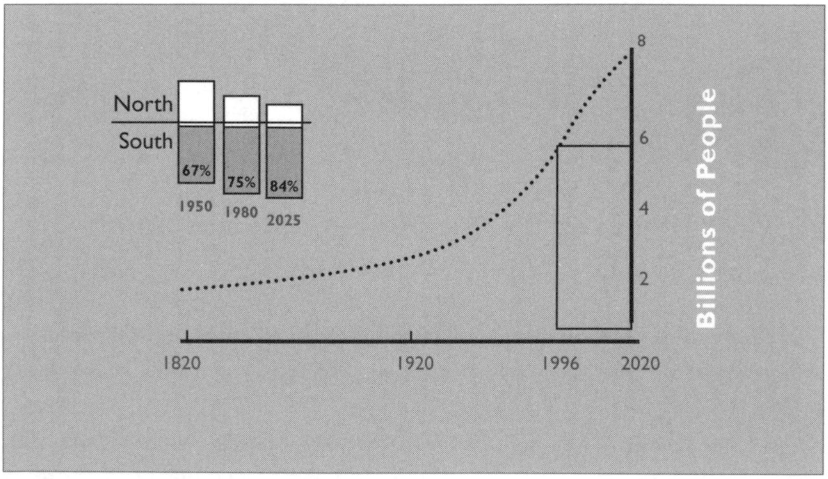

Source: Modified from UNDP/HDR (1990), p. 25

people was achieved in 1960, after 30 years. And then the fourth billion took 13 years; the fifth billion, 12 years; the sixth billion, 11 years. So there has been a huge acceleration in the growth rate of the world population, and this is one reason why we have become concerned about population and resources. Figure 1-2 shows the trend in world population as of 1996, when it was less than 6 billion. It is more than 6.5 billion now, and it is still increasing. Based upon 1990 data, the UN indicated that it would increase to more than 10 billion by 2050, following their median population estimates, and that it might rise as high as 13 billion before stabilizing. Just to show how quickly population forecasts can change, as of 2002 the UN experts expected the world population to level off at between 9 to 11 billion. A difference of 2 to 4 billion is rather large, considering that the total world population in 1975 was only 4 billion.

The Ehrlich Identity

To help analyze the interaction of factors causing environmental impact, the American environmentalist Paul Ehrlich suggested the relationship, I=PAT, popularly known as the Ehrlich Identity. The identity relates in a multiplicative way population, P, affluence, A, and technology, T, to environmental impact, I. (This identity fits into a long line of "production" functions in economic analysis. The best known is the Cobb-Douglas production function, where production output, O, is related nonlinearly to capital inputs, K, and labor inputs, L, by the equation $O = K^a L^b$, where a and b are the output elasticities of capital and labor, respectively.)

Box 1-5. Ehrlich Identity: I=PAT

Environmental Impact (I) = Population (P) times Affluence [consumption per capita (A)] times Technology per capita (T)
I = PAT

A small change in each, ΔP, ΔA, and ΔT, gives the new impact
$(I+\Delta I) = (P+\Delta P) (A+\Delta A) (T+\Delta T)$

Dividing through by the identity I = PAT yields
$(1+\Delta I/I) = (1.0+\Delta P/P) (1.0+\Delta A/A) (1.0+\Delta T/T)$

where $\Delta I/I$ etc. is the percentage increase in impact, population affluence, and technology.

Ehrlich has written several books, commencing with *The Population Bomb* (1971), predicting dire consequences from the rapid growth of human population. Fortunately, so far his predictions have not been borne out, but he (like Malthus) might be right in the long run. In any event, I=PAT provides a useful way of looking at the impact of population, consumption per capita, and technology per capita. These three factors constitute some of the major influences on the environment.

For example, I=PAT can help us understand the relative causes of the impact of lead from automobiles on the environment from 1946 to 1968. During those 22 years, the US population increased by 42%. The measure of affluence in terms of vehicle miles driven per capita rose by 100%, and the measure for technology in terms of lead emitted per vehicle mile rose by 81%. Therefore, the increase in environmental impact can be described as

$$(1+\Delta I/I) = (1.0+0.42)\ (1.0+1.0)\ (1.0+0.81)$$
$$(1+\Delta I/I) = 5.14$$

This amounts to a 414% increase. What caused the increase? Clearly it was not simply a population effect, but the joint effect of affluence and technology working together. Fortunately, lead was phased out from gasoline in the US fuel system starting in 1973.

What is the carrying capacity of the globe? As the Ehrlich Identity suggests, the level of per capita consumption is very important in determining the impact on the environment or the carrying capacity. But then, too, technology changes and income rises, and both these changes are associated with the use of resources.

These factors need to be taken into account when population growth in third world countries is compared with such growth in industrialized countries. Third world countries do not consume very much. Industrialized countries have low rates of population growth but high rates of consumption of resources like energy. In many instances a person in an industrialized country consumes as much energy in six months as an Indian villager consumes in a lifetime. Per capita consumption is thus probably the most important component in such comparisons of technology change. In planning for the future we typically want per capita consumption to increase; hence, to reduce the impact on the environment the multiplicative effects of the other components need to be reduced. Perhaps we need to focus more on the third factor: technology change. Such an emphasis is the basis of much of the cornucopians' optimism about the future.

Life Cycle Analysis and Sustainability

The choice of a simple disposable coffee cup is a trivial example, but it can demonstrate how we could improve sustainability by examining each of our small life style choices—a small achievement, but an important demonstration of the power of life cycle analysis in establishing sustainability. This relates to the environmental impacts of paper cups compared with polyfoam, or Styrofoam cups. The debate over this issue goes back many years. It appears that in many quarters, paper cups have won this debate. The question is, which is the most environment-friendly of these cups? How can we ascertain which is more sustainable? Does the paper cup provide the right answer? We will have to do some analysis to find out. Consider Table 1-2 comparing some obvious features of a typical paper cup and a typical polyfoam cup.

Table I-2. Paper Cup vs. Polyfoam Cup: An Environmental Summary I

Item	Paper Cup	Polyfoam Cup
	per cup	
Raw materials:		
Wood and bark (g)	33 (28 to 37)	0
Petroleum fractions (g)	4.1 (2.8 to 5.5)	3.2
Other chemicals	1.8	0.05
Finished weight (g)	10.1	1.5
Wholesale cost	2.5 ×	×

Source: Based on M. Hocking (1991)

When we are examining sustainability, it is important to look at the life cycle of the device in question, including production, use, and ultimate disposal. In Germany, for example, there is an attempt to make automobiles fully recyclable. This has not yet been achieved, but large portions of German automobiles are now recyclable, and greater portions will become recyclable in the future.

As indicated in the table, the raw materials in the paper cup include wood and bark, since it is made of paper. Paper cup raw materials also include petroleum. Actually, there is more petroleum used in paper cup production than in a polyfoam cup, which is made almost entirely of petroleum products. Some may find that surprising. Also, a lot of chemicals like chlorine are used to bleach the paper in the paper cups to make them look nice. Binders such as glue are used to stick paper cups together. All of these ingredients for paper cups cost about two and a half times as much as cups made of polyfoam.

Now consider the environmental impacts during production of the cups, summarized in Table 1-3.

The production of the cups requires steam, power (electricity), and cooling water. Water effluent for each cup is measured by volume, suspended solids, biochemical oxygen demand (BOD), organochlorines, and metal salts. Air emissions are measured in terms of chlorine, chlorine dioxide, reduced sulfates, particulates, chlorofluorocarbons, pentane, and sulfur dioxide. The table shows that in most cases polyfoam cup production causes much less environmental impact than paper cup production.

What about the reuse and recyclable potential and ultimate disposal of paper cups versus polyfoam cups? (Tables I-4 and I-5.) The ability to reuse paper cups is likely low, since they can disintegrate when reused. Very few people reuse paper cups. However, polyfoam cups are easy to wash, and reuse. Paper cups burn well, but produce a hot melt adhesive. If paper cups are not completely burned, these adhesives will linger in the environment.

Table 1-3. Paper Cup vs. Polyfoam Cup: An Environmental Summary II

Item	Paper Cup	Polyfoam Cup
	per metric ton of material	
Utilities:		
Steam (kg)	9,000-12,000	5,000
Power (kWh)	980	120-180
Cooling water (m³)	50	154
Water effluent		
Volume (m³)	50-90	0.5-2.0
Suspended solids (kg)	35-60	Trace
BOD (kg)	30-50	0
Organochlorines (kg)	5-7	0
Metal salts (kg)	1-20	20
Air emissons		
Chlorine (kg)	0.5	0
Chlorine dioxide (kg)	0.2	0
Reduced sulfides (kg)	2.0	0
Particulates (kg)	5-15	0.1
Chlorofluorocarbons (kg)	0	0
Pentane (kg)	0	35-50
Sulfur dioxide (kg)	10	10

Source: Based on M. Hocking (1991)

Table 1-4. Recyclable Potential of Paper Cups and Polyfoam Cups

Item	Paper Cup	Polyfoam Cup
	Recyclable Potential	
To primary user	Possible, though washing can destroy	Easy, negligible water uptake
After use	Low, hot melt adhesive or coating difficulties	High, resin reuse in other applications

Source: Based on M. Hocking (1991)

Table I-5. Ultimate Disposal of Paper Cups and Polyfoam Cups

Item	Paper Cup	Polyfoam Cup
Ultimate Disposal		
Paper incineration	Clean	Clean
Heat recovery (MJ/kg)	20	40
Mass to landfill (g)	10.1	1.5
Biodegradable	Yes, BOD to leacheate, methane to air	No, essentially inert

Source: Based on M. Hocking (1991)

Potential heat recovery from a polyfoam cup is twice that of a paper cup. The mass to landfill ratio of paper to polyfoam cup is 8 to 1. Are these two types of cups biodegradable? Polyfoam cups do not seem to be biodegradable. Walking the beaches of Massachusetts, one finds lots of old polyfoam that was not disposed of in a correct way.

Which is the best cup depends on what we think are bad results. A lot of people seem to think that the litter of polyfoam on the beaches of the world is much worse than all of those other environmental insults produced by paper cups. If polyfoam cups were collected and disposed of properly by incineration, there would be no question about which would be preferred.

SUSTAINABILITY ON THE HIGHWAY PRODUCED BY THREE KEY SOURCES OF ENERGY

Comparing vehicles powered by electricity, gasoline, and diesel is a bit like comparing apples and oranges, and bananas. A comparison of these vehicles is possible only if it is based on their respective performance levels in use and over their entire life cycle. In the following example, based upon typical sized gasoline, diesel, and electric cars in France in the late 1990s before hybrids were available, the cars were assumed to be similar in all performance and travel conditions.

In this case, life cycle costs are calculated on the assumption of 45 kilometers a day. First, when all of the private costs from purchase price to energy use, maintenance, battery replacement, and the like are considered, it turns out in Figure 1-3 that the new gasoline vehicle is the most expensive, the cost of a new diesel is the least expensive, and the cost of an electric vehicle lies in between. This result is based upon very low electricity rates in France due to the large amount of nuclear electricity on the base load. In the US the new electric car would have had the highest private costs. Diesel vehicles are a lot cheaper. How would one make a choice? If one is a rational

Figure I-3. Life Cycle Costs per Kilometer: *Private Costs*

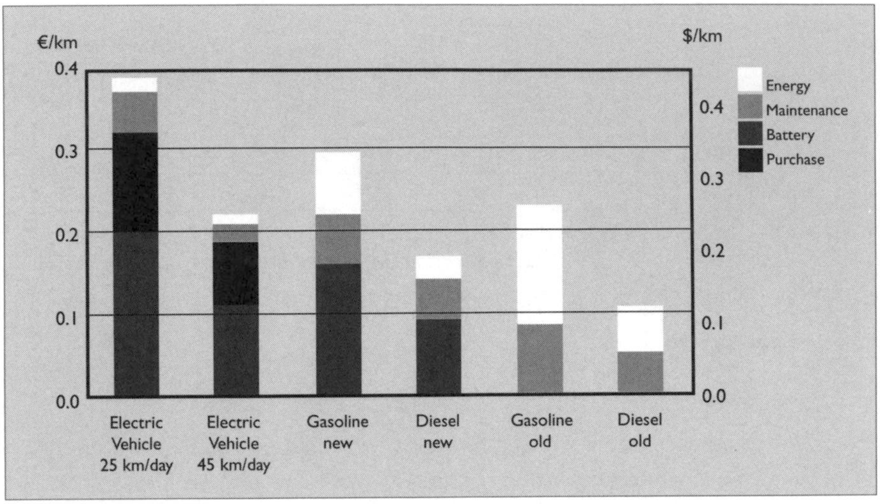

Source: Funk and Rabl (1999)

Table I-6. Calculated Damage Costs of Common Air Pollutants

Pollutant	Damage Cost (euro/kg)[a]
Greenhouse gases, CO_2 equivalent	0.029
Secondary pollutant, per kg of primary pollutant	
SO_2 via sulfates	10.0
NO_2 via nitrates	14.5
NO_2 via ozone	1.50
NMVOC via ozone	0.93
Primary pollutants from refineries	
PM10	15.4
Primary pollutants from cars	
$PM_{2.5}$ Paris	2190
$PM_{2.5}$ highway, Paris-Lyon	159
$PM_{2.5}$ rural France	22
SO_2 direct, Paris	28
SO_2 direct, highway, Paris-Lyon	2.2
SO_2 direct, rural France	0.3
CO_2 Paris	0.02
CO_2 highway, Paris-Lyon	0.002

[a] 1€ = $1.16

Source: Funk and Rabl (1999)

Figure I-4. Life Cycle Costs: Including Social Costs

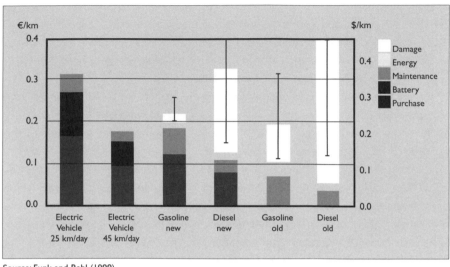

Source: Funk and Rabl (1999)

consumer, focusing on the overall cost of running and owning a car, one would buy a new diesel car or an old diesel car, because either one costs less based on euros spent per kilometer.

However, use of these vehicles results in damages caused by the pollution they produce over their life cycle. To calculate these damages, we need to know the damages caused by primary and secondary pollutants. Primary pollutants are emitted from refineries and from fuel use, and secondary pollutants consist of sulfates, nitrates, and ozone generated in other parts of the life cycle. The primary pollutants from cars are provided in terms of driving in a city or driving on a highway, and greenhouse gases (use of all fossil fuels produces greenhouse gases). Table I-6 reports the estimates used to calculate the impacts of the conventional pollutants. Also we need to add in the cost of greenhouse gases estimated at about $20 per ton of carbon dioxide (CO_2).

Different vehicular activities have different damage costs based on health damages (mortality damages were not considered). Figure I-4 shows what the relative attractiveness of the automobile choice is now when these externalities are factored in. An old diesel vehicle, which is really cheap to buy and use based upon the private costs, has high social costs because it produces a great many particulates that are very damaging to human health. If all of these costs are added together, the life cycle cost per kilometer, including social costs, is high. Many consumers, however, do not wish to be concerned with social costs; they wish to pay only private costs. However, a policy designed to find a solution that takes into account everyone in a community, not just those who purchase low-cost vehicles, will encourage the purchase and use of electric vehicles. Indeed, electric vehicles, which can be driven 45 kilometers per day, become competitive with old gasoline vehicles after taking into consideration average values of damages.

How can we make consumers respond to social costs rather than the private costs? Some would suggest manipulating costs, particularly fuel costs, and removing direct and indirect subsidies, in order to make the private cost look more like the real social cost. When attempting full life cycle analysis, social as well as private life cycle costs have to be considered. We must also factor in the damage to the environment. Each of these three points of view may provide entirely different answers, all of which are important to achieve sustainability.

By looking behind the numbers and ascertaining the impacts, we could start modifying motor vehicle technology. For example, sports utility vehicles (SUVs) were often considered the worst vehicles from the sustainability point of view because they were big and consumed a great deal of fuel. Ford has now produced a new, small, hybrid SUV powered by gasoline and electricity. As advertised, the new SUV has improved fuel efficiency by 81% and reduced emissions by 60%, and this SUV is now enjoying brisk sales. Americans often prefer bigger mid-sized vehicles than Japanese consumers. So now American consumers can buy an SUV and feel better about it from the environmental point of view. From the environmental point of view, however, everyone should be driving small cars or taking public transportation, if such is available.

On the public transit side there are also potential moves towards sustainability. For example, Seattle recently bought 235 new diesel electric buses, each with a hundred seats. Compared with previous buses, these have a potential improved fuel economy of 60% and reduced particulates of 90%. Also note that Seattle has many tunnels where these buses will be used, powered only on electric cycle in the tunnels. The ability to drive significant distances on only electricity has other significant advantages in stop-and-go traffic, because most of the emissions come from low-speed driving.

Recall the I=PAT identity and note that we are now rapidly changing the technology we use, which will lead at the same time to reducing consumption. These are major technical improvements with major potential for changing per capita use of petroleum resources. How long does it take to roll over from one type of vehicle in the United States—ten years or 15 years? If these new technologies do indeed catch on, then we can expect that US petroleum demand by 2020 could be substantially lower than currently projected.

One important reason to believe that we are due for such an accelerated change of technologies in the direction of more sustainability is the current and growing competition for petroleum-based fossil fuels. In 2004, the PRC imported about 90 million tons of petroleum products, while the US imported about 400 million tons. By 2020, the PRC will import 400 million tons. Also India imported about 90 million tons of oil products last year, and India's demand in 2020 will be significant, though not as high as the PRC's. The world market for oil may not be able to supply these amounts at reasonable prices. Something has to give. Unless there is a radical shift in the availability of fossil fuels, we are heading for one of those proverbial train wrecks. To avoid such disaster, we are already starting to see the adoption of alternative-fueled vehicles. This suggests that we will muddle through because we are smart enough to figure out that we do not want to be wiped out by such a train wreck. The two examples of new technologies for hybrid SUVs and Seattle's purchase of new hybrid buses are quite hopeful. If other parts of the world such as India, where there are several hundred thousand buses, take similar initiatives, major environmental and social improvements can be achieved. However, without a radical technology shift, we will face significant problems. The good news is, people are actually buying and using new technologies.

Life cycle analysis of every proposed change is imperative to achieve sustainable development. We often fall short, because most of our analyses are based purely on private costs, on manufacturing costs, and on costs to purchase goods and services in the marketplace without sufficient attention to what is important. Why were little plastic bags filled with air designed for packing purposes? Not so long ago Germany required all packaging to be returned to the manufacturer. Before this change, US producers were flying thousands of computers packed with Styrofoam to Germany. With this new requirement the Styrofoam had to be flown back to the US. While flying computers packed in Styrofoam is probably a profitable activity, flying Styrofoam-filled 747s back to the US for disposal clearly is not. Manufacturers had to find a new way of packing the computers. Because bags full of air are a lot cheaper to bring back home than bulky Styrofoam, they were rapidly adopted.

These changes in technology for packaging were induced by environmental concerns, new legal requirements, and resulting economic costs, as suggested by the above example of the electric vehicle, which was superior, but only if based on the social costs.

A LOOK FORWARD

This introductory chapter has explored many of the key issues to be confronted in achieving sustainable development, including the triple bottom line of environmental, social, and economic considerations in the face of such global environmental issues as population growth, consumption, production, pollution, effects of legal requirements, as well as some of the causes and effects of poverty. The book will consider other issues, including sustainable development indicators; environmental assessment and management trends; international law, including multilateral environmental agreements; and national environmental accounts.

The book concludes with a review of what international financial institutions and others are doing to achieve sustainable development, together with a quick look into the next 50 years. The Epilogue focuses on the challenges posed by terrorism, climate change, the global food system, and globalization. It will be argued that the most serious indicators of losing our path to a sustainable 2050 would be an increase in absolute levels of poverty in the world, increasing gaps between the rich countries and the poor countries, and increasing gaps between specific countries. Since sustainable development requires social sustainability as well as economic and environmental sustainability, we believe that increased polarization between the rich and the poor could lead to increased terrorist violence, failed states, further deterioration of the environment, and mass migrations for economic survival and environmental reasons. To avoid such consequences and provide for a better world, we all need to work toward achieving sustainable development throughout the world.

CHALLENGES OF SUSTAINABLE DEVELOPMENT

CONCEPT OF SUSTAINABILITY

The concept of sustainability explores the relationship among economic development, environmental quality, and social equity. This concept has been evolving since 1972, when the international community first explored the connection between quality of life and environmental quality at the United Nations Conference on the Human Environment in Stockholm. However, it was not until 1987 that the term "sustainable development" was defined as "development that can meet the needs of the present generation without compromising the ability of future generations to meet their own needs" (World Commission on Environment and Development, 1987.) This definition established the need for integrated decision making that is capable of balancing the economic and social needs of the people with the regenerative capacity of the natural environment. Sustainable development is a dynamic process of change in which the exploitation of resources, the direction of investments, the orientation of technological development, and institutional change are made consistent with future as well as present needs. According to the Brundtland Commission, sustainable development, in the final analysis, must rest on political will of the governments as critical economic, environmental, and social decisions are made. There are many definitions and concepts of sustainable development as depicted in Table 2-1. Besides, there is a vast literature on sustainable development, which also provides other definitions, concepts, principles, criteria, indicators, and references (see: http://www.iisd.org/ie/info/ss9504.htm and http://www.gdre.org/sustdev). Reviewing these and other relevant references constitutes a major task in trying to understand the meaning and significance of the term "sustainable development."

Table 2-1. Sustainable Development: Definitions, Principles, Criteria, Conceptual Frameworks, and Indicators

Subject	Number
1. Definitions	57
2. Principles	19
3. Criteria	12
4. Conceptual frameworks	4
5. Indicators	28 sets

(See: <http://www.sustainableliving.org>)

Three Components

Sustainable development has three dimensions: economic, environmental, and social. These are frequently referred to as the triple bottom line, and are used to gauge the success of a particular development program or project. It is critical that each component be given equal attention in order to ensure a sustainable outcome. This balance becomes obvious when each component is examined individually.

1. **The economic approach: Maximize income while maintaining constant or increasing stock of capital.**

> *[T]he core idea of sustainability is that current decisions should not impair the prospects for maintaining or improving future living standards. This implies that our economic systems should be managed so that we can live off the dividends of our resources.* (Robert Repetto, 1986)

By "resources" Repetto includes natural and otherwise, considering them as an endowment fund. The interest rate is the regenerated capacity of the natural environment or of a human-made environment, plus the managed capacity for expansion. As he was connected at the time with the World Bank, it is understandable that Repetto's definition relies heavily on economic concepts.

> *Sustainable economic growth means that real GNP per capita is increasing over time and the increase is not threatened by "feedback" from either biophysical impacts (pollution, resource degradation) or from social impacts.* (David Pearce et al., 1989)

> *Sustainable development argues for: (1) development subject to a set of constraints which set resource harvest rates at levels not higher than managed natural regeneration rate, and (2) use of the environment as a "waste sink" on the basis that waste disposal rates should not exceed rates of managed or natural assimilative capacity of the ecosystem.* (D. Pearce, 1988)

In this definition, note the phrases "managed natural regeneration rate" and "managed or natural assimilative capacity." This is a definition that is somewhat quantifiable and can be translated in mathematical terms. For example, with reference to forest management:

If: X_1 = m³ biomass removed/unit time

X_2 = m³ biomass regenerated naturally and/or reforested/unit time

Then: X_1 should be less than X_2 for sustainable forestry

Similarly, in terms of water quality, if there is, in a given wastewater effluent, Y_1 parts per million of biochemical oxygen demand (BOD) per day being discharged into a receiving body of water, and Y_2 is the parts per million of BOD per day that the receiving body of water can satisfy in terms of its dissolved oxygen content, then Y_1 has to be less than or equal to Y_2 in order for the natural body of water to retain its sustainable character. That is:

If: Y_1 = ppm BOD discharged/unit time

Y_2 = ppm BOD satisfied/unit time

Then: Y_1 should be less than or equal to Y_2

> *Sustainable development means basing developmental and environmental policies on a comparison of costs and benefits and on careful economic analysis that will strengthen environmental protection and lead to rising and sustainable levels of welfare.* (World Bank, 1992)

This definition regards the classification of sustainability as a balance between a desired environmental end and the costs involved in achieving that end. Here, the World Bank tries to balance the three dimensions of sustainability, but "sustainable levels of welfare," which refers to the social dimension, is not very clear.

> *Sustainable development is an approach that will permit continuing improvements in the quality of life with a lower intensity of resource use, thereby leaving behind for future generations an undiminished or even enhanced stock of natural resources and other assets.* (Mohan Munasinghe and Ernst Lutz, 1991)

This is yet another definition given by the World Bank. It refers to future as well as present generations only in terms of enjoying the stock of resources and assets. The social dimension is partly ignored, which is the definition's inherent weakness.

2. The ecological approach: Maintain the resilience and robustness of biological and physical systems.

> *Sustainable development is about maintenance of essential ecological processes and life support systems, the preservation of genetic diversity, and the sustainable utilization of species and ecosystems.* (IUCN, WWF, UNEP, 1987)
>
> *The term "sustainable development" suggests that the lessons of ecology can, and should be applied to economic processes. It encompasses the ideas in the World Conservation Strategy, providing an environmental rationale through which the claims of development to improve the quality of (all) life can be challenged and tested.* (Michael Redclift, 1987)

3. The socio-cultural approach: Maintain the stability of social and cultural systems.

> *Sustainable economic development is directly concerned with increasing the standard of living of the poor, which can be measured in terms of increased food, real income, education, health care, water supply, sanitation, and only indirectly concerned with economic growth at the aggregate.* (Edward Barbier, 1987)

Maurice Strong, the first Executive Director of the United Nations Environment Programme (UNEP) and the Secretary General of the United Nations Conference on Environment and

Development (UNCED) in Rio in 1992, offers this definition, which runs beyond the economic, environmental, and social boundaries.

> *Sustainable development involves a process of deep and profound change in the political, social, economic, institutional, and technological order, including redefinition of relations between developing and more developed countries.* (Maurice Strong, 1992)

There are many definitions of sustainable development contained in the Brundtland Commission report and related references on the subject.

Operational Criteria for Sustainable Development

Considering many definitions and concepts of sustainable development, there seem to be three operational criteria. These criteria should evaluate each objective of the triple bottom line with the following three caveats:

Box 2-1. Balancing Project Benefits

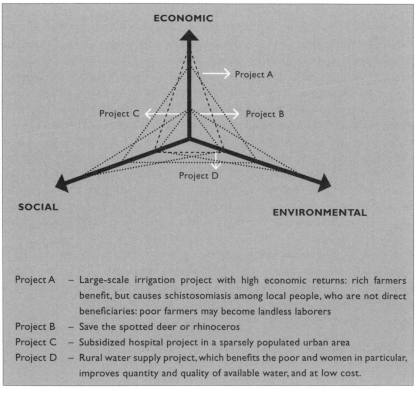

Project A — Large-scale irrigation project with high economic returns: rich farmers benefit, but causes schistosomiasis among local people, who are not direct beneficiaries: poor farmers may become landless laborers

Project B — Save the spotted deer or rhinoceros

Project C — Subsidized hospital project in a sparsely populated urban area

Project D — Rural water supply project, which benefits the poor and women in particular, improves quantity and quality of available water, and at low cost.

Source: D.V. Smith and K. F. Jalal (2000), p. 3

- Economic objectives should not be maximized without satisfying environmental and social constraints.
- Environmental benefits should not necessarily be maximized without satisfying economic and social constraints.
- Social benefits should not be maximized without satisfying economic and environmental constraints.

Operationally speaking, sustainable development is about maximizing economic, social, and environmental benefits subject to a set of constraints. (See Boxes 2-1 and 2-2.)

Box 2-2. Project Types

Let us consider the following typology of projects (See Box 2-1).

Project A, a large-scale irrigation and flood control project with a very high benefit-to-cost ratio, favors large farmers more than poor farmers, and causes waterborne and snailborne diseases such as malaria and schistosomiasis. These diseases affect the local people, most of whom may not be direct beneficiaries of the project. The poor marginal farmers who are living within the project area eventually become landless laborers.

How does that occur? Mainly it happens through the confluence of modern science and modern farming techniques. The large farmers are aware of the benefits of irrigation; of high yielding seeds; and, nowadays, genetically modified seeds; of pesticides; and so on—the fruits of science in the service of the Green Revolution. These agribusiness persons can produce five times more crops per unit of land, making the land itself more valuable. So they go to the small farmers and ask, "How much are you getting out of your land in terms of income?" They then convince the poor farmers to sell their land to them. Thus, the formerly independent small farmers may become laborers or tenants on what was once their own property. Obviously, this kind of a project is less likely to be sustainable.

Project B is about maximizing environmental objectives at the cost of social and economic objectives, using the spotted deer or the rhinoceros as an example. If the multilateral development banks (MDBs) decide to fund one of these projects, they should identify and integrate social and economic benefits into the project.

Project C exemplifies a situation that maximizes social objectives at the cost of environmental and economic objectives, and therefore is not considered as sustainable.

Project D is a sustainable development project such as a rural water supply project that benefits the poor (women in particular, since they are the ones usually responsible for fetching household drinking water) and improves the quantity and quality of the water supply at low cost. This is the kind of project that should be regarded as sustainable. Does this mean that the MDBs should not finance those projects with high economic payoff? The answer is no; they may do so provided that the projects can be redesigned to take into account environmental and social considerations while maximizing economic benefits.

FACTORS GOVERNING SUSTAINABLE DEVELOPMENT

The key factors governing sustainable development are poverty, population, pollution, participation, policy and market failures (including good governance), and prevention and management of disasters. These can be regarded as the major pillars on which sustainable development rests.

According to estimates made by the United Nations Development Programme (UNDP), the wealthiest 20% of the global population earns 82.7% of the total global income. This bracket also accounts for 81.2% of world trade, 94.6% of commercial lending, 80.6% of domestic savings, and 80.5% of domestic investment. By contrast, the share of total global income of the poorest 20% is a mere 1.4%. Their contribution to world trade (1.0%) and commercial lending (0.2%) is statistically negligible.

Plotting these figures yields a graph that is commonly called a champagne glass (Figure 2-1). Clearly, most of the investments, income, trade, and lending are attributed to the first 20% of the global population.

Figure 2-1 Distribution of World Income and Disparities

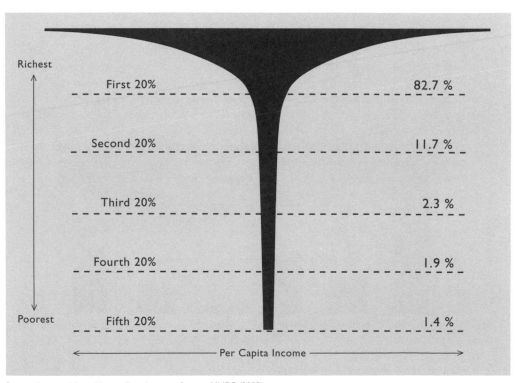

Source: Extracted from Human Development Report, UNDP (2005)
Website: http://hdr.undp.org

47

Where do these poor people live? Most of them live in South Asia (550 million), followed by Sub-Saharan Africa and then the Middle East and North Africa (Figure 2-2). A recent study (Cavanagh and Anderson, 2004) indicates that there are now 497 billionaires in the world, whose collective wealth is greater than the combined wealth of the poorest half of humanity of over three billion people. According to another article (*Economic Development Futures Web Journal,* 2004), the number of millionaires in the world has soared to 7.7 million, and the number of poor people earning less than a dollar per day increased from 1.1 billion (in 1992) to 1.3 billion in 2004. A more recent (2007) report says, the number of millionaires in the world now stands at 9.5 million. Figure 2-3 shows the global income distribution and disparities drawn up by UNDP in 1992; the agency's 1999 Human Development Report (HDR) suggests that global income inequality has worsened since then. However, a 2003 International Chamber of Commerce (ICC) paper states that "new research shows that, contrary to popular belief, it is precisely during the recent period of increased globalization of the world economy that poverty rates and global income inequality have most diminished." The ICC study undertaken by Prof. Sala-i-Martin of Columbia University points out that the HDR of UNDP "computed its poverty ratios using current exchange, therefore ignoring the fact that the cost of living is lower in developing countries." Once adjusted for purchasing power parity, Sala-i-Martin finds that the poverty ratio of the richest 20% to the poorest 20% of the global population has actually started to diminish over the last two decades.

In his recent (2005) book entitled "The End of Poverty", Jeffrey Sachs, professor of Columbia University, and adviser to the UN Secretary General on poverty alleviation, states: "The share [of

Figure 2-2. Regions Where the Poorest People of the World Live

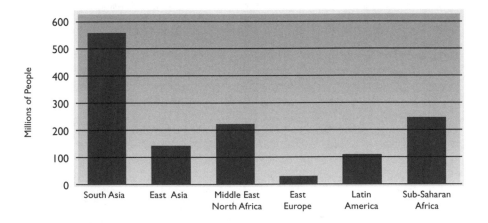

Source: (1) J. Cavanagh and S. Anderson (2004)
(2) *Economic Development Futures Web Journal* (June 2004)
(3) Merrill Lynch and Capgemini (2007): Eleventh Annual World Wealth Report

world resources] devoted to helping the poor has declined for decades and is a tiny fraction of what the US has repeatedly promised, and failed to give." Except for a few developed countries of the world (such as the Scandinavian countries and the Netherlands), most industrialized countries have failed to fulfill their global commitment of 0.7% of their GDP for international assistance to reduce poverty. Current resource allocation for addressing the plight of the poor by the US is only 0.15% of its GDP. According to Sachs, our generation can choose to end poverty provided that we are able to mobilize resources from the developed world, in accordance with commitments made at the Earth Summit held in 1992 in Rio de Janeiro, Brazil, and reiterated by the World Summit on Sustainable Development (WSSD) held in 2002 in Johannesburg, South Africa. He also recommends adoption of a new method that he chooses to call "clinical economics." In his view, clean water, productive soils, and a functioning health care system are just as relevant to sustainable development as pure economic growth. Says Sachs: "In the past quarter century, the development economics imposed by rich countries on the poorest countries has been too much like medicine in the nineteenth century, when doctors used leeches to draw blood from their patients, often killing them in the process." Having given this two-pronged prescription, it is not certain if it will work to change the plight of the poor.

Figure 2-3. Income Disparity Between the Richest 20%
and Poorest 20% of the World's Population

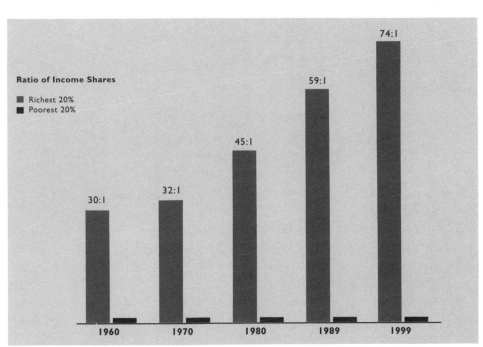

Source: UNDP/HDR (1992) and UNDP/HDR (1999)

Box. 2-3. Some More Facts About Poverty and Global Priorities in Spending

- Today across the world 1.3 billion people live on less than one dollar/day; 3 billion (half the world population) live on less than two dollars/day; 1.3 billion people have no access to clean water; 2 billion have no access to electricity; and 3 billion have no access to sanitation.
- Also today consider the following as global priorities in spending:

Item of Expenditure	Annual Spending US$ billion
Cosmetics in the US	8
Perfumes in Europe and the US	12
Ice cream in Europe	12
Pet foods in Europe and the US	17
Business entertainment in Japan	35
Cigarettes in Europe	50
Alcoholic drinks in Europe	105
Narcotic drugs in the world	400
Military spending, global	780

- And yet some of the basic needs of poor humanity, the cost of which are as follows, are not being met:

	Annual estimated cost in $US billion
Basic education for all	6
Water and sanitation for all	9
Basic health and nutrition for everyone	13
Reproductive health for all women in the world	12

Sources: Anup Shah (2006)

LINKAGES AMONG SUSTAINABLE DEVELOPMENT, ENVIRONMENT, AND POVERTY

To achieve sustainable development, two vicious circles, which feed on themselves, must be broken (Figure 2-4).

The left circle illustrates how poverty causes resource depletion and degradation in perpetuity. By the sheer necessity of survival, the poor pollute the environment and erode the land, both of which, in turn, further entrench poverty. Former Prime Minister of India Indira Gandhi once called this vicious loop the "pollution of poverty."

The right-hand vicious cycle demonstrates how development leads to resource depletion, degradation, and climate changes. These environmental problems then retard, if not stop, the development process, because the resources of the environment are also the resources of development.

These two circles have to be broken if development is to be sustainable.

Figure 2-4. Linkages Between Sustainable Development, Environment, and Poverty

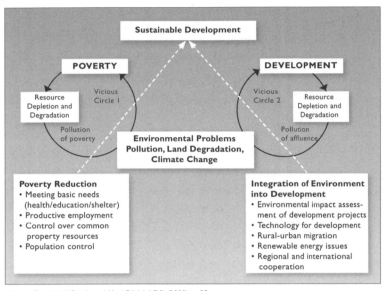

Source: Douglas V. Smith and Kazi F. Jalal, ADB (2000), p. 55

Poverty must be reduced by meeting basic needs: health, education, shelter, productive employment, control over common property, and population management. Similarly, to minimize the environmental and social consequences of development, a strategic assessment of policies and plans must be undertaken. Projects must be assessed for their impact upon the environment and society. To successfully achieve sustainable development, the community of nations must also stop the unfavorable impacts of rural-to-urban migration in developing countries, consider renewable energy issues, and promote regional and international cooperation.

There are at least five myths about the relationship between environment and poverty:

1. Myth 1: Most environmental degradation is caused by the poor.

In fact, it is the other way around: The wealthier classes are responsible for the most serious forms of environmental degradation. By the sheer necessity of survival the poor may overgraze the land and deplete the forest of fuel wood, resulting in local deforestation, subsequent topsoil erosion, and surface water contamination and runoff causing flooding. However, the pollution from the nonpoor is driven by profit maximization. There is a world of difference between the two, especially in the magnitude and extent of the damage incurred.

2. Myth 2: Poverty reduction necessarily leads to environmental degradation.

Reduction of the income gap and environmental stress are closely related. If the income gap is reduced, the stress on the environment should also be reduced. Furthermore, poverty reduction is not likely to create overconsumption, which could, in turn, enhance environmental degradation. When the poor increase their earnings from one dollar per day to two dollars per day, they will be less likely to pollute the environment, because they will finally have the resources and a reason to protect the very environment upon which their survival depends.

3. Myth 3: Population growth necessarily leads to environmental degradation.

An increasing population could place increasing demands on natural resources, which can lead to environmental degradation and an unsustainable demand for natural resources. However, environmental impact depends not only on population growth but also on GDP (see Chapter 11) and development of technology. This can be demonstrated in the Ehrlich Identity (see Box 1-5).

4. Myth 4: The poor are too poor to invest in the environment.

The Department for International Development (DFID) of the United Kingdom (UK) has done several studies at the local level showing that poor communities are willing to invest in their environment but under certain favorable conditions, such as when they have property ownership and control over their common resources. However, they are reluctant to invest in the environment if the area is controlled by outsiders, such as a logging company or the government, leaving them with no stake in their surroundings. Given the proper conditions, particularly land title or tenure, the poor are willing to provide what they can to upgrade their environment—usually labor, since they have little cash.

5. Myth 5: Poor people lack the technical knowledge for resource management.

While poor people may fall short of modern technical knowledge for resource management, their indigenous knowledge is often more appropriate or even better suited to support their habitat. Unfortunately, this type of indigenous knowledge is too often ignored. Furthermore, when modern technology is imposed upon the poor, it tends to undermine their indigenous knowledge. Modern technology and machinery also fail to do the job because the community often does not know how to utilize and/or maintain the alien technology.

As an example, in Bangladesh during the 1970s, the United States Agency for International Development (USAID), in an ill-advised flood control program, built multimillion-dollar embankments in coastal areas so that farmers could continue working during the rainy season. However, instead of keeping the floods out, water accumulated inside the embankments, sinking the farms under even deeper water. Eventually, the farmers had to breach the embankments to let the water out. In another effort to introduce modern irrigation technology from Germany in Dinajpur District, also in Bangladesh, deep tube wells (>60 meters) were sunk into the soil to provide a steady source of irrigation water. Everything worked fine during the first year, but then the wells broke down. The foreign engineers were long gone, and no one there knew how to maintain and repair the wells. While the poor have limited skills, it is not true that they lack technical knowledge. What they need is enhanced capacity to solve problems using their indigenous skills and local resources.

Population Planning

Population planning is another significant factor in sustainable development. Between 1820 and 1920, the world population doubled from one billion to two billion. However, in the subsequent 100 years, 1920 to 2020, it will climb up to eight billion, a fourfold increase (Figure 1-2). Throughout the history of humankind the rate of population growth has never been higher than it is now; nor is the rate likely to get any higher. It is significant that, while the overall world population is rapidly increasing, it is actually decreasing in many of the developed countries. In 1950, 40% of the world's population lived in developed countries and 60% in developing countries. By 2025, 80% will be living in developing countries and only 20% in developed countries. By 2050, India will surpass the PRC to become the most populous country in the world and will continue to remain so for a long time, if not forever. In terms of population planning, therefore, managing population increases in the developing countries between now and 2020 is the biggest challenge.

While population growth may cause some environmental degradation, it is not as significant as that caused by other types of activities. Also, the poor may cause limited environmental degradation, but they do so out of necessity of survival and have little choice. It has also been demonstrated that, if the poor experience a slight improvement in their income, they will probably do something else to earn their livelihood rather than take as much as they can from the land and the sea. There are many reasons why population growth is not such a significant factor in environmental degradation. A good example is the PRC, where the burgeoning population is matched by rapid industrialization and growing affluence; and as we have seen, increasing economic activities strain the environment far more than does increasing population. It should also be borne in mind that environmentally unsound technology can be, and probably is, a far more important governing factor in determining sustainability of development than population growth.

The best estimate of global population increase by the year 2050 is 9.13 billion from 2.55 billion in 1950 (Negative Population Growth, 2004; also see Figure 2-5). The average annual growth rate of population in the world varies from 2.19% (1962 1963) to 0.46% (estimated for 2050). By 2050, the global population is expected to be stabilized (at about 9.3-9.6 billion), based on current demographic trends (World Resources Institute, 1998. However, the assumption is that determined efforts to plan population growth will be made by the world community on the basis of recommendations of the World Population Conference in Cairo and the United Nations Population Fund (UNPF) action program of recent years. However, demographers say programs toward population stabilization by region will continue to remain the biggest challenge in population planning.

With expanding population, the competition for land and water resources intensifies. Under such a situation, social tensions are likely to grow to a point where conflicts (ethnic, religious, and other types) are likely to increase. Such expanding world population has reduced the land area under food grain production from 0.23 hectares/person in 1950 to 0.11 hectares in 2000 (Lester Brown, 2004). This not only threatens the nutrition of a global population living at subsistence levels in areas with depleted soils, but also threatens its survival. As a consequence, conflicts build up among social groups competing for survival. Already, in parts of India, Sudan, Nigeria, and Mali, such conflicts have cut down thousands, if not millions, of human lives. Growing global population has also given rise to

Figure 2-5. Projected Growth in World Population, 1950–2050

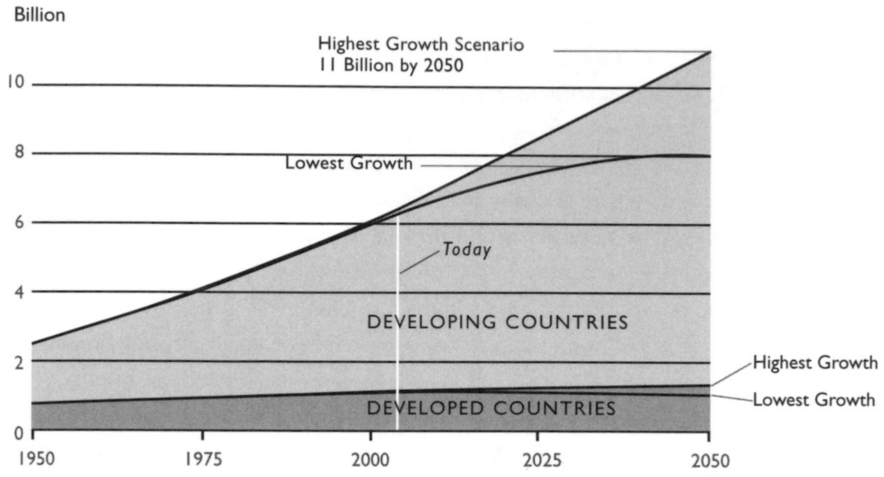

Billion
Highest Growth Scenario
11 Billion by 2050
10
8
Lowest Growth
6
Today
4
DEVELOPING COUNTRIES
2
Highest Growth
Lowest Growth
DEVELOPED COUNTRIES
0
1950
1975
2000
2025
2050

Source: Based on United Nations Population Division (2005) Population Challenges and Development Goals and UN (2005) World Population Prospects (2004 Revision)

Figure 2-6. Projected Growth in World Economy, Population, and Chemical Production, 1995-2020

1995=100
200
180
160
140
120
100
Chemical Industry Production
Gross World Product
Population
1995
2000
2005
2010
2015
2020

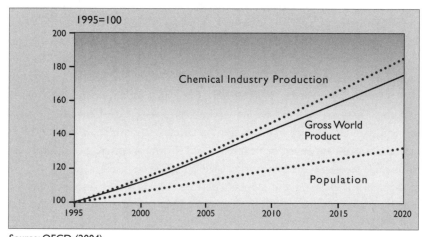

Source: OECD (2004)

conflicts between and among countries on shared water resources as in the case of India, Pakistan, and Bangladesh, which draw water from the Indus and Ganga-Brahmaputra rivers; and Thailand, Laos, Cambodia, and Vietnam, which are watered by the Mekong River. Similar conflicts have existed for many years among the countries of Central Asia sharing the Amudarya and Syrdarya rivers. Conflicts among local groups involving water sharing have also become common in the PRC and India, where cities with a larger power base deprive rural areas of water on which farmers depend for their livelihood (Lester Brown, 2005). Therefore, unless population growth is slowed down and stabilized quickly, the world is likely to continue to see scarcities of land and water, giving rise to increasing social tensions and conflicts. Under such conditions not only development, but also life on earth, cannot be sustainable.

Taking 1995 as the baseline, the global population will increase by 30% as of 2020 but the gross world product will increase by 70% (Figure 2-6). One segment alone, chemical production, will increase by over 80%, and this increase will be accompanied by numerous problems arising from the types of chemicals being produced (see Boxes 2-4 and 2-5).

Box 2-4. Types of Chemicals

Environmentalists categorize industrial materials into four groups:
• less toxic/less persistent
• less toxic/more persistent
• more toxic/less persistent
• more toxic/more persistent (most chemicals being produced today)

		Less Persistent	More Presistent
Less Toxic		**Group 1** • Cellulose • Carbohydrates • Carbohydrates (soap) •Biopolymers	**Group 2** • Iron • Silicon • Aluminum • Copper • Polyolefins
More Toxic		**Group 3** • Acids and bases • Ethers • Alcohols and thiols • Alphatic amines • Aromatic amines • Ethylene/propylene • Ethanol/methanol • Phenols • Aromatic hydrocarbons	**Group 4** • Halogenated alphatic hydrocarbons • Lead • Mercury • Cobalt • Cadmium • Halogenated aromatic hydrocarbons (PCBs, DDT) • Dioxins and furans

Source: Kenneth Geiser (2001)

Box 2-5. Lead and Mercury

The global production of lead and mercury, both highly dangerous substances, during the mid-1990s illustrates the situation. Production of lead was 119,259 tons per year, while production of mercury was 2,235 tons per year. At first glance, comparing these figures with those from 1983, one notices a reduction of 64% in the production of lead and a 37% reduction in the production of mercury. This would seem to be good news, except that these reductions occurred only in developed countries such as Japan, the US, and Western Europe, where stringent regulations were implemented and enforced. In the Third World, where laws and enforcement are weak, production went up. In fact, when quantifying the distribution of persistent toxic chemicals and overall pollution, the situation in the developing world is currently disastrous.

Source	Lead	Mercury
	(tons per year)	
Vehicular traffic	88,739	--
Stationary fossil fuel combustion	11,690	1,475
Nonferrous metal production	14,815	164
Iron and steel production	2,976	29
Cement production	268	133
Waste disposal	921	109
Others		325
Total emissions, mid-1990s	119,259	2,235
Change since 1983	-64%	-37%

Source: Jozef M. Pacyna and Elisabeth G. Pacyna (2001)

As part of a study called *Emerging Asia: Changes and Challenges* (ADB, 1995), the Harvard Institute for International Development (HIID) was engaged by ADB in 1997 to quantify the pollution levels found in Asia in relation to the rest of the world (Figures 2-7 and 2-8). HIID and ADB compiled daily data over a 30-year period to measure air pollution in major urban centers and water pollution in major inland rivers. The results in terms of particulate concentrations in the main Asian cities were found to be 250 micrograms per cubic meter, compared with only 125 micrograms per cubic meter in the rest of the world. Compared with the member countries of the Organisation for Economic Co-operation and Development (OECD), the Asian figures were five times higher.

The Emerging Asia study divided Asia into regions to determine where pollution was most pernicious. Air pollution in South Asia was overall the worst. South Asia had close to 450 micrograms per cubic meter of air pollution in terms of particulates (Figure 2-7). Within South Asia, Bangladesh, India, Nepal, Sri Lanka, and Pakistan were the worst cases.

Figure 2-7 Air Pollution: Particulates

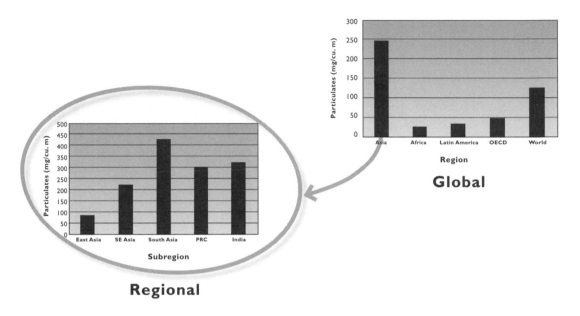

Source: ADB and HIID (1997)

Figure 2-8. Water Pollution: Organic Pollution

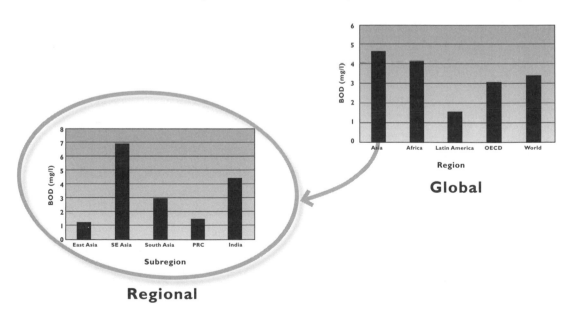

Source: ADB and HIID (1997)

Figure 2-9. Forests

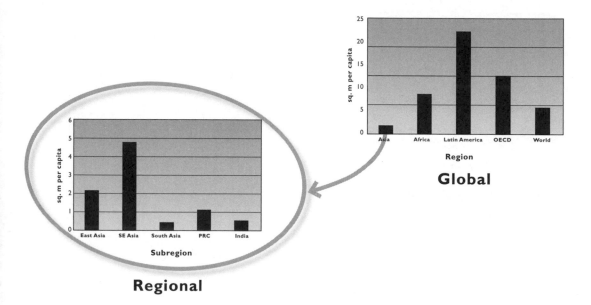

Source: ADB and HIID (1997)

In terms of water pollution, Asia again topped the list (Figure 2-8). Water pollution is measured in terms of BOD, which is measured in milligrams per liter (mg/liter) of water and is indicative of the organic pollution level in water. The world average was 3.5 mg/liter for major inland waters. In Asia it was close to 5 mg/liter. In this case, Southeast Asia, which is the most industrialized/urbanized subregion, was highest with a BOD level close to 7 mg/liter, or double the world average.

Not only are the air and water polluted in Asia, but the land is being depleted as well. The 1997 publication by ADB and HIID indicated that the world's average forest cover was 6 square meters per capita (Figure 2-9). In Asia it was about 2 square meters per capita; and within Asia, South Asia had less than 0.5 square meter of forested area per capita. However, Southeast Asia, primarily Indonesia and Malaysia, had roughly 4.8 square meters of forest per capita.

Participation

Another major factor that affects the sustainability of development is participation. Participation is a process through which stakeholders can influence and share control over development initiatives and the resources used to fund them through engagement in decision making.

Stakeholders include the citizens who benefit from the development, including the poor, disadvantaged groups of people such as women, children, indigenous minorities, and other ethnic groups, and the complex communities in which they live (Figure 2-10). They are also the government, private sector, and civil society (including academies and research institutes, labor unions, religious organizations, political parties, the media, foundations, and especially social service or advocacy-oriented nongovernment organizations or NGOs) at local, district, provincial, and national levels. International donor governments, NGOs, and financing institutions like the World Bank and ADB are also stakeholders.

Participation may take a range of forms or levels, from shallow to deep. Participatory planners must decide which forms to employ with which stakeholders at different times depending upon skills required to make particular decisions. The forms are discussed as follows.

1. Information sharing

Stakeholders, in particular the people affected by a project, should be informed in advance about what is being planned and what is expected to happen, and how much money is being invested in their communities. Alternatively, they may be asked to provide information by responding to survey questionnaires, contributing to data that others will use. While essential, information sharing involves minimal engagement.

Figure 2-10. Participants in Development

Source: ADB (2000)

2. Consultation

Discussion of proposed activities, their consequences and implications, provides an opportunity for stakeholders to respond to new ideas. Though information flows two ways, stakeholders usually have limited opportunities to contribute to or change the basic design.

3. Collaborative decision-making

Scope for stakeholder influence over decisions is considerably increased in this mode of participation. Through debate and discussion or shared responsibility for drafting documents, stakeholders raise concerns and work together to build consensus.

4. Empowerment

When people are given an opportunity to take an active role in planning, implementing, and monitoring projects that affect their own development, they develop a sense of ownership of the activity and are motivated to make the necessary effort to ensure its success. As individuals and groups learn through experience, as well as from training programs and ongoing support, their capacity to manage activities and plan new ones is enhanced. Trust-based networks, or social capital, typically expand, grow stronger, and support continued social stability and economic growth. Long-term development impacts improve. Participation often has a multiplier effect, as it promotes the empowerment of citizens, communities, and organizations.

A large range of tools and methods has been developed to facilitate effective and cost-efficient information sharing, consultation, collaboration, and empowerment; and facilitators have been trained around the world to use these to maximize outcomes. Participation requires respect for the deep understanding of local conditions that only residents can have, a supportive institutional and policy environment that helps groups to act on decisions they make, willingness to learn and share, and skilled application of these tools. Special approaches to planning, budget management, participatory monitoring, partnerships between public and private sector organizations, and decentralized governance and service provision have been created in the past 12-20 years as participation is "scaled-up" from individual communities to wider social contexts.

Policy and Market Failures

Policy and market failures constitute another key factor in determining sustainable development Policy failure can be the result of a sin of omission—not intervening when it is necessary and beneficial—or of commission—stepping in when intervention is unnecessary or even detrimental.

An example of policy failure is the coexistence of overuse, waste, and inefficiency with growing resource scarcity. Take the case of the large-scale irrigation projects in Pakistan, where water from the Indus River is being used to irrigate grain farms. A side effect is causing parts of the river basin to become increasingly waterlogged and saline, taking almost 32 million hectares of land out of production. The problem stems from a multitude of sources, most notably operational

Box 2-6. More Examples of Policy and Market Failures

- *Putting a resource into a single use when its multiple use would generate a greater net benefit.* Many tropical forests in Asia and South America are exploited almost solely for timber production although the same forest can yield fruits, medicinal plants enhancing biological diversity, beehives for honey, and a host of other environmental services such as water and soil conservation.
- *Irreversible loss of unique sites and ecosystems for marginal economic benefits.* The uniqueness of historical sites and some threatened environments could be of immense value that should not be lost except in case of emergency (such as famine) or when significant indisputable benefits are derived from such a loss. Unfortunately, however, in some of the developing countries, wanton destruction of coral by driftnets and deforestation are occurring, bringing marginal, temporary benefits to some people who may or may not even be the direct beneficiaries.

Source: The Environment Program, ADB (1994)

inefficiencies, including overirrigation and lack of land leveling. As a consequence, many farms become flooded, while others do not receive sufficient water. In both cases, crops are damaged.

Market failure occurs when freely functioning markets produce prices that do not reflect the social and economic value of an action.

In the developing countries it is assumed that air, water, and unclaimed land are free resources. As such, they have become dumping grounds for wastes and emissions. It is also assumed that raw materials generally demand the lowest market prices, intermediate goods are priced a little higher, and finished products command the highest prices. These price differentials are primarily technology driven. There are numerous examples. Jute, Bangladesh's chief export, is considered a raw material and is accordingly sold to the UK at the bottom of the pricing scale. The jute is then processed in the UK into finished products and resold to Bangladesh at a higher price. A further example is coffee. It is incumbent therefore on developing countries to pursue policies that add more value to their raw materials locally in accordance with their comparative advantage.

Policy and market failures often go together. They occur most often when a primary resource that could otherwise be managed as a renewable resource is not (see Box 2-6). The rate of deforestation is a classic example. The rate of logging is almost always higher than the rate of reforestation. Because of poor policy facilitation, local communities are deprived of their customary rights of access, even though they may be the most effective resource managers. Those who dwell near the forest and depend on it for survival also, by necessity, possess very specialized knowledge as to how to protect it. Unfortunately, governments sometimes leave forest management to the loggers and not to the people who have a major stake in it and whose survival depends upon the regeneration of the trees.

Yet, with a little bit of thought, and sometimes a little bit of science, it is possible to formulate policies that are environmentally sound and sustainable. An example is the Malaysian palm oil industry. Malaysia is the largest exporter of raw palm oil in the world. In the past, the effluent from the palm oil mills, which has a BOD level of 30,000 mg/liter (raw domestic sewage has a BOD of 300 mg/liter), was being discharged directly into the rivers, creating severe oxygen depletion in the receiving water. A sustainable solution was developed 20 years ago when the UN Economic and Social Commission for Asia and the Pacific (ESCAP), with the help of the Asian Institute of Technology, devised a method to treat the palm oil effluent and to make it harmless as a solid waste byproduct that is used as animal feed and fertilizer. This was a real win-win solution to a serious environmental problem.

Good Governance

Good governance is an integral part of and a necessary precondition of avoiding market and policy failure. *Webster's Dictionary* defines governance as "the manner in which power is exercised in the management of a country's economic and social resources for development." Poor governance constrains, retards, and distorts the process of development and has a disproportionately negative impact on the poor.

Lawrence Summers, former President of Harvard, discussed this issue of poor governance when, as the then US Treasury Secretary, he said, "Economic history has provided a clear, natural experiment regarding the efficacy of finance without conditions. Again and again, natural resources windfalls have financed presidential planes and palaces and entrenched official corruption, while producing very little in the way of lasting economic benefits."

Summers raised a very important issue: What would be the point of increasing the external aid flow and imposing the Tobin Tax (see Chapter 13) if funds go to the developing countries or wherever the sustainable development problems are, only to see those funds used to finance either nonsustainable development activities or corruption? This has been emphasized again and again: Most of the development finance institutions (DFIs) today have adopted "anticorruption" and "good governance" policies that the borrowing member countries must follow in order for them to be eligible to borrow from these banks.

The policies of multilateral financing institutions (MFIs), such as the World Bank and ADB, provide for adherence to four principles of good governance.

1. Accountability

This involves making public officials answerable for their behavior as public servants. It also demands establishment of criteria by which accountability will be measured.

2. Participation and decentralization

Since people are the major stakeholders in a nation's development process they are also the major beneficiaries. A principle of good governance is to involve all the stakeholders in the policy of government. Decentralization improves the manageability of participation, which, in turn, improves governance. However, decentralization in the absence of good local governance can be a cause of increasing poverty.

3. Predictability

Laws, regulations, and policies must be fair and consistently applied so that people can predict the consequences and the outcomes of violating them.

4. Transparency

Information on government actions and policies, before and after an action, must be available to the general public.

These four elements of good governance hold true for the policymaking bodies of corporations and NGOs as well. In recent years, people have seen in the US how bad corporate governance erodes stockholders' public funds and savings.

The World Bank took the lead in formulating a policy on good governance, which is now advocated by the regional development banks as well.

Prior to adopting a governance policy, the policy of the World Bank was that, as long as borrowers repay the money with interest, the lenders have no business demanding good governance, which is the internal affair of a borrowing government. Today, however, all the member nations of the MFIs have accepted good governance as a conditionality of borrowing.

Prevention and Management of Disasters

Disasters are defined by the United Nations Disaster Relief Organization as "abnormal or infrequent hazards to communities or geographical areas that are vulnerable to such events causing substantial damage, disruption and often casualties, leaving the affected community unable to function normally." One area of sustainable development that cannot be overlooked is disaster management. A recent study shows that natural disasters have immense adverse economic, environmental, and social impacts on a country.

A distinction is commonly made between a natural disaster and disasters being caused by humans, such as the Chernobyl nuclear power plant meltdown or the explosion at the Bhopal pesticide plant. Since the events of September 11, 2001, though, a further distinction has been made between disasters caused by humans that are technological/accidental and those that are deliberate.

With the issues of climate change, the rising sea level, and the increasing frequency of killer storms caused by long-term environmental degradation, and with the rise of technological disasters and terrorism, disaster management has come to be regarded as one of the major factors in promoting sustainable development.

The International Federation of Red Cross and Red Crescent published a study by region, covering the years 1972 to 1996, of the percentage of people killed, injured, rendered homeless, or otherwise affected by natural disasters (Figure 2-11). In Africa, the mortality rate was 59%; in

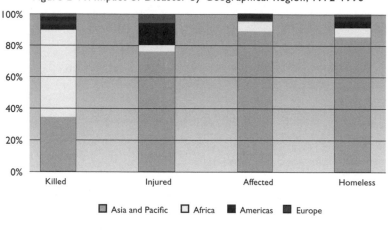

Figure 2-11. Impact of Disaster by Geographical Region, 1972-1996

■ Asia and Pacific   ☐ Africa   ■ Americas   ■ Europe

Source: Isabel Ortiz (1998)

Asia, 33%. The disasters that killed Africans were presumably famine and drought, whereas the disasters that killed Asians were typhoon-related (i.e., winds, floods, and tidal waves). In Asia, 77% of the affected population sustained disaster-related injuries, while more than 80% were left homeless.

Between 1987 and 2005 the most common disasters on earth were:

- high winds (tornados, cyclones, typhoons, and hurricanes),
- floods,
- quakes (including earthquakes, tsunamis, and volcanic eruptions),
- droughts and famines,
- wild fires, and
- landslides (including pyroclastic flows).

While floods and high winds affect mostly Asia and parts of Latin America, drought and famine are the major causes of disasters in Africa. In fact, floods and high winds are also now causing problems in the developed countries such as the US due possibly to climate changes.

Natural Disasters

The tsunamis and seaquakes in Asia in December 2004 and March 2005 raise new issues and questions as to how to rehabilitate the survivors and protect vulnerable populations in the future. In particular, Indonesia and its neighboring coastal countries such as Thailand, Malaysia, Sri Lanka, and India are adversely affected. An estimated 150,000 people were killed by the tsunami/seaquake in Asia. In addition, tens of thousands of people were injured, or displaced. (Lareef Zubair, 2005) An early warning system is currently being established for the region. Experts predict more tremors in the region in this decade than in the past several ones. Several tsunami websites have recently been established to provide environmental, economic, and social information on these events.

Technological disasters and terrorism are also affecting the developed countries of the world. Thus, disaster management is currently considered as an important prerequisite for sustainable development in the world.

In the twenty-first century, the world will continue to be quite concerned about the possible economic, environmental, and social impacts of disasters induced by humans and in particular about terrorists. When a state or a group of nonstate actors directs violence against the civilian population of its own or of another state, it is called terrorism (Mark Selden and Alvin Y. So, 2004). The prospects of increased terrorist threats to the national as well as individual security of people in a country are becoming frightening. Terrorism is on the rise since the incidents of 9/11. Ethnic and religious conflicts and killings are becoming more frequent. Such rampant lawlessness, insecurity of life, and violence not only cost the governments around the world (both developed and developing) billions of dollars, but also disturb the peace of mind and the behavior of citizens. People worry about security of their lives most; they also are concerned about loss of employment and loss of income from trade and tourism. In the future, the risk of using a nuclear weapon in a regional conflict or by a terrorist is predicted to be on the rise (Martin Rees, 2003). According to the US Central Intelligence Agency, the nuclear materials and technology to build bombs are more accessible to terrorists now than at any time in history. This, together with the possibility of increased frequency and severity of natural disasters, may become one of the key factors governing the sustainability of development in this century. Today, sustainable development has a significant implication for world peace.

DETERMINANTS OF SUSTAINABLE DEVELOPMENT

The three determinants of sustainable development are consumption, production, and distribution. In examining these determinants, one should turn the question around and ask what makes development unsustainable.

Obviously, in the case of consumption, the issue is the use of resources beyond the reasonable limits set by nature through regeneration. For example, the forest has a regenerating capacity through both natural and artificial methods. So its limit is the sum of the two. Any logging beyond that limit is unsustainable. Unsustainable production is characterized by gross inefficiencies and mismanagement in the use of water, energy, and minerals. Examples include large-scale irrigation projects along the Indus River in Pakistan. These were designed to increase production, but because of failed operating procedures and policies, vast tracts of land passed out of production due to flooding and salinity. Finally, inequitable distribution is unsustainable. A prime example is the distribution of global income, where the gap between the richest 20% and the poorest 20% is enormous and is growing wider with the passage of time.

Consumption

When talking about consumption, it is important to examine not only the amount of resources consumed but also the patterns in which they are consumed. There are five reasons to examine these patterns:

1. **Economic efficiency alone cannot meet the natural resource appetite following current consumption patterns.**

Many people strive for eco-efficiency, believing that if we can achieve it, we will have reached a sustainable plateau. This is not true. No matter how efficient we become ecologically, the natural resources appetite of the present generation can never be met by eco-efficiency alone. Consumption must be reduced. This can be achieved only by developing strong normative policies on regulating the environment and enhancing policy mechanisms to reflect the degree of environmental damage that current consumption patterns impose on the world.

2. **Consumption is the key to understanding policy challenges, as they focus on the demand side.**

If we study the consumption patterns of water and energy, we will soon realize that many subsidies meant to help the poor usually end up not helping them, since subsidies reduce costs, inducing an increase in demand by both the poor and the wealthy. Finally, we will realize that, because demand has increased in response to low prices, precious resources like water and energy are being wasted. This creates a vicious cycle of inefficiency and pollution.

3. **Examining consumption patterns reveals what is being consumed and whether it is meeting the basic needs of the people.**

Considering what is being consumed, whether basic goods or luxury items, is very important, as it will tell us whether the consumption pattern meets the basic needs of people and whether development will be sustainable.

4. **The pattern will illustrate vividly that the poor not only consume less, but also pollute less, and they are directly affected if the environment is degraded.**

Polluted water affects the health of the poor directly. Exposed to dirty air 24 hours a day, seven days a week, the health of the poor in urban slums and squatter settlements, where as much as 40% of the total population of a developing country may live, is endangered. Likewise, water and land polluted by agrochemicals and solid wastes can adversely affect the health of farmers.

5. **Consumption patterns tell a great deal about problematic relationships among economic growth, the satisfaction of basic needs, and human aspirations.**

In one country, GDP growth may be low, and a large number of people may live below the poverty line. In another country, GDP growth may be the same, but few people are below the poverty line. In the first instance, the production and consumption patterns may be more geared toward luxury goods, and toward increasing economic benefits at the cost of environmental and social benefits. In the second case, GDP growth is likely to be utilized toward satisfying the basic needs of the people. Therefore, with the same GDP, consumption patterns and the incidence of poverty may vary widely, with countries in the former category presenting greater challenges to sustainable development.

Even within a poor community or a poor household, there is a problematic relationship between groups of powerful people and groups of disadvantaged people. For example, among the poor families in India, the power structure is such that women have little voice in decision making. At a meeting between a group of villagers living in an Indian desert and representatives of a development bank to discuss poverty reduction in their village, only a few women were invited. They came but would not speak. Afterwards, away from the men, the women spoke freely. They suggested that the primary reason for the village's poverty was the way their meager incomes were spent: The men drank; any income or savings was spent on alcohol. Therefore, these families had no financial cushion for emergencies or future needs. These women were powerless, and the men abused them. This case study emphasized the need for gender-segregated consultation.

The role of local governments in nurturing sustainable development cannot be overemphasized. In this case, ideally the local government, not the development bank, should be addressing these women's problems. But life is rarely ideal. The power structure in the village is made up of the people who drink, but they are also the heads of the families. Therefore, they have more say in the matter—and they have the ear of the local officials in charge of the village. It goes back to the issue of governance and corruption.

The patterns of food consumption among the poor are also quite different. The women are responsible for gathering and cooking food, but they eat last, only after the husband and children have eaten. So while the patterns of consumption and power structure between the rich and the poor are very important, it is also necessary to understand the dynamics within poor families, particularly gender discrimination.

The Religious Revolt Against Consumerism

In 1998, UNDP did a study on how the world's various religions treat consumption. The finding was that almost every religion has strictures against excessive consumption (Box 2-7).

Mahatma Gandhi once said this world has enough to meet the "needs" of everybody, but not the "greeds" of everybody.

Keeping those religious thoughts and Gandhi's maxim in mind, one could look at what is happening in the real world: 76% of the world's population live in the developing countries as compared with 24% who live in the developed countries. Yet, as Table 2-2 shows, people living in developed countries are consuming 64% of the meat, almost half the cereals, over 80% of the metals, over 86% of the chemicals, and 92% of the cars. In terms of per capita consumption, Americans consume 52 times as much meat, have 320 times the number of private vehicles,

Box 2-7. Some Religious Strictures Against Excessive Consumption

- Christianity – "Watch out! Be on your guard against all kinds of greed; a person's life does not consist of an abundance of possessions."

- Confucianism – "Excess and deficiency are equally at fault."

- Buddhism – "By the thirst for the riches, the foolish man destroys himself as if he were his own enemy."

- Hinduism – "When you have the golden gift of commitment you have everything."

- Islam – "It is difficult for a person laden with riches to climb the steep path that leads to bliss."

- Taoism – "One who knows he or she has enough is rich." (There have been great secular thoughts along this line, too.)

Source: D.V. Smith and K. F. Jalal (2000), p. 27

and use 245 times as much copper as average Indians. With these figures, one can, once again, appreciate that eco-efficiency alone cannot satisfy the demand for food, natural resources, and other consumer goods of the global population. The consumption pattern must be changed. If, for example, Americans would reduce the amount of meat they eat to about one fifth their present consumption, and paper use to one tenth, they could make a noticeable contribution toward creating a more balanced consumption pattern, wherein eco-efficiency could begin to play an important role.

In a 2005 article, Lester Brown notes that, although the US has long consumed the lion's share of world resources, the PRC is taking over on almost all fronts, excepting the use of corn and oil. For example in 2004, the PRC consumed 64 million tons of meat as against 38 million tons in the US. Steel consumption in the PRC is currently more than double that in the US (250 million tons in the PRC against 104 million tons in the US). Similarly in the PRC, consumption of electronic and household appliances has soared in the recent past; the number of cell phones in the PRC is now over 270 million versus 160 million in the US; consumption of TV sets in the PRC currently exceeds 375 million against 245 million in the US. Of course, on a per capita basis the US consumption still exceeds consumption in the PRC.

Similarly, the consumption patterns of Europe and of other developed regions are very high. Consumption all over the developed world needs to be reduced.

The question that may legitimately arise is, why should people in the developed world reduce their consumption patterns to satisfy the needs of teeming millions of poor Africans or Asians, who are not making any serious effort toward reducing their own populations, and who are not increasing their efficiency of operation?

Let us talk about food consumption. Aside from moral and ethical reasons, it has been demonstrated that drastic reductions in consumption are needed to release resources, seeds,

Table 2-2. Who Consumes?

Product	Developed World Share (%)	Developing World Share (%)	Per Capita Consumption: United States/India (units)
Cereals	48	52	6
Milk	72	28	4
Meat	64	36	52
Sawn wood	78	22	18
Paper	81	19	115
Fertilizer	60	40	6
Cement	52	48	7
Copper	86	14	245
Iron and steel	80	20	22
Aluminum	86	14	85
Inorganic chemicals	87	13	5
Organic chemicals	85	15	28
Cars	92	8	320
Commercial vehicles	85	15	102
Population	24	76	.28
Total energy	75	25	35
Electricity	79	21	40

Source: Smith and Jalal, ADB (2000), p. 24

and more land, which could be allocated to growing food for the poor. For example, if people were to shift to a vegetarian diet, it would make a significant difference in terms of increased grain supply. Reducing consumption by 1 kilogram (kg) of poultry would release about 3-4 kg of grain. Another good reason to reduce food consumption is health. Vital Signs, the 2001 World Watch Institute annual report, focuses on obesity. A person is considered obese if his or her body/mass index (BMI) is greater than 30. BMI is the measure of body fat based on height and weight. The index is defined as weight divided by height squared. The Institute noted that a large percentage of the population in developed countries is obese. In the US, obesity among the total population has increased from 15% in 1980 to over 33% today. In the UK, obesity increased from 7% in 1980 to approximately 25% in 2004. The frightening aspect of these numbers is that they hold true for the rest of the developed world. Obesity is considered an illness that affects some 1.1 billion people who are sick or incapable of working normally, a condition leading to low productivity. On the other hand, the world has 1.3 billion who earn less than $1 a day, who are also suffering from malnutrition and other illnesses and are unable to produce as much as a

Box 2-8. Ecological Footprint Calculation[a]

Section I: Food

1. How often do you eat animal-based products?
2. How would you describe your average daily food intake?
3. How much of your purchased food is thrown out rather than eaten?
4. How much of the food that you eat is locally grown, processed, or in-season?

Section II: Transport

5. How much do you drive each year on average?
6. On average, how often do you drive with someone else?
7. What kind of fuel efficiency does your car get (put the average if you drive several cars)?
8. On average, how many kilometers do you travel on public transportation (bus, rail) each week?
9. How many hours each year do you spend flying?

Section III: Housing

10. How many people live in your home?
11. How big is your home?
12. Does your home use electricity from a "green" electricity provider (e.g. solar, wind, micro-hydro)?
13. Do you use energy-efficient appliances and light bulbs?

[a] Go to Google search on "Ecological Footprint" calculation to measure your actual footprint. There are 13 questions, divided into three sections as above. To calculate footprint, answer the questions and click on "Go." The calculation presented is obviously a gross simplification and does not take into account many details that will add or subtract from your footprint. This calculation will perform poorly for people outside North America, since it is calibrated to the average North American lifestyle. Also, those North Americans who live an atypical lifestyle, for example, by avoiding owning cars and new products, by growing their own food, by living on a boat, or by buying fewer material goods, may not be represented accurately by this calculation.

normal human being. Thus, a total of 2.4 billion people, because of malnutrition or obesity, cannot engage fully in economic and other activities. Changing food consumption patterns could not only create a healthier world population, it could also ensure greater productivity by the entire world population. This is, of course, based on the simple assumption that the food released by reducing the consumption of the rich will be available to increase consumption of the malnourished or the poor.

The ecological footprint is essentially a representation of the environmental consequences of consumption expressed in terms of land and water areas required to satisfy the food, transportation, and housing needs of a person or a country (Box 2-8). Although calculation of the ecological footprint has shortcomings, it is the first time that the global consumption pattern has been expressed in quantitative terms. It is a complicated formula in which three parameters come into play—consumption of food, transportation, and housing.

Food consumption is measured in terms of the land and water areas needed to produce a given quantity of food; housing consumption is measured on the basis of the plinth area a person occupies in a home, or the land area the house occupies; energy and transport requirements are measured in terms of the areas of forest that have to be planted to absorb the emissions of CO_2 produced. (This is not the best way of calculating energy consumption, because developed nations might be using very efficient energy systems, while people in Nepal, for instance, may be using inefficient cooking stoves or motor vehicles. Obviously, there will be some distortion in the figures.)

Worldwide there are only 1.8 hectares of biologically productive area per person. Against this figure, an average American's ecological footprint is 10 hectares, over five times the world average. This is one more piece of evidence of why eco-efficiency cannot, by itself, solve the problem of resource shortage in this world.

Production

The second determinant of sustainable development is production. It is possible that the twenty-first century needs a new production revolution through a process that will take into account not only the economic benefit of production but also its ecological and social benefits. This is also referred to as the triple "p" or the triple bottomline to sustainability: profits, people, and planet (Brian Nattrass and Mary Altomare, 1999). We have to develop a production pattern that will satisfy the needs of most of the consumers who are in the middle-income to low-income to poor category.

What is wrong with production patterns? There are five basic problems with our current production patterns.

1. Use of materials and processes that cause environmental degradation and health hazards

Materials and processes employed in the industrial production of many developing countries result in large quantities of toxic emissions—gaseous, liquid, and solid. These pollutants endanger the health of not only the industrial workers and their immediate family members, but also many people living downstream. The concept of cleaner production (as against the concept of cleaner technology) has brought about some positive changes; but it still has a long way to go.

2. Inefficiency of production, which causes system losses and environmental degradation

Again, as an example, one can look at the irrigation systems in Pakistan (see "Policy and Market Failures," p. 60). One can also look at the aluminum cola can, which is more complicated and costlier to produce than the cola itself (see Box 2-9). This is a striking case study of the complexity of industrial production, revealed in describing the origins and pathways of an English cola can.

3. Failure to reflect negative externalities in product costs

The third important problem is one that has already been discussed under the challenges of market failure. When a product is manufactured, particularly in developing countries, air, water, and land are considered free goods. This is especially true when there are no regulations or no one follows the regulations. Accordingly, a tree standing deep inside a forest does not have a dollar value. Only when the tree is felled and brought to the mill is it assigned a monetary value. This is a grossly erroneous concept when pricing a product. The failure to reflect negative externalities in the product cost must be corrected if the production revolution is to succeed. To remedy the situation, a natural resources accounting procedure has to be introduced (Chapter 11).

4. Energy, water, and fertilizer subsidies, which benefit mostly the nonpoor

In a study on subsidies in the energy and water sectors, the World Bank found that just withdrawing the subsidies would release $125 billion a year worldwide. What is more, these subsidies, established in the name of helping the poor, actually go to the nonpoor. There are just too many examples, supported by data, showing that in developing countries poor people pay 5-10 times more for water than many of those who are wealthy and who have access to urban piped water. Due to failure of the local government to supply water to all its citizens, the poor buy their water from vendors at a much higher price.

5. Transaction costs, which are significantly higher for the poor

Because large farmers or affluent urban dwellers have the advantage of scale, they can access water and other resources much more easily than poor farmers and poor citizens.

A new production revolution is imperative to ensure sustainable development in the world to overcome the five problems mentioned above. Whereas resolution of the first three problems pertains more to a new industrial revolution, the remaining two problems are more relevant to a new agricultural revolution. This is also termed in this book as the "Green 2 Revolution" for reasons explained later.

According to Paul Hawken et al. (1999), such a New Industrial Revolution has been triggered in the industrialized countries. Hawken describes "natural capitalism" as the future of industrialization in which business and environmental interests overlap and business can make increasing profit and at the same time help environmental problems. Industrialization through the natural capitalist approach suggests four major interlinked changes in business practices:

- Dramatically increase the productivity of natural resources by reducing the wasteful and destructive flow of resources. Such an increase will be effected through concurrent changes in process design, technology, and good housekeeping.

Box 2-9. The Origins and Pathways of a Cola Can

A striking case study of the complexity of industrial metabolism is provided by James Womack and Daniel Jones in their book *Lean Thinking* [1996], where they trace the origins and pathways of a can of cola in England. The can itself is more costly and complicated to manufacture than the beverage. Bauxite is mined in Australia and trucked to a chemical reduction mill, where a half-hour process purifies each ton of bauxite into a half-ton of aluminum oxide. When enough of that is stockpiled, it is loaded on a giant ore carrier and sent to Sweden or Norway, where hydroelectric dams provide cheap electricity. After a month-long journey across two oceans, it usually sits at the smelter for as long as two months.

The smelter takes two hours to turn each half-ton of aluminum oxide into a quarter-ton of aluminum metal, in ingots 10 meters long. These are cured for two weeks before being shipped to roller mills in Sweden or Germany. There each ingot is heated to nearly 900 degrees Fahrenheit and rolled down to a thickness of an eighth of an inch. The resulting sheets are wrapped in 10-ton coils and transported to a warehouse, and then to a cold rolling mill in the same or another country, where they are rolled tenfold thinner, ready for fabrication. The aluminum is then sent to England, where sheets are punched and formed into cans, which are then washed, dried, painted with a base coat, and then painted again with specific product information. The cans are next lacquered, flanged (they are still topless), sprayed inside with a protective coating to prevent the cola from corroding the can, and inspected. The cans are palletized, fork lifted, and warehoused until needed. They are then shipped to the bottler, where they are washed and cleaned once more, then filled with flavored syrup, phosphorus, caffeine, and CO_2. The sugar is harvested from beet fields in France and undergoes trucking, milling, refining, and shipping. The phosphorus comes from Idaho, where it is excavated from deep open-pit mines—a process that also unearths cadmium and radioactive thorium. Round-the-clock, the mining company uses the same amount of electricity as a city of 100,000 people in order to reduce the phosphate to food-grade quality. The caffeine is shipped from a chemical manufacturer in England.

The filled cans are sealed with an aluminum "pop-top" lid at the rate of 1,500 cans per minute, then inserted into cardboard cartons printed with matching color and promotional schemes. The cartons are made of forest pulp that may have originated anywhere from Sweden or Siberia to the old-growth, virgin forests of British Columbia that are the home of grizzlies, wolverines, otters, and eagles. Palletized again, the cans are shipped to a regional distribution warehouse, and shortly thereafter to a supermarket, where a typical can is purchased within three days. The consumer buys 12 ounces of the phosphate-tinged, caffeine-impregnated, caramel-flavored sugar water. Drinking the cola takes a few minutes; throwing the can away takes a second. In England, consumers discard 84 percent of all cans, which means that the overall rate of aluminum waste, after counting production losses, is 88 percent. The US still gets three-fifths of its aluminum from virgin ore, at 20 times the energy intensity of recycled aluminum, and throws away enough aluminum to replace its entire commercial aircraft fleet every three months.

Source: Hawken et al. 1999: 49-50, as cited in D.V. Smith and K.F. Jalal (2000), p. 45

- Shift to biologically inspired production models so that waste will be eliminated, rather than minimized.
- Move to a solution-based business model that, for example, will provide illumination instead of selling light bulbs.
- Reinvest in natural capital so that the ecosystems can yield services and resources more abundantly.

The Green 2 Revolution

Like the new industrial revolution, a new agricultural revolution is also needed to achieve sustainable development in this world. This is called the Green-Green or Green 2 Revolution. The first Green Revolution was initiated in the 1960s in South Asia, where the sole objective was to increase total food production to save people from starving. While the program produced more food, in the process it also increased the number of landless laborers. Many small farmers became agricultural workers for the large farmers who bought up their lands. The small farmers' choices were further limited by bad governance. The prevailing government policies favored the large farmers when it came to providing access to better seeds, fertilizers, irrigation water, roads, and communal storehouses. A good example of this type of favoritism is in the case of diesel fuel. During the Green Revolution the government of Bangladesh imported diesel fuel, with the honest intention of selling at subsidized prices to local communities to run their irrigation pumps. The principal customers, it so happened, were large farmers. When the small farmers tried to buy the subsidized fuel they were turned away, forcing them to buy it from private venders at three times the government price. In short, the rich farmers had high visibility and a voice in local politics, which the poor farmers did not have. It became increasingly difficult for the poor farmers to modernize, and if they could not farm efficiently, the benefit-cost ratio of their lands was the same as it was, under rain-fed conditions. It is not surprising, then, that during the first Green Revolution the income gap between the rich and the poor actually increased, even though the total production of food crops increased.

But this type of Green Revolution does not promote sustainable development. What is needed is a Green-Green Revolution based in part on key elements of good governance. The Green 2 Revolution will have to be based on participation by all affected parties, including those who will be adequately compensated for the sale of portions of their land and the poor farmers, who will have to learn to work productively in an environment friendly way with their new land and modern inputs (see, e.g., Box 2-10).

There are essentially five policy elements of a Green 2 Revolution:

1. A redistributive policy that favors the poor by providing them access to land and modern inputs

Since good governance includes predictability, fair compensation pursuant to law will be required for a successful redistributive policy.

2. Increased public funding for less favorable agricultural land

In Asia alone, as much as 48.5% of the agricultural land is considered barely or not productive. These "bad" lands are found in marginal deserts, on steeply sloping hills, or in other inhospitable locations. Huge tracts of sorely needed agricultural land either have been ignored entirely or have received minimal attention. Government attention has mostly been on the irrigated agricultural land, which constitutes about 1.5% of the total. However, due to intense farming, this land's full potential has already been realized, and its productivity is now decreasing. Once again, the solution is obvious: Governments must redirect their attention and their human and financial resources toward lands which can be improved.

3. Increased attention to the needs of smallholder farms and landless laborers, including credit

Increased attention will have to be given to small farmers and landless laborers to increase production (in terms of agricultural extension services and inputs, but not subsidies). Microfinance often requires a year to educate smallholders and the landless poor who will avail of it. However, with proper preparation, microfinance can be profitable, with losses from bad loans often less than those incurred by traditional banks.

Box 2-10. The Coffee Connection

A 29 July 2001 edition of the Boston Sunday Globe reported that a Guatemalan coffee farmer gets 34 cents per pound for planting, growing, and harvesting coffee beans, which are then sold in high-end cafés in Boston for $8 per pound. True, there are downstream costs such as processing, packaging, and shipping costs, and profit. But the return received by the farmer and the return that the coffee shop receives are widely disproportionate. The farmers say their rights have been violated—not just their right to work but their families' rights. Their children get sick because the farmers cannot afford to buy proper food. Issues presented by this case can be addressed in developed countries through the purchase of coffee from buyers who take steps to assist with the plight of the coffee farmers, an option presented to purchasers of coffee at the World Bank, as described in Chapter 10. In developing countries, governments and others can assist coffee farmers and members of their families to obtain better education and access to technology so these farmers can diversify the products they sell in accordance with their comparative advantage.

A big debate occurred at the WSSD during a seminar on indigenous people and their rights. Such rights are clearly stated in at least half a dozen laws and international agreements accepted by various states and their governments. Yet time after time, these laws have been breeched or ignored in many developing countries and sometimes even in developed countries. The aborigines in Australia have been exploited for years and have been crying in vain for the government to help them.

4. **Increased investment in rain-fed agricultural areas in both Asia and Latin America**

Governments tend to ignore agricultural areas that receive ample rain, believing they are self-irrigating. But there is also a need for land leveling, for example. If land is not leveled, one farm gets flooded while another might be parched. Other inputs such as seeds, organic and limited quantities of inorganic fertilizers, and extension services may be needed.

5. **Decentralized agricultural research, development, and extension systems focusing on particular issues such as soil and water management**

Researchers at the International Food Policy Research Institute in Washington, D.C., have suggested that agricultural resource management is highly location specific. Centralized agricultural research, development, and extension systems or universal policies that would be applicable universally do not work to improve land productivity.

Each of the elements contained in the aptly named Green 2 Revolution will have a clear and significant impact on poverty reduction, which is a major objective of promoting sustainable development. These five elements of the new agricultural revolution need to be in place before development can become sustainable.

Distribution

The third determinant of sustainable development is the distribution of resources. It is a complex issue. We have already examined poverty and its linkage with sustainable development. We have also seen how the income gap between the rich and the poor is widening over time. What can be done about it?

Definitions of poverty fall into two categories: (i) the "objective," based on per capita annual income, expenditure, and assets; and (ii) the "subjective," meaning people's perception of poverty. An objective definition is people who earn less than $1 per day. But how do the poor define poverty in a subjective way? And how do they see their role in sustainable development?

To answer this question, the World Bank surveyed 60,000 people worldwide who subsisted at the poverty level. The results of the survey were published in the World Development Report 2000. According to the report, people who are not well off materially consider themselves poor. People who are not well off physically also consider themselves poor, regardless of their income level. Security and the ability to cope with emergencies also lead to the perception of poverty. In addition, the poor feel that they are denied choices, that they are rarely given the opportunity to be part of decision-making processes, and that they lack the freedom to take action. That food was far down on their list of responses was another revelation. The general feeling was, "Okay, I'm eating less and earning less, but if I feel well and secure I can endure." Basically, what the survey revealed was that people interviewed would not feel poor if they did not have to worry about feeling threatened, if they had the wherewithal to cope with emergencies, if they could participate in those choices that control their lives, and if they had affordable access to basic health care.

How can we help the poor help themselves? Providing community health care, ensuring security, and propagating emergency disaster planning are some obvious solutions. Another is offering the poor the financial resources to broaden their choices in the form of microcredit. The poor have been routinely excluded from the commercial banking system. Many have never stepped inside a bank. Ordinary commercial loans for the poor are completely out of the question. Yet a poor person, like any entrepreneur, often needs funds to start a new business, to expand an existing business, or just to stay in business. The importance and success of microcredit organizations is best demonstrated with a story.

A woman who was the village beggar was approached by a representative of a microcredit institution, who wished her to take a $5 loan. "How can I take a loan?" she asked, "I am a beggar. I could never repay it." The lender, however, was insistent and said, "I will not only give you the loan, but I will show you how you can pay it back." The loan agent told her to use the loan to buy bamboo. He then showed her how to fashion the bamboo into baskets. "Now," he said, "go into the village and sell your baskets." She came back two months later looking like a new person. "Here is your loan, and here is your interest," she said. "And this is the money that I earned." But it obviously was not just the money that renewed her spirit and self-confidence. She went on, "Previously I used to go to the houses in the village and the people would slam their doors in my face or tell me to come back on Friday, which is alms day. Now when I go to their homes, they not only open the door, they invite me in, give me a glass of water to drink, and then ask what I have to sell today. I may sell one or two items or nothing that day. It doesn't matter. Now people respect me." This is one of several factual stories told by the well-known founder of Grameen Bank of Bangladesh—Muhammad Yunus (Muhammad Yunus, 2003).

Microcredit organizations have filled the void between banks and the poor. Often the loans might be as little as a few dollars, offered with a fair repayment schedule and at normal bank interest rates. Not only are microcredit loans going a long way toward reducing poverty, the lending institutions are finding that microcredit is sound business. The experience of Grameen Bank—a leading micro-credit organization in Bangladesh—reveals that repayment rate is very high among the poor borrowers.

However, there has been some rethinking about the role and potential of microfinance. It is now recognized that microfinance is not a panacea for poverty reduction; microfinance may not always have an impact on poverty. Microfinance can help the working poor, but not generally the poorest of the poor, who cannot afford to take on additional debt.

The money borrowed enables the poor to produce their goods and then sell them at a price that allows them to pay off the loan and provide their families with an income. Living on one's earnings, even though small, not only puts food on the table but gives the wage earner dignity, an important factor in not feeling poor. In a world where the richest 20% of the population earn more than 80% of the global income, development cannot be sustainable unless the income gap is reduced. Some people try to dissociate the questions of poverty and income distribution. In reality, however, inequitable distribution of income is one of the major determinants for several reasons.

First, statistical evidence shows that inequality (especially in the distribution of assets) hinders economic growth. Some have suggested that the effects of inequality may be nearly twice as significant for the poor as for the general population. Second, societies with a higher income gap are also likely to exclude a large number of poor people from opportunities that the nonpoor enjoy – water and sanitation, health care, education, credit, insurance, and employment. Third, a major but often underestimated tool for poverty reduction is the redistribution of income and assets. This is the way the Republic of Korea, the PRC, and Japan have successfully reduced poverty and achieved a high economic growth rate. Finally and most importantly, in the present context of global insecurity, statistical evidence suggests that there is a close relationship between income inequity and the level of violence and political instability (P. D. Fajnzylber, D. Lederman and N. Loayza, 1998).

The Role of Civil Society

Civil society refers to associations of citizens (outside their families, friends, and businesses) entered into voluntarily to advance their interests, ideas, and ideologies. The term does not include profit-making activity (the private sector) or governing (the public sector). It does include mass organizations (such as organizations of peasants, women, or retired people), trade unions, professional associations, social movements, indigenous people's organizations, religious and spiritual organizations, the academe, and public benefit NGOs. Civil society must play an important role in sustainable development in terms of agitation, information, and the distribution of resources. How will this be achieved? Civil society must make stronger demands, organize, and mobilize its efforts better, and push for improved accountability on the part of government and industries. Specific actions by civil society follow.

1. Demand rights to life and health.

If the government is corrupt or not doing its job effectively, then citizens need to assert their rights in order to safeguard life, health, security, and safety. Even in developed countries, things can change when all of the people who constitute civil society know what their rights are and what they can demand from the government.

2. Demand access to land, water, and other services.

Citizens should demand protection when threatened by large infrastructure projects or privatization of what used to be common property resources.

In many countries in the developing world, forests and rivers, which are common property resources, have been closed off to the indigenous population, who might have been living in the area for hundreds of years. Agricultural land has been converted from small farms into technofarms producing goods for export and leaving the original population little to till and little to eat.

3. **Form user groups to manage common property resources sustainably.**

In some Asian countries, small farmers have been able to form cooperatives to protect their interests and to demand that they be given equal access to the modern agricultural inputs. The formation of cohesive groups of farmers in the form of farmer cooperatives is a very effective means of empowering people and making things happen in favor of the poor.

4. **Mobilize individual households and community resource groups for improving the environment.**

People generally know what is right and what is wrong, and if they know what demands to make for sustainable development, that is where sustainable development begins.

5. **Share information and resources with other groups about common environmental and political concerns.**

Those who understand environmental issues and political concerns should build this capacity for understanding among other people in the community to make them more aware of these issues.

6. **Pressure industries to clean up, and hold businesses accountable.**

Even though there is a business council for sustainable development and a chamber of commerce and industry, civil society needs to put pressure on businesses and industries to clean up their mess, and to hold the private sector accountable for what it does.

7. **Increase group empowerment.**

Group empowerment is the ability of a group of people to be heard and to get things done. Unfortunately, the people who need it most are least able to harness this power. Nor do they often have the money to act on their own behalf. Women in a village in India hesitate to demand their rights and therefore do not play a role in sustainable development. They need to be empowered with information, knowledge, capacity, legal authority, and legal support.

8. **Pressure governments and developers into taking seriously the rights and needs of marginalized people.**

Those who have the resources should pressure governments and developers into taking seriously the rights and needs of marginalized people—people who are at a big disadvantage because of poverty, because of being indigenous, because they are women or children, or because they are disabled.

Violence, conflict, and corruption also affect the poor, who are often the first to become victims and the last to be protected. Corruption has been cited as one of the reasons why villagers do not like some of their local government officials. Many say they are better off without these officials and without a police force in the village.

Box 2-11. Sustainable Development in Asia: Case I

Cooking Stove Improvement Project in the PRC*

The use of improved cooking stoves in the PRC provides an example of a successful sustainable development project. The World Health Organization discovered that there was an unusually high rate of respiratory diseases among rural women in the PRC. Further investigation revealed the culprit to be the stove. The women were cooking on very inefficient coal- and wood-burning stoves in traditional kitchens with no windows. In the 1980s, a project was started to improve the stoves in order to protect the health of the women. The project ran for 15 years without any government subsidies. In the end, more than 700 million rural families benefited from new, safer stoves. The credit goes to the initiative of the communes and the people who desired these benefits.

The strategy behind the implementation of the project was to begin in areas where the people showed a desire for improved stoves. The communities had to agree that they wanted new stoves and that they were ready to commit either labor or monetary resources to the project.

Research and development were then geared toward designing stoves to match local conditions, such as the type of fuel used for cooking and heating. Most of the PRC uses coal, while Inner Mongolia, for example, uses wood. The researchers designed stoves, depending on fuel and usage (extensive or less cooking), to meet the needs of the people.

With the new stoves in place and operational, the program was closely monitored to see how it was progressing in terms of health and efficiency. Since its inception, government contributions have been small, about 15% of the total budget, and restricted to training, administration, and promotion.

*Source: D.V. Smith and Kazi F. Jalal (2000)

CASE STUDIES ON SUSTAINABLE DEVELOPMENT

Having discussed the challenges of sustainable development, it would be prudent to document several successful case examples of sustainable development from all over the world. However only two case studies from Asia will be presented here due to limitation of space (Boxes 2-11 and 2-12). The lessons learned and results achieved are more generic based on many other examples received by the authors.

Lessons Learned

These case studies suggest that the necessary conditions for grassroots sustainable development are often end-targeted programs that the people want and need, coupled with a minimum of government involvement. Looking at both costs and profits, if the private sector is

Box 2-12. Sustainable Development in Asia: Case II

Rainwater Harvesting Project in India*

A project to harvest rainwater in the desert province of Rajasthan in India in the mid-1980s was at the time, according to a media report, the largest mobilization of people for an environmental regeneration project ever. The problem was drought. The wells of the affected villages were dry, and the water table was low. There was not enough drinking water or water for irrigation. An NGO called Tarn Bharat Sing stepped in. A local voluntary organization, it assisted a village in building three small rainwater-harvesting structures called check dams to catch the rainwater. The check dams stored the monsoon rains, then used the water to irrigate fields and to percolate through the ground to raise the water table. It was an inexpensive, workable solution that proved so successful that there are now some 3,000 check dams in 650 villages throughout Rajasthan. The project resulted in regeneration of 6,500 square meters of land, a rise in the water table by 6 meters, and the perennial flow of five formerly seasonally dry rivers.

A successful sustainable project produces a ripple effect. Benefits accrue down the line. Due to the availability of water from check dams, Rajasthan's forests increased by 33%. The new vegetation, mostly fast-growing shrubs imported from Israel, was used to check sand shifting in the desert. Five rivers that previously flowed only during the monsoon season now flow all year round. Agriculture is more productive and self-sustaining, increasing the annual per capita income by $19.78 or 6%. For every dollar invested in check dams, economic production in the villages increased by $4.20, yielding an extremely high benefit-cost ratio.

The project also had social impacts. It helped reverse the migratory trend associated with environmental degradation. The people no longer move out of their villages because of hardship to other townships that do not wish to support a growing migratory population, or crowd into already congested urban areas.

Other positive social benefits include an increase in school attendance and a reduced crime rate. Apparently, because their incomes went up, families could afford to send their children to school. With the young in school and the older members of the community busy working in the fields, few have time for mischief. Even the women have benefited, since they spend less time fetching and distributing the family's water supply. For a similar example, see Smith and Jalal (2000) on Indian watershed development.

*Source: D.V. Smith and Kazi F. Jalal (2000)

the project initiator, then chances are the size of the related bureaucracy will be minimal. If the government is involved, and it should be, the project often works best if the government limits its role to initiator and leaves implementation and administration to the private sector.

The community, participating NGOs, the private sector, and stakeholders must also have an active role; all must share in the responsibility for the project. This will maximize the possibility of everyone involved feeling some sense of ownership in it. This was the strategy behind the cooking stoves in the PRC.

A project must also prove to be commercially viable. Many people think that whatever the government or the private sector does for the poor is free. But nothing is free, and no project or strategy will be successful unless there is a full-cost recovery plan. There may not even be a need to subsidize the very poor. As has been seen, the poor need very little, and in the case of micro-borrowing, their repayment rate is extremely high.

Results Achieved

That small, local sustainable development projects work is undeniable. Witness the kind of success they had in India. Similar projects are being carried out in dozens of small, isolated communities as well. So the question raised at the WSSD becomes: Does it make a difference in this world? The answer is "yes and no." Yes, it will make a difference if these success stories can be replicated in millions of other places. And no, they will not be success stories if they stay in those communities and nobody hears about them; they might have an impact on the pertinent community, but not on the global community.

Putting aside the global view, the positive results of these local projects within the communities are obvious. Marginalized groups derive economic and environmental benefits, investors make money on both short- and long-term loans, occupational hazards are minimized, affected communities cooperate and develop better understanding of the benefits of such projects, and NGOs and the private sector are fostered. These results have been achieved in all the case studies. Market and policy failures were minimized if not eliminated, and development became more meaningful and sustainable.

C H A P T E R   3
GLOBAL ENVIRONMENTAL ISSUES

What are the major global issues regarding environmental sustainability? Population, income, urbanization, health care, food, fisheries, agriculture, materials, and energy are just some of them. The amount of fossil fuel that we consume, even following a modest lifestyle, is going to catch up with us. So transportation is becoming a big issue, as are global atmospheric changes. We also have to consider natural resources such as forests and water. All these are heavily implicated in the ecosystem's sustainability.

Population, Income, and Urbanization

Population growth entails good news and bad news. The bad news is that population has been increasing steadily. The current world population is slightly more than six billion. In 1973, it was only four billion. The good news is, while the numbers are going up, the rate of increase is going down.

Census Taking

Of course, the actual numbers are an educated guess. Some countries rarely conduct a census, because they do not want to upset the status quo, be it religious or political. In other countries the government just does not know where its people live. Fortunately, two very large countries, the PRC and India, do a very good job of census taking. It is part of their culture, their heritage, and their history. When the Indians and the Chinese do a population count, they mobilize millions of people as census takers. In the US, doing a census every 10 years is a constitutional requirement.

A big issue among those involved with global population is whether or not to eliminate the traditional census and instead rely on sampling. Some feel that sampling would yield more accurate results, and the larger, more progressive countries have indeed done quite a good job on enumeration. However, although the aggregate errors are small, they are probably big enough to populate entire countries. Yet it is better than depending on conventional wisdom. For instance, people have assumed for the last 50 years that Nigeria is the most populous country in Africa. But no one has a good idea as to how many people actually live there. The UN has a Population Division that works hard to get fertility and mortality data through birth and death certificates, and other similar records. For many countries, it succeeds. It is those countries that will not or cannot count their people that make census taking difficult.

Population Trends

Global population continues to rise. The UN's Population Division has made a number of breakdowns showing where the population is most likely to increase. According to the agency, the population in Africa is growing much more rapidly than the population in Asia, whose growth rate is now on a downward trend. Europe and North America have very low rates of population growth. Europe is below the replacement mark (the population is actually shrinking), and, if current trends continue, the US will also soon be in the same situation.

The good news here is that the population growth rate is declining all over the world. This trend can be attributed partly to the efforts of the UNFPA. It is also the result of a combination of factors, including family planning, income growth, and the education of women. However, in some countries like Bangladesh, there has been a tremendous decrease in fertility rates that has not been accompanied by a large increase in per capita income. It is difficult to create an effective, comprehensive hypothesis as to why this is happening other than to suggest that some form of disembodied modernization is taking place.

Figure 3-1 suggests that GDP growth in the poor countries has been doing slightly better than in the rich countries. Note that the aggregate GDP growth was positive over the entire period. More recent data (after 2000) suggest that some other countries may be experiencing a negative GDP growth rate.

Figure 3-1. GDP Growth (annual %)

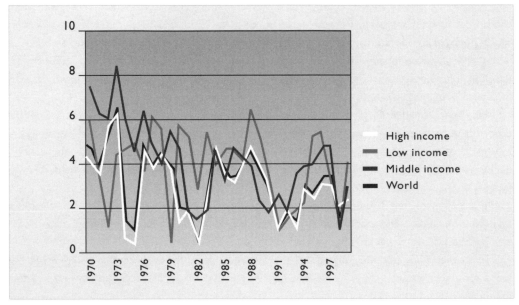

Source: World Bank (2001); World Development Indicators

Population and Income

While the world's average fertility rate is declining, the overall population is going up. Worse, the increases are among the poorest people—those who, according to the UN definition of poverty, live on $1 a day. Even those living on $2 a day are not doing very well. Our mention of these two definitions of poverty suggests that there are problems in defining poverty.

Another problem is the growing disparity of income. Western Europe and the US are on top: their average per capita income of about $25,000 in 1997 has now grown to about $34,000. That spells a big difference between the West and, say, countries in Africa, with less than $2,000 per capita. The numbers are in terms of purchasing power parity (PPP). The simplest way to calculate purchasing power parity between two countries is to compare the price of a "standard" good that is in fact identical across countries. Every year *The Economist* magazine publishes a light-hearted version of PPP: its "Hamburger Index" that compares the price of a McDonald's hamburger around the world. More sophisticated versions of PPP look at a large number of goods and services. One of the key problems is that people in different countries consume very different sets of goods and services, making it difficult to compare the purchasing power between countries (Werner Antweiler, 2006). Instead of doing a straight comparison of the exchange rate, we measure how much the money will buy. Based on a parity scale, there is still a tremendous difference between the developed, high-income OECD countries and the rest of the world.

Urban Migration

One of the big problems when discussing population is the growth of urbanization. For a long time, populations grew but the people stayed in the rural areas, where there was more room to absorb the increases. Recently, however, even the rural areas have become overwhelmed, causing people to migrate to the cities. Cities around the world gain a million people a week. It is not difficult to understand why. Cities have become synonymous with economic opportunity. Bangkok, for instance, which has 7.4 million people or 12% of the Thai population, produces 40% of Thailand's economic output.

However, many Third World cities lack sanitary sewage disposal, and about 50% of the people do not have an adequate supply of drinking water. Furthermore, because most of these cities are in tropical countries, where population growth is most rapid, public health issues are compounded. Bacteria thrive in temperatures of 75° Fahrenheit, or 24° Celsius and above. For them, it is like living in an incubator.

Currently India has 32 cities with populations exceeding one million. By 2015, it will have more than 50 such cities. India's population is growing more rapidly than that of the PRC, and, in fact, it is projected that India will be bigger than the PRC by 2015.

With that many people, congestion becomes a problem. For instance, Sao Paulo, Brazil, has more private helicopters than almost anywhere else in the world. The road traffic is so bad that the wealthy take to the sky.

To appreciate the way cities are growing, one must only realize that in 1950 New York City was the only city in the world that had a population above 10 million. It was the only megacity. By 1975, there were five such cities: New York, Tokyo (which was by then bigger than New York), Shanghai, Mexico City, and Sao Paulo. By 2001, there were 17 megacities. Based upon these figures, it is predicted that the world will have 21 cities with more than 10 million people by 2015. In 1965, Dhaka had a population of 385,000; today it has 13.2 million. Why has this happened? Bangladesh, a tiny country the same size as the state of Wisconsin in the US, has a population of 150 million people. There is no more open land in the countryside to accommodate the excess population, so people gravitate toward Dhaka. The UN predicts that Dhaka's population may reach 22 million in the next two decades.

These numbers are real and projections are the nightmares of sustainable development. How do we deal with these cities, many of which are no longer functioning? Most do not have adequate sanitation or safe drinking water, and the people are choking on air polluted by industrial and automobile emissions. Automobiles are a real problem, because they are usually the first major purchase people make when they begin to earn above the subsistence level.

Asia will be responsible for the major problems we are going to face in terms of urbanization, water supply, transportation, air pollution, and all the negative aspects related to population growth. There is no avoiding it, because the PRC and India, both with over a billion people, are trying to develop rapidly. Over 40% of the sewage in Delhi, which has 14 million people, is not treated, creating an urban river system that is turning black with pollution.

HEALTH CARE

All these problems translate into health and health-care expenditures. As a rule, the more a nation spends on health care, the healthier its citizens will be. High-income countries spend an average of $2,505 per capita per annum on health care (Table 3-1). Their public expenditures, as a percentage of GDP, are 6.2%; in addition, private expenditures are 3.7%, bringing the total to 9.9%. In the US, the percentage spent on private health care is even higher.

Compare the amount of money high-income countries like the US are spending on health care with the per capita spending of other regions: Sub-Saharan Africa is $84; South Asia, $69. There is a huge difference. This is a problem aggravated by unique regional health burdens, such as waterborne diseases, associated with developing regions such as Sub-Saharan Africa, India, the PRC, and Bolivia.

FOOD, FISHERIES, AND AGRICULTURE

World grain production in 2001 was about 1,840 billion tons or 303 kg per person. Thus, when it comes to food production, the world is doing well, although estimates for 2002 show a 3% drop in total production to 1,833 million tons.

In 1974, the World Food Summit in Rome predicted that the world would not be able to feed itself by the year 2000. This did not happen. In fact, food production almost doubled in those 27 years. We were able to increase food production at about 3% per annum in comparison with the 2.2%-2.5% population growth rate, so we have kept ahead of consumption needs. Since 1960, average yields have gone up by more than 150%, as indicated in Figure 3-2, thanks to modern agricultural practices, use of more fertilizer, better water control, different species of crops, and different cultivars of traditional crops.

Genetically Modified and Genetically Engineered Seeds

Once again we are at a pivotal point where technology has run ahead of the public. Depending upon one's point of view, with or without hard information, we can now disseminate genetically modified (GM) and genetically engineered (GE) seeds. Large countries like India and the PRC have already decided that GM farming is what they need to feed their populations in the future. Other countries are still debating the issue.

Table 3-1. Health Care Expenditures per Capita and as Public, Private, and Total Share of Gross Domestic Product, by Region, Mid-1990s

Region	Per Capita (dollars)[a]	As Percent of Gross Domestic Product		
		Public	Private	Total
High-Income[b]	2,505	6.2	3.7	9.9
Latin America and the Carribean	461	3.3	3.3	6.6
Eastern Europe and Central Asia	355	4.0	0.8	4.8
East Asia and the Pacific	154	1.7	2.4	4.1
Sub-Saharan Africa[c]	84	1.5	1.8	3.3
South Asia	69	0.8	3.7	4.5
World	561	2.5	2.9	5.5

[a]Currency conversion based on purchasing power parities. [b]Australia, Canada, Israel, Japan, New Zealand, the United States, and Western Europe. [c]All African countries except those bordering the Mediterranean.
Source: Based on World Bank data (2000)

GM crops have become controversial, and involve scientists, farmers, politicians, and large corporations as well as UN agencies (FAO, 2004). The International Rice Research Institute (IRRI) in Laguna, Philippines, a proponent of GM cultivars, points out that there are no food crops today that have not been genetically modified. An ear of modern table maize (corn) looks nothing like what the Native Americans served to the Pilgrims. Maize has been crossbred for size, appearance, consistency, and resistance. It is just that previously we had to let nature do the cross-pollination. Today, scientists can do it much faster in the laboratory, with predictable results. And therein lies the conflict. Some people feel crossbreeding the way Gregor Johann Mendel did it in the mid-nineteenth century is natural, whereas using high-tech biochemistry is unnatural, producing "Franken-food."

Even those involved in the production of GM seedlings are not in total agreement. Some point out that there is a difference between GM seeds that have been modified to increase productivity and yield, and those that have been modified to increase the profits of the seed bank selling them. Third World rice farmers are terrified that they will become hostage to an expensive multinational seed supplier whose GM rice seeds will force out their low-cost traditional plants.

Another point of contention among scientists is the wisdom of interspecies crossbreeding—GE seeds—which introduces vitamins, bacteria, or viruses that are alien to the subject plant. By natural selection, that is unlikely to happen, but in the laboratory all things are possible. IRRI was able to introduce vitamin A into a rice strain by manipulating the plant's deoxyribonucleic acid (DNA). While the introduction of vitamins is manifestly beneficial, many believe this type of research is a very narrow and dangerous road to tread.

Figure 3-2. Yields Are Up But Growth Is Slowing

Global Changes in Cereal Yields
and Yield Growth Rates, 1961-96

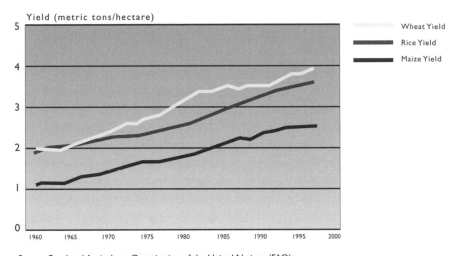

Source: Food and Agriculture Organization of the United Nations (FAO),
FAOSTAT Statistical Database, FAO (1997)

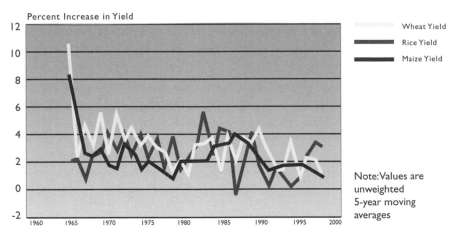

Note: Values are
unweighted
5-year moving
averages

Source: Food and Agriculture Organization of the United Nations (FAO),
FAOSTAT Statistical Database, FAO (1997)

The whole debate becomes even more volatile when we add in urban (or perhaps rural) legends. Some say it began with the butterfly kill in the US. Even though scientists linked the absence of butterfly migration to other causes, the story that it was a "GM pesticide" will not die.

The Green Revolution and Traditional Approaches

At some point, though, many argue that we will no longer be able, through any means, to increase our food supply, and then there will be serious trouble. Smith and Jalal (2000, pp. 46-51) suggest in part that we will not successfully come to the end of the road unless we follow a different course of action from the current emphasis on the Green Revolution.

As indicated in Figure 3-2, the yield growth rates in cereal production rose from 1961 to 1996 as a result of the Green Revolution, but the growth rates are slowing. If we continue with an agriculture based on the Green Revolution, and even more fertilizer, productivity will not increase much above present levels. But if we put less emphasis on irrigated agriculture arising from the Green Revolution, and more emphasis on neglected areas such as rain-fed agriculture and on agricultural extension and research, productivity will likely go up (Mark W. Rosegrant and Peter Hazell, 1999, p. 191).

At some point the maximum increase is reached, and then it begins to decrease or at best remains at the same level. This is not inconsistent with technology, because, although new breeding methods and plant strains will continue to be produced, they are mostly geared toward irrigated agriculture.

Traditional approaches such as rain-fed agriculture might very well be able to continue increasing yields for another 10-15 years. (See also Chapter 2.)

Increased Income Equals Increased Consumption

Another problem in food production is that increased income changes eating habits. When we reach a nine billion world population, we are going to need a big boost in agricultural production, because people eat nonlinearly. In the PRC and India, for instance, as income increases we see that former vegetarians are becoming meat (mostly chicken and beef) eaters. But that puts a strain on the grain supply. When grain is used as animal food, it takes ten times as much to produce an equivalent amount of table food.

Now we have a dilemma. While we need more crops, we are faced with diminishing yields and an objection to using GM seeds. Thus, the question arises: Why not reinvigorate the soil by adding more nutrients?

Fertilizers

The problem is soil depletion. If we are growing a product that yields one ton per hectare, it depletes the soil of nitrogen, phosphorus, potassium, and micronutrients in a set ratio. By adding more fertilizer, we can replace the nitrogen, potassium, and phosphorus, but we have not replaced the micronutrients that were also used by the plants. Many places in the world, such as the US Midwest and the Pampas in Argentina, have very deep soil. Under those conditions people can continue to use naturally occurring micronutrients by mining the soil. But in parts of the PRC and India that have been cropped for many hundreds of years, there is a shortage of naturally occurring micronutrients, and they must be replaced chemically.

Another problem with using fertilizers is cost. Almost all of today's fertilizers are petroleum-based, and the cost of petroleum fluctuates significantly, the direction usually being up. As the price goes up, farmers are able to buy less. Sometimes this causes a whole sector of the economy to collapse, as it did in the former Soviet Union. There the collective farms used a prodigious amount of fertilizer until 1992, since it was essentially free. When communism collapsed, fertilizer became a market item and people stopped using it. The end result was that farm production went down dramatically.

On the other hand, the PRC, which had very low fertilizer application early on, is now heavily fertilizing its fields (256 kg/ha). But as we have seen, the very thing that improves farm yield eventually destroys it through depletion of micronutrients, breakdown of soil structure, and lack of higher yielding plant cultivars. Lester Brown of the World Watch Institute thinks that by 2015 or 2020 the PRC will have to import 100 million tons of grain per year, about 50%-60% of the total grain that is currently marketed worldwide, because its agricultural technology has reached a plateau, and cropped area under cereals is decreasing. The Food and Agriculture Organization (FAO, 2004) has a much more benign view of the grain situation in the PRC, at least in the short run. In contrast, India's farms have more time before they reach the same situation.

More fertilizer, more food, more pollution—this is a problem in countries like Holland, which uses prodigious amounts of fertilizer (450 kg/ha, second only to Ireland). The nitrates have caused serious eutrophication in the watercourses and nitrate pollution in the groundwater. The Dutch are, however, trying to remedy the situation by a wide variety of methods to reduce their total fertilizer usage.

Food Supply and Demand

Progress in being able to feed a population varies widely by region. Millions still go hungry. Although the overall figures are decreasing, millions are still suffering from malnourishment and malnutrition. And this is occurring while we actually have food surpluses.

Countries like India and Bangladesh are actually exporting food while many of their citizens are suffering from malnutrition. The food is there, but the people cannot afford to buy it, and there is no mechanism through which they can demand the food. The annual trade in agricultural products, according to FAO, is estimated at about $417 billion, up from $150 billion in constant terms since 1960. The growth in such annual trade has been declining, however, over the last several years, again, not because people have enough food to eat, but because they do not have enough money to buy the food. While the supply is available, there is a shortage of effective demand.

Fisheries

Fish, an important part of the human food chain, are abundant, thanks to fish farming. Fish farms quadrupled between 1984 and 1995. The salmon sold in the US, for instance, is now grown in farms in Norway and Canada. The actual catch from oceans has remained fairly stable, around 85 million tons of fish per year, even though the sustainable catch is thought to be around 70 million tons. Technology is causing overfishing. Due to better fish-finding apparatus and more trawlers, the North Atlantic fisheries of the US were the first to collapse from overfishing. They are trying to rebuild the stock, but they are meeting resistance from the fishing interests. It is difficult to tell a commercial fishing concern that has a large investment in boats and equipment that they can send their boats out for only a short season.

The fish harvest in the Northwest Atlantic peaked in 1967 and has been declining since then, forcing the fishing fleets to go farther out. The Central Pacific is still a fertile fishing ground. In the marine exclusive boundary of the Marshall Islands, hundreds of Chinese fishing boats are scooping up almost every fish that can be caught for shipment to the PRC.

Birds

Bird populations are also under siege. Birds are a particularly good indicator of pollution and excessive development. When the wetlands get filled in, the migratory birds suffer. Sometimes, when we try to improve the situation, something bad happens as a side effect. Communities build parks and golf courses, adding green spaces where there were none. But the greenery fools migrating birds into discontinuing their journeys. Heavily fertilized large agricultural tracts, such as those found in the US, the PRC, and Russia, are also a danger to migratory birds.

Materials and Energy Flows

Materials flow measures how many of one item is equivalent to how many of another item. For instance, how many bushels of wheat have to be sold to buy one barrel of oil? In 1950, that ratio was about 1:1. Now it takes 10 bushels of wheat to buy a barrel of oil (36.8 bushels of wheat equal one metric ton). This is important, because it says that the terms of trade have shifted badly against agriculture. It also means that people are not growing as many crops, because many inputs in crop production are dependent upon the cost of oil.

The US agricultural system is about the same size as India's in terms of cropped area. They are also about the same in terms of energy usage. But in the US, only one third of the energy is used for growing crops. The rest is used for transportation and marketing. The price of what is grown is determined by the cost of energy used and then by the cost of bringing it to market. Of all the entrepreneurs involved in agriculture, the farmer earns the least. This is one of the reasons why farming is often not profitable. Then, too, farmers have to buy not only oil but also manufactured items such as cars, appliances, and machinery, all of which have heavy energy and materials inputs. When a bushel of wheat could still buy a barrel of oil, farmers had a decent chance, but perhaps not anymore.

This applies to both individual farms and large corporate farms. Although large farms can probably produce a bushel of wheat more efficiently and, therefore, at less expense, they are certainly feeling the same pain as the small farmer. It is merely a matter of degree. Since farming is vital, the question then becomes, how do we break the cycle in such a way that we can make farming more attractive?

In 1973, to artificially raise prices, the Organization of Petroleum Exporting Countries (OPEC) nations severely cut oil production. One year later, US Secretary of State Henry Kissinger suggested that farmers do the same thing—withhold the food supply. In other words, use food as a weapon. It did not work. In North America and Western Europe, the food supply was always plentiful, and there was still a great demand for oil. OPEC won that battle. The countries that suffered were those that had neither a plentiful supply of food nor oil.

Finally, we should examine how industrial economies use up materials as inputs. A group in Wuppertal in northern Germany looks at economies not in terms of GDP, but in tonnage of materials used. It found that the annual amount of materials used per capita in Germany, the US, and the Netherlands is about 85 tons per capita. Japan registers a smaller figure. The less material consumed, the smaller the environmental impact is more likely to be and the less damage caused to sustainable systems.

We consume a lot of materials indirectly—things we do not see. We know we consume cars, washing machines, and the like. But in order to make a car or a washing machine, somebody has to spend a lot of money to build a plant. A huge amount of material is mobilized in the fuel, the concrete, and the steel. When we talk about indirect industrial consumption, Europe and the US are about the same. So when the Europeans claim that the US is driving the world into disaster with its big automobiles and wasteful consumption, it is not true, at least not in terms of total materials mobilized per capita. The picture may change if the value of the materials is used as the index of consumption.

Fossil Fuel Use

Germany, the Netherlands, and the US burn fossil fuels. However, Germany's consumption of coal far exceeds that of either the US or the Netherlands. Part of the reason is that Germany burns a great deal of soft coal, which is less efficient. The other reason is that Germany may be overly dependent upon coal because of its strong mining unions. It has been estimated that the German government spends over $100,000 per mining job in subsidies, so there is a financial incentive to use coal. The US actually uses more energy per capita than Germany, but the US use of soft coal is lower, because the US also consumes other fuels such as oil and high-grade coal. When assessing energy consumption, it is important to look beyond the total energy use and look at the details of the composition of the fuels used.

Materials Flow

Japan stands out as a country that is able to have a very high quality of life with a very small throughput of materials. Part of its success is the result of efficiency and miniaturization. This, in turn, results in a high standard of living. If the Germans or the Americans could live like the Japanese, they would be well on their way to a sustainable future in terms of materials flow. The reliance of the West on heavy, large-scale manufacturing produces carbon dioxide (CO_2), and other greenhouse pollutants that impact the global atmosphere.

By contrast, the Netherlands, a small country, consumes a lot of energy and materials. It does so overseas, however, not at home. Most of the materials it uses are already manufactured when they reach Holland. Thus, when we look at consumption figures, the Netherlands seems small, although actually the amounts are quite large. The Japanese also do a lot of offshore manufacturing, but they are also doing a better job in terms of overall materials usage.

Computers were supposed to bring about the paperless office, but we know that has become a bad joke. We have gone from the simple yellow pad, which often lasted a month, to reams of paper flying out of the ubiquitous printer. A lot of paper is used worldwide, but the US and Canada are far ahead of the others in terms of paper consumption. This is a sore issue in Europe, because it recycles, and, for the most part, North America does not recycle domestically. Rather North America dumps its waste paper on the world market, which further annoys the Europeans, as this badly impacts European paper manufacturers, who complain that American waste paper is too inexpensive.

Obviously, if we use a lot of paper we need to produce a lot of paper, and producing it involves the use of chemicals, bleaches, and energy. It also means deforestation and its attendant problems. The answer, of course, is domestic recycling. Even Central America is considerably ahead of North America in that area. Most of its paper products are made from recycled materials.

Energy Flow

The US uses a lot of energy, but on a per dollar of GDP basis, it is actually in the middle range of countries, even though it uses twice as much total energy as Japan and some European countries. In rejecting the Kyoto Protocol, US President George W. Bush, while acknowledging that the US uses a lot of energy, pointed out that the answer lies not in cutting back on usage but rather in constantly improving efficiency to cut down harmful emissions. It is not clear, however, if such an approach is realistic in the face of increasing per capita incomes and increasing consumption patterns.

Energy Sources
1. Fossil fuels

The use of fossil fuel per dollar of gross national product (GNP) (see Chapter 11) has been declining globally, mostly because of its high price. In current dollars, oil is a very expensive input. From a sustainability point of view, however, oil is not expensive enough. If it were more expensive, we would be forced to shift to other energy sources. We might finally have to drive smaller, more efficient cars, or manufacture hybrid cars on a large scale. The technology for hybrid cars is in place, but the cost of oil is not yet high enough to force a transition to newer technology, so there is little demand for it. Similarly, industrial oil consumers do not yet feel the fuel price is high enough to demand retrofitting their operations or looking for alternate energy sources.

Despite the implementation of the Kyoto Protocol, total global energy use is constantly rising. Today, some of the fuels used are decarbonized because we are using less coal and more natural gas, which releases fewer carbon atoms per unit of energy. From an environmental point of view, the best fuel source is natural gas, then oil, and finally coal. There are ways to increase energy use and still hold production of CO_2 at about the same level.

2. Nuclear energy

When it was first introduced, nuclear power seemed like a panacea: clean, efficient, abundant energy at a very low price; "too cheap to meter" was attributed to the head of the US Atomic Energy Commission. It did not live up to its billing. Nuclear power plants are expensive to build and maintain, and there have been several very serious accidents in the US and abroad. While the French are still building new plants, almost all other countries are taking them off line. The US is still the largest producer of nuclear power (generated from existing plants), but not the most dependent on it. France is, with 79% of its electricity coming from nuclear plants.

3. Wind

Wind is among the safest of the renewable energy sources, and one that is probably the closest to being economically viable. Wind farms in Europe and the US generate sufficient energy to be included on national electrical grids. The drawbacks are expense and reliability. But basically wind power is here, it works, and it is a good technology. As it becomes more popular, many of the early flaws are being ironed out. In fact, there is an active industry to service and maintain the equipment. Surprisingly, it is not without opposition from environmental groups. For example, there is opposition to deployment of wind farms off the shore near Cape Cod in Massachusetts because they are perceived to be a visual intrusion on the natural beauty of the area.

4. Tidal power

Tidal power is being investigated in some remote areas, such as Rance in southern France. There is a big experimental OTECH (Ocean Technical Services, Inc., http://www.oceantech.com/) pilot project currently being developed in Hawaii that is tidal powered, using the temperature difference between deep water and surface water to generate electricity. While it is a natural way to produce energy, the drawback is that it is expensive and intrusive in the marine environment.

5. Solar energy

Solar energy has been a dream for a long time, but the technology has not yet caught up with the dream. Solar panels are still very expensive, and an array of panels is needed to run anything more than a 50-watt bulb and a black-and-white television. Unfortunately, in areas where alternative methods are not available, diesel generators are still the cheapest way to generate electricity. It may not be so if diesel fuel cost $60 a barrel. So far, direct solar electricity is not competitive.

Particulate Matter from Energy Use

Energy use emits large amounts of pollutants into the atmosphere—CO_2, hydrocarbons, oxides of nitrogen, sulfur oxides, and other products of combustion. Many of these combine to form particulate matter, which precipitates out of the atmosphere, often after undergoing chemical transformations and long-range transport. Particulate matter, especially the fine particulates (those that have an average size of 2.5 microns or less, referred to as PM 2.5) and ambient concentrations of particulates are worst in the urban areas of the PRC, India, and Mexico.

The US has solved these problems fairly well, but the Latin American cities still have problems. Two countries—the PRC and India—will be the countries with the most difficulties in terms of particulates in the air.

TRANSPORTATION: THE AUTOMOBILE INDUSTRY

As soon as transportation is mentioned, people immediately think of automobiles and trucks. Currently there are close to a billion motor vehicles in the world, and that number is going to go up very rapidly. The US has 750 motor vehicles per thousand people. The number of cars per driver is even higher when those too young or too old to drive are subtracted. It is apparent that the US has a surfeit of automobiles. The Japanese are catching up in the number of cars per population, but with a difference. Japan is among the major automobile manufacturers in the world, and the Japanese support the industry by buying cars. However, it is very expensive to use an automobile in Japan. High registration fees make it difficult for the Japanese to afford to drive their cars. Coupled with an inferior road system, it is easier, cheaper, and faster to take a train, and the Japanese have one of the finest railroad systems in the world. Compared with New York City and London, Tokyo has the highest usage of public transportation. Yet Tokyo is also the city with the highest automobile ownership. The Japanese have found the perfect solution: buy a car to expand the economy and then do not use it. That is how they keep CO_2 and other emissions out of the air!

In terms of car purchases, Europe, where the bicycle was once king, is catching up with the US, where bicycles are merely playthings for children. It is now estimated that there are 270 cars per thousand people in Europe, and the number is rising steadily. Paris has a superior mass transit system, with a Metro station on almost every major corner, but the lowest ridership among big cities. At last count there were about three million private cars in Paris alone.

When the PRC and India opened their markets to the World Trade Organization (WTO), automobile manufacturers rushed in. All the popular makes and models are now available. In India, which has only a few kilometers of single restricted access highway, one can buy a $400,000 Ferrari.

The worst part about the automobile trade in developing countries is that it cannot keep out second-hand automobiles. Almost all of Asia drives three- and four-year old Japanese automobiles, trucks, and buses. That would be fine, except when buying an old car one also buys old technology. The governments are trying to enforce Euro 1, Euro 2, Euro 3 emissions standards for diesel and gasoline vehicles (http://www.dieselnet.com/standards/eu/ld.html), but people are buying what they can afford—second-hand automobiles.

The Chinese aim to manufacture hundreds of millions of automobiles in addition to the 14 million already in use. Electric bicycles would have seemed to be a nice option, but they have recently been banned. Now instead of bicycles there are severe traffic jams. The PRC government believes that automobile production could become a leading sector of the economy. It looks at the European automobile industry and wishes to emulate Europe's success. The automobile industry is not just the automobile companies. An army of suppliers is scattered throughout a given country. One plant makes windshield wipers, another makes the fabric for the seats, and so on. The industrial base is expanded a thousand fold. It is very hard to counteract the argument that the automobile industry provides great benefits by pointing out that cars cause pollution, congestion, and traffic fatalities.

Worldwide vehicle production set new records in 2000: 40 million vehicles were built worldwide. What is alarming is that manufacturing was only at about 70% of capacity. Manufacturers could easily add another 30% any time demand calls for it. Even while operating at reduced capacity, the global vehicle fleet grew by nine times from 1950 to 1996. These are huge numbers with serious consequences for sustainable development.

Americans drive 1.5 trillion kilometers per year, about 5,000 miles for every man, woman, and child. That number is expected to go up to five trillion kilometers in 2020. Not only is the automobile dangerous, it is dangerously inefficient. The spark-fed internal combustion engine is only 13%-18% efficient in real world conditions and is responsible for 30% of the CO_2 emissions and perhaps 40% of the particulate emissions in the US. Only 13% of every tank of gasoline is used to run a car. The other 87% is wasted. A hybrid car, which can use some of the car's normal energy to recharge its batteries, might run at 40% efficiency. That is still 60% going out the tail pipe. Because of the internal combustion engine, 1.4 billion people worldwide breathe unhealthy air. Due to poor air quality, we are approaching the same level of damage to health that we already have with inadequate water and sanitation. Certainly, this is a very inefficient technology that we somehow backed ourselves into, and we have done so for a long time and wasted colossal amounts of precious fossil fuel.

The strange thing is that alternative power sources for cars have been around since the beginning of the twentieth century. In the early 1900s, a car buyer could choose among a steam car, an electric car, a gasoline car, and a car with a diesel engine. And even though each had a different operating system, all were priced about the same. The electric cars in those days actually outperformed the gasoline cars. They had four electric motors, one in each hubcap, providing excellent traction without the need for limited slip differentials to maintain control on turns. The only drawback of electric cars was their limited range. But at that time there were not many gasoline stations, either. Motorists using gasoline had to take large fuel cans with them, which was dangerous. Steam cars could be refueled easily; the only drawback to the steam car was that the boilers occasionally exploded.

It is too bad that the gasoline engine rendered the others obsolete. But once the technology was settled upon, all anyone could do was to optimize it. And we are seeing this right now. The Japanese, and now the US hybrids, have made a start, and while they are still using internal combustion engines, their efficiency has improved markedly.

Before we leave cars and energy sources, we should look at another innovation, which, however, has yet to realize its potential. That is the car powered by hydrogen. Hydrogen burns efficiently and has proven to be an effective propellant for cars. The best part of it is that the emission from a hydrogen engine is water. The drawback is that a hydrogen-powered car at this stage of development is extremely expensive, and there are not many stations at which to fill the tank.

PRECAUTIONARY PRINCIPLE

The impact of future economic growth, coupled with an increasing population, means that we will need more energy. It is equally disturbing that we have not been able to end our reliance on fossil fuels. We are working on alternate energy sources—wind, solar, geothermal, and so on—and we already have nuclear power. The remaining scientific uncertainties surrounding nuclear energy are not grounds for complacency, but the application of the "precautionary principle," which is found in Principle 15 of the Rio Declaration on Environment and Development adopted at UNCED:

> In order to protect the environment, the precautionary approach shall be widely applied by States according to their capabilities. Where there are threats of serious or irreversible damage, lack of full scientific certainty shall not be used as a reason for postponing cost-effective measures to prevent environmental degradation.

The fates of industrialized and developing countries are linked more than most people realize. We are in the midst of a giant political and economic transition, and we are discovering that globalization does not just mean having Japanese cars and water from France. It also means that the fate of mankind is intimately involved in the issue of sustainability.

Global Atmospheric Change

There are numerous reasons to take action on climate change. A primary one is that all human life and behavior are dependent on the climate. Climate has a big effect on how we live (Figure 3-3). Life in St. Petersburg, Russia, for instance, involves about six months of continuous sunshine and almost six months of darkness. Psychologically, this does very strange things to people. Another factor to consider is that climate disruption may be further along and harder to reverse than most people think.

There is currently a lot more CO_2 in the atmosphere than over the preceding hundreds of thousands of years, and many think because of that we are experiencing anomalous weather patterns. Stabilizing emissions of CO_2 will likely take significant efforts over a long period of time. Significant declines in chlorofluorocarbon (CFC) production have been achieved since 1986. Perhaps similar declines in CO_2 levels in the atmosphere could be achieved in the next 20 years.

John Holdren, Professor of Environmental Policy at Harvard University, suggests six reasons to take action on climate change:

- Human well-being is more dependent on the climate than most people think.
- Climate disruption is further along and harder to reverse than most people think.
- The impact of future growth in population and energy use will be greater than most people think.
- Remaining scientific uncertainties are not grounds for complacency (the precautionary principle).
- The time lags in implementing effective evasive action are longer than most people think.
- The fates of industrialized and developing countries are more linked than most people think.

Figure 3-3. Temperatures Have Warmed Over the Past Century

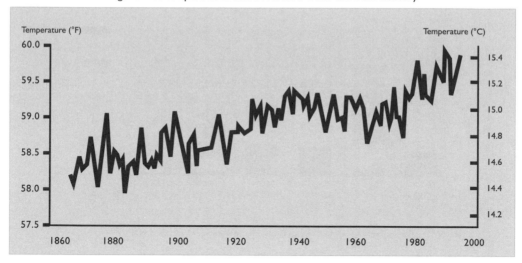

Source: University Corporation for Atmospheric Research (UCAR) and the National Oceanic and Atmospheric Administration (NOAA) (1997), p. 20

FORESTRY

A great many of the earth's original forests have been cleared or degraded.

As suggested in Table 3-2 and Figure 3-4, nearly 40% of the world's frontier forest is under threat.

WATER RESOURCES

Countries with low per capita income levels are especially vulnerable to water scarcity, and these nations have higher population levels than high per capita income countries (Figure 3-5). One reason for some optimism is that agriculture dominates the use of water now, but its share will decline as countries grow richer (Figure 3-6).

VALUATION OF NATURE'S SERVICES

What is nature worth to us? "The Value of the World's Ecosystem Services and Natural Capital," a paper by Robert Costanza et al. (1997), tried to assess what nature is worth to us (Figure 3-7). To make the assessment understandable, the team assigned these services monetary values. They pointed out that, while the global GDP (see Chapter 11) stood at about $18 trillion, the value of the

Figure 3-4. The Current State of the Earth's Original Forests

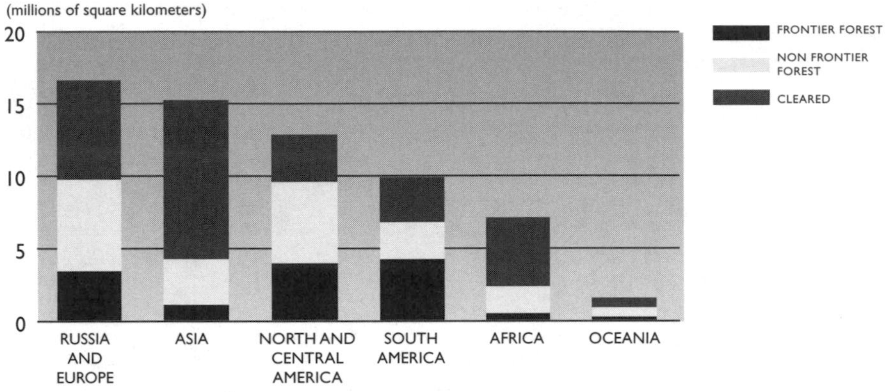

(millions of square kilometers)

Legend: FRONTIER FOREST / NON FRONTIER FOREST / CLEARED

Source: Dirk Bryant, Daniel Nielsen, and Laura Tangley, World Resources Institute (1997)

Table 3-2. Frontier Forests Suffer a Variety of Threats

REGION	PERCENTAGE OF FRONTIER FOREST UNDER MODERATE OR HIGH THREAT[a]	PERCENTAGE OF FORESTS AT RISK FROM				
		LOGGING	MINING, ROADS, AND OTHER INFRASTRUCTURE	AGRICULTURAL CLEARING	EXCESSIVE VEGETATION REMOVAL	OTHER[b]
Africa	77	79	12	17	8	11
Asia	60	50	10	20	9	24
North and Central America	29	83	27	3	1	14
North America	26	84	27	2	0	14
Central America	87	54	17	23	29	13
South America	54	69	53	32	14	5
Russia and Europe	19	86	51	4	29	18
Russia	100	80	0	0	20	0
Europe	19	86	51	4	29	18
Oceania[c]	76	42	25	15	33	27
World	39	72	38	20	14	13

[a] Frontier forests are considered under immediate threat, as a percentage of all frontier forests assessed for threat. Threatened frontier forests are places where ongoing or planned human activities are likely, if continued over coming decades, to result in the significant loss of natural qualities associated with all or part of these areas. [b] "Other" includes such activities as overhunting, introduction of harmful exotic species. isolation of small frontier forest islands through the development of surrounding lands, changes in fire regimes, and plantation establishment. [c] Oceania consists of Papua New Guinea, Australia, and New Zealand.

Source: Dirk Bryant, Daniel Nielsen, and Laura Tangley, World Resources Institute (1997)

Figure 3-5. Population in Areas of Relative Water Scarcity

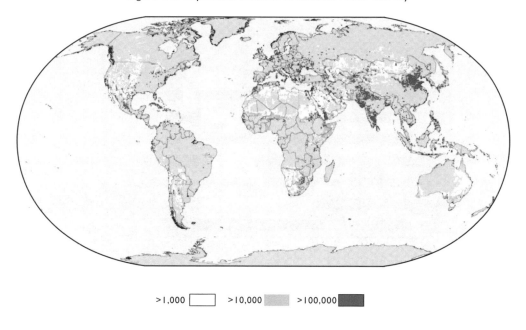

>1,000   >10,000   >100,000

Notes: An area suffers from relative water scarcity if the mean demand for domestic, industrial, and irrigated agricultural uses is greater than 40 percent of the mean annual surface and subsurface runoff area. The tints indicate the population in each area of water scarcity.

Source: Vörösmarty et al. (2000)

services the ecosystem rendered was about $33 trillion, and all these gifts from nature were free! The conclusion is obvious: the ecosystem—consisting of soil formation, recreation provided by nature, nutrient cycling, water regulation, climate regulation, temperature, precipitation, habitat for species, flood and storm protection, food and raw materials, genetic resources, atmospheric gas balance, and pollination—is too valuable a resource to destroy (see Chapter 10).

Soil Formation

Nature's most valuable service is, according to Costanza et al. (1997), soil formation. Without soil there would be no farming (not considering aqua farming and other exotic methods). How do we put a value on this loss? We do so by measuring the amount of topsoil lost in centimeters each year and computing how much it would cost to replace it. When we examine sustainability indicators (see Chapter 4), we will note that in the PRC the largest component in GDP is the cost of remediation for soil lost. In fact, the most damaged ecosystem in that country is the soil, and its continuing degradation is catching up with the PRC in terms of agricultural

Figure 3-6. Agriculture Dominates Water Use, But Its Share Will Decline

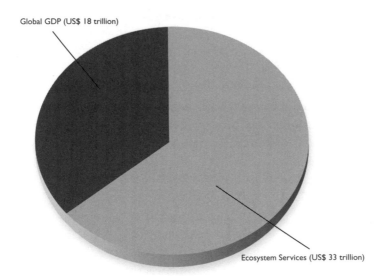

Source: FAO, Aquastat

Figure 3-7. Estimate of Human Activities and Ecosystem Services

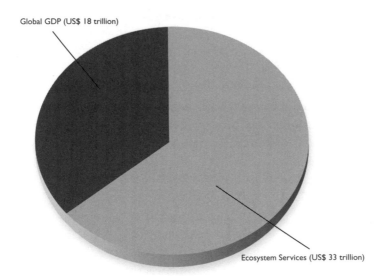

Sources: Adapted from R. Costanza et al. (1997), p. 256, Table 2

productivity loss. The PRC will have to spend a huge amount of money to regain a viable soil system in the not-too-distant future.

Pollination

If we are loathe to rely on GM and GE seeds, then we will have to continue relying on pollination to cross-fertilize and restore our crops. Pollination is important, and provided an interesting contribution leading to this book. In the nineteenth century, Gordon McKay, a shoe manufacturer from Lowell, Massachusetts, established several professorships at Harvard University, including a professorship for one of the present authors. Even though McKay was never an academic and never even understood the mechanics of an ecosystem, he was an innovative entrepreneur. Noticing that agriculture in the Midwest was becoming big business, he decided that it would be profitable to supply bees for pollination. He bought a wagonload of beehives and set off to rent the use of bees to farmers in order to pollinate their crops. Unfortunately, all the bees died on the journey. McKay did not realize that a species cannot just be transplanted into an alien environment and be expected to prosper. And often, if such a transplanted species does survive, it is at the expense of a native species. Bee farms, however, do exist today where the bees have been indigenized, and farmers do, indeed, pay to ensure that the crops will be pollinated. For them pollination is not free, and, like soil, it is a quantifiable service.

COPING WITH GLOBAL PROBLEMS

How can we cope with global problems, and how do we know how far we have come? We start by identifying some of the problems we have been dealing with—overpopulation, income distribution, and rural to urban migration, to cite a few examples. We also take into account new technologies and what interventions we can make. We consider tastes and preferences. Are we dealing with a consumer society or a nature-friendly society? It makes a difference. In some Scandinavian countries, for instance, people would rather hike than drive. And then there are the issues of globalization and the resistance to globalization. Many factors must be considered.

How Far Are We?

It helps to start with a base year. Since it can be arbitrary, let us take 1990 as the base year. We then go back to our charts and graphs to look at population, water withdrawals, crop production, CO_2 production, food grain consumption, and so on for that year. What do we see? There were both large water withdrawals and high crop production in Asia. Asia tended to dominate all of the consumption items. It also had the largest population. Looking at motor vehicles, North America had the largest percentage, the percentage for Europe stayed about the same, and Asia's number was small. So we can more or less assume that the world looked pretty much the same then as it does today. Income distribution has not changed. The poor have stayed poor and still consume like poor people. The more interesting scenario would be if the poor were no longer poor. When the poor become middle class, there will be a tremendous difference. Poor nations begin to take on aspects of Western culture in terms of consumption. If Asia were to end up with 33% of the motor vehicles in the world, we could have significant new problems. So if we go forward with incomes increasing and larger numbers joining the middle class, we will end up with a world in which it is much more difficult to survive. When the middle class formed a minority in most developing countries, there was not much of a problem. But what if the middle class encompasses six billion people emulating America's rate of consumption? It just will not work. We discuss this further in Chapter 14.

Environmental Policies and Programs

The US has transportation energy policies, but the regulatory agencies are not strictly enforcing them, and the federal government has recently been watering them down. Citizens should insist that environmental safety regulations are followed and strengthened, and that automobiles actually work the way they are supposed to. They should also make their government initiate aggressive incentives that would give manufacturers the flexibility to build programs that can transform old technologies. But instead, the government has been cutting back on its environmental programs, so automobile companies are not under any pressure to produce fuel-efficient cars. However, the newly proposed energy bill passed by the US Senate in May 2007 has tightened the vehicle fuel efficiency standards to be met by 2010.

There are plenty of new policies that governments should implement. They should reward innovation and early adoption of new technologies, regulate CO_2 (something that was promised but may not happen on a global scale), and develop international antipollution policies.

One sure way to cut automobile emissions immediately is to make gasoline very expensive. Americans are driving 2.5 trillion miles per year, and the Department of Energy is predicting a 30% increase over the next 15 years. The Department also predicts a 40% increase in the engine power of American cars in that same period, which will consume even more fuel. A hefty tax at the pump might turn things around, but it could be political suicide for its proponents.

CHAPTER 4

SUSTAINABLE DEVELOPMENT INDICATORS

When examining the world with a concern for sustainable development, we obviously want to know if our actions, however marginal, will have a positive or negative impact in terms of meeting our criteria for sustainability. These impacts include not only physical consequences for the environment, but also associated social consequences and economic costs. To make rational policy choices based on predicted or observed impacts, we need indicators.

Indeed, most big international firms today, among them British Petroleum of the UK, produce company reports with a triple bottom line, one indicating profit, the two others showing the social and environmental consequences of their actions. All the big accounting firms provide services to produce such reports. These reports are valuable to stockholders as well as to those who make decisions about financial risks.

The indicators discussed in this chapter are concrete and quantitative measurements. If only generic definitions of quality are used, it is very difficult to make measurements at the margin.

Indicators, especially environmental indicators, often relate specifically to the phenomenon or object of observation. For example, one indicator for assessing the impact of human actions on the climate may measure megatons of CO_2 emitted into the atmosphere, while another may measure the rate at which the ice sheets are melting. To compare different indicators, it is often necessary to convert them into economic costs or benefits. While economic costs can usually be measured using fairly standard and well-accepted techniques, perhaps not exactly but at least within acceptable parameters, we have more trouble measuring benefits. Yet both are important measures of a project, policy, or any other type of intervention that affects the environment. The question is, can we truly determine the costs and benefits to society of changes in our environment? Probably not, but a look at the literature shows that environmental economists keep trying.

Hidden behind the dollars and cents of any economic calculation are very important, and often debatable, value judgments. There is no simple conversion factor that relates the amount of smog in the air to the economic cost to society. Is it possible to objectively quantify the quality of our environment and the impact that our actions have on environmental quality? It is a question that must be answered if we are working toward sustainability.

NEED FOR INDICATORS

A concerted effort to enhance habitability of our planet is unlikely to succeed unless we know "where we are" and "where we want to go." To answer these questions, we must first consider exactly what we include in the term "environment." If we restrict our definition to overly simplified definitions, such as the amount of a specified pollutant in the air, we have very little difficulty in measuring the environment. However, as we broaden our definition to include all physical components, or all the physical and biological, or all the physical, biological and cultural ones, environment becomes exponentially more difficult to describe (William A. Thomas, 1972).

This is really a paraphrase of the Chinese proverb that says, "if you don't know where you're going, any road will get you there." But we do want to know where we are and where we want to go. To do that, we must have accurate data—a map of some sort. To get accurate information, we must first know what exactly it is that we want to assess, and we must define the scope of our inquiry. If we restrict our definition to, for example, the amount of a specified pollutant in the air, we have little difficulty in measuring the environment, as mentioned by Thomas. However, as we broaden our definition to include all the physical, biological, and cultural components, it becomes exponentially more difficult to describe. We are good at measuring physical and chemical phenomena, but once we try to rationally assess the biological, social, and cultural aspects of the environment, we have serious problems.

To quantify quality, we need some indicators. Laudable attempts have been made to compile lists of sustainable indicators (IISDnet, 1995). However, the results are often voluminous and not very well focused. The problem with many of these compilations is that they are highly co-linear; all are related to each other. It is hard to find indicators that measure one dimension and not another. For example, does the rise in US fuel consumption over the past decade indicate a trend toward less efficient vehicles, a higher number of vehicles, longer driving times, or a combination of these factors? Now combine this one indicator with another that measures changes in urban air quality and the causes and effects become even harder to disentangle.

Measuring several dimensions at once and finding a precise interpretation can become very difficult. The "seven plus or minus two" law was propounded apparently by a social psychologist, George Miller (1956). A normal human being can think of about five to nine independent facts at any one time if they are part of a linear problem. Computers can deal with thousands of different indicators and variables at the same time, but at some stage humans have to interpret the data, and they are limited by the above perceptual rule. The dimensionality of the problem, hence, the number of variables, has to be reduced to something that is manageable by human decision-makers.

Benefits of Environmental Protection and Sustainable Development

Many years ago Emil Salim, a former Indonesian minister for population and environment, claimed that he needed environmental benefit data to support his ministry's concerns at government meetings because he was tired of being told that his approach was too costly. Yet, at the time, he was in no position to assess the real benefits of environmental protection and sustainable development, because the measurements did not exist. So he demanded that environmental scientists develop indicators that he could use to compare the losses in environmental resources against national productivity in monetary terms.

Salim's story encapsulates the problems we still face today. When something that might be environmentally sound is proposed, we are told it is too expensive without looking at the benefit side of the equation. We see a major focus on the cost of a proposal in terms of its effect on the GDP, which can be fairly accurately estimated. But sustainable development requires more; it requires the estimation of the economic costs and benefits of sustainability.

Obtaining Accurate Data

Environmental indicators gained popularity in the early 1970s after the formation of the US Council on Environmental Quality (CEQ). The CEQ's purpose was, and still is, to inform the American people about the quality of their environment. The CEQ and the Environmental Protection Agency (EPA) invested a great deal of money in hiring scientists to undertake theoretical and practical research on indicators that would allow them to methodically gauge air and water quality (see Ott, 1978, for a state of the art review at that time). This type of research petered out in the early to mid-1980s, when the CEQ and the EPA realized that they were not getting accurate or useful analyses and therefore could not make insightful comparisons.

Environmental Measurements

Some categories of pollution are not difficult to measure. It is fairly easy to characterize water pollution by variously using 20, 30, 40, or 80 parameters. For instance, in the US, drinking water must be tested for 86 chemicals that must be assessed and that have standards to be met. If the 86 chemicals were to change uniformly in the same direction each time the water is tested, it would be easy to judge whether the water quality is safe or not. But the individual chemicals vary: some might be high on one sample and low on another. Even though we can measure the water's chemical contents, how do we know whether the quality is getting better or worse? A similar dilemma arises when measuring air quality.

Some water and air pollutants are harder to measure than others. When dealing with water, we have to contend with factors like loss of terrestrial systems and habitat, eutrophication, loss of breeding grounds, and coastal pollution. Then there is also the loss of intrinsic or cultural value, loss of recreational capacity, loss of solitude, or simply loss of aesthetic pleasure. When examining air resources we have to factor in effects like loss of visibility and damage to human health. These factors may or may not be local. The landscape of the Grand Canyon is not as visible as it was a few years ago because of the number of automobiles in Los Angeles and the coal-fired electric power plants in the desert.

Environmental Indicators

What are environmental indices? (An index is a ratio or other number derived from a series of observations and used as a measure; *Webster's New International Dictionary*, 1961). We need them because national governments and international agencies need to know how the environment is affected by development, what can be done about it, and how much remediating the damages will cost.

It is interesting to put the costs of environmental protection into meaningful numbers. Recently the US has been spending about 7% of GDP for defense and about 2% for environmental protection. The latter is not small in dollar terms, but is it large enough? The 2% figure represents the combined expenditures of the government and the private sector. In the US, corporations spend a lot of money on improving the quality of the air and water. For developing countries funding also comes partly from international agencies. Those agencies must be able to assess their investment portfolios accurately and make difficult choices between countries and sectors. For instance, should a funding agency help the Chinese improve their water quality, or should it help them improve their manufacturing capacity, which, in turn, would help raise the standard of living but might also make their water quality worse?

How can these decisions be made? Who makes them? Clearly, a poor person would rather have bread on the table than a clean environment. It is a dilemma that international agencies frequently face, because they prefer that people have both a clean environment and food. Depending upon the agency, one aspect or the other receives the money and attention. It was pointed out at the 2002 WSSD in Johannesburg that there were really two issues that needed to be addressed: The less developed countries were concerned more with development and sustainability, and the developed countries with sustainability and environmental protection. There was a mismatch in goals, when ideally the two should have been merged.

There is a need to integrate our thinking. There are ways to increase industrial development in a manner that is also environmentally friendly. It means doing things differently than we have in the past. Of course, this is hard, given fixed views on technology. Current measures relying solely on economic costs are not considered entirely satisfactory. As the Indonesian minister pointed out, there is another side to the equation. But there is a need to establish the marginal cost of improvements. We have to know what the improvement is, and we have to be able to relate it directly to the cost of the project.

How Best to Describe the Environment

So how do we describe the environment? There are three major types of issues that require indicators;

- **Type I, Brown Issues.** Brown indicators deal with conventional pollution issues (urban, rural, industry, agriculture, mining, forestry, and nonpoint sources of pollution). These are traditionally measured in terms of emissions in tons per day. We can set emission standards and then look at the cost of meeting them.

- **Type II, Green Issues.** Green indicators have to deal with broader environmental and ecological issues (biological diversity, soil and land conservation, aquatic ecosystems).

- **Type III, Red Issues.** Red indicators have to deal with environmental policies, institutions, and legislation.

  Creation of indicators for these types of issues relies upon the ingenuity of the analysts. As mentioned above we can often use total emissions as proxies for some of the brown and green issues, but often it is necessary to use ambient concentrations. Emissions do not kill people directly. It is the ambient concentrations of the emissions (again the brown approach) that kill or harm people and damage the environment. So instead of using "tons per day" when discussing air or water quality, we should be assessing micrograms per cubic meter (or milligrams per liter for water quality). We can set ambient standards and then look at the cost of meeting them.

For the green and red issues, it is more traditional to create indicators of impacts, using physical parameters. What we are really interested in is not the ambient concentrations per se, but their impact once they are transported and diffused throughout the environment. What we are ultimately interested in is mortality, morbidity, and economic and ecosystem damage. Some of these factors can be measured in terms of performance standards. We can map the spread of ambient pollutants, and then we can look at the impacts in terms of human health and ecosystem damages.

Note that the focus of most of the literature has been on brown indicators for pollution but not so much on green, and very rarely on the red. The brown indicators, which are almost uniformly negative, include pollution of water, air, and land. The green indicators, which typically represent habitat loss and intrinsic values in aquatic systems, air resources, and terrestrial systems, are the indicators that can be most helpful when looking for positive outcomes.

Metrics of Measurement

1. Nominal scales

The simplest type of measurement is nominal measurement, which essentially involves separating and classifying the objects to be measured into distinct categories and then counting the members of each category. Bird species could be an example of categories used to classify observations on a bird watching trip. For each species, we can assign some arbitrary tag (e.g., species 1 or species A2531). The tag itself, which could be a number, word, or any identifying mark, has value only in its function as a label (i.e., species 2 is not "greater" than species 1, even though there may be more individuals of species 2). Once different classes are formed, we can count the number of members of any particular class.

There are some mathematical operations that can be applied to individual observations. First is identity. If A equals B, then A is in the same class as B, and B is in the same class as A. Or we can use transitive logic: If A is preferred over B, and B is preferred over C, then A is preferred over C. Or if A and B are in the same class, and B and C are in the same class, then A and C are in the same class.

We can also use nominal scales of measurement in regression analysis. Dummy variables, which represent different classes, can be set to a value of one when that class is the one for that particular observation, or zero otherwise. All classifications can be broken down into binary relationships. In fact, classification, or taxonomy, is the first step in most scientific investigations.

2. Ordinal scales

The next level of measurement is ordinal – the ordering of classes and individuals. With this type of measurement, objects are assigned to classes, and the classes are ranked with respect to one another; or alternatively, the objects themselves can be ranked directly (i.e., each class has only one member). For instance, students in a class can be ranked according to their test scores (e.g., student 1, student 2, etc.). With ordinal scaling, if A is greater than or equal to B, then B cannot be greater than A. Transitivity is still valid in this case: If A is greater than B and B is greater than C, then A is greater than C. For ordinal measurements, we cannot say anything about the distance between different rankings. For instance, if A, B, and C are along a continuum, we cannot say anything about the magnitude of the distance between A and B or B and C, but we can say that the continuum from A to C is the sum of both increments. To return to the example of student rankings based on test results, the ordinal measurement refers only to the rank and not the score on the exam. Hence, there is no way to tell how far apart the test scores of different students are if we only know their rank.

Mathematical operations on ordinal measurements cannot use addition and division, but only inequalities. Many indices are based on some sort of ranking, which then violates these mathematical rules when people try to sum up the ranks. Further unscrupulous analysis complicates matters by adding the ranks. For example, if we took 10 students out of a class of 30 and tried to determine their average score on the exam by finding their "average" rank (i.e., summing the ranks and dividing by 10), the result is meaningless. Relying on these numbers causes flawed results, because the methodology is illogical and mathematically illegitimate.

3. Interval and ratio scales

The highest level of measurement is the interval or ratio scale. The two are similar except that a ratio scale requires the meaningful definition of a nonarbitrary zero-point. Temperature, for instance, is an interval scale. We can observe the difference between cool and warm temperatures, and we can measure the magnitude of that difference. But it is not a ratio scale, because, 40° is not twice 20°. Kelvin temperature does represent, however, a ratio scale, because the definition of absolute zero temperature is minus 273° Kelvin.

Income is usually considered a ratio scale because it has a nonarbitrary origin of zero dollars, but neither a ratio nor an interval scale may strictly apply because of behavioral factors such as the decreasing marginal utility of value of money. For instance, a dollar is not worth as much to a rich person as it is to a poor person. When the UN created its human development index (HDI), it attempted to take this fact into consideration (http://hdr.undp.org/).

STATISTICAL PROCEDURES

Statistics is the interpretation or manipulation of data. Statistics allows us to make inferences about large numbers, when direct observation is expensive or impossible. In the Annex at the end of this chapter, we give the details of the statistical measures that we typically use in assessing environmental issues.

Population and Sampling

The relationship between population and sampling is important because we will very seldom be able to measure a population of things, such as the temperature at all points on the earth's surface, directly. But we can take samples from the population and thus simplify our data gathering and analysis, by applying various statistical concepts and rules. These rules enable us to make inferences about the whole population without measuring each individual item.

Graphical Analysis of Statistical Data

An extremely important task when communicating the results of any quantitative study is determining how to present the data. It is usually impossible to communicate all of the data at once in one table. Also too many tables make it hard to assess underlying trends. A graph can illustrate a wealth of information quickly and efficiently, without requiring a long list of numbers.

EMISSIONS, DIFFUSION, AND IMPACT MODEL

A basic framework, originally due to OECD, that can be used to assess the impacts of pollutant emissions on humans and the environment is known as the emissions, diffusion, and impact model, shown in Figure 4-1. In Table 4-1 we show how some of these emissions, and impacts may be measured over regions and over time.

Emissions can be controlled through a variety of means. Generally, polluters are either legally bound to reduce their emissions or are encouraged to do so through some form of financial incentive, such as a pollution tax. While these mechanisms for controlling emissions are often unwieldy and imprecise, they can still have significant effects in reducing levels of pollution. For example, emission controls imposed on automobiles in California have significantly reduced levels of air pollution around Los Angeles.

Pollutants can travel through soil, water, air, or a combination of more than one medium. We need to understand the impact that these substances have once they are ingested or inhaled by humans or as they reside in the environment. Typically, the human impact is modeled by a dose response curve, which essentially relates the threat to human health vis-à-vis the amount of exposure. Similarly, impact models can be developed for flora and fauna, ecosystems, or even human-made structures. Acid rain, for instance, not only affects forests, lakes, and other natural ecosystems, but can also cause significant corrosion of buildings and other structures.

We control emissions by telling people that they can emit only so much sulfur oxide into the atmosphere, and they have to use a special type of fuel. There are other solutions, not as successful, but in use anyway. In Japan, people wear facemasks during high pollution periods.

There is also aesthetic pollution. At one time, before budget constraints cut back services, cities fielded street cleaners who picked up litter. They were not stopping emissions, merely controlling them.

Almost everyone concerned with climate change is worried about the large amount of CO_2 being dispersed into the atmosphere. Being unable to deal with the impacts and treating the ambient atmosphere, and certainly being unwilling to reduce the use of fossil fuels, much attention is now being given to sequestration of the CO_2 after the combustion takes place. Depending upon how this is carried out, it may be too expensive, or, even where it is cost effective, the ability to

Figure 4-1. Emissions, Diffusions, and Impact Model

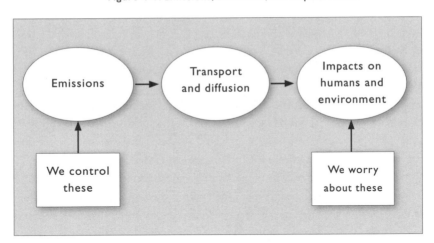

Table 4-1. Emission-Ambient-Impact Measurements

	Emission based	Ambient based	Impact based
Measures	acres deforested	concentrations opacity	mortality morbidity economic losses ecosystem losses climatic effects
Regions	local national depends on data collection	river basins airsheds normal averaging regions	political boundaries urban/rural national transboundary effects
Dynamics	days weeks years	acute chronic long period short period	all time periods
Data	easy	hard expensive	hard expensive conceptually difficult
Typical indices	tonnage of solid waste	ambient quality index	damage functions excess mortality

sequester CO_2 for long periods of time and in the quantities being produced may not be technically possible.

Weighting Schemes

How we respond to a given environmental problem depends a lot on how we assess or measure it. Which yardstick do we use when measuring the tons of pollutants emitted into the air and water; the hectares deforested; the opacity of the air and its impacts on mortality, morbidity (indicative of disease), economic losses, and ecosystem losses? It depends on who is doing the calculations.

There are many ways of doing these calculations, as suggested in Figure 4-2.

Emission-based data are easy to come by. Ambient data are hard to obtain, and it is both difficult and expensive to estimate health, mortality, and morbidity impacts. For example, we have air quality standards for the city and for the country. In the Boston area there are seven monitoring stations. One of them is in Kenmore Square, near a traffic light. The readings during a red light are low, because the engines near the sensors are idling. When the light turns green, the cars accelerate, spouting burned and unburned fuel into the air. The question is, is Kenmore Square representative of the air in Boston? It is clearly not, but the city has sensors taking measurements at several other locations. How should they be weighted together?

It is expensive to measure air quality: approximately $2,000 per month per station per species being measured. With that kind of money involved, it is fair to ask if we are measuring the right things.

Figure 4-2. Structure of Indicators by Environmental Issue

	PRESSURE	STATE	RESPONSE
	Indicators of environmental pressure	Indicators of environmental state	Indicators of social response
Issues			
Climate change			
Ozone layer depletion			
Eutrophication			
Acidification			
Toxic contamination			
Urban enviromental quality			
Biodiversity			
Landscape erosion			
Waste			
Water pollution			
Forest depletion			
Fish resources			
Soil degradation			
General indicators			

Source: OECD, 1998

Obviously we are more interested in the impacts, the intake fraction, or how much of a pollutant actually gets into people's lungs. But the problem is methodology. Do we issue everyone in Boston a sensor badge similar to those worn in nuclear or biohazard plants? That would be exorbitantly expensive. We could, however, sample various groups that might be at risk from elevated levels of pollution.

Indoor pollution is another problem. Often the air inside a closed space is worse than what is found outdoors. It depends a lot on the cooking fuels used, how tight the houses are, and so on. Therefore, should we think about monitoring indoor air quality, factoring in how much time people spend indoors as opposed to outdoors. Obviously it is a complicated matter.

We worry about what is in the rivers, because we are worried about the ecosystem. We also worry about what people drink. Because of low standards, someday we may have nothing safe to drink but bottled water and canned or bottled drinks.

Natural Weighting

One entire group at the OECD in Paris is devoted to environmental indicators. It has defined the pressures on the environment—emissions, ambient concentrations, and impacts—and has compiled a huge database for environmental indicators such as climate change, ozone layer depletion, eutrophication, acidification, toxic contamination, urban environmental quality, biodiversity, landscape erosion, waste, water pollution, and forest depletion.

Once we have this information, what do we do about it? Determining how to combine different indicators to make an informed statement about environmental quality is not a trivial exercise. Somehow we have to find a way to weigh different indicators based on their relative impact. A number of weights are based on objective scientific laws, and these are called "natural" weights. For instance, different greenhouse gases vary in their effectiveness at trapping heat within the atmosphere. We can formulate an aggregate index that measures climate forcing (i.e., heat flux per unit area) based on the ambient concentration of a number of different greenhouse gases by their heat-trapping effectiveness. We can calculate how many watts per square meter increment we get in this combination of gases. For this type of assessment, chemistry will back us up. Similarly, if we know how much carbon, nitrogen and phosphorus are present in a stream, we can predict eutrophication, using well-established scientific principles.

Science can help when we have natural weighting. However, if we do not have natural weightings or if we have them only for physically independent processes that we want to combine (e.g., greenhouse gases and eutrophication in water), then we have to find a more subjective weighting scheme that involves people's values and preferences.

During the administration of US President Bill Clinton, a survey was taken of how much value people put on global warming. It seemed a reasonable way of assessing a situation. We might also ask the experts, but experts and citizens do not always agree. And when there is disagreement, whom do we believe? The experts have all the data, but the citizens understand the problem's impact on their lives a lot better than somebody who has spent his or her life in the laboratory looking at the science. How do we resolve the problem between experts and non-experts? We suggest that the best way is to derive entirely new indicators relying heavily on economic benefits.

AGGREGATING INDICATORS

There are three common methods for weighting indicators: "natural" weighting, "expert" or "citizen" weighting, and weighting based on economic benefits. "Expert" and "citizen" weighting schemes are derived from the opinions of either the experts or citizens on the relative importance of different indicators in an aggregate index. For example, an indicator for quality of life can be aggregated from per capita income, health care access, educational level, green space, and so on by surveying experts or citizens on the relative importance of each indicator.

Figure 4-3. Fundamental Issues in Aggregating Indicators

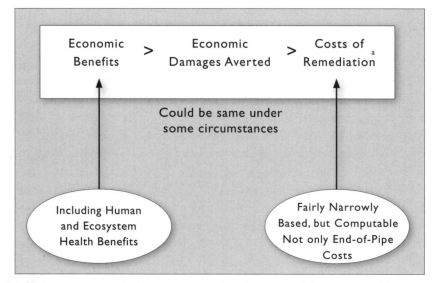

a Remediation is what a nation should spend annually on the environment to maintain what it has, while trying to improve environmental areas that are in trouble.

The advantage of employing economic benefits is that it can pull together indicators that do not have a common "natural" or physical basis, while veering away from the subjectivity of either experts or citizens. However, it does require a methodology for translating a given indicator into financial terms, which may involve some subjectivity concerning the value of a human life, for instance. Figure 4-3 shows how economic indices can be used and how some simple ones relate to each other.

It creates a set of logical relationships. The economic benefits from sustainable development are greater than the economic damage averted, which is greater than the cost of remediation. Some people think that this is a pious hope, and there are some equations and some instances where we might end up with these inequalities not being valid. But if assessing economic benefits and costs proves difficult, measuring the cost of remediation will likely be easier. This follows because, generally, economic benefits are hard to measure, and economic damage, "medium-to-hard." If this relationship holds true in a particular case, then calculating the cost of remediation, which is the lower-bound estimate of the economics, is often easier.

One index that relies on some subjectivity in the weighting scheme is the air pollution standard index. Beijing newspapers routinely publish a pollution standard index (PSI) for many Chinese cities based on seven sub-indices: total suspended particulates (TSP), sulfur dioxide (SO_2), CO, CO_2, ozone (O_3), nitric oxides, and TSP times SO_2 (Figure 4-4). The developers of the index say that air pollution is not just about the suspended particles by themselves, but about the combination of the sulfur compounds that attach themselves to the particulates like aerosols and sulfuric acid derived from the SO_2, which enters the lungs.

Figure 4-4. Air Pollution in Major Chinese Cities for a Day in January

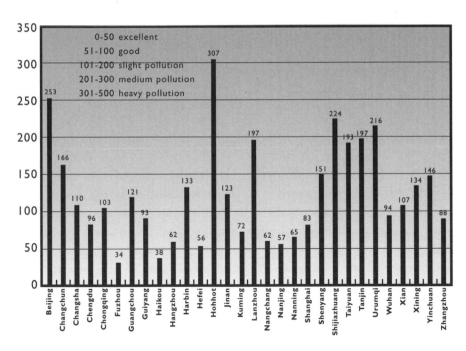

Source: Based on China Environmental Monitoring Center data

117

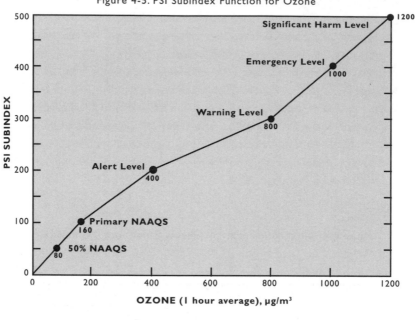

Figure 4-5. PSI Subindex Function for Ozone

NAAQS = National Ambient Air Quality Standard

Source: Wayne Ott (1978)

Indices can be normalized such that the maximum allowable value is set at a convenient number. For example, in Figure 4-5 we see that a PSI above 100 violates the National Ambient Air Quality Standard (NAAQS) of 160 micrograms per cubic meter for ozone, from the Clean Air Act enacted by the US Congress. (Congress sets the standards for air quality, while the EPA, a quasi-independent body, is responsible for water quality.) The EPA and the states have charts such as Figure 4-5 for tracking air pollution in the form of curves that indicate specific levels: 400 micrograms per cubic meter is the alert level; 800, the warning level; 1,000, the emergency level, and 1,200 micrograms per cubic meter, the significant human health harm level; the PSI approach has been adopted by other places in the world such as Mexico City, Beijing, and Taipei.

Such graphical environmental indicators allow us to monitor, measure, and show to the citizenry the state of the environment. Many European cities use such indicators, often displayed in the main square, to let the people know how the ambient air quality is and whether the environment is getting better or worse. Quantifying the amount of pollution, it is hoped, will cause people to modify their behavior and/or demand better management policies.

OTHER WEIGHTING SYSTEMS

A weighting system based upon best technical information can also be used. An example can be found in a study done in Canada during the 1970s by a group led by Herbert Inhaber (1976). Inhaber established (Rogers et al. (1997), p. 16) four components of the environment to measure: air, water, land, and miscellaneous.

Inhaber also created indices for interurban air quality, overcrowding in cities, visibility at airports, and industrial emissions. Indices for rural areas consisted of forestry maintenance and resources, insect and disease damage, forest fires, land quality due to forestry, industrial emissions of sulfur oxides from eroded rural areas, and industrial emissions. Other indices were access to national and provincial parks, strip mining, and sedimentation.

Air Quality Index

The construction of the air quality index is shown schematically in Figure 4-6 and mathematically in Box 4-1.

Water Quality Index

The database for water quality included industrial and municipal effluent index, ambient water quality index, turbidity, and the amount of mercury found in fish. Inhaber was referring to items for which it already had data, but one could think of other factors to measure. In any case, Inhaber's water quality index was computed in the same way as the air index was computed.

Figure 4-6. Air Quality Index

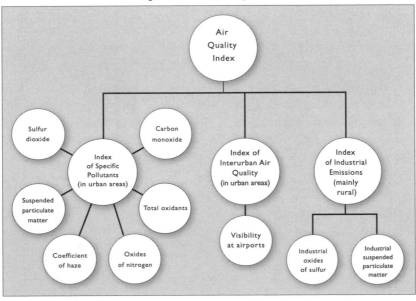

Source: Inhaber (1976)

Box 4-1. Aggregating Air Quality and Comprehensive Environmental Quality index

Air Quality Index

$$I_{AIR} = \sqrt{0.2\, I^2_{SO_2} + 0.1\, I^2_{SPM} + 0.1\, I^2_{COH} + 0.2\, I^2_{CO} + 0.2\, I^2_{O_x} + 0.2\, I^2_{NO_x}}$$

where

I_{SO_2} = Index for sulphur dioxide

I_{SPM} = Index for suspended particulate matter

I_{COH} = Index for coefficient of haze

I_{CO} = Index for carbon monoxide

I_{O_x} = Index for total oxidants

I_{NO_x} = Index for oxides of nitrogen

Comprehensive Environmental Quality Index

$$I_{EQ} = \sqrt{0.3\, I^2_{AIR} + 0.3\, I^2_{WATER} + 0.3\, I^2_{LAND} + 0.1\, I^2_{MISCELLANEOUS}}$$

Air Indices are based on ratio of average annual concentrations in the atmosphere to the prescribed atmospheric standard.

Source: P. Rogers et al. (1997), p. 16

Figure 4-7. Land Quality Index

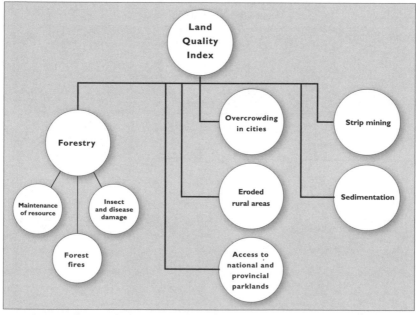

Source: Inhaber (1976)

Land Quality Index

The land quality index is an amalgam of forestry, urban overcrowding, and impacts from mining. These are shown schematically in Figure 4-7.

Bringing Indices Together

Inhaber created an index for each of the four categories and added them together to create the comprehensive index of environmental quality. What we see in Box 4-1 is an index of air quality that is the square root of the sum of 0.2 times the concentration squared of SO_2, plus 0.1 times the concentration squared of suspended particulate matter, 0.1 times the concentration squared of the coefficient of haze, and so on. The sum of all of these multiplying factors is unity. This allows the weighting of coefficients relative to each other. If we feel that SO_2 and the production of O_3 are very important and that oxidants such as nitric oxides are less important, we can weigh them by taking the square root of the assembled numbers to produce an index for air quality. The various components can be measured, and numbers assigned. But what if the numbers are arbitrary? We can measure SO_2, particulate matter, and the coefficient of haze. All these have operational numerical values. But then we take the square root of the sum of the squares of those numbers multiplied by some mysterious weighting factors. The weightings make a big difference, but where do they come from?

Inhaber then applied the same type of formula for land, water, and miscellaneous factors at the bottom of Box 4-1, weighting all four categories—0.3, 0.3, 0.3, and 0.1—to get the index for environmental quality. This is a comprehensive index of the environmental quality for Canada, but the question remains, is it a useful number?

Since Inhaber published his initial findings, there has been a lack of follow up studies. Perhaps, ultimately, there was some doubt concerning the usefulness of this approach.

Human Development Index

Before we go to further discussion of remediation, let us go back to adding, subtracting, and lists. Every year UNDP (ndr.undp.org/reports/) publishes the HDI rankings of all countries (Box 4-2). The index, devised by Nobel Laureate Amartya Sen (en.wikipedia.org/wiki/Amartya_Sen), is claimed to be an improvement over the use of GDP per capita as a measurement of human development. The criteria Sen decided to measure were life expectancy at birth, two thirds of the adult literacy rate plus one third of the mean years of schooling, and income. The index was designed to provide a true measure of human development based on longevity, knowledge, and earnings. There is also a parameter for—the marginal utility of income. It is a way of skewing the income to reflect the marginal value of income; an increment of income is worth more to the poor than to the rich.

Norway, Canada, or Switzerland routinely comes out as the country with the highest HDI, closely followed by the US, France, Germany, and Britain. At the bottom of the list are nations like Zambia. For the 2006 Report based upon 2004 data, Norway, Iceland, Australia, Ireland, and

Box 4-2. Human Development Index

HD = f {longevity, knowledge, income}

longevity   =   life expectancy at birth
knowledge   = $^2/_3$ (adult literacy rate) + $^1/_3$ (mean years schooling)
income   =   utility of income w(y) expressed by the logarithm of the
                  per capita GDP

Each factor is scaled by maximum and minimum

$$\text{e.g., for longevity} = \frac{\text{actual LE} - \text{min LE}}{\text{max LE} - \text{min LE}} = \frac{48.4 - 25}{85 - 25}$$

Source: P. Rogers et al. (1997), p. 38

Sweden were the top five (averaging 0.958), with the US coming in at eighth place. The bottom five were inea-Bissau, Burkina Faso, Mali, Sierra Leone and Niger (averaging 0.335).

The data do not change much from year to year. A change in the life expectancy at birth takes decades to show a significant effect, as do changes in literacy and years of schooling. Income, however, might change by a fair amount from year to year.

One may be tempted to ask if the HDI is really a new measure. The rank order correlation of HDI with GNP per capita is about 0.98. HDI is strongly correlated with GDP per capita, which it was supposed to improve upon and ultimately replace. The close correlation is due to the fact that life expectancy is highly correlated with GDP per capita. What is called knowledge is actually literacy and years of schooling, which are also highly correlated with GDP per capita. Income, of course, is GDP per capita. In the end, what we have is a wonderful system that pretty much reproduces GDP per capita, and it does that because of the highly interdependent nature of the sub-indices.

The correlations in assessing human development are very complex and open to all sorts of manipulations, interpretations, or simply tampering. This is why we can find all manner of versions of the HDI. There was one that weighted women's employment much more highly than men's employment. Another version weighted women's life expectancy more strongly. We need only to change things slightly to drastically change the results. Nevertheless, the HDI is becoming popular in making intercountry comparisons, particularly for countries with similar GDP per capita.

USE OF PRINCIPAL COMPONENT ANALYSIS

To get around the problem of multi-colinearity—the fact that different components of an index are highly correlated with each other—we can use what is called principal component analysis. Essentially, principal component analysis combines and modifies the data from interdependent categories such that a new set of mutually independent categories arises. Once we take out all the cross-correlations from the data, we can work with a new set of variables.

In 1994, ADB and the Government of Norway cofinanced a study executed by Harvard University's Environmental Systems Program to develop a set of indices to monitor environmental changes among ADB developing member countries (Rogers et al., 1997). At that time, approximately 30% of ADB's loans were for environmental and socially sustainable issues, amounting to $2 billion to $3 billion per year. The question was how to assess the environmental quality of ADB developing member countries with such different ecological conditions as the PRC and the Marshall Islands.

To do this, a large database consisting of 79 environmental indices in 146 countries was examined, which uncovered several difficulties. Although every year the World Bank, ADB, the UN, and the World Resources Institute compile huge databases encompassing a large number of indicators, the coverage for each country for each of the indicators is poor. So the list ended up with data for 33 indices covering only 17 countries.

Moreover, the indices were highly multi-colinear; i.e., when measuring one dimension they also measured a little bit of another dimension. We rotated the axis upon which all of the indices were measured until we got 33 indices that were entirely independent of each other and expressed as linear functions of the original indices. It was found that the first four principal components (the first four new indices) explained about 70% of the total variance in the database.

This is what data reduction is about. We started with 33 indices and boiled them down to just 4; and those 4 indices were composed of pieces of the original 33. With the number of indices reduced, serious numerical analysis is possible. It turned out, fortunately, that the variables or the new indices that were derived were exactly what the ADB team had thought to be important. The first principal component had many air pollution indicators embedded in it; in a similar fashion the second was devoted to deforestation and soil degradation; the third related to biodiversity and endangered species; and the fourth dealt with water quality.

THREE ENVIRONMENTAL QUALITY INDICES

In assessing the current and potential future states of the environment in the developing member countries of ADB, three comprehensive environmental quality indices based upon the four principal components were found to be especially useful: the cost of remediation, environmental elasticity, and the environmental diamond.

Cost of Remediation

The cost of remediation (COR) is the cost of moving the present state of the environment to an acceptable level based on a set of predetermined standards. The concept entails three steps: assessment of the existing environmental emissions and degradation, establishment of a set of environmental standards, and estimation of the aggregated costs of achieving these environmental standards.

Most countries in the world have already adopted the water quality standards of the World Health Organization (WHO), the European Union (EU), or EPA. Much uniformity exists in national standards. So if urban air quality is at 600 micrograms per cubic meter and we want it to be down to 60 micrograms per cubic meter, we can calculate the cost of remediation. See Box 4-3 for air, water, and land pollution targets.

Box 4-3. Air, Water, and Land Pollution Targets

Air and Water
- Pollutants: Five pollutants, including chemical oxygen demand (COD), suspended solids, and heavy metals (water); TSP and sulfur (air)
- Targets: 90% reduction in water and air pollutant emissions (1990 levels) in 10 years

Land Components:
- Soil Erosion Control
    - Target: 70% of total land cover within 10 years
- Municipal Solid Waste Management
    - Target: All municipal wastes will be collected and disposed of immediately

Source: P. Rogers et al. (1997)

To estimate the COR, we estimate the aggregate cost of meeting the environmental standards. This is a monetary unit that can be an effective counterweight to traditional economic indicators such as GDP. The COR of different components of the environment may be added or subtracted freely. We are not adding apples and oranges; we are adding or subtracting costs. The COR avoids the problem of weighting environmental indices. These are numbers that we can work with on a spreadsheet and are responsive to what Indonesian minister Emil Salim was seeking—a measure of environmental losses in economic terms.

There are data banks for remediation costs. Indonesia has a ten-year plan for building national parks or conservation areas that includes cost. The PRC has excellent cost data on air, water, and land remediation. The World Bank has costs on solid waste management. We do not know the cost of the loss of a species, but we do know the cost of national parks and conservation areas, since the World Conservation Union (IUCN) and the World Wildlife Fund (WWF) can provide cost data for ecosystem management. ADB has used a cost remediation process in assessing the environment for several of its developing member countries since 1994. It has been able to accurately report where the major problems were, and which countries needed to spend a lot to remediate and maintain their environment (Table 4-2).

Table 4-2. Annualized Cost of Remediation (COR)
for ADB Developing Member Countries ($ million in 1990 US$)

Country	Water	Air	Land	Ecosystem	COR (total)
BANGLADESH	13.70	30.34	321.47	52.39	417.89
BHUTAN	0.16	0.35	8.50	24.45	33.45
CAMBODIA	0.31	0.70	78.11	30.85	109.97
LAO PDR	0.26	0.58	38.46	33.18	72.48
MONGOLIA	5.91	13.08	2,773.26	13.39	2,805.64
MYANMAR	3.56	7.87	260.74	65.20	337.36
NEPAL	0.78	1.74	115.60	48.90	167.02
PAKISTAN	53.97	119.49	867.20	36.09	1,076.76
SRI LANKA	3.5	7.76	65.12	147.86	224.24
VIET NAM	12.97	28.71	200.75	251.48	493.91
PRC	1,430.13	3,166.07	12,657.97	299.79	17,553.96
INDIA	418.97	927.53	4,882.97	852.23	7,081.70
INDONESIA	100.10	221.61	953.92	296.30	1,571.93
PAPUA NEW GUINEA	1.73	3.82	12.94	70.44	88.92
PHILIPPINES	39.59	87.65	319.67	160.67	607.57
THAILAND	67.00	148.32	557.63	47.73	820.68
FIJI	0.52	1.16	7.48	20.37	29.53
KOREA, REP. OF	199.84	442.41	203.24	61.71	907.19
MALAYSIA	43.15	95.52	138.78	329.48	606.93
SINGAPORE	24.42	54.07	14.65	14.55	107.70
TOTAL	2,420.58	5,358.76	24,478.44	2,857.06	35,114.83

Source: P. Rogers et al. (1997)

A nation like Viet Nam must spend about 8% of its GDP for remediation. Countries that have maintained a good environment can spend less—for instance, the Netherlands, 2%; Switzerland, about 2%; the US, about 1.8%, and the UK, almost 1.5% (P. Rogers et al., 1997). Of the western nations, France spends the least, about 1.3%, perhaps because the French have done such a good job of protecting the environment in the past. The Netherlands, however, takes environmental problems more seriously, spending more of its GDP on maintaining and enhancing its environment.

The COR enables one to assess demands for external financial assistance. The study determined that if the COR divided by GDP is less than 1%, there is probably no demand for external financing. On the other hand, if the COR is more than 4.5% of GDP, external funding would be needed. Or, following Kuznets' argument, a country can raise its GDP and then finance its COR.

The PRC is really pressing very hard on its environment. It is a huge country, but it consists mostly of deserts and mountains; it has very little living space. Mongolia, though mostly underdeveloped, also has very little living space. It has also been reduced to mostly desert by overgrazing. The Mongolians have cut down most of what little forest they had.

Table 4-2 shows that the major COR in the PRC is for land. There is tremendous soil erosion, partly due to the poor quality of the soil and partly because of overfarming (the Chinese have been farming the same soil for more than 3,000 years). Conventional wisdom might say that the main problem of the PRC is air pollution (recall Figure 4-4), but the air is relatively inexpensive to clean up. Remediation of the land is by far the most important and expensive task.

Box 4-4. Environmental Elasticity

Environmental Elasticity's Principal Merits

Environmental elasticity is the ratio of the aggregate percentage change in the environment to the aggregate percent change in the economy.

Environmental elasticity is based on price and income elasticity found in the economic literature.

The principal merits of environmental elasticity are twofold:
- It is dynamic, using data for two points in time to capture environmental changes with respect to economic trends.
- It is a trend indicator as opposed to a state indicator.

Source: P. Rogers et al. (1997)

Figure 4-8. Map of Environmental Elasticity

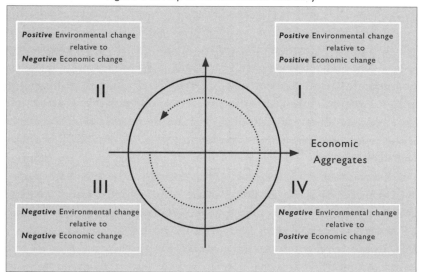

Source: P. Rogers et al. (1997)

Environmental Elasticity

The second comprehensive index is called Environmental Elasticity and is akin to the price and income elasticities used in economics. The principal merits of environmental elasticity are its dynamics. Using data from two points in time on two axes, it captures environmental changes with respect to economic trends, making environmental elasticity a trend indicator as opposed to a state indicator. The cost of remediation tells the state of the environment; environmental elasticity tells the direction of the trends. Box 4-4 summarizes the definition.

If we set up a chart with environmental aggregates and economic aggregates as our two variables, it is possible to track the rate of economic and environmental changes and the percentage of change, as suggested in Figure 4-8.

Quadrant I in the upper right corner of Figure 4-8 indicates a positive environmental change relative to a positive economic change. Sri Lanka is an example of a country that has achieved Quadrant I status. This is a healthy balance: both an improving economy and an improving environment. Quadrant IV in the lower right corner shows an improving economy, while environmental quality is declining. This is where many rapidly developing nations, such as the PRC, are. Quadrant II in the upper left corner shows an improving environment and an economic downturn. The classic example of this is found in Russia. Threatened with bankruptcy, after the break up of the Soviet Union, Russia closed down many of its factories. The positive side effect was that its air and rivers became cleaner. Finally, Quadrant III shows that it is possible to have both negative environmental change and negative economic growth.

Development Diamonds and Environmental Diamonds

Development diamonds and environmental diamonds, shown in Figure 4-9, are graphs that illustrate a country's or region's relative performance with respect to four indicators. Ideally, these indicators should be independent from each other. The development diamond was introduced by the World Bank (2004). Notice how the four criteria are similar to the HDI, which utilizes three of them.

The development diamond is especially useful in showing a particular country's performance with respect to a regional average. The first step in constructing a development diamond is to determine the regional average for each of the four indicators. The axes on the diamond plot are then scaled according to the percentage of the regional value. The regional average diamond is then plotted with four equal sides with the vertices at 100% on each axis. Each indicator is then plotted for the hypothetical country as a percentage of the regional average. If all the indicators are "good" indicators (e.g., concerning access to safe water, life expectancy, etc.), then a diamond larger than the regional average signifies a country that is performing much better than its neighbors. From the figure, we see that the hypothetical country is performing better than average in terms of schooling and GDP per capita, but worse than average for access to safe drinking water and life expectancy. The usefulness of the development diamond approach is the ability to quickly assess the performance of a given country with respect to a regional average (Figure 4-10).

Figure 4-9. Generic Development and Environmental Diamonds

Development Diamond

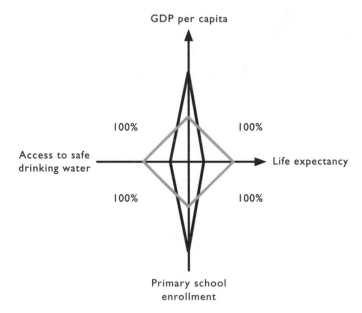

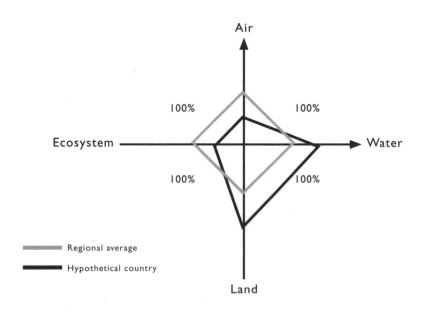

Regional average

Hypothetical country

Figure 4-10. Environmental Diamonds for the PRC and Pakistan

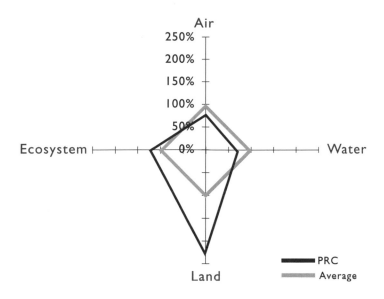

Source: Rogers et al. (1997)

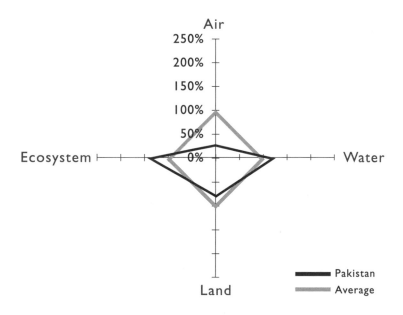

Source: P. Rogers et al. (1997)

129

While it is tempting to measure the relative area under each triangle and compare the countries based on the areas of their diamonds, this operation is flawed. We have four dimensions shown on a flat piece of paper, and if we calculate the diamond area, we will have committed a cardinal sin in mathematics. The diamond is really a tetrahedron, with four independent dimensions, not a diamond flat on the paper. It is easy to see the problem with calculating the diamond area if you reorder the axes. If primary school enrollment and life expectancy are switched, we obtain a diamond with a different area. Since there is no inherent reason guiding the ordering of the axes, there is obviously a problem with trying to calculate the area.

It is possible to construct an environmental diamond by plotting on the four independent axes the cost of remediation for the ecosystem, water, land, and air. Again, the actual values plotted would be percentage values with respect to some regional average.

Figure 4-11. Eight health/education indicators for Africa

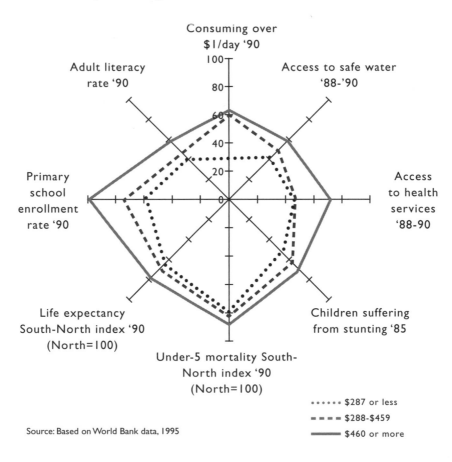

Source: Based on World Bank data, 1995

A slightly more complicated graph related to development and environmental diamonds is known as a "snowflake." Figure 4-11 shows eight indicators plotted on a snowflake with eight, not four, independent axes. Again, values are plotted as percentages with respect to averages in the World Bank's African region. The Japanese environmental protection agency uses a slightly modified version showing seven indicators. These plots are called star diagrams.

In Figure 4-11, the solid line is the average for countries with GDP over $460 per capita, and the dotted and dashed lines are the average values for even poorer countries. Small is not necessarily beautiful in this case. For six of the indicators it would be better to be bigger than the average, while for two (under-5 mortality and children suffering from stunting) being below the average is better. The problem with environmental diamonds, snowflakes, and stars is that their shape is deceptive. Four (or 7 or 8) dimensions cannot be plotted on a flat, two-dimensional sheet of paper. The areas within the different shapes are deceiving. If we make comparisons based upon the relative areas of the diamonds, etc., we have violated the laws of topology

Adding the four indices in an environmental diamond creates a "thermometer." The height of the thermometer (shown in Figure 4-12) can allow us to make a judgment on the relative magnitudes of the impacts in a fairly unbiased way. We are still confronted with the problem of setting relative weights for various indices.

Figure 4-12. An Environmental Thermometer Showing Four Components of Environmental Quality Equally Weighted

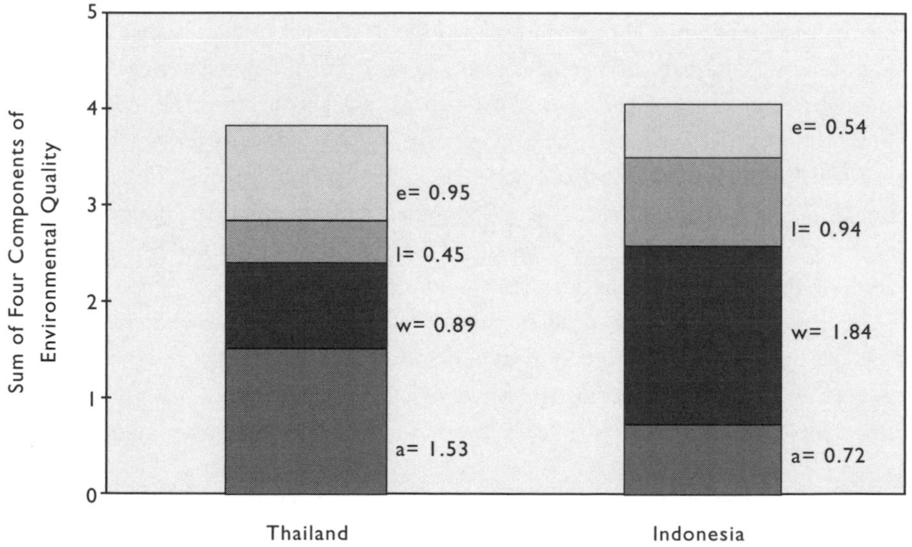

(a=air, l=land, w=water, and e=ecosystem).

Source: A. Gelber and P. Rogers (Aug. 2002)

The math, the graphs, the charts, and other special devices such as the development and environmental diamonds are all tools employed toward an end: economic and environmental assessment that allows environmentally aware developers and financial institutions to predict both the impacts and full costs of sustainable development.

SUMMARY

In assessing economic, environmental, and social development, it is important to have clear, simple, and reliable indicators of progress or lack thereof. The discipline of economics is the most advanced in providing such quantifiable and reproducible indicators. Measures of GDP, savings rates, and price and income elasticities are among some of the most useful. The field of environmental science also has a wide range of useful indicators for measuring environmental quality. The field of social indicators also provides a broad set of somewhat less focused indicators. Unfortunately, the developing field of sustainability science, which relies upon indicators from the other fields, is not well developed, and has to rely upon combinations of these for indicators of progress. P. Rogers et al. (1997) attempted to expand the use of indicators for broad environmental assessment at the national and regional scale. This chapter reports some of the results.

To use many of the indicators, it is necessary to recall some of the basic tenets of arithmetic, in particular, the avoidance of confusion associated with the inappropriate arithmetic manipulation of ranked data. In addition, the Annex to this chapter points out some of the issues associated with measures of centrality and dispersion when the underlying distributions are nonsymmetric.

A major problem with indicators is the aggregation of one carefully measured and statistically reliable index with another index in order to broaden the usefulness of the resulting indicator. In many cases, even where the data are purely physical (as in air pollution), the aggregated indicator may be a poor indicator of the joint effects of the indices brought together. The most important observation in this chapter, however, is how to remove multicolinearity from the data used in describing sustainability issues. Principal component analysis can be employed to convert highly correlated data into uncorrelated indices. It is imperative that all indicators of sustainability be subject to this rigorous exercise. In many cases this will rule out a large number of redundant variables, allowing the planner to focus upon fewer and more relevant ones.

While we have developed the complex cost-of-remediation and environmental elasticity indicators, we fully endorse simpler approaches such as environmental diamonds and snowflakes. The chapter, however, also warns of the pitfalls associated with environmental snowflakes and diamonds, and suggests a simple "thermometer" as an easier and more honest representation of data.

ANNEX
SOME USEFUL STATISTICAL DEFINITIONS

Measures of Central Tendency

There are several measures of central tendency; they are meant to reflect the locations where most of the observations lie. Of these the mean, the median, and the mode are the most useful. A few other measures are used in environmental assessment, which are influenced by the scaling of the data. The geometric and harmonic means are two such measures.

- **Mean.** The arithmetic mean (or "average" in common parlance) is the sum of all the values in a set of numbers divided by the number of values. When doing a population study, it is important to remember that the mean of a sample will usually not be exactly equal to the mean of the population. However, as the size of the sample, which is usually denoted as N, increases, the sample mean will approach the population mean. Every time we take a bigger sample we get closer and closer to the population mean and ultimately, when N equals the size of the population, we get the true mean.

  N is an interesting number in statistics, and there is a lot of debate as to what is big. Is 50 big enough for a sample size? It will depend upon how accurately we want the sample mean to be. It may be hard to take a large sample, particularly in the social sciences, where sampling and experimentation are expensive. However, if the sample data contain an extreme value (as in the sample 1, 3, 5, and 1,000), the computed mean might not realistically reflect the middle value, or the population mean derived from a larger sample.

- **Median.** The mean is the most common tool for getting a sense of a "typical" or "middle" value. However, a more accurate or more useful measure of "middleness" is often achieved by calculating the median. The median is the central number in a group of numbers. For instance, in the series 4, 5, 6, 9, 13, 14, 19, the median is 9. If we have a symmetrically distributed population or sample, then the mean and the median are the same. In a "normal" population distribution (the Gaussian bell curve), 50% are above the mean, and 50% are below the mean (Figure 4-13). The median is a good indicator if we are interested in where half of the population falls as opposed to the population average. For instance, if we wish to determine income distribution in a fixed populace, we would look for the median income rather than the mean, simply because extreme values (e.g., a few billionaires) tend to skew the results, and the mean does not necessarily represent a "typical" income. If we average in the wealthiest segment of the population and the poorest, we would get spurious results.

- **Mode.** The mode is the most commonly occurring value in a set of numbers. In the sequence 1, 2, 3, 3, 3, 3, 4, 4, 5, 6, 6, the mode is 3. When plotted on a graph, the above series looks something like a sloppy bell curve.

- **Harmonic mean.** We can use other yardsticks such as the harmonic mean. In certain situations, this statistic gives a more accurate measure of an average value, as suggested in the following example: If one travels at 40 mph for a half of the distance of a car trip, and 60 mph for the other half, the average speed is calculated using the harmonic mean. In this case, the average speed would be 48, which is less than the arithmetic mean. The formula for the harmonic mean, H, of N observations follows.

$$H = \frac{N}{1/x_1 + 1/x_2 + \ldots + 1/x_N}$$

- **Geometric mean.** The geometric mean is defined as the product of all the values in a set of numbers raised to the power of the reciprocal of the number of values in the set. The formula for the geometric mean, G, is

$$G = (x_1 \cdot x_2 \cdot \ldots \cdot x_N)^{1/N}$$

As we can see, there are a number of different ways to calculate the "average" value for a set of numbers. Depending on what these numbers represent and what we are trying to find, the geometric mean might be more useful than the harmonic mean or median calculations, for example, when we are showing rates of change. A useful relation to remember is that the harmonic mean is always less than or equal to the geometric mean, and the geometric mean is always less than or equal to the arithmetic mean.

Measures of Data Dispersion

As we move on to refine data, the computations become more complex. Whether measuring water or air pollution, income, or resource distribution, we need to know how the data are dispersed within the sample. There are several measures of dispersion.

Box 4-5. Variance and Standard Deviation

Application of these measurements is illustrated in determining population variance and standard deviation:

The sample variance, denoted below by s^2, is the sum of the squared deviations from the mean, x_m, divided by the number of samples N, minus one. The standard deviation is the square root of the sample variance. If N is very large, then N minus 1 is practically the same as N, and the sample variance is a close estimate of the population variance.

s^2 = sample variance = $\sum (x_i - x_m)^2/(N - 1)$

SD = standard deviation = $\sqrt{s^2}$ = s

For example, consider the following five numbers: 3, 5, 7, 14, and 21; the mean is 10 and $s^2 = [(3 - 10)^2 + (5 - 10)^2 + (7 - 10)^2 + (14 - 10)^2 + (21 - 10)^2] / 4$. Computing these results, $s^2 = 55$ and SD = 7.4.

Figure 4-13. Normal Distribution

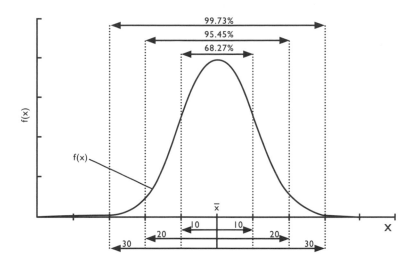

- **Variance and standard deviation.** Variance measures how spread out the distribution of values is from the mean. Standard deviation is the square root of the sample variance.

- **Range of data.** This is the distance between the extreme (lowest and highest) data points gathered. Because the calculation of sample variance averages the square of the distance from the mean, a value that is far from the mean will be weighted more heavily than one close to the mean, and hence will have a larger influence on the final result. The range is less influenced by extreme values.

Box 4-6. Range of Data

Another approach that considers the linear, as opposed to squared, distance from the mean is to measure the range or interquartile range. The total range is simply the distance between the two extreme data points. Obviously, this approach says nothing about how the data are spread within the range, and by definition it is influenced by extreme points.

To determine the interquartile range, we first sort the data according to magnitude and then determine the first three quartiles (Q_1, Q_2, Q_3). The first quartile is the median of the lower half of the data, and the third quartile is the median of the upper half. The second quartile is the median of the entire data set. The interquartile range is the distance between the first and third quartiles $(Q_3 - Q_1)$. Therefore, the data are ranged so that 25% are below the range, 25% are outside the range, and 50% lie within the range.

- **Box-and-whisker plots.** Another useful statistical tool is known as box-and-whisker plots, which graphically show summaries of environmental quality data. A box-and-whisker plot reveals the spread of the data by plotting three values: the two extremes (forming the "whiskers"), standard deviation (the ends of the "box"), and the mean. The following chart shows how this statistical tool can be used. Each box and whisker represents a set of measurements at a particular well location, MW1, MW2, MW3, and MW4, showing varying mean, range, and standard deviation of arsenic concentration in the water at four monitored well locations.

Figure 4-14. Monitoring Well Location

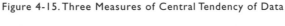

Source: McBean and Rovers, 1998

Figure 4-15. Three Measures of Central Tendency of Data

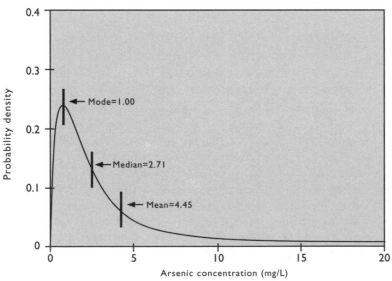

Source: McBean and Rovers, 1998

136

• **Skewness.** For a normal distribution, 50% of the samples fall below the computed mean and 50% above the computed mean. Deviation from the normal distribution is called skewness. The term is defined as having some elements on opposite sides of a mean line reversed or unbalanced. The formula for skewness is:

$$A=n\Sigma(x_i-mean)^3/(n-1)(n-2)s^3$$

A is a positive number for a skew to the right tail and a negative number for a skew to the left tail.

Schematic Depiction of Three Measures of Central Tendency of Data

The plotted data in Figure 4-15 show unimodal distribution that is positively skewed. Along the horizontal axis, the mode appears on the left, the median in the middle, and the mean on the right. If the order were reversed and the tail extended to the left, then it would be a negatively skewed distribution.

What does this graph reveal about the arsenic in the groundwater? Should a health standard be based on the mean, the median, or the mode? There are such big differences among the three figures that could determine whether the standard is met or not. The answer will depend upon how we value the negative health effects of large but rare concentration of arsenic in the groundwater. At high levels, arsenic poisoning can be fatal. In writing a standard, it is necessary to obtain more information on typical distributions of arsenic measurements and the health impact of arsenic exposure to come up with an appropriate statistic or combination of statistics for the standard.

We should be careful about drawing strong conclusions. One way to check the quality of the measurements is to divide the standard deviation of all the measurements by the mean. This statistic is referred to as the "coefficient of variation," which will be very high if there is a wide spread in the magnitude of the measurements. As a rule of thumb, when the coefficient of variation is greater than one, the data are considered very noisy, and it is a good idea to recheck the measurements. The long whiskers indicating wide dispersion that are shown in the figure are typical of these kinds of sample data, as accurate data on environmental conditions are often hard to come by. This difficulty should provide a warning when working with only average values, which can be quite misleading.

CHAPTER 5

ENVIRONMENTAL ASSESSMENT

I n this chapter we are going to explore environmental impact assessment (EIA). At one time no one thought about environmental impact. They just went out and built highways and bridges, and never took a second look. The only concerns were completing the job on time and on budget. The "E" word was efficiency, not environment.

Now we know better.

We will examine the various methods used to make EIAs, and the techniques that predict impacts, whether on land, air, or water. Since all the methods cannot be considered in detail, we will restrict ourselves to one particularly useful framework. The example of a coherent method to carry out an EIA to be discussed in some detail is taken from an ADB tutorial on EIA.

NATIONAL ENVIRONMENTAL POLICY ACT OF 1969

In the US, the National Environmental Policy Act (NEPA) was passed during the Nixon Administration in 1969. President Nixon got good marks from environmentalists, because during his term some very important legislation was passed, of which the NEPA is an outstanding example. The mandate of the NEPA was to be a trustee for the environment for succeeding generations. It predated the concept of sustainability and the formation of the Brundtland Commission by more than a decade. The NEPA came about at a time when the federal government was becoming concerned about the environmental degradation it was witnessing—rivers catching fire, polluted groundwater, indiscriminate handling of waste materials—and decided to do something about it. It was essentially a top-down approach from the federal government to the states and local governments. There was little, if any, participation of civil society.

The NEPA also had to do with aesthetics. It wanted to assure all Americans safe, healthful, productive, and culturally pleasing surroundings. Written into its preamble was the vow to attain the widest range of beneficial uses of the environment without risk to health or safety and without other undesirable or unintended consequences. It meant to preserve important historical, cultural, and natural aspects of the national heritage and to maintain an environment that supports diversity and a variety of individual choices.

The NEPA could be considered a Magna Carta for the environmental movement in the US and later in many other countries. It gave citizens and citizens' groups legal standing on a host of environmental issues that they did not previously have. Under the NEPA the citizenry could participate in the decision-making process, which formerly had been reserved for government agencies operating without the need for consultation.

Council on Environmental Quality

The NEPA inevitably led to the establishment of the Council on Environmental Quality (CEQ) at the beginning of 1970. CEQ would assess the state of the nation's environment, and the EPA would set standards, implement regulations, and administer the law. For a while, CEQ served as a vital control body, attracting some of the most important environmentalists of the time, including Russell Train and Gus Speth. Unfortunately, today one would have to think hard to name anyone currently on CEQ, or for the last 10 years for that matter. It has been seriously downgraded.

But during its early years, CEQ not only monitored the environment but also was required by law to make an annual report on the state of the environment in the US. These reports, from 1970 through 1990, have become collector's items. They contain some very serious environmental thinking, establishing indicators and indices of the state of the environment in the country. These papers tell us that the environment was in bad shape in 1968 and 1969, then began improving.

When CEQ was established, it was supposed to be an independent agency. That is no longer the case. The reporting is now done by the affected agencies. For example, instead of having independent experts review what the Department of Agriculture is doing concerning the environment, we have to take the department's assessment of its own performance, which can make its reports subject to question.

The reports are still collated annually, but they are no longer dated with a particular year, and they are increasingly difficult for citizens to obtain. That renders them almost useless as a scholarly tool and indicates that recent administrations have put the environment, or at least environmental assessment, on the back burner.

Learning the Three "E's"

The NEPA required project planning and decision making to include integrated consideration of the three "E's": engineering, economics, and environment. While now it may seem obvious, at the time the concept was quite revolutionary and, as it turned out, hard to accomplish.

What did the Department of Agriculture know about environmental and social consequences? These were never part of their brief. After a while, the big civilian agencies and the military establishment did learn their "E's," creating strange anomalies. The largest employer of landscape architects in the US, for instance, is the Army Corps of Engineers.

It is interesting to see how the NEPA actually works in the real world. Under the NEPA, America's national heritage must be safeguarded and promoted. In Michigan, for instance, the Army Corps of Engineers is assigned to maintain the locks of Lake Superior, which are considered part of the national heritage. The installation also contains a museum. So the Corps, which formerly concentrated solely on military infrastructure, now has a historical division under a chief historian. The study of history, the upkeep of public museums, and the beautification of the locks are excellent and environmentally sound ways to spend tax money. The Corps is also partnered with EPA in administering wetland development permits, which involves large amounts of detailed ecological research and knowledge.

The NEPA "contains provisions that are intended to force" (Roger Findley and Daniel Farber, 2000) government agencies to do things according to the three "E's," but it was not easy. All of a sudden these agencies were required by law to take environmental inventories, do EIAs, and produce an environmental impact statement before they could put up a bridge or irrigate a field.

If an agency is told by CEQ that its project might have a significant negative impact on the environment, it has to go back and reassess the project proposal and redo the environmental impact statement, then resubmit it to CEQ. This causes delays, but, as we will see, often saves money by avoiding projects or programs that would have proved disastrous.

Impact studies are, if anything, comprehensive. The environmental impact statement for the Alaska pipeline consists of 22 volumes. Environmental impact statements for interceptor sewers in Boston are 14 or 15 volumes. Some think this is too comprehensive. Who wants to read 14 or 15, let alone 22 volumes? It has been suggested that perhaps 120 pages of clear prose would be sufficient.

The NEPA's Goals

The NEPA also set goals (Section 101, 42 United States Code, Section 4331). One was to achieve a balance between population and resource use that would permit a high standard of living. There were economic considerations, too, namely efficiency in resource use. Another goal was to enhance the quality of renewable resources by maximizing the recycling of resources that are being depleted. Again, this was quite revolutionary, especially the part that dealt with enhancing renewable resources. The US is one of the major consumers in the world of nonrenewable resources such as oil. In 1970, the country imported 40% of its petroleum needs. By 2003, the figure had climbed to almost 60%.

Environmental Inventory – Providing the Baseline Data

Under the NEPA, before a project or a program can be undertaken, an environmental inventory must be undertaken (40 Code of Federal Regulations Section 1508.9) unless certain exemptions apply, such as "Conflicts with statutory obligations," "Express statutory exemption," or "Functional equivalence of NEPA" with other statutes excusing an agency from taking action under NEPA (Linda Malone, 2003). This should consist of a complete description of everything that will be affected by the project. However, in reality, it includes only those items deemed important as specified under the law. It is obviously impossible to include, for example, all the species and their numbers of earthworms in a given region. (Actually, there is a nationwide biological survey under way, a census of everything alive. However, it will be a long time before useful data emerge.)

The environmental inventory is therefore limited, complying with a NEPA checklist that includes the physical, chemical, biological, cultural, social, and economic environments. Interestingly, the NEPA inadvertently revived some quite arcane professions. Archaeologists, for instance, used to be people who sat in dusty libraries and occasionally dug holes in the ground. The idea of archaeology becoming a boom profession was fairly remote. Today, archaeologists are in big demand. Now they spend a lot of their time two steps ahead of the bulldozers as they prepare studies for road projects and sewer pipelines. The same is true for botanists, agronomists, and geologists. Protection of endangered species is an activity that has received a great boost from the NEPA.

In this regard, note the problems encountered in dealing with endangered and threatened species introduced into recently created environments. For example, the Salton Sea in California contains brine shrimp, a threatened species. Recently created canals have leaked into the desert, creating in part a salty sea, to which sea gulls, or other travelers, have brought brine shrimps. Should these brine shrimp be protected when providing such protection can trump any other development? Taking drainage water from the Colorado River and California's Imperial Valley to California has thus created a unique but major problem.

The environmental inventory provides the baseline data. The next step is to find out if the intended program or project is going to make things better or worse. In other words, how will it impact on the environment?

ENVIRONMENTAL IMPACT ASSESSMENT

The purpose of an EIA is to identify and evaluate systematically the potential impact of a project or program. Note that not just traditional projects but also programs are included. So the 401 Program of the Clean Water Act, enacted to protect the American wetlands, has to be examined from an environmental point of view. If the NEPA is to be enforced, all major undertakings will have to pass environmental tests, even enterprises like space exploration and war equipment. Before the B1 stealth bomber went into production, it underwent a secret environmental impact study.

Sometimes this methodology may be considered as going too far. One would not normally consider projects or trade programs undertaken in some remote area outside of one's country relevant, even if they are debilitating for that area's environment.

That environmental assessments have achieved almost universal acceptance was dramatically underscored when the People's Congress Committee on Environment proposed EIA legislation for the PRC. The PRC has EIA laws that look very similar to those of the US, including public participation in the formulation of environmental programs and projects.

This suggests that good environmental policy is also good social policy. A single act like the NEPA is opening up democratic channels in nations that previously had only limited areas in which citizens were able to interact with, interfere with, or change policy.

While the NEPA is a federal act in the US, most states have their own versions, which we will call NEPA-like laws. Many of the state environmental laws have to do with privately financed projects such as housing and golf courses. State laws also consider the size of a project. Obviously, the bigger the project, the closer the scrutiny.

Project Alternatives (Including the No-Build Option)

Although the NEPA is decades old, implementation is still painful. A project proponent always believes that its proposed project will be beneficial. It is hard to point out that a multimillion dollar project will not work out from an environmental standpoint, especially when the degradation of the environment happens elsewhere or the impact seems miniscule. A famous example concerns the snail darter, an endangered species of fish in a remote area in the Tennessee Valley that stopped the Tellico Dam, a major construction project. When the requirements of the law could not be satisfied, Congress allowed the project to proceed, but only after much acrimonious debate.

There are options, many of them "doable," such as changing the size of a project or its location. The most painful of all is the "no-build" option. It is hard to tell a highway department not to build a road. Building roads is what they do. Yet, because of NEPA-like laws, that is exactly what has happened. And that is why there is no major interstate highway linking a few of the key cities in the American northeast.

Maintaining Long-Term Productivity

Part of an environmental assessment is to examine the relationship between local short-term use of the environment and the maintenance of long-term productivity. This is a sustainability issue. Not only do we worry about what is going to happen to, say, an irrigation project, in the next 20 years, but we want to know if after 50 years the land is going to be so saline that it cannot be used. That is what happens if an irrigation project is not properly designed. It will work fine for 10, 20, or 40 years, and then all of a sudden the soil will become badly salinized and unfit for agriculture. Normally, looking 20 years down the road seems reasonable, but the NEPA requires an even longer view. The economic assessment also asks if there are any irreversible and irretrievable commitments of resources involved, and whether these are reasonable and plausible. We now see the sustainability issue coming to the fore. That there are long-term projects is obvious, but some must be considered in millenniums. In a recent federal court ruling, it was decided that Nevada could not block the use of Yucca Mountain as a nuclear waste repository, but the court ruled that EPA should assess and ensure the safety of the facility not for 20,000 years, which the EPA had proposed, but for 100,000 years!

Satisfying CEQ's Requirements

It is CEQ's job to assist the President with environmental concerns (NEPA S105, 42 U.S.C. Section 4342) but its "main responsibility…is to issue guidelines to interpret NEPA's requirements" (L. Malone, 2003). When it was first formed, CEQ reviewed up to 2,000 environmental impact statements a year. Since then, the number has fallen to 400-500 a year. New projects are being implemented, but the agencies are doing things right. After a few years of living with the NEPA, people learned what they were supposed to do and understood the law. So many projects that would have been rejected were never started. It became a filtering process. If the numbers do not tell the whole story or a good story, they do tell us that people learn from their mistakes. Another reason for fewer reviews is that exclusions (categorical and noncategorical) have been built into the laws.

The Army Corps of Engineers has about 18 categorical exclusions that do not require an impact statement. Most exclusions deal with land tract transactions, transferring land from the private sector to the public domain. Another exclusion relates to the Corps renovating its own infrastructure. Even though many of the Corps' projects are free from NEPA oversight, the Corps set up its own internal mechanisms to evaluate the environmental impact of the cumulative effect of these individual projects and to make sure they will not cause problems.

Most significant projects fall under the category of noncategorical exclusions and need to be assessed (L. Malone, 2003). If a Finding of No Significant Impact is awarded by CEQ, then the project can proceed immediately. If there is a significant impact anticipated, then the project has to be revised, resubmitted, significantly altered, or abandoned. Many projects have to go through this procedure several times. CEQ is not a rubber stamp.

Assessment Review Based on Policies, Plans, Programs, and Projects

Let us examine the assessment procedures for a proposed road, assuming it has already passed the "no-build" criteria (Figure 5-1). Four levels of government are involved: national or federal, regional or state, subregional, and local. For each of the four levels of government, there are four categories: policies, plans, programs, and projects. The first three need a strategic environmental assessment (SEA); the fourth category, projects, calls for an environmental impact study (EIS). As the process moves down to the regional, subregional, and local levels, the impact statements must become more specific. For instance, when the federal government mandates a five-year road-building program, the builder simply has to show that the road network will do no harm. But at the subregional and local levels, the builder must not only report on the environmental impact that the roads will have, but must also demonstrate how the project will benefit the local economy and infrastructure. This type of action and assessment review is widely used in many countries that not only consider projects, but also look at policies, plans, and programs as part of environmental impact assessment.

Figure 5-1. Actions and Assessments within a Broad EIA Framework

Level of government	Level-use plans (SEA)	Category of actions and type of assessment (in parentheses)			
		Sectoral and multisectoral actions			
		Policies (SEA)	Plans (SEA)	Programs(SEA)	Projects (EIS)
National/federal	National land use plan	National transport policy →	Long-term national roads plan →	5-year road building program →	Construction of motorway section
		National economic policy ↘			
Regional/state	Regional land use plan		Regional strategic plan ↘		
Subregional	Subregional land use plan			Subregional investment program ↘	
Local	Local land use plan				Local infrastructure project

Source: Canter (1996), p.19. This is a simplified representation of what, in reality, could be a more complex set of relationships. In general, those actions at the highest tier (i.e., national policies) are likely to require the broadest and least detailed form of SEA.

Strengthening Efforts: ADB and the World Bank

ADB and the World Bank are two publicly owned institutions that do a great deal of project work around the world. These two institutions and many others, including bilateral agencies such as USAID, have been under fire for a long time for not doing as good a job on environmental issues as have some of the private banks that lend to developing countries. Part of the problem relates to the nature of development banks such as ADB and the World Bank; they are basically banks, and their traditional function has been to lend money. Once there was the view that it was primarily the responsibility of the borrower to use the money wisely. This form of reasoning, though, is simplistic. Obviously, multilateral development banks (MDBs) should worry about how the money will be used. If the projects they are being asked to fund promote sustainable development, then the loans should be easy to access. If any of these projects would significantly impact the environment negatively, the loan should be denied.

After being severely chastised for their participation in projects like the Narmader Dam in India, under pressure from their shareholders, the World Bank tightened up its environmental requirements. Since the mid-1990s, both banks have made serious efforts to rectify the situation, as have the Inter-American Development Bank (IADB) and many smaller development banks, and at least the major privately held development banks. By contrast, some private lending institutions are sometimes happy to step in, requiring only fiscal responsibility on the part of the borrower. Some countries employ selective borrowing. When they need loans for controversial projects or environmentally damaging projects, they go to private banks that lend funds while taking few steps to ensure implementation of guidelines and regulations arising from environmental considerations and social dimensions. At the same time, these countries have billions of dollars in their accounts at the World Bank, sitting unused. One could say that these are poor countries that need money, but they do not need money so badly as to allow the World Bank to tell them what may sometimes be difficult to do.

Controversy over Laws

The NEPA and its sister legislation, the Endangered Species Act (16 United States Code Sections 1531-1544, 1988; L. Malone, 2003), are not without their critics. Many feel that following these stringent laws to the letter slows down progress. There is no question that agencies administering these two acts are under a great deal of pressure. If proponents have their environmental impact statement turned back, they are in serious trouble in the sense that they either have to reformulate the project or abandon it. The only other choice is litigation. However, the original intent of the acts was not to become involved in endless litigation. The idea was to help improve the performance of government and introduce more democratic participation in decision making. Besides, if a project is slowed down, perhaps it deserves to be.

Thinking and then doing is always better than doing and then thinking later. A good example is the proposed Dickey-Lincoln Dam project. If it had gone ahead, it would have flooded a huge area of Maine just to produce a small amount of electricity. Here is where the value of assessment comes in. A study showed that it would have been better to have a small wood-fired power plant and chop down some of the trees than to flood a huge area and lose so many more trees. This is an example of an EIA that was doing exactly what it should.

PROJECT CATEGORIES BASED ON ENVIRONMENTAL IMPACTS

The type of scrutiny a project receives depends upon its impacts, categorized as A, B, or C by ADB and the World Bank. These are the broad categorizations; but projects are fluid, and a project that starts out as a B may end up a C after an environmental evaluation is made.

- **Category A** projects are those deemed to have significant environmental impacts calling for in-depth studies. One example would be forestry. Extensive alterations of forested land change the whole ecosystem in an area because they affect the flora and fauna in a major way. Other Category A projects include irrigation, large-scale new water source development, large water impoundments, new railways and mass transit, and ports and harbors. Medium- and large-scale thermal power plants also fall under Category A, because they affect water and air quality and may rely on nonrenewable resources as fuel.

- **Category B** projects have less environmental impact. They include agricultural industries, small-scale water projects, small processing industries, harnessing of renewable energy, small power plants, watershed development and rehabilitation of watersheds, and water supply without impoundment.

- **Category C** projects are unlikely to have a significant adverse environmental impact. Many of these undertakings, while large, are surveys or teaching projects such as forest research and extension programs and agriculture programs, where experts help the indigenous populations to do a more efficient job. Other programs like primary and rural health surveys, and geological and mineral surveys (but not mining) are Category C projects, as are education, family planning, and some other physical planning projects. Many of these projects are not necessarily small in scope and may have budgets of $100 million or more.

IMPACT IDENTIFICATION METHODS

The methodology used to make a scientific environmental analysis is quite complex and often unwieldy. (See L. Canter, 1996, for details.)

Matrices

The simplest way is to lay out the pros and cons of a project in a matrix, of which several types have been devised. (See Table 5-1.) An early model called the Leopold Matrix, developed by Dr. Luna Leopold and his colleagues at the US Geological Survey (Leopold et al., 1971), sets up, in columns and rows, the actions causing an environmental impact and the environment impacted

Table 5-1. Concept of an Environmental Baseline Matrix

Identification	Evaluation		
Environmental elements/units	Scale of importance	Scale of present condition	Scale of management
	1 2 3 4 5 low high	1 2 3 4 5 low high	1 2 3 4 5 low high
Biological: flora fauna ecological relationships **Physical-chemical:** atmosphere water earth **Cultural:** households communities economy communications **Biocultural linkages/units:** resources recreation conservation			

Source: Canter (1996), p. 78

upon. It has 90 rows and 100 columns, and each cell is divided into two parts—one for the magnitude of the impact, and the other for the importance of the impact—both scaled from 1 to 10. The problem is, if a project involves a tropical rainforest, it might have something like 18,000 entries in the matrix. Take just one species. There are hundreds of actions that could impact upon it, and the magnitude of each and how important each is to everything else have to be figured out.

Step matrixes are better, because they feature a matrix with connections to another matrix, which cascade until the data are complete.

The idea in all these matrixes is to form a baseline for pertinent data: biological, physical, chemical, cultural, biocultural, and so on. The scale of importance, scale of present condition, and scale of management are according to numbers. However, the assignment of values becomes a judgment call and therefore loses scientific validity. There is also the problem of the quantity of data. No one can read and digest the data contained in a filled-out Leopold Matrix. The best one can do is arrive at the conclusion that a lot of facts and figures were collected and choose those that help one's case.

Environmental Impact Prediction Techniques

Most data used come from technical research. Air pollution is a good example, because it has been extensively studied, and the people working on measuring air pollution have done a good job. They have created urban statistical models, receptor models, and box models. Other investigators have created quantitative models (see Figure 5-2) to study surface water, point and nonpoint waste loads, aquaculture water quality, and waste load allocations.

EPA has sponsored much of this research, and so there are models that can actually be applied to groundwater, pollution source survey, soil and groundwater vulnerability indexes, leachate testing, individual source propagation models, statistical models of impact, and noise impact indices.

Noise pollution is an interesting environmental problem. There are many models for testing noise level. Although the health factors of noise are generally not as serious as the health factors associated with water quality, people seem more aware of noise; so it often gets more attention. New York City has proposed noise abatement legislation to limit the allowable decibel count on construction equipment, including jack hammers, and has changed traffic patterns in residential neighborhoods. Similarly, many cities, including New York, have altered flight paths to reduce airplane noise on take-offs and landings over populated areas.

Biological, historical, and visual techniques can predict decibel levels on a given project before it is built. Today, using virtual reality software, computers allow us to measure noise and sound suppression techniques before a structure is ever built. But prior to the advent of sophisticated computer programs, engineers and scientists were already dealing with noise abatement. Before a major American limited access road was begun, scientists and acoustical engineers built a model road. Using the model and computer projections, they could predict traffic patterns and usage. Being able to "see" any portion of the highway under any conditions, day or night, allowed the engineers to create indexes and make necessary changes. Today's powerful computers permit drive-throughs and walk-throughs in virtual reality, allowing scientists and engineers to easily and accurately prod, poke, measure, and assess projects while they are still on the drawing board.

ENVIRONMENTAL IMPACT ASSESSMENT PROCESS

The EIA process follows the fate and transport of pollutants through the various parts of the ecosystem. It begins when a pollutant is released into the air, water, or soil. The factors to be considered are the nature of the pollutant, the nature of the environment, the distribution of the pollutant, and how it will be distributed. We also want to know how it will affect the population. So it is a linear process of emission, transport, and dispersion, plus impacts on the receivers—the factors to be measured and assessed.

We also have to assess exposure or the level of danger. To simply say the quality of the air is bad is not enough. We want to know who is exposed, how many people will be affected, and at what level of exposure. We also want to know what the causes are, and what will be the effects. Because of the complexity of the problem, the solutions are quite difficult.

Stopping Pollution at the Source

Often site A can be polluted by activities in region B, but B is somewhere else entirely— maybe even in another country. Lake Superior is heavily polluted by mercury, but a quick assessment shows there is no mercury near the lake. So where is the pollution coming from? It is being transported by the wind from farmlands farther west, where the soil is treated with a phosphate-based fertilizer that contains mercury. Mercury is also found in significant quantities

Figure 5-2. Fate and Transport of Trichloroethylene

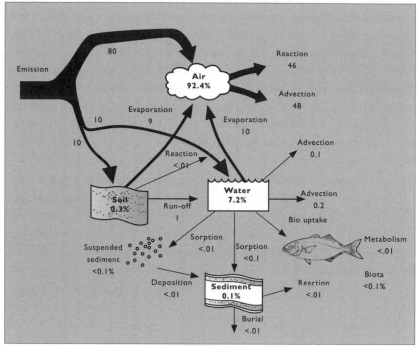

Source: Lohani et al. (1997), p. 42

due to the combustion of mercury-bearing coal in tiny doses. In this system, the wind is called a latent transport system.

Part of an EIA is following the pathways of these latent transport systems, making the job of discovering where contaminants are going to end up complicated and often quite expensive.

Consider the journey of trichloroethylene, an industrial solvent used to degrease machinery (Figure 5-2). Of 100 units of emission, 80 units are released into the air, while the remaining 20 enter the soil and water. Here, what is needed is a life cycle analysis for the pollutant.

The best way to stop pollution is at the source. Once the genie is out of the bottle, it is very difficult to put it back in. Production processes must be modified so that they do not produce pollutants that will seep into the environment and contaminate it. Devising solutions in a piecemeal fashion is an arduous and costly task. Once a contaminant gets into the biota, for instance, it is hard to deal with it. We can ban fishing in Lake Superior, thus wiping out an industry and a recreational area, or we can convince the farmers out west to use a more benign fertilizer.

ADB's Tutorial CD on EIA

ADB has created a computer program that demonstrates how an EIA is undertaken through a hypothetical study of the expansion of a pulp mill (a good choice, because even small mills can be very messy). The program works almost like a video game.

- **Game Characters.** The characters in the game are the Developer or project proponent; the Government Agent, perhaps someone from the bureau of forestry or mines; the Environmental Planner, a citizen who will be affected by the project; the ADB Project Manager, who will be responsible for ensuring that all the appropriate regulations are being followed; and the ADB Senior Manager.

- **The Game's Background Setting.** The mill, with its headquarters in Washington, D.C., is located somewhere in Asia. It has been in operation since 1960 and has been recently sold. The new owners want to expand its operations at a cost of $500 million. They ask ADB for a loan. The mill now becomes subject to the ADB environmental assessment process.

  So here is a project to be undertaken by a multinational corporation that is regulated by the host country. For the project to push through, its proponents have to meet the country's requirements. To secure the ADB loan they also have to meet the environmental requirements of ADB. As noted earlier, if the pulp owners had gone to a private lending institution all they might have had to do is meet the environmental regulations of the country, which may not be as stringent as requirements imposed by ADB. Then again, some private lending institutions are as stringent or more stringent than ADB.

  Under the recent guidelines adopted by many development banks, anyone applying for a loan must follow their procedures, including the employment of consultants who work pursuant to agreed upon terms of reference. ADB's procedures for assessing a project are comprehensive, so that a developer cannot take advantage of deficient procedures in a host country. These procedures may require some time and effort to follow, but they work well in the field, and they might even help avert an environmental catastrophe.

- **How the Game Works.** Once the Developer approaches ADB for a loan, an initial environmental examination (IEE) is carried out. In this case, ADB's staff initially categorizes this project as a B. This means that in all probability an EIA will not be necessary, although it calls for more study. Based upon further study, ADB's consultant screens the project for significant environmental issues and recommends that more information be collected on two pertinent factors—the aquatic environment and air quality. Subsequently, since there is sufficient concern about the aquatic environment, forestry resources, and public health to justify a full EIA, the project is reclassified as Category A. This is the heart of the matter: an initial assessment was made, but it was superficial. When a consultant examined the details in accordance with ADB standards, possible environmental problems surfaced.

  So the executing agency retains an independent private consulting firm to undertake the EIA. While ADB does not restrict the project proponent from hiring its own environmental consultant, it does strongly recommend that someone from ADB's own list be chosen. The list contains the names of companies that have a proven track record and frequently operate in just one part of the world.

  The consulting firm completes its EIA, a five-volume, 1,100-page report containing data on the deficient areas. The summary and the full EIA are then submitted to ADB for review

Figure 5-3. Environmental Impact Assessment and the Project Cycle

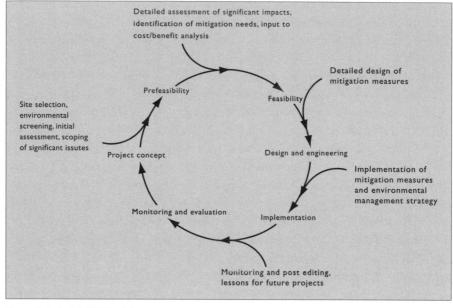

Source: Lohani et al. (1997), p. 1-6

and to the government for publication at least 120 days prior to the date of consideration of loan approval by the ADB Board of Directors. The summary of the EIA is reviewed by the Board, which may then approve the loan subject to a number of conditions.

Once again, the differences between a development bank and some commercial banks become apparent. Since this loan comes from ADB, ADB's involvement does not end when it hands over the initial tranche of the money (Figure 5-3). The borrower is expected to meet ADB's requirements, which is also a requisite for releasing the loan's next tranche and potentially for other loans by ADB in this sector.

If the project proponents meet ADB's recommendations and satisfy the environmental requirements stipulated in the loan agreement for the project, then a document such as an environmental clearance document may be signed by an appropriate ADB officer.

Modifications may begin to occur during the construction phase, in compliance with the environmental monitoring plan. Again, this is part of a development bank's list of requirements and is part of the whole EIA process. Monitoring does not end when construction is completed; it is a continuing process. The requirement is often built into the loan agreement. It should be noted that long-term monitoring is important beyond the project at hand. The data collected over a period of time will become a baseline for future projects. What is learned helps make the next project better.

The ADB Project Manager submits a post-audit evaluation, which includes the data collected from the environmental monitoring plan, to ADB's environmental specialists for review. Those data then become part of ADB's environmental library at its headquarters in Manila.

The time frame for this project is six years from the proposal stage to coming on line, which is quite fast.

While going to a development bank like ADB might seem to slow things down, in the end it is to the proponent's advantage. True, they could have cut environmental corners and strong-armed the local government to approve the project, but now their project has received accreditation from a major institution, so they have a verification that it is environmentally sound. They followed the EIA methodology as outlined by ADB, and they have verification of compliance from ADB.

Reconciling EIA Compliance with Production Norms

Conforming to environmental regulations often runs counter to the norms of production. For example, the standard method of producing paper requires the use of a lot of bleach, the effluvia of which are chlorinated organics. To alleviate this problem, the Philippine EPA proposed that all mills be required to reduce their chlorinated organic waste to 1.5 kg per ton of pulp produced. The estimate the agency stipulated also includes an interim target of 2.5 kg per ton. Even so, these targets are beyond the reach of most plants unless the industry modernizes its production methods—a costly undertaking.

In the case of the model paper mill, the company estimated the cost of meeting the EPA control objectives to be $70-120 million.

Part of the IEE is a description of the environment, including a map. The description must include the geography and geology of the affected region, jobs in the area, and even recreational activities. Had the mill retained its B classification, none of these concerns may have been addressed.

When there are no established procedures such as this one, the results for the environment and the people who live in the affected area can be disastrous.

Implementation and Enforcement of Environmental Standards

Noise, wildlife, land use, land fill, water, and so on are factors that impact a project or are impacted upon, and the EIA must describe each. But who is going to be responsible for setting the standards and enforcing them? It is important to have institutions to implement parameters. Part of the problem in the past was the willingness of banks to lend funds in places where there were no functioning institutions. For a project to be sustainable, there must be institutions that can regulate all the related activities and monitor what is actually happening.

More and more countries around the world are adopting European or American health standards for the amount of acceptable air pollution. For example, such standards do not permit more than about 60 mg of TSP per cubic meter. But in Beijing or New Delhi, which use the western standards, the average level of pollution can be over 400 mg per m³. No wonder some people cough, and pollution can be seen in the air when the sun shines brightly. The law is in place, the standard is in place, but the implementation is not. The solution to this implementation problem may include a combination of enhanced public awareness, stronger political will, and stronger enforcement institutions, including more vigorous law enforcement on the part of prosecutors and judges.

Soliciting Opinions from Project Site Residents

As has been pointed out, an EIA must factor in how a project will impact upon the people living in the affected area and what they say about that project. In the ADB model, there is a fairly typical response from a female respondent: "Well, I think ADB sort of got carried away ... We're worried about the forest. Where is all this wood going to come from when they expand the size of the mill? Are they going to chop down the forest? We live in this forest. Our livelihood comes out of the forest." She does not think that the project proponents and ADB have given the sustainability issue enough consideration. The woman lives in the affected area. In effect she is saying, "Wait a minute! You will build this huge paper mill and chop down all the trees. But where do we fit into this picture? Yes, we get jobs initially, but in the final analysis we'll end up the losers."

Her response is typical, and it is what makes this ADB program a valuable tool. It realistically captures the assessment of a project. The developers are being brash, saying, "I don't see what the problems are." The Government Agent is portrayed as being accommodating, while the Project Manager remains professional. He says, "We are balancing project objectives and environmental and social concerns."

A New Way of Doing Business

The good news is that a great many companies understand that the way business is conducted has changed. The EIA process is leading us into a different world. It is not happening all at once; nor is it universal. For local companies in the PRC, where the government owns the means of production, very few regulations may be implemented. But once we move into a globalized setting where there are multinationals involved, we not only have development banks regulating what businesses can and cannot do, but the companies have become sensitive to public opinion. A project has to look sound even when a company owns only a small portion of it, because the company's name is associated with it. Even if these corporations are not delighted about spending money on environmental upkeep, they realize that not doing so will hurt their business in other areas. This is one of the positive aspects of globalization.

When talking about EIAs we are also talking about democracy—allowing people to participate in the management of their own environment. Happily, we are seeing this even in the Third World. The mill model accurately depicts the voices of those who previously never had a platform where they could express their opinions. Of course, governments and developers may try to alter unsolicited opinions, but generally there is the beginning of a sense that people understand that they can do something, that they can actually participate in the development process.

Evaluating a Project's Viability

Part of the discussion can and should be on whether the project is at all viable. In the case of our model, the question seems to be whether the mill should be expanded or whether a second mill should be built. Which makes more sense—to begin constructing a new mill with modern equipment or to build on the existing infrastructure using the roads that are already in place? This is addressing the issue of alternatives. If the software includes a no-build alternative, it is even better; in the real world, that is always an option to consider.

EIA's Contributions to the Government

Finally, the positive effects an EIA has on the government must not be minimized. The government may know that the air quality and water quality are bad and are probably getting worse, but it may not know how bad, and it does not have the money to find out. The EIA, however, requires that people monitor the affected environment, so all of a sudden there is money and technical expertise being devoted to study the quality of the air and water. Now the government has an environmental assessment that it may not have had to pay for, a way of learning how to do future assessments, and quite probably high-quality equipment and monitoring devices that will be left in place.

Although the hypothetical mill is only one case study, it includes much detail on how and why an EIA is begun, what the terms of reference are, what is in the project cycle, and in what order one proceeds.

CHAPTER 6

ENVIRONMENTAL MANAGEMENT: TRENDS AND POLICIES

Environmental management is not about management of the environment; it is about management of developmental activities within the limits of the assimilative capacity of the environment. Environmental management can be approached at every level—from each individual to the firm or company level; to the municipal and subregional levels; to national, regional, and global levels. The approach at each level is different. We begin with a review of some global milestones in the concept and practice of environmental management.

MILESTONES IN ENVIRONMENTAL MANAGEMENT

Conceptual thinking about the environment began in the 1960s. However, the concept of environmental management at that time was limited mostly to abating pollution caused by development in the developed countries.

In 1972, the first UN global meeting to discuss the issue of environment and its impact on humankind was held in Stockholm. Called the United Nations Conference on the Human Environment (UNCHE) and attended by world leaders and top environmental scientists, it was not without controversy. Many of the developing nations felt that the conference was a ploy of the developed world to discourage development in their countries. Some of them pointed out that the conference was designed by heavily urbanized and industrialized developed nations; in fact, the island countries of the Pacific decided not to attend. In this sense, UNCHE was only a modest success.

In 1975, based on UNCHE outcome and recommendations, a new international organization was established—the United Nations Environment Programme (UNEP). With the aid of UNEP, many countries began forming their own environmental committees, agencies, and ministries. Some nations, based on UNCHE recommendations, started to set environmental standards and formulate environmental legislation. UNEP held the world's first ministerial level conference on the environment in 1982, adopting the Montevideo Program for the development of international environmental law, which Kiss and Shelton (2000, p. 88) described later as having "framed most of its normative activities."

Pursuant to a UN General Assembly resolution passed in 1983, the World Commission on Environment and Development (WCED) was established in 1984, chaired by Gro Harlem Brundtland, who was at that time Prime Minister of Norway. According to Kiss and Shelton (2000, p. 66), WCED was an independent body linked to, but outside of, the UN system. Later more commonly known as the Brundtland Commission, its mandate was to examine critical environmental and developmental issues and formulate realistic proposals for dealing with them; to propose new forms of international cooperation on these issues in order to influence policies toward needed changes; and to raise the levels of understanding and commitment to action of individuals, organizations, businesses, and governments.

The Brundtland Commission published its report in 1987 (WCED), introducing the concept of sustainable development, and emphasized the need for an integrated approach to development in the context of sound environmental policies. The work of the Brundtland Commission and the contents of its report led to the convening of the United Nations Conference on Environment and Development (UNCED), also called the Earth Summit, in Rio de Janeiro, Brazil, in 1992. The environment was given an expanded focus, including issues like poverty and population. The title of the conference covered environment and development, reflecting environment as an integral part of development as documented in the Brundtland Report. The UNCED, among others, adopted a plan of action for the twenty-first century on environment and development, known as "Agenda 21."

In the 1990s, UN agencies and bodies organized a number of other global summits on various themes. The first conference in 1991 was devoted to child welfare. The Scandinavian countries, in conjunction with the UN, sponsored the Population Summit in 1992 in Cairo. In 1995, three significant milestones were established: the Social Summit in Copenhagen; the Women's Summit in Beijing; and the establishment of the WTO to deal with the issues of trade, environment, and development. Other meetings included the Habitat Conference in 1996 in Istanbul and the World Food Summit in 1996 in Rome. In 1997, the progress of implementation of the 1992 UNCED was reviewed by the UN General Assembly after five years.

Despite all these conferences and discussions, the environmental situation continued to worsen in most developing countries. This came about because one of the recommendations made at the 1972 Stockholm Conference was that every country needed to establish a ministry for the environment and to enact environmental legislation. Without these prerequisites the environmental situation could not improve. While this may be true, it turned out that the efforts that went into implementing the recommendations were not very sound, simply because laws and policies alone could not solve a nation's environmental problems. In the first place, an environmental Ministry or Agency must have the power to act on its findings and concomitantly be equipped with a realistic budget. Such a Ministry/Agency usually had neither. Second, in their rush to formulate legislation, developing countries used the laws and standards of developed countries as models. After adopting those alien laws and policies and following the pattern of institutions that developed nations had created for environmental management, developing countries discovered that the laws and policies would not work and were not practically enforceable. Similarly, the developing countries found that they could not sustain the institutions from both the budget and capacity points of view. The countries also found that environmental policy is not going to be effective until sector policies on environment are in place. The ministry of environment can formulate an umbrella policy on environment, but that does not solve the problem if, for example, the ministry of industry is not formulating a policy on industrial pollution, and the ministry of water is not formulating a policy on the conservation of water. Governments of many developing countries thought one ministry could do it all, forgetting that other line ministries have a greater role to play. Realizing this, many governments in developing countries began to redress the problem gradually. The environmental legislation and policies that were initiated in the 1970s after the Stockholm Conference were revisited in the early 2000s to address the more complex issues of poverty, trade, technology transfer, financing, and other matters related to the overall environment and development picture.

The next important environmental summit took place in New York under the aegis of the UN General Assembly. Held in 2000, it was aptly called the Millennium Summit. At this conference, the UN delegates had set certain international development goals and targets, called the Millennium Development Goals or MDGs (see Box 6-1 for details).

Box 6-1. UN Millennium Development Goals

By the year 2015, all 191 UN member states have pledged to meet these goals.

GOAL 1	ERADICATE EXTREME POVERTY AND HUNGER
TARGET 1	Halve, between 1990 and 2015, the proportion of people whose income is less than $1 a day
TARGET 2	Halve, between 1990 and 2015, the proportion of people who suffer from hunger
GOAL 2	ACHIEVE UNIVERSAL PRIMARY EDUCATION
TARGET 3	Ensure that by 2015, children everywhere, boys and girls alike, will be able to complete a full course of primary schooling
GOAL 3	PROMOTE GENDER EQUALITY AND EMPOWER WOMEN
TARGET 4	Eliminate disparity in primary and secondary education, preferably by 2005, and at all levels of education no later than 2015
GOAL 4	REDUCE CHILD MORTALITY
TARGET 5	Reduce by two thirds, between 1990 and 2015, the under-five mortality rate
GOAL 5	IMPROVE MATERNAL HEALTH
TARGET 6	Reduce by three quarters, between 1990 and 2015, the maternal mortality rate
GOAL 6	COMBAT HIV/AIDS, MALARIA, AND OTHER DISEASES
TARGET 7	Have halted by 2015 and begun to reverse the spread of HIV/AIDS
TARGET 8	Have halted by 2015 and begun to reverse the incidence of malaria and other major diseases
GOAL 7	ENSURE ENVIRONMENTAL SUSTAINABILITY
TARGET 9	Integrate the principles of sustainable development into country policies and programs and reverse the loss of environmental resources
TARGET 10	Have halted by 2015 the proportion of people without sustainable access to safe drinking water and basic sanitation
TARGET 11	Have achieved a significant improvement by 2020 in the lives of at least 100 million slum dwellers
GOAL 8	DEVELOP A GLOBAL PARTNERSHIP FOR DEVELOPMENT
TARGET 12	Develop further an open, rule-based, predictable, nondiscriminatory trading and financial system (including commitment to good governance, development, and poverty reduction, nationally and internationally)

TARGET 13	Address the special needs of the less developed countries (including tariff and heavily indebted poor countries and cancellation of official bilateral debt; and more generous official development assistance for countries committed to reducing poverty)
TARGET 14	Address the official needs of landlocked countries and small island developing states (through the Programme of Action for the Sustainable Development of Small Island Developing States and the outcome of the 22nd special session of the General Assembly)
TARGET 15	Deal comprehensively with debt problems of developing countries through national and international measures to make debt sustainable in the long term
TARGET 16	In cooperation with developing countries, develop and implement strategies for decent and productive work for youth
TARGET 17	In cooperation with pharmaceutical companies, provide access to affordable, essential drugs in developing countries
TARGET 18	In cooperation with the private sector, make available the benefits of new technologies, especially information and communication

Source: World Bank (2005), p. xxii

2001: International Conference on Fresh Water, Bonn

In December of 2001, the International Conference on Fresh Water was held in Bonn, Germany. The Ministerial Declaration for this conference, while noting "that 1.2 billion people live a life in poverty without access to safe drinking water, and that almost 2.5 billion have no access to proper sanitation," indicated that "governments, the international community, the private sector, the nongovernmental organizations and all other stakeholders need to base their action on the following: governance, funding gap, role of the international community, capacity building and technology transfer, gender and next steps."

Concerning governance, the ministers stated that the "primary responsibility for ensuring the sustainable and equitable management of water resources rests with governments. Nevertheless, the ministers urged "the private sector to join with government and civil society to contribute to bringing water and sanitation services to the unserved and to strengthen investment and management capabilities." (See < http://www.water-2001.de/>.)

2002: Conference on Financing for Development, Monterrey

Leaders from developing and developed countries discussed matching commitments and action at the 2002 International Conference on Financing for Development in Monterrey, Mexico, so that political and economic reform by developing countries would be supported by developed countries in the form of aid, debt relief, investment, and trade. The heads of states and governments declared: "We...have resolved to address the challenges of financing for development around the world, particularly in developing countries." Since that conference many of the problems of financing remain.

2002: World Summit on Sustainable Development, Johannesburg

In August and September of 2002, the largest gathering of heads of states and governments and delegates from countries around the world – both developing and developed—met in Johannesburg, South Africa, to work out a plan of action to save planet Earth from unsustainable development. The heads of states and governments signed a political declaration making a commitment to the achievement of sustainable development. The conference delegates agreed upon a "Plan of Implementation" introducing actions including poverty reduction, changing unsustainable patterns of consumption and production, protecting and managing the natural resource base, meeting the challenges of globalization, and protecting human health.

REVISITING COMPLEX ISSUES

While the conferences and summits elicited a multitude of promises and pledges, accompanying action and the required financial resources did not seem to be forthcoming. The situation necessitated revisiting the complex issues to begin redressing the problem. The environmental policies and legislation that were initiated in the 1970s after the Stockholm Conference were reviewed: (i) to make them enforceable in practice, and (ii) to address the issues of poverty, trade, financing, and other matters related to the entire environmental picture.

Sustainable Development Policy Defined

One crucial area that is missing in the UN's list of issues is a sustainable development policy.

What is a sustainable development policy and how is it defined? The book *Our Common Future*, based on the Brundtland Report, defined sustainable development as "ensuring that it meets the needs of the present without compromising the ability of future generations to meet their own needs." Sustainable development policy comprises institutional and environmental safeguards that will protect the environment and the economy as a whole, as well as another set of guidelines and principles on economic and social sustainability. Each of these policy components, in turn, will rest on different sets of policies as depicted.

Institutional Safeguards

Many feel that the most important of the four principles of sustainable development is institutional safeguards, because it enables the other three (economic sustainability, social sustainability, and environmental safeguards) to be in place. Institutional safeguards consist of good governance, disclosure of information, anticorruption, and inspection policies. Many of the countries of the world have problems of rampant corruption. According to an International Monetary Fund (IMF) report, as much as 10% of the GDP of a country is wasted by corruption. As a countermeasure, the World Bank and ADB have set up policies on anticorruption and inspection. According to their inspection policies, a project can be stopped, even if it has been approved, if the stakeholders make a complaint about violation of some of the policies of the institution financing it.

Environmental Safeguards

Environmental safeguards integrate environmental dimensions into a development project at the planning stage. An EIA is a mandatory requirement for many major development projects. Monitoring has also become mandatory so that a project's adherence to its stated goals is observed.

Economic and Social Sustainability

Economic sustainability depends on a set of sector policies in various areas, including energy, forestry, water, agriculture, and fisheries. Some of these sector policies are discussed in this chapter. Social sustainability hinges on such policies as gender, involuntary resettlement, indigenous people, cooperation with NGOs, and poverty reduction. These social policies are addressed in Chapter 8.

To make development sustainable, social and economic sustainability policies must go hand-in-hand with the policy on environmental and institutional safeguards.

SECTOR POLICIES CONCERNING THE ENVIRONMENT

As stated earlier, environmental management implies management of development activities within the assimilative capacity of the environment. Consequently, an environmental policy comprises an umbrella policy related to monitoring the overall environment, setting environmental standards, and setting policy and guidelines for EIA. Beyond this, environmental policy essentially comprises a set of sector policies on the environment. For the purpose of illustration, three sector policies for environmental sustainability will be considered: water, energy, and forestry.

Water Policy

Table 6-1 is a summary of the state of the world's water supply. It shows that (i) on a per capita basis, availability of fresh water in this world is lowest in the Middle East and North Africa, followed by South Asia; (ii) the percentage of population having access to an improved water source is lowest (55%) in Sub-Saharan Africa; and (iii) agriculturally, the percentage of fresh water is very high (from 63%-93%), the highest (93%) being in South Asia.

Six unique characteristics of water as a sector must be noted before an effective water policy can be developed. The first is water's unitary nature. Water is a peculiar commodity because it is a liquid compound of oxygen and hydrogen (H_2O) that is absolutely essential to maintain life, ecosystems, and agricultural and industrial activity. Its unitary nature implies that it can be easily substituted from one source to another. Second, water is not distributed equally over the globe. It is highly variable in location, and its location is in natural hydrologic units that do not necessarily follow geographical boundaries. Third, water is a diversified sector in terms of both supply and demand. On the supply side are surface water, groundwater, rainwater, and seawater. On the demand side water is provided for drinking, sanitation, irrigation, drainage, navigation, fisheries, and hydropower generation. The fourth characteristic is related to the second one: water has a highly multidimensional institutional framework. At the national level, even if there is a ministry dealing with water, it is a sector dealt with by several—ministries—fisheries, agriculture, shipping and navigation, health (for the domestic water supply), and energy. Fifth, water is not a simple economic good; sometimes it exhibits the attributes of a public good and sometimes that of a private good. Within a hydrologic unit, fresh water may be limited, but almost any quantity can be traded between users and uses, or it can be imported from another hydrologic basin, at a cost.

And, finally, water has very important cultural, religious, and political dimensions. Most ancient civilizations originated along riverbanks. In Thailand, water is worshipped during the Songkran and Loy Krathong festivals. In India, the Ganges is sacred; bathing in the Ganges, even though it is polluted, is believed to clean people spiritually as well as physically.

Table 6-1. State of the World's Water Supply

REGION	Population in 1999 (million)	Freshwater Resources per Capita (m³)	Improved Water Source (% of total population)	Agricultural Withdrawal (% of freshwater water withdarawal)
World	5,978	8,240	81	70
East Asia and Pacific	1,837	-	75	80
South Asia	1,329	2,854	87	93
Europe and Central Asia	474	12,797	90	63
Latin America and Carribean	508	27,919	85	74
Middle East and North Africa	290	1,145	89	89
Sub-Saharan Africa	643	8,248	55	87

Source: Based on World Bank data (2000)

Based on these characteristics, ADB has developed a water policy for Asia (see http://adb.org/Documents/Policies/Water/default.asp?p=wtrrefs), the core elements of which are as follows:
- Promote effective national water policies and action programs.
- Invest in water resource management in priority river basins.
- Improve water services through autonomous and accountable providers.
- Foster the efficient and sustainable use and conservation of water in society.
- Increase the mutually beneficial use of shared water resources within and between countries.

- Facilitate stakeholder consultation, participation, and partnerships.
- Improve governance through capacity building, monitoring, and evaluation (http://www.adb.org/
  Publications/product.asp?sku=010796).

Although a water policy should address the main issues related to the water sector in a given country or region, these core elements are usually common to all situations.

Energy Policy

Table 6-2 presents a summary of global energy use and its consequent CO_2 emissions. In terms of global energy use and its impact, a few observations can be made: (i) in terms of per capita use of commercial energy, Europe and Central Asia top the list with 2,637 kg of oil equivalent emitting almost 3.3 million kilotons of CO_2 every year. This translates into 6.9 metric tons per capita of CO_2 emission, the highest in the world.

Table 6-2. Global Energy Use and Air Pollution

REGION	Population in 1999 (million)	Commercial Energy Use per Capita (kg oil equivalent)	Percent of Electricity Generated from Coal	Total CO_2 Emissions, Industrial (1,000 kt)	CO_2 Emissions, per Capita (metric tons)
World	5,978	1,659	38.4	23,868.2	4.1
East Asia and Pacific	1,837	857	61.2	5,075.6	2.8
South Asia	1,329	445	64.7	1,200.5	0.9
Europe and Central Asia	474	2,637	30.3	3,285.6	6.9
Latin America and Carribean	508	1,183	4.7	1,356.4	2.8
Middle East and North Africa	290	1,344	1.8	1,113.6	4.0
Sub-Saharan Africa	643	700	71.2	501.8	0.8

Source: Based on World Bank data (2000)

Essentially there are at least nine core environmental elements of a sound energy policy. These are

- Tackle environmental issues before they occur.
- Utilize high-grade (low-sulfur) coal for energy supply.
- Practice coal washing at the mines.
- Undertake large-scale afforestation programs to create carbon sinks as well as to enhance the fuelwood supply.
- Develop nonconventional sources of energy (solar, biomass, wind, etc.).
- Continue development and research on the technologies of nuclear power, nuclear fusion electricity, and fuel cells.
- Practice demand-side management by energy conservation in industrial, commercial, and residential installations.
- Put a fair price on energy and withdraw energy subsidies.
- Secure energy installations.

The mission statement of the World Bank Group's Energy Program (2002) concerning Poverty Reduction, Sustainability and Selectivity "supports" the "objectives of reducing poverty and increasing sustainable economic growth in developing and transition economies." To achieve these objectives, "sustainable and affordable energy services" need to be provided "for all, including the poor, and… these services can best be provided by creating efficient markets in energy—markets that are open to investors and enterprises, both large and small, private and public, centralized and decentralized." The mission statement closes by indicating that "expansion of access to energy services for the poor needs to be based on markets that function on sound commercial principles and on the preservation of the environment."

The key elements of the ADB energy policy are

- poverty reduction (impact of energy services on the poor, approach to rural energy, approach to subsidy).
- private sector participation and sector restructuring (public sector monopoly, hydrocarbon subsector restructuring, power subsector restructuring, energy pricing, good governance).
- regional and global environmental impact (acid rain, greenhouse gas abatement, renewable energy use).
- regional cooperation (regional energy trade, export-oriented power projects).
- impact of financial crisis (impact on energy demand and investment, role of build-operate-transfer projects).

Forestry Policy

The world's forested areas are in a state of flux (Table 6-3). Global tree cover is deteriorating rapidly and needs attention. The world has 38.6 million square kilometers of forest comprising 29.7% of the total land mass. Most of the forests are found in two regions: Europe and Central Asia, and Latin

America and the Caribbean. Currently, the annual rate of deforestation in Europe and Central Asia as well as in the Middle East and North Africa is −0.1%, and in Latin America and the Caribbean, 0.5%. In 2000, both regions had roughly an equal amount of forested land, which was approximately 9.4 million square kilometers each. However, at the prevailing rate of deforestation, Latin America and the Caribbean will soon be trailing far behind Europe and Central Asia.

Once again, as could be expected, the most precarious condition is found in the Middle East and North Africa, which account for only 168,000 square kilometers of forest area out of the world total of 38,609,000 square kilometers. South Asia has the lowest percentage (16.3%) of forest area as a percentage of the total land area.

Table 6-3. State of World's Forests

REGION	Population in 1999 (million)	Forest Area (1,000 km²)	Forest Area per Capita (km²)	Forest Area as % of Total Land	Annual Rate of Deforestation (%)
World	5,978	38,609	0.006	29.7	0.2
East Asia and Pacific	1,837	4,341	0.002	27.2	0.2
South Asia	1,329	782	0.0006	16.3	0.1
Europe and Central Asia	474	9,464	0.02	39.7	-0.1
Latin America and Carribean	508	9,440	0.02	47.1	0.5
Middle East and North Africa	290	168	0.0006	47.1	-0.1
Sub-Saharan Africa	643	6,436	0.01	27.3	0.8

Source: Based on World Bank data (2000)

Some of the many causes of forest destruction and degradation follow.

1. Destructive logging

The first and most obvious issue in any discussion of deforestation is excessive and destructive logging. Some estimate that 4.4 million hectares of forest is logged annually just to satisfy the timber needs of Europe, North America, and Japan. Japan has a forest cover of 67%, possibly the highest of any country in the world. Yet Japan is importing timber and other forest products from Southeast Asia and the Pacific in order to keep its forests intact. While this is a good national forestry policy for Japan, it has negative consequences on the state of forests in Asia and the Pacific region.

2. Crop and livestock expansion

The second reason for the disappearance of the forests is crop and livestock expansion. The World Bank estimates that expansion of crops and livestock is destroying 70% of the forests in Africa, 50% in Asia, and 35% in Latin America. Africa still has much of its forest intact, mainly because of its small population in a very large land area. In many countries of the world, large aquaculture farms (especially shrimp farms) and the charcoal industry are depleting the mangrove forests. This is a dangerous move, since mangroves are a first line of defense against typhoons. In Bangladesh, for instance, since the coastlines have been cleared of mangrove forests, deaths related to storms along the coast have dramatically increased. In November 1970, an estimated 300,000 people living along the coast died during one major storm (http://www.disastercenter.com/disaster/TOP100K.html).

Roads through forestlands are another danger. Once a road is built through a forest, it opens the forest to other activities. When mid-sized hydroelectric power plants were built in the PRC and Indonesia, all the construction materials were brought in by helicopter. Had roads been built through the forests to reach the sites, they would have become a permanent invitation to loggers and poachers.

Increased migration by rural populations into forested lands is another issue that should be examined. People clearing the forests for cultivation, fuel wood, and fodder is understandable, but not necessarily benign.

Governments are also culpable for deforestation. Tenure for large logging companies, low taxes, tax relief, plus pricing policies favorable to removal of the forest are encouraging institutional logging. Environmentalists say that government-based conversion of forests to other forms of land use is one of the leading causes of deforestation.

3. Lack of ownership

Another issue is ownership. Who owns the forests? Why are forest communities reluctant to invest their time and money in forest management? One would think that, since the forest is the main source of their income and livelihood, protecting it would not only make sense, but would be their only choice. Yet they do not, because these communities do not have any sense of ownership, since the forests belong to the government and are not common property resources.

4. Forest fires

Forest fires, both caused and naturally occurring, such as destructive wildfires, are major environmental issues in the US. In an Indonesian forest, a carelessly started fire created a smoke haze throughout Southeast Asia in 1998. Experts believe that the unprecedented floods in the PRC and Bangladesh in 1998 were caused by the destruction of upstream forests due to one reason or another, including forest fires.

Some of the environmental issues that must be considered in formulating forestry policy are as follows:

1. Forest zoning regulation

One core issue is the need for forest zoning regulations that differentiate between production forests and protection forests. The principle is similar to urban zoning. A protected forest cannot be harnessed for human use; a production forest is where timber can be felled on a sustainable basis.

2. Impact of intersector development

The second issue recognizes the impact of intersector development on the forestry sector. There are competing demands for crop production, particularly cash crops; for human settlements; for expansion of industries; and for commercial areas.

3. Access to timber resources

The third core issue is restricting access to timber resources. This policy element will hopefully require the people who hold forest leases to bear the full cost of timber production, including the cost of timber, forestry management and maintenance, and environmental conservation. However, in practice the full cost has never been realized from the lessees of the forest. Hopefully, this policy element will encourage the growth of high-yielding marketable trees in selected degraded lands. The Lao People's Democratic Republic (Lao PDR) has an area that is a degraded slope. The government is using this land to build an industrial plantation that will grow wood for commercial use and for fuel. This should take the pressure off the country's primary forests.

4. Public consultation

The fourth core issue is the need for public consultation on forestry development with the affected people, local communities, and NGOs prior to financing any forestry projects. Consultations should be designed to explain the purpose of the development and to make the participants feel that they are part of the decision-making process. Shared ownership allows the people a stake in a project that the government is undertaking.

5. Active role of forestry agencies

Reorienting forestry agencies to play an active role in the planning and management of forests is another issue regarding forestry policy. Too often botanists manage forests purely from the viewpoint of their discipline; they think that the only issue is the number, variety, and growth rate of the plants that make up the forest. What they fail to consider is the interaction between the forest and the forest dwellers, whether they be human or wildlife. These forest managers also fail to distinguish among different types of forests. For example, a mangrove forest has a primary productivity many times more than that of an upland forest. Yet in many countries, the same group of people, using the same guidelines as for upland forests, manages mangrove forests.

The answer is to form an interdisciplinary panel comprised of people who know about not only the forest but also the forest dwellers and the interaction between the forest and the ecosystem. These are the people who should be put in charge of forest planning and management.

Figure 6-1. Institutional Framework for Environmental Management

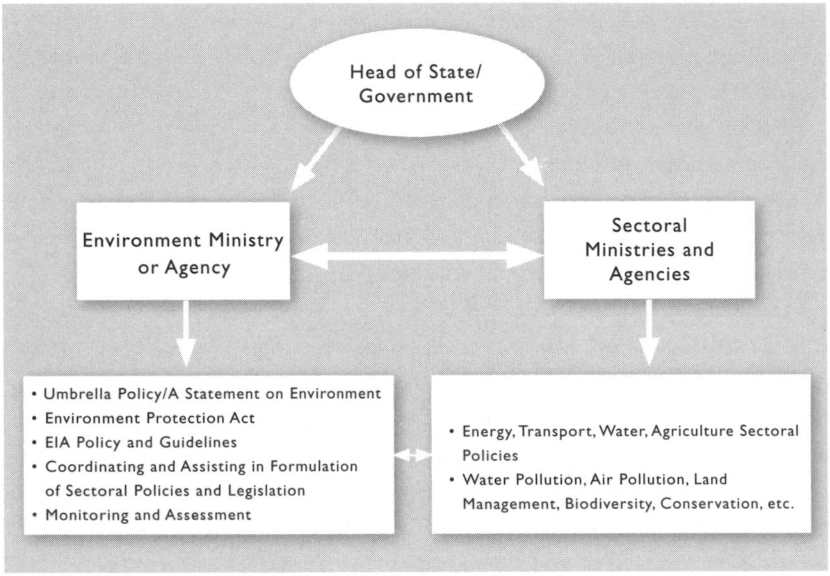

Head of State/
Government

Environment Ministry
or Agency

Sectoral
Ministries and
Agencies

- Umbrella Policy/A Statement on Environment
- Environment Protection Act
- EIA Policy and Guidelines
- Coordinating and Assisting in Formulation
  of Sectoral Policies and Legislation
- Monitoring and Assessment

- Energy, Transport, Water, Agriculture Sectoral
  Policies
- Water Pollution, Air Pollution, Land
  Management, Biodiversity, Conservation, etc.

Figure 6-2. World GDP Growth

World GDP, 1995$

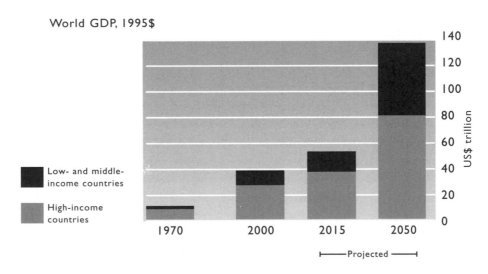

Low- and middle-
income countries

High-income
countries

US$ trillion

1970   2000   2015   2050

├── Projected ──┤

Source: *The Economist* (July 6-12, 2002), p.4, quoting World Bank

ENVIRONMENTAL IMPACT ASSESSMENT (EIA)

Whether an impending project will involve forestland, water, or air, to find out what its impact will be one must do an EIA. In most countries this assessment is required by law. The formulation of law and policy related to EIA is the overall responsibility of the environment ministry or agency and constitutes a part of the umbrella environment policy.

Project Classification

The multilateral development banks (World Bank, ADB, African Development Bank, and IADB) classify projects into three categories:

- Category A: projects with significant environmental impacts as predicted by an Initial Environmental Examination (IEE);
- Category B: projects with adverse environmental impacts, but of less significance than those in Category A; and
- Category C: projects unlikely to have adverse environmental impacts.

(See Chapter 5 for details.)

Preparing the EIA

A typical summary EIA report can run from about 13 to 20 pages. It begins with an introduction to the project (1/2 page) and contains topics like anticipated impacts and mitigation (4-6 pages), alternatives (2-4 pages), cost-benefit analysis (2-4 pages), and a conclusion (1 page).

Figure 5-3 in Chapter 5 illustrates where the EIA fits into the overall project cycle. The project starts from developing a concept and undertaking a prefeasibility study. Then a full feasibility study is carried out, and design and engineering studies are undertaken. Finally, the project is implemented. Monitoring and evaluation of the project follow. The results of the evaluation become data that are fed back into a new project cycle.

During this project cycle, the activities are matched up against the EIA. At the concept stage, during site selection, an environmental screening is done to make an initial assessment. It is necessary to draw up a qualitative list of significant issues that might be involved in the project. Based on the list, one can make some preliminary assessments. Following the prefeasibility study, a detailed assessment of significant impacts is made, and identification of mitigation measures is done. For a Category A project, this entails significant documentation. In the detailed design of mitigation measures, it is not enough to identify the environmental issues and problems. It is also necessary to identify the steps that will be taken toward solving these problems. After implementing design and engineering data, the implementation of mitigation measures and environmental management strategies must be fed into the project cycle. These must be specific as to what kind of environmental management strategies should be built into the project. Finally, there will be monitoring and post-auditing lessons for future projects. For further discussion on EIA, please refer to Chapter 5.

Figure 6-3. World Exports

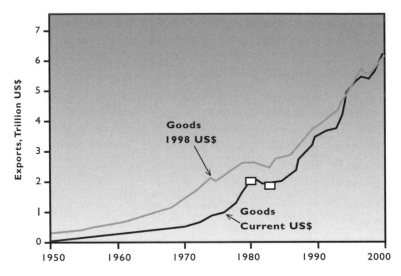

Source: Bjørn Lomborg (2001), p.8

Figure 6-4. Access to Water in the Third World

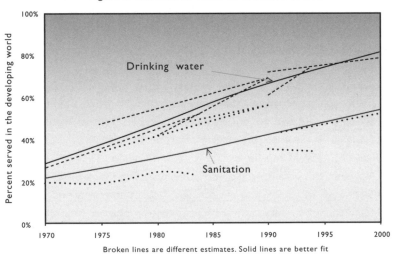

Source: Bjørn Lomborg (2001), p.22

Figure 6-5. Infectious Disease Death Rates

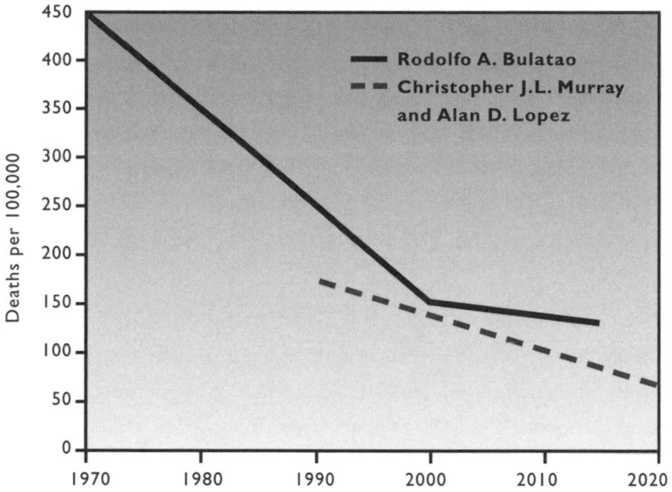

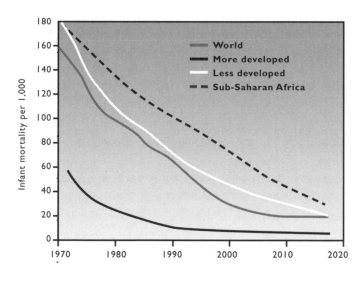

Source: Bjørn Lomborg (2001), p.26

Figure 6-6. Infant Mortality

Infant mortality per 1,000 live births. Prediction from 2000.

Source: Bjørn Lomborg (2001), p.55

INSTITUTIONAL FRAMEWORK FOR ENVIRONMENTAL MANAGEMENT

Figure 6-1 suggests the institutional framework in which an environment ministry or agency works within a government. It is not always easy for one such environmental ministry to influence the actions of many other ministries and agencies. Even if legislation and/or regulations are in place, the integrity of the prosecutorial and judicial systems may be tested in the implementation of environment policies.

ACHIEVEMENTS IN ENVIRONMENTAL MANAGEMENT

There has been a lot of activity between the 1970s and the present regarding the economic development and rehabilitation of the environment. Between 1970 and 2000, world GDP grew from $10 trillion to $40 trillion. By 2050, according to World Bank projections, it is going to reach $138 trillion (Figure 6-2). Similarly, world exports grew from $0.5 trillion in 1970 to $6 trillion in 2000, a growth factor of 12 (Figure 6-3). Access to safe water in the developing world also increased, though not as significantly (Figure 6-4).

In 1970, 30% of the population in the developing world had access to safe water; in 2000, the figure was 80%. Unfortunately, the numbers for sanitation did not keep up, even though sanitation coverage doubled in the target years, from 22% to 44%. Although more than half of the developing world population still does not have access to such facilities, death rates from infectious diseases have gone down significantly, from 450 per 100,000 to only 150 per 100,000 (Figure 6-5). Likewise, infant mortality decreased from 160 per 1,000 to 25 per 1,000 (Figure 6-6). Life expectancy at birth now stands at 60-70 years, and gross enrollment in secondary schools increased from 20% to 60% (Figure 6-7). These numbers indicate that, on the whole, human civilization has done very well in terms of economic growth, exports, health, water supply, and sanitation coverage. However, the world needs to do much more, particularly in the areas of environmental pollution, natural resources degradation, and social equity.

PEOPLE'S PERCEPTION OF THE ENVIRONMENT

It is important to find out how people perceive their environment. In 1992, a worldwide poll called Health of the Planet was taken in 12 developed and 12 developing nations. The respondents were asked to rate the environment in their local community, their nation, and the world. The results, except for one or two surprises, were what one would expect (Figure 6-8). In the developed countries, most of the respondents felt that their local and national environments were not too bad, but the global environment was in trouble. The big surprise was Japan, where more than 50% of the people felt that the national environment was bad. That was the same number posted by the Philippines.

Figure 6-7. Better Lives—Past 30 Years

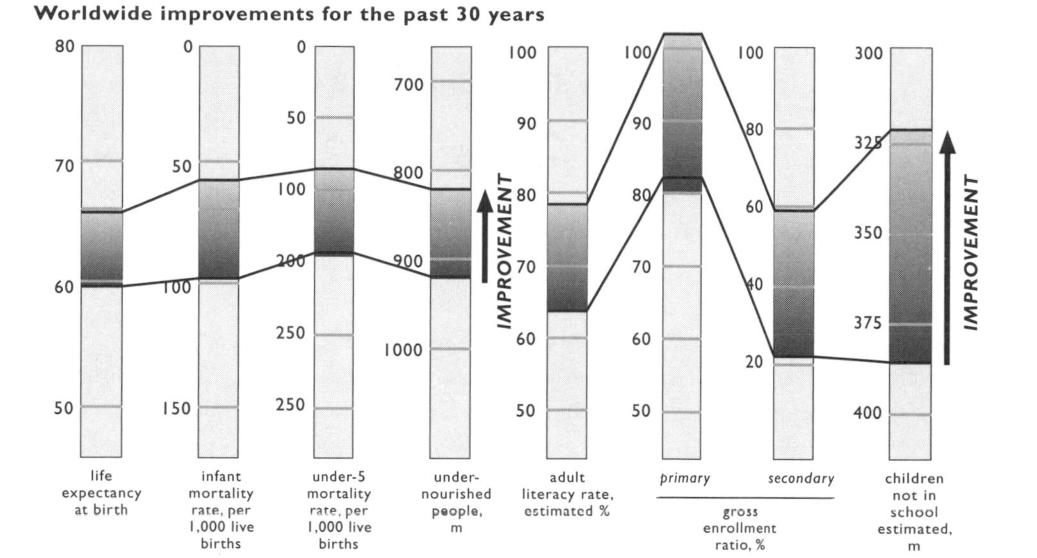

Worldwide improvements for the past 30 years

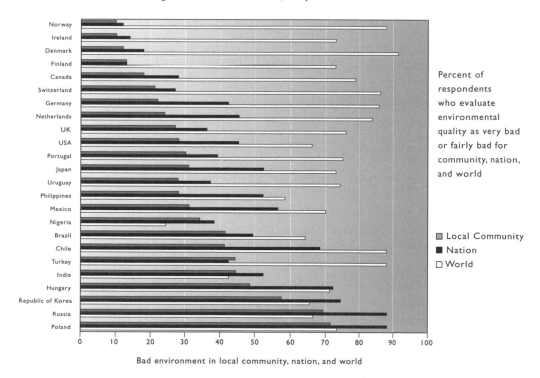

Source: UNEP (2002), p. 33

Figure 6-8. Environment Quality: Public Evaluation

Percent of respondents who evaluate environmental quality as very bad or fairly bad for community, nation, and world

Bad environment in local community, nation, and world

Source: Bjørn Lomborg (2001), p.35

175

On the other hand, all the developing nations felt that their local and national environments were bad. In the case of India, Republic of Korea, and Russia, the people felt their national environment was worse than the global environment.

WHY IS THE ENVIRONMENT BAD?

The question is, despite all the progress and achievements in economic growth, human health, and so on, why is it that the environment is perceived to be so bad globally, and in developing countries nationally and locally as well? There are two possible explanations.

Ecological Threshold

The first explanation relies on a modified version of Kuznets' Curve.

The traditional Kuznets Curve suggests that, as income per capita grows, environmental degradation initially increases up to a certain point, beyond which the environmental situation improves. There is, however, a concept called "ecological threshold," which says that if the environmental situation deteriorates beyond a threshold, the process becomes irreversible. At that point, the environmental conditions cannot be reversed, or improved (see Figure 1-1).

In a situation where subsidies for energy or water are removed, property rights are well defined, and externalities are internalized, coupled with better environment policies, the Kuznets Curve will lie below the ecological threshold. Professor Theodore Panayotou, then of HIID, discovered that if the annual income level in the developing countries is between $5,000 and $7,000 per capita, the air pollution level in urban areas is likely to start improving.

So in theory, higher income per capita is expected to bring an improvement in the environmental situation. However, some environmental experts disagree.

Unique Characteristics of Environment Problems

The second explanation as to why the environment is getting worse has to do with certain unique characteristics found in environmental problems (see World Bank, 2001):

- **Delayed Impacts.** Many potential environmental changes have significantly delayed impacts. Delayed environmental impacts argue for a long lead time in implementing appropriate prevention or mitigating measures. An example would be the release of toxic substances into the environment. After ingestion or inhalation, it takes time before health problems begin to appear. Therefore, corrective measures must be taken before the toxic substances are released.

- **Spatial Impacts.** Sources and environmental impacts are often separated in space (for example upstream/downstream or hills/valleys), making it necessary to have a framework that can address diverse stakeholders' interests. An example would be an irrigation system built in a developing country without leveling the land. The result is that some stakeholders' farms are flooded while others are left arid because they are located above the project site. Unless there is a framework that includes consultation with various stakeholders about their interests, spatial impacts are bound to adversely affect the environmental situation.

- **Cumulative Impacts.** Individual actions often have little effect on the environment, but the cumulative effect of many such actions can be substantial. Bangkok, for example, has 70,000 small-scale industries and factories, which, taken individually, have little impact on the environment. But taken on the whole, the cumulative effect is tremendous. In fact, their cumulative negative impact is greater than that of the big industries like distilleries and breweries located in the same city.

- **Irreversible Damage.** A significant number of environmental outcomes are fundamentally irreversible, and the implications of such changes are hard to predict. There are rivers and lakes in Asia, like the Bagmati River in Katmandu, which are polluted beyond recognition and therefore dead or the damages irreversible.

- **Need for Government Intervention.** Environmental problems are often a consequence of market failures. Without government intervention to introduce regulations and create markets where they do not exist, the private sector alone cannot achieve optimal environmental outcomes. The private sector has a role to play, but the government must also be there to see to it that regulations are in place and that they are enforced.

- **Multisector Links.** Environmental problems surface across a range of sectors through many pathways, calling for coordinated policies and concerted efforts by various ministries and agencies.

- **Regional and Global Implications.** Many environmental impacts have broad cross-boundary and global effects that require international frameworks and agreements to deal with them.

Millennium Development Goals

To chart the progress and results of the MDGs (see Box 6-1), the developing world was divided into seven regions: East Asia and the Pacific, Europe and Central Asia, Latin America and the Caribbean, the Middle East and North Africa, South Asia, Sub-Saharan Africa, and Developing Countries. These are designations of regions as given by the World Bank. The Secretary-General of the UN reported on the progress of implementation of the Millennium Declaration to the UN General Assembly (Secretary-General of UN, (Doc.A/58/323, 2000)). A similar report is also available online (http://www.un.org/millenniumgoals/).

Figure 6-9. Development Goals for Poverty

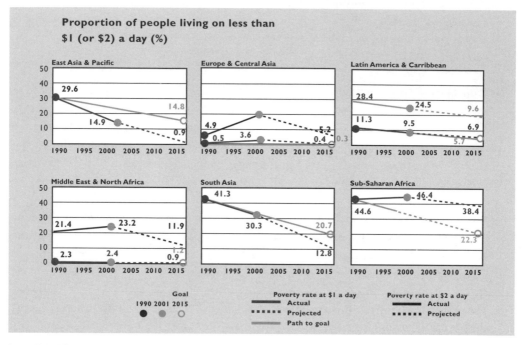

Source: World Bank data (2004)

According to the UN Secretary General's report, "A sustained and broad-based annual per capita income increase of 3 percent is the minimum needed to lift people out of poverty at a rate sufficient to meet the goal of reducing by half, by 2015, the proportion of people living on less than a dollar a day." Since almost two thirds (approximately 800 million) of the world's poor earning less than $1 a day live in Asia, the chances of reducing abject poverty worldwide by half will be determined mostly by the GDP growth rate per capita in the PRC and India. With both these countries making good progress and keeping on track, the world has a fair chance of meeting the global goal of poverty reduction by 2015. However, regional and national variations will continue to exist. Sub-Saharan Africa presents the gloomiest picture, even though some countries in that region (e.g., Cape Verde, Mauritius, Mozambique, and Uganda) have achieved sustained growth above the 3% benchmark in the recent past.

A 2005 report by the Secretary-General of the UN, entitled "The Millennium Development Goals Report 2005," claims that the MDGs are people-centered, time-bound, and measurable. They are based on global partnership and have unprecedented political support. Therefore, the Secretary-General concludes, "they (MDGs) are achievable." In forwarding this report, the Secretary-General stated: "We will not enjoy development without security, we will not enjoy security without development, and we will not enjoy either without respect for human rights. Unless all these causes are advanced, none will succeed."

Figure 6-10. Development Goals for Water

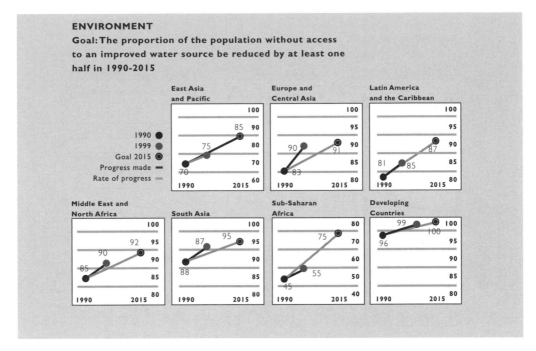

Source: Based on World Bank data: Global Economic Prospects (http://www.developmentgoals.org)

Goals to Eradicate Extreme Poverty and Hunger

The goals to eradicate extreme poverty and hunger in developing countries are to reduce the problem by at least half between 1990 and 2015 (Figure 6-9).

In 1990, the percentage of the population in the East Asia and Pacific region, which includes the PRC, earning less than $1 per day was 29.6%. In 2001, the figure dropped to 14.9%. The goal for 2015 is 14.8%, or half the 1990 figure. In this case, given the prevailing trends, it looks like the goal will be achieved. On the other hand, in Eastern Europe and Central Asia, the incidence of poverty actually increased from 0.5% of the population in 1990 to 3.6% in 2001. This, of course, is a special case, because the time span included the collapse of the Soviet Union. With most of its factories closed, the environmental situation in the former Soviet Union improved, because there was much less polluted air, but the GDP growth rate went down and poverty went up. South Asia saw an 11% decrease in the poverty, but Sub-Saharan Africa registered a slight increase in poverty from 1990 to 2001.

What the figures indicate is that developing countries are generally not doing too badly, with Sub-Saharan Africa falling behind and the Middle East and North Africa missing the goal by a small margin. An optimistic view is that the world as a whole and even the regions should be able to achieve the goal of reduction of abject poverty by 2015, which cannot be said regarding any other of the MDGs. Asia is leading all other developing regions in achieving the goal of poverty reduction.

Figure 6-11. Development Goals for Gender Equality

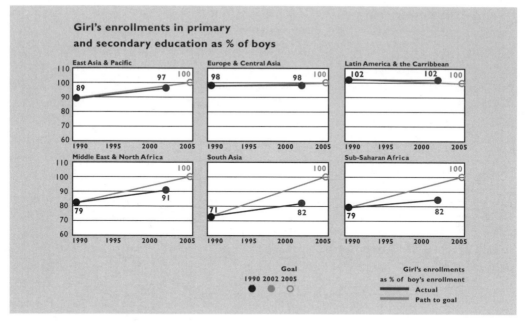

Source: Based on World Bank data (2004)

By contrast, the number of people below the poverty line in Sub-Saharan Africa increased between 1990 and 2001.

Goals for the Environment

One aspect of the development goals for the environment focuses on the proportion of the population without access to an improved water source and to sanitation. The target is to reduce that number by half by 2015 (Figure 6-10). The other targets are (i) integrating principles of sustainable development into country policies, (ii) halting by 2015 the proportion of people without sustainable access to safe drinking water and basic sanitation, and (iii) achieving significant improvement in the lives of at least 100 million slum dwellers by 2020. With regard to target (i), critics say that it is vague compared to the others.

In some countries the target for water and sanitation will be achieved; in others it will not. Take East Asia and the Pacific. If the proportion of the population with access to an improved water source, now estimated at about 75%, is below 85% in 2015, the goal may not be achieved. By contrast, the goal of 91% in Europe and Central Asia will likely be achieved; as of 1999, 90% of the regions' populations already had access to safe water. In the high-income countries the percentage of population with access to good water was 100%, and it is projected to stay at that level.

Goal in Gender Equality

The gender goal calls for the empowerment of women, to be demonstrated by eliminating gender disparity in primary and secondary education by 2005, not 2015 (Figure 6-11).

Figure 6-11 reveals that the target is unlikely to be achieved except in high-income countries and, apparently, in the Middle East and North Africa.

The disparity is calculated by the ratio of girls to boys in primary and secondary schools, as a target. For example, in East Asia and the Pacific, the ratio of girls to boys in primary and secondary schools was 89% in 1990. In other words, for every 100 boys in the primary and secondary school system, there were 89 girls. By 2002, the percentage had climbed to 97%. While five of the seven regions showed some improvement, two did not. In Sub-Saharan Africa the numbers are almost flat – about 79% in 1990 and about 82% in 2002. In Latin America and the Caribbean, the figure remained strong at 102% from 1990 to 2002 The MDG report (2005) in the quoted website reflects progress against each of the eight MDGs.

Goals for Infant and Child Mortality

The goal for infant and child mortality is to reduce death rates for infants and children under the age of five years by 2015 by two thirds of the 1990 level.

Unlike universal primary education, the numbers in this category seem to indicate that most countries, except those in Sub-Saharan Africa, are on the mark. Hopefully, the Middle East and North Africa will catch-up (decrease child mortality at higher rates than in the past decade) in 2005-2015.

Goals for Maternal Health

The maternal health goal is calculated by births attended to by skilled health personnel.

Again, all the regions showed improvement except Sub-Saharan Africa. It is of concern that in 1990, only 50% of the births in that region were attended to by skilled personnel, but in 1998 the percentage had dropped to 46%. According to this trend, Sub-Saharan Africa cannot possibly reach the maternal health goal, which means it is also not going to reach the goal set for infant mortality. Obviously, children born without attending medical care will have a higher mortality rate. The situation in Asia (excluding the PRC and India) is also quite alarming; with the present rate of progress, by 2015 less than 40% of childbirths are likely to be attended to by skilled health personnel. According to the report of the UN Secretary-General submitted to the UN General Assembly (2003), women in Sub-Saharan Africa and Asia are likely to die during childbirth 175 and 20-60 times more, respectively, than women in a developed country. It appears that no region, including the so-called high-income countries, will be able to achieve this target by 2015. Obviously, it is not only economic reasons, but also religious, cultural, and physiological ones that stand in the way of achieving this goal. The UN therefore should consider revisiting and revising the goal.

Goals for Reproductive Health

The goal for reproductive health care is to make contraception available to all married women by 2015.

CONCLUSION

During the past 40 years, the concept of environmental management moved from pollution and no action to global environmental protection and sustainable development by means of a proactive global strategy based on economic, ecological, and social considerations. The Millennium Development Goals (MDGs) are seen as quantitative indicators of environmental management and sustainable development at the global, regional, and national levels. As time is running out on meeting the MDGs, developing countries should continue to improve their performance and developed countries should fulfill their commitments to increase financial contributions and adjust trade barriers and subsidies so as not to isolate a majority of the global population from the great economic opportunities of the twenty-first century. It would also be necessary to strengthen the involvement of the private sector and the civil society in playing increasingly important roles in environmental management and sustainable development.

CHAPTER 7
LEGISLATION, INTERNATIONAL LAW, AND MULTILATERAL ENVIRONMENTAL AGREEMENTS

To achieve sustainable development and protect the environment, the communities, countries, regions, and continents of the world need reformed policies and laws as well as increased capacity of both new and existing institutions. Legislation and international law will play an important role in making these changes and developing these capacities. Multilateral Environmental Agreements (MEAs), a form of international legislation, will play a significant role in this process and in the achievement of sustainable development. National judiciaries as well as international courts of justice and arbitrational tribunals will be required to implement, under the rule of law, applicable international and national environmental laws as well as the concept of sustainable development, which will include efforts to combat poverty.

To consider these reforms and developments, we first need to examine some of the basic concepts of international law as well as obstacles to the implementation of some of the key MEAs. We need to make such an examination because we want to find out how polluting states can be made to obey rules established outside their borders, and how polluting states unable to clean up their activities due to local politics can be compelled to do so by international law. We also need to explore how activists can use local and international courts to advance international environmental law standards, and we must examine, briefly, the evolution, from the legal point of view, of the concept of sustainable development, plus recent legislative developments to implement this concept.

To begin our review of some of the basic concepts arising in the context of international law and legislation, let us consider the following four questions:

- Did the Declaration of the United Nations Conference on the Human Environment in 1972, also known as the Stockholm Declaration, which helped establish UNEP as a key initiator of international environmental action, "create" or "develop" international environmental law?
- When the UN General Assembly passed two resolutions in 1974, entitled "Declaration on the Establishment of a New International Economic Order" and "Charter of Economic Rights and Duties of States," did it "create" or "develop" international environmental law?
- Did the UNCED in Rio de Janeiro in 1992 "create" or "develop" international environmental law when it adopted Agenda 21 and the Rio Declaration on Environment and Development?
- Is "sustainable development" a general principle of international law?

Definitions

To answer these questions we will first consider the definitions of law, international law, and environment.

1. Law

The *Oxford English Reference Dictionary* (1996, p. 810) defines law as "a rule enacted or customary in a community, and recognized as enjoining or prohibiting certain actions, and enforced by the imposition of penalties." Note that this definition includes those rules that are "customary in a community" as well as those that are enacted. In *Gorky Incident*, Mark

Twain suggested (*Bartlett's*, 2002, p. 562) which of these two is more important: "Laws are sand, customs are rock. Laws can be evaded and punishment escaped, but an openly transgressed custom brings sure punishment."

2. International law

The US uses the following definition of international law as a "standard of conduct" pertaining to both "states" and "other entities":

> *International law is the standard of conduct, at a given time, for states and other entities subject thereto. It comprises the rights, privileges, powers, and immunities of states and entities invoking its provisions, as well as the correlative fundamental duties, absence of rights, liabilities, and disabilities* (Whiteman, 1963, Vol. I, p. 1).

3. Environment

Professors of law Alexandre Kiss and Dinah Shelton point out (2000, p. 2) that the European Convention on Civil Liability for Damage Resulting from Activities Dangerous to the Environment describes the "environment" as including the following:

- natural resources both abiotic and biotic, such as air, water, soil, fauna, and flora, and the interaction between the same factors;
- property, which forms part of the cultural heritage; and
- the characteristic aspects of the landscape. [footnote omitted]

Furthermore, as Kiss and Shelton note, the International Court of Justice (ICJ), in its opinion on the Legality of the Threat or Use of Nuclear Weapons (1966, pp. 241-242, para. 29) includes a social dimension in the definition of the environment, stating that "the environment is not an abstraction, but represents the living space, the quality of life, and the very health of human beings, including generations unborn." See Box 7.1.

Box 7-1. Environmentalism

Environmentalism: active engagement in protecting the environment. Two kinds of approach underlie it.

Anthropocentrism: the natural world and non-human life do not have intrinsic value independent of us and are there for human beings to use sustainably. Biocentrism: the natural world or the environment is not simply there for humans to use; non-human life has an intrinsic value independent of human interests, and therefore humans ought to respect nature.

Source: Nigel Dower, *An Introduction to Global Citizenship*, Edinburgh University Press, 2003, pp. xi and xii

SOURCES OF INTERNATIONAL LAW

Article 38(1) of the international agreement establishing the ICJ (Statute of the International Court of Justice), which forms the apex of the judicial branch of the UN, describes the following four sources of international law:

- international conventions, general or particular, establishing rules expressly recognized by the contesting States;
- international custom, as evidence of a general practice accepted as law;
- the general principles of law recognized by civilized nations; and
- subject to the provisions of Article 59, judicial decisions and the teachings of the most highly qualified publicists of the various nations, as subsidiary means for the determination of rules of law.

According to Kiss and Shelton (2000, p. 2), "Article 38 represents the authoritative listing of processes deemed capable of creating rules binding on states." To understand the first of these sources of international law, we have to go back to basic definitions.

International Conventions or Treaties

Black's Law Dictionary (1999) states, "A convention is an agreement or compact among nations. . . ." Thus, an international convention includes agreements that are often called treaties. The Vienna Convention on the Law of Treaties (1969) reads in part in Section 1(a) of Article 1:

> For the purposes of the present Convention: (a) "treaty" means an international agreement concluded between States in written form and governed by international law, whether embodied in a single instrument or in two or more related instruments and whatever its particular designation. ...

Since a treaty may exist "whatever its particular designation," and since such agreements have been negotiated for thousands of years, treaties have been designated with a wide variety of titles, including agreement, compact, protocol, and the like. One of the earliest treaties, written on a clay tablet, was between King Silis of the Hittites and Ramses II of Egypt. That was in 1269 B.C., more than 3,200 years ago, or about the same time as Moses was receiving yet another set of clay tablets.

International Custom

Professor of law Anthony D'Amato, in an article quoted by law professors David Hunter, James Salzman, and Durwood Zaelke (2002, pp. 310-311), states that "customary rules represent regularities of behavior" while noting three qualifications:

> First, the approach is empirical rather than normative. It attempts to describe the existing norms that govern the relations among states, but does not advocate or prescribe new norms. . .

> *Second, customary rules are not equivalent to simple behavioral regularities. ... Customary norms depend not only on state practice (that is, on observable regularities of behavior), but also on acceptance of these regularities as law by states. ...*
>
> *Finally, customary rules represent regularities, but not necessarily uniformities, of behavior. The behavioral approach requires a general congruence between rules and behavior. If a purported rule says one thing and states generally do something else, one can no longer say that the rule "governs" behavior. Nevertheless, mistakes and violations of rules are possible.*

General Principles

Hunter, Salzman, and Zaelke (2002, pp. 315-316), while pointing out that "what is included within [general] principles is a matter of debate," quote professor of law Ian Brownlie, who states that

> *"General principles" may refer to "rules accepted in the domestic law of all civilized States," or alternatively, to the general principles of private law used within all or most States. ... insofar as those principles are applicable to relations of States. General principles, then, fill in the gaps in international law that have not already been filled by treaty or custom.*

Significantly, general principles include principles that have emerged from municipal legal systems, and are therefore tried and tested in domestic law before they have been imported into international law.

Judicial Decisions and the Teachings of the Most Qualified

Law professor Antonio A. Oposa Jr., perhaps best known for the landmark case providing judicial recognition of the principle of intergenerational equity (Box 7-2), gives the following description (2003, p. 445) of the role of judicial decisions and scholarly writings in the articulation of international law:

> *International Law may also be expressed through the judicial decisions of international courts and tribunals, and of national courts. It must be noted that a judicial decision is not, by and of itself, the International Law. Rather, the judicial decision is said to be only an expression or an articulation of the principle of International Law which is applied to a particular controversy or case at hand. In other words, it is not International Law itself but only evidence of the existence of the legal principle involved.*
>
> *So also with the writings and learned explanations of the "most highly qualified" scholars. The writings of these scholars, who through years of labor, research, and experience, have become intimately acquainted with the principles and practice of international law, are in a position to explain what it is.* [footnote omitted]

Box 7-2. Oposa v Factoran and Intergenerational Equity

Law professors Donna Craig, Nicholas N. Robinson, and Koh Kheng-Lian (2003, Vol. I, pp. 720, 728) summarize this landmark case handed down by Hilario Davide, Jr., then Justice and later Chief Justice of the Philippine Supreme Court, in part as follows:

The Petitioners, minors represented by their parents, and the Philippine Ecological Network, Inc., sought to have the defendant, the Secretary of the Department of Environment and Natural Resources, ordered to rescind all existing Timber License Agreements (TLAs) and to desist from receiving, renewing or approving new agreements. The judgments...decided only upon the validity of the cause of action, not the merits of the case. It was argued [by Professor Oposa in behalf of his children as the petitioners] that the granting of the TLAs constituted a breach of numerous positive laws, the Constitution and natural laws. The cause of action rested upon the argument that these elements combined in Filipino law to create a right to the environment that had been breached. The defendant argued that the complaint raised no cause of action and was a political question.

The case is a landmark for judicial recognition of the principle of intergenerational equity. This principle was accepted in so far as the petitioners were permitted to represent unborn generations in their pursuit of the right to a healthy environment. ... [T]he matter was held to be a valid class suit with the plaintiffs representing all present and future citizens of the Philippines. Davide Jr., J.[Justice] held unequivocally that Sec. 15 and 16 of the Constitution combined to constitute "a fundamental legal right—the right to a balanced and healthful ecology."

[He proceeded to find that these rights are "assumed to exist from the inception of mankind." It was held that, without the forests which were threatened by the TLAs, a balanced and healthful ecology would...not be achievable. Therefore, the decision to grant the TLAs infringed upon the rights of the people. ...]

A key sentence in the Davide, Jr., opinion, quoted by Hunter, Salzman, and Zaelke (2002, p. 401), states in part that "the minors' assertion of their right to a sound environment constitutes, at the same time, the performance of their obligation to ensure the protection of that right for the generations to come."

THE FOUR QUESTIONS IN THE CONTEXT OF INTERNATIONAL LAW

Armed with these definitions, we can go back to our original questions about how international law would interpret the Stockholm Declaration of 1972, the vote on General Assembly resolutions dealing with new international economic declarations and charters, and the adoption of Agenda 21 and the Rio Declaration at the WSSD in 1992. First, would any of these satisfy the definition of a convention or treaty, the first source of international law? No, they would not. When states acted on these three instruments through their representatives, they did so without the requisite intent to be bound to an international convention or treaty.

However, this is not to suggest that these instruments are unimportant. Documents such as the Rio Declaration are often referred to as "soft law," which *Black's Law Dictionary* (1999, p. 1397) defines in part as "[g]uidelines, policy declarations, or codes of conduct that set standards of conduct but are not directly enforceable."

Stockholm Declaration

Would all or portions of the Stockholm Declaration qualify as "international custom, as evidence of a general practice accepted as law," which is the second source in Article 38(1) of the ICJ charter? Kiss and Shelton indicate (2000, p. 42) that two norms formulated in the Stockholm Declaration—Principle 21 dealing with environmental damage across international borders, and Principle 24 concerning the duty to cooperate—do qualify as the articulation of international custom. Thus, though the entire Declaration itself may not give rise to legal obligations, specific provisions, such as those found in Principles 21 and 24, may constitute an "articulation of custom." In other words, a "mere" declaration may either restate custom or contribute to custom by being referred to in state judicial opinions or influencing state practice, but the true "source" of the obligation is still custom.

Kiss and Shelton (2000, p. 42) also point out that the customary rule of international environmental law that "no state may cause or allow its territory to be used to cause damage to the environment of other states…first arose in international jurisprudence and was formulated in Principle 21 of the Stockholm Declaration before being adopted and reaffirmed in numerous other binding and nonbinding international instruments." Principle 21 of the Stockholm Declaration provides that "States have, in accordance with the Charter of the United Nations and the principles of international law, the sovereign right to exploit their own resources pursuant to their own environmental policies, and the responsibility to ensure that activities within their jurisdiction or control do not cause damage to the environment of other States or of areas beyond the limits of national jurisdiction."

Other commentators, including Hunter, Salzman, and Zaelke (2002, p. 177), agree that "'Principle 21,' as it is known to all international environmental lawyers, continues today as an important statement of customary international environmental law."

UN General Assembly Resolutions

Can a resolution of the UN General Assembly, which constitutes legislation within the UN system, contribute to the development of international law? If three particular conditions are satisfied, the answer is in the affirmative. This was explained by Robert Rosenstock, US Representative to the Sixth Committee (Legal) at the United Nations, in a November 11, 1977 statement dealing with "how such a resolution may in exceptional cases contribute to the development of international law," as reported in a US Government publication (*Digest of US Practice in International Law, 1978,* p. 53). Rosenstock, then a senior lawyer of the US Department of State, made this statement while taking exception to commentary in the UN *Report of the International Law Commission* on its 29th session, which suggested that the "UN General Assembly had only recently reiterated and developed" the "principle of permanent sovereignty over natural resources" by passing General

Assembly Resolution 3201 entitled the "Declaration on the Establishment of a New International Economic Order" and General Assembly Resolution 3281 entitled "Charter of Economic Rights and Duties of States." Rosenstock noted three "ifs" or conditions required for such a UN General Assembly resolution to contribute to international law:

> This Assembly is not a lawmaking body. Its resolutions, in the ordinary course, do not enact, formulate or alter international law, progressively or regressively. In the exceptional cases in which a General Assembly resolution may contribute to the development of international law, it can do so only if the resolution gains virtually universal support, if the members of the General Assembly share a lawmaking or law-declaring intent—and if the content of that resolution is reflected in general state practice.

Unlike UN General Assembly resolutions, UN Security Council resolutions, such as Security Council Resolution 1373, adopted on September 28, 2001, following the terrorist attacks on September 11, 2001, are "legally binding on all member states of the United Nations," as pointed out by legal expert Herbert V. Morais and ADB Counsel Motoo Noguchi (2003, p. 9), when "a Security Council Resolution [has been] adopted in response to a threat to international peace and security, pursuant to Chapter VII of the United Nations Charter." Chapter VII is entitled "Action with Respect to Threats to the Peace, Breaches of the Peace, and Acts of Aggression." The most famous of these authoritative Resolutions intended to be law is the Declaration on Principles of International Law Concerning Friendly Relations and Cooperation Among States in Accordance with the Charter of the United Nations (Resolution 2625, adopted October 24, 1970). The long title for this 1970 Resolution suggests the lengthy negotiations that went into its drafting, precisely because it would be authoritative.

Rio Declaration on Environment and Development, and Agenda 21

The Rio Declaration on Environment and Development, adopted at the 1992 UNCED, is one of three nonbinding instruments that emerged in Rio de Janeiro. The other two are Agenda 21 and the Forest Principles. The legally binding instruments that emerged in Rio were two international conventions—the UN Framework Convention on Climate Change, and the Convention on Biological Diversity—both of which were signed in Rio and subsequently entered into force. As pointed out by law professor Philippe Sands (1994, p. 320), in this sense "Rio represented an advance on the Stockholm Conference," since the Stockholm Conference did not result in the signing of any international convention.

The Rio Declaration of 1992 consists of a preamble and 27 principles that contain, in the words of Sands in his article on "International Law in the Field of Sustainable Development" (1994, p. 322), "provisions more specific and precise than those adopted at Stockholm" 20 years earlier.

Kiss and Shelton suggest that the Rio Declaration contains principles that may be placed under four categories: legal, policy, economic, and public policy. Concerning those principles, Kiss and Shelton (2000, p. 71) point out that

> Principle 2, which concerns transboundary effects, is similar to Principle 21 of the Stockholm Declaration, but adds the word "developmental." Other legal norms can be found in Principle 10, affirming rights of public information, participation, and remedies; Principle 13, which calls for the development of liability rules; and Principles 18 and 19, which require notifying other states of emergencies and projects that may affect their environment. The formulation of then-emerging principles includes the precautionary principle (Principle 15), and the "polluter pays" principle that requires internationalization of environmental costs (Principle 17). Principle 11 stresses the importance of enacting effective environmental legislation, although it notes that standards applied by some countries may not be appropriate to others because of the economic and social costs involved.

In the view of many, the key to the Rio Declaration is found in Principle 3, which is a restatement of the definition of sustainable development proposed in the Brundtland Report. Principle 3 states that "The right to development must be fulfilled so as to equitably meet developmental and environmental needs of present and future generations." (UN Doc. A/CON.151/26 Vol. I.)

Principles 1 and 5 of the Rio Declaration focus on people in general and on the poor, respectively. Principle 1 provides (*ibid*) that "Human beings are at the center of concerns for sustainable development. They are entitled to a healthy and productive life in harmony with nature." Principle 5 declares (*ibid*) that "All States and all people shall cooperate in the essential task of eradicating poverty as an indispensable requirement for sustainable development, in order to decrease the disparities in standards of living and better meet the needs of the majority of the people of the world."

Financial institutions such as ADB implement this principle in development projects that are designed to eradicate poverty by applying the conceptual tool known as the "logical framework" or "logframe" or "project framework" to analyze, plan, and manage such projects (1998, p. 15). In some instances, poverty eradication is pursued in conjunction with other Rio principles, such as Principle 20, which declares that "Women have a vital role in environmental management and development" and that "Their full participation is therefore essential to achieve sustainable development." (Maldives, 2001, pp. 62-76.) A similar approach is taken to implement Principle 22 of the Rio Declaration, which states that "Indigenous people and their communities and other local communities have a vital role...in the achievement of sustainable development." (Plant, 2002, pp. 9-10.) Poverty eradication can also be pursued through reforms of a national judiciary. (See Box 7-3.)

Box 7-3. Poverty Eradication by Improving the Legal Basis for the Judiciary
and Administrative Reforms

One of the most significant ADB poverty reduction loans is for the Access to Justice Program (AJP) in Pakistan, approved on December 20, 2001, which consists of two policy loans equivalent to a total of US$350 million, plus a technical assistance loan equivalent to US$20 million to finance institutional development for the AJP. In addition, ADB provided a technical assistance grant equivalent to US$900,000 to support a program management unit within the Ministry of Law, Justice, Human Rights and Parliamentary Affairs, which is the executing agency for the AJP. According to the ADB Report and Recommendation of the President (pp. i and ii) for the AJP, the "key development objective of the AJP is to assist the Government" by "supporting five interrelated governance objectives":

"(a) providing a legal basis for judicial, policy, and administrative reforms;

(b) improving the efficiency, timeliness, and effectiveness in judicial and police services;

(c) supporting greater equity and accessibility in justice services for the vulnerable poor;

(d) improving predictability and consistency between fiscal and human resource allocation and the mandates of reformed judicial and police institutions at the federal, provincial, and local government levels; and

(e) ensuring greater transparency and accountability in the performance of the judiciary, the police, and administrative justice institutions. "

The Report and Recommendation of the President indicates (pp. ii and iii) that the "term 'judicial,' unless the context indicates otherwise, includes institutions responsible for the delivery of administrative justice, such as the offices of the ombudsman at various levels."

Of interest to environmentalists is a component in the AJP (p. i) that "support[s] the enforcement of environmental laws through the establishment of environmental tribunals already provided for in the law, and by ensuring that any conflict of interest is removed by different persons heading the provincial environmental agencies ... and the provincial environment departments." Also (p. iii) "civil society groups will be able to access the LEF [Legal Enforcement Fund] to raise environmental awareness and provide assistance for enforcement of environmental rights."

As Kiss and Shelton (2000, p. 72) conclude, the Rio Declaration is a very important statement of environmental principles and "includes several principles of an unambiguous, if general character." Principle 2, according to them (2000, pp. 43-44), "reiterated the duty" found in Principle 21 of the Stockholm Declaration and thus articulates a general principle of law.

The Rio Conference adopted Agenda 21, which is a program of action containing 40 chapters and a nonbinding action plan for sustainable development. In answer to the question "What contribution will Agenda 21 make, if any, to the progressive development of international law?" Sands responds in part as follows:

> It should be recalled that it only has recommendatory status, and that the
> immediate legal consequences which flow directly from the text are few. Its principal
> recommendations include the creation of a new Commission on Sustainable

*Development, and the improvement of co-ordination among UN and other bodies,
and the further development of international law.* [footnote omitted] *It also commits
all States to prepare national implementation reports.*

In the view of another commentator, Professor of Law John C. Dernbach (2002, p. 49),
"The Agenda 21 commitment is not binding in international law, but it does represent a political
commitment."

Sustainable Development as a Concept or General Principle

As pointed out by Kiss (2003, p. 8), in the case concerning the Gabcikovo-Nagymaros Project
(Hungary/Slovakia) in 1997, the ICJ explained (1997, p. 75) the "concept" of sustainable development,
though a dissenting opinion, argued that sustainable development is a "principle of international
law." In this case the ICJ had been requested to decide on the basis of the 1977 Treaty on the
Construction and Operation of the Gabcikovo-Nagymaros dams, which concerned a system of
dams on the Danube River designed to produce electrical energy and improve the "navigability of
the Danube, flood control and regulation of ice-discharge, and the protection of the environment."
The ICJ was also requested to decide the case on the basis of "rules and principles of international
law as well as such other treaties as the court may find applicable." (Kiss and Shelton, 2000, p.
423.) The judgment, delivered by the 15 Judges of the Court, with Stephen M. Schwebel serving
as President, included the following paragraph 140 (Gabcikovo-Nagymaros Project [Hungary/
Slovakia)] 1997, ICJ,) dealing with "effects upon the environment," "risks for mankind—for present
and future generations," and the "concept of sustainable development":

> *[140] ...Throughout the ages, mankind has, for economic and other reasons, constantly
> interfered with nature. In the past, this was often done without consideration of the
> effects upon the environment. Owing to new scientific insights and to a growing
> awareness of the risks for mankind—for present and future generations—of pursuit
> of such interventions as an unconsidered and unabated pace, new norms and
> standards have been developed, set forth in a great number of instruments during
> the last two decades. Such new norms have to be taken into consideration, and such
> new standards given proper weight, not only when States contemplate new activities
> but also when continuing with activities begun in the past. This need to reconcile
> economic development with protection of the environment is aptly expressed in the
> concept of sustainable development.*

Having described "sustainable development" as a concept, the ICJ then ruled in part that "the
Parties together should look afresh at the effects on the environment of the operation of the
Gabcikovo power plant" and "[i]n particular they must find a satisfactory solution for the volume
of the water to be released into the old bed of the Danube and into the side-arms of both sides
of the river." (Gabcikovo-Nagymaros Project [Hungary/Slovakia] 1997, ICJ, p. 78.)

As Kiss (2003, p. 8) points out, the Vice-President of the ICJ at that time, Judge Christopher Gregory Weeramantry, opined that sustainable development is a principle, not a concept, of international law:

> In his dissenting opinion, on the contrary, Judge Weeramantry presents sustainable development as a principle of international law. He recalls that after the early formulations of the concept of development, it was recognized that development cannot be pursued to such a point that substantial damage results to the environment within which it is to occur. Therefore, development can only be sought in harmony with the reasonable demands of environmental protection. He stresses that:
> It is thus the correct formulation of the right to development that that right does not exist in the absolute sense, but is relative always to its tolerance to the environment. The right to development as thus defined is clearly part of modern international law. It is compendiously referred to as sustainable development.

In his separate opinion, Weeramantry describes in part the evolution of sustainable development, noting that the ICJ refers to sustainable development as a "concept," while he "considers" sustainable development to be "a principle with normative value" and "a principle of customary international law" (Gabcikovo-Nagymaros Project [Hungary/Slovakia] 1997, ICJ, pp. 89-107.)

> The Court has referred to it [sustainable development] as a concept in paragraph 140 of its Judgment. However, I consider it to be more than a mere concept, but as a principle with normative value which is crucial to the determination of this case. ...
> I would observe, moreover, that both Parties in this case agree on the applicability to this dispute of the principle of sustainable development. Thus, Hungary states in its pleadings that: "Hungary and Slovakia agree that the principle of sustainable development, as formulated in the Brundtland Report, the Rio Declaration and Agenda 21 is applicable to this dispute. ..."

For a discussion of the legal status of "sustainable development" and what international law requires of states and international organizations concerning sustainable development, see Box 7-4 entitled "The Legal Status of Sustainable Development." See also Box 7-5 on "Sustainable Development and Unsustainable Arguments."

Box 7-4. The Legal Status of Sustainable Development

Alan Boyle and David Freestone (1999, pp. 16-18) describe the legal status of sustainable development as follows:

No easy answer can be given to the question whether international law now requires that all development should be sustainable.

... It is difficult to see international court reviewing national action and concluding that it falls short of a standard of "sustainable development." The International Court of Justice did not do so in the Case Concerning the Gabcikovo-Nagymaros Dam, preferring instead to address more readily justiciable questions such as the equitable allocation of waterflow or the applicability of international environmental standards in the operation of the hydroelectric system. ...

Normative uncertainty, coupled with the absence of justiciable standards for review, strongly suggest that there is as yet no international legal obligation that development must be sustainable, (Gunther Handl, "Environmental Security and Global Change: The Challenge to International Law" [1990] Yearbook of International Environmental Law 25. ... See also Handl, "The Legal Mandate of Multilateral Development Banks as Agents for Change towards Sustainable Development" [Multilateral Development Banking: Environemental Principles and Concepts Reflecting General International Law and Public Policy 2001]) and that decisions on what constitutes sustainability rest primarily with individual governments.

This is not the end of matter, however. A more plausible argument is that although international law may not require development to be sustainable, it does require development decisions to be the outcome of a process which promotes sustainable development. Specifically, if states do not carry out EIAs, or encourage public participation, or integrate development and environmental considerations in their decision-making, or take account of the needs of intra- and inter-generational equity, they will have failed to implement the main elements employed by the Rio Declaration and other international instruments for the purpose of facilitating sustainable development. There is, as we shall see below, ample state practice to support the normative significance of most of these elements. Moreover, an interpretation which makes the process of decision-making the key legal element in sustainable development, rather than the nature of the development, is implicitly supported by the case concerning the Gabcikovo-Nagymaros Dam. In that decision, while not questioning whether the project was sustainable, the International Court of Justice did require the parties in the interests of sustainable development to "look afresh" at the environmental consequences and to carry out monitoring and abatement measures to contemporary standards set by international law. 92 AJIL 642. (1997) ICJ Reports, 7, at para. 140] Such an approach enables international courts to further the objective of sustainable development in accordance with the Rio Declaration while relieving them of the impossible task of deciding what is and what is not sustainable.

An argument of this kind would thus focus on the components of sustainable development, rather than on the concept itself. ... whether or not sustainable development is a legal obligation, and as we have seen this seems unlikely, it does represent a goal which can influence the outcome of litigation and the practice of states and international organizations, and it may lead to significant changes and developments in the existing law. In that very important sense, international law does appear to require states and international bodies to take account of the objective of sustainable development, and to establish appropriate processes for doing so. ...

Box 7-5, Sustainable Development and Unsustainable Arguments

Vaughan Lowe (1999, p. 21) argues that the concept of sustainable development is not a "binding norm of international law" but nevertheless "a concept with great potential value":

... the argument that the concept of sustainable development is now a binding norm of international law in the sense of the "normative logic" of traditional international law as reflected in Article 38(1) of the Statute of the International Court of Justice is not sustainable, but ... there is a sense in which the concept of sustainable development exemplifies another species of normativity which is of great potential value in the handling of concepts of international environmental law.

Noting the "two different views concerning the nature of sustainable development," Kiss asks: "Is it a concept as the International Court of Justice qualified it or is it a principle?" He begins his reply (2003, pp. 8-9) by trying to "clarify the two notions" as follows:

A concept is an abstract creation of the human mind without having a material content. Principles are, on the contrary, fundamental norms for the orientation of persons, authorities or others, materializing the content of legal, moral or intellectual concepts, without necessarily being directly applicable. In this sense, the state is a concept, while its Constitution proclaims principles in order to establish the fundamental rules of its functioning. In application of such principles, specific laws are enacted to govern the functioning of the state's organs and the behaviour of persons.

Kiss then suggests (2003, p. 9) that "sustainable development should be considered as a concept while several principles have been proposed to establish its concrete content." Noting that the "2002 Johannesburg World Summit on Sustainable Development focused a large part of its work on sustainable development," (*ibid.*) Kiss refers to a declaration on the principles of international law in the field of sustainable development adopted at the April 2002 Conference of the International Law Association held in New Delhi. That declaration, which did not emanate from a meeting of states but merely from a private group, proposed seven basic principles followed by explanatory comments:

1. **The duty of the States to ensure sustainable use of natural resources**

   While, in accordance with international law, all States have the sovereign right to use their own natural resources pursuant to their own environmental and developmental policies, they are also under a duty to manage natural resources, including natural resources within their own territory or jurisdiction, in a rational, sustainable and safe way so as to contribute to the development of their peoples and to the conservation and the protection of the environment, including ecosystems. States must take into account the needs of future generations. The Declaration stresses that all relevant actors, including States, industrial concerns and other components of civil society are under a duty to avoid wasteful use of natural resources and promote waste minimization policies. ...

2. The principle of equity and the eradication of poverty

The New Delhi Declaration recalls that the principle of equity is central to the attainment of sustainable development. It refers to both intra-generational equity and inter-generational equity. The first means the right of all peoples within the current generation to fair access to the Earth's natural resources. The second imposes the duty upon present humanity to take into account the long-term impact of its activities and to sustain the resource base and the global environment for the benefit of future generations. "Benefit" is to be understood in this context as including inter alia, economic, environmental, social and intrinsic benefit. From the recognition of the right to development flows the duty of States to cooperate for the eradication of poverty. Whilst it is the primary responsibility of the State to aim for conditions of equity within its own population and to ensure, as a minimum, the eradication of poverty, all States which are in a position to do so have a further responsibility to assist other States to achieve this objective.

3. The principle of common but differentiated responsibilities

All States and other relevant actors, international organizations, corporations, non-governmental organizations and civil society should co-operate in the achievement of global sustainable development and the protection of the environment. The special needs and interests of developing countries and of countries with economies in transition should be recognized. Developed countries bear a special burden of responsibility in reducing and eliminating unsustainable patterns of production and consumption and in contributing to capacity-building in developing countries.

4. The principle of the precautionary approach to fields such as health, natural resources, and ecosystems

According to the Declaration, a precautionary approach commits States, international organizations and civil society, particularly the scientific and business communities, to avoid human activity which may cause significant harm to human health, natural resources or ecosystems, including in the light of scientific uncertainty. Such approach should include accountability for harm caused, where appropriate, State responsibility, planning based on clear criteria and well-defined goals, effective use of environmental impact assessment and establishing an appropriate burden of proof on the person or persons carrying out or intending to carry out the activity.

5. The principle of public participation and access to information and justice

The Declaration stresses that public participation is essential to sustainable development and good governance. It is a condition for responsiveness, transparency and accountability both for governments and civil society organizations, including industrial concerns and trade unions. The text adds that the vital role of women in sustainable development should be recognized. Public participation requires effective protection of the human right to hold and express opinions and to seek, receive and impart ideas. It also requires a right of access to appropriate, comprehensible and timely information held by governments and industrial concerns regarding the sustainable use of natural resources and the protection of the environment. Non-discriminatory access to effective judicial or administrative procedures should be ensured in the State where the measure has been taken to challenge such measure and to claim compensation. [footnote deleted.]

6. **The principle of good governance**

The Declaration proclaims that civil society and non-governmental organizations have a right to good governance by States and international organizations.This means the adoption of democratic and transparent decision-making procedures and financial accountability, effective measures to combat corruption, the respect of the principle of due process, of rule of law and human rights and the implementation of a public procurement approach. Good governance also calls for corporate social responsibility and socially responsible investments and a fair distribution of wealth among and within communities.

7. **The principle of integration and interrelationship, in particular in relation to human rights and social, economic, and environmental objectives**

This principle reflects the interdependence of social, economic, financial, environmental and human rights aspects of principles and rules of international law relating to sustainable development as well as of the interdependence of the needs of current and future generations of humankind. According to the Declaration, States should strive to resolve apparent conflicts between competing economic, financial, social and environmental considerations, whether through existing institutions or through the establishment of appropriate new institutions.

Kiss concludes (2003, p. 11) that "On the whole, these principles are rooted in the Declaration of the Conference of Rio de Janeiro and in Agenda 21 and can be considered as generally accepted, although their legal nature can be discussed." He further notes (2003, p. 14) in conclusion of his discussion of sustainable development that "the Implementation Plan of the WSSD…seems to somewhat ignore law or legal rules, [and thus] could be considered as particularly counterproductive in this regard." However, he points (*ibid.*) out that "policy measures are necessarily linked with law. …":

> *At the highest level, law, as the expression of the common concern of a community, has to determine the values to be protected and, after defining and adopting the policies which serve that objective, needs to fulfill the proposed tasks. Almost every paragraph of the Implementation Plan contains the word "policy" which means that in reality its implementation involves legal measures. Further, when good governance is proposed, it also includes good institutions and good norms, which again mean law and mainly environmental law.*

The "conceptual approach to sustainable development," suggested by Kiss (2003, pp. 14-15), from fundamental values, concepts, principles, and policies to legal tools, follows:

* *Fundamental values of humanity: definition by global legal instruments*
  - *Peace (UN Charter)*
  - *Human rights (UN Charter; Universal Declaration of Human Rights; Covenants on Civil, Political Rights and Economic, Social and Cultural Rights)*

- *Environment (Declarations of Stockholm and of Rio de Janeiro, WSSD Declaration and Plan of Implementation)*

• *Concept of sustainable development (Declaration of Rio de Janeiro) - Principles flowing from the concept:*
  - *sustainable use of the environment;*
  - *pollution control;*
  - *equity and eradication of poverty;*
  - *common but differentiated responsibility;*
  - *prevention of harm and precautionary approach (health, natural resources, ecosystems);*
  - *public information, participation and access to justice;*
  - *good governance; and*
  - *integration and interrelationship in particular in relation to human rights and to social, economic and environmental objectives.*

• *Policies (Stockholm: Action Plan; Rio: Agenda 21; WSSD: Declaration and Plan of Implementation). They include in particular:*
  - *land-use planning;*
  - *health care;*
  - *habitat;*
  - *energy;*
  - *ecosystem management;*
  - *soil protection; and*
  - *education, awareness-raising, training, capacity building.*

• *Legal tools implementing the policies adopted for enhancing sustainable development:*
  - *international conventions;*
  - *constitutional rules;*
  - *framework laws;*
  - *laws concerning basic services (water and sanitation, energy, transport, health care, town and country planning, etc.);*
  - *laws concerning specific environmental sectors (water, sea, air, biodiversity) and sources of environmental deterioration (polluting substances, wastes, nuclear material, etc.);*
  - *regulations adopted at different levels (national, regional, subregional in accordance with the principle of subsidiarity) implementing such laws or framing economic instruments; and*
  - *judicial decisions.*

MDBs have been established pursuant to international conventions and thus provide examples of how international conventions can support sustainable development. See Box 7-6 describing in part the relationship between development banking and sustainable development.

Professor Gunther Handl (2001, pp. 23, 31, 33, 34, 35; see also 1998, p. 642 and following) describes the legal mandate for MDBs as agents for change toward sustainable development as follows:

... the banks have metamorphosed into true development institutions, i.e., have abandoned their original narrow focus on economic development as measured in terms of "satisfactory" rates of increase in gross national product, and have embraced human resource development, and protection of the environment as legitimate development ends in their own right..[footnote omitted]

(p. 23)

The Legal Mandate of Multilateral Development Banks

... the conclusion arrived at here: As members of the international community, MDBs are subject not only to evolving international public policy and general international law (custom and general principles of law), but also to the normative reach of those MEAs that have been adopted precisely to lay down principles and standards of global applicability. [footnote omitted]

(p. 31)

... MDBs which, as their name already implies, occupy a special position in the sustainable development process, represent also key addressees of the emerging norms of the international law of sustainable development. Whereas it is true that MDBs have no special international mandate to vindicate human rights generally and hence are subject to only (functionally) limited affirmative obligations regarding the enhancement of human rights, international financial institutions (and development agencies) have been entrusted with a broad and universally recognized role in promoting sustainable development. That mandate entails a responsibility: MDBs must actively promote the objectives of international normative concepts, extant or emerging, that bear directly on sustainable development. Thus the normative implications of, for example, "women in development" suggest that the banks not only refrain from acting in defiance of, or at cross-purposes with, the environmental and social objectives the normative concept seeks to capture, but also act affirmatively towards their realization. It goes without saying, however, that such an affirmative obligation is neither absolute nor unlimited. Rather, MDBs will be only required to take reasonable steps in support of sustainable development. [footnote omitted]

(p. 33)

Conclusions

It should be evident, then, that the Banks have not only an inherently economic and political incentive, but also a clear international legal obligation to avoid causing environmental harm in developing member countries, and indeed to incorporate environmental protection and social development objectives into all of its activities in DMCs [developing member countries]. In this sense, international public law and policy merely underline the status of MDBs as critical agents of change towards sustainable development. [footnote omitted]

(p. 34)

... variances in how MDBs approach private as against public sector operations are explainable first and foremost in terms of the different scope of development objectives that MDBs can pursue legitimately in financing respective sector projects. Otherwise the Bank's general international legal obligations apply mutatis mutandis to private sector activities. ... [footnote omitted]

(p. 35)

Source: Gunther Handl (2001)

It is important to emphasize that this declaration on the principles of international law in the field of sustainable development adopted at the April 2002 Conference in New Delhi lacks the authority that might follow from a declaration made by representatives of states, but it may have a clarity that a private group can provide when acting without constraints imposed by states.

MULTILATERAL ENVIRONMENTAL AGREEMENTS (MEAs)

Characteristics of Environmental Treaties

Kiss and Shelton describe (2000, p. 33) seven main features of environmental treaties:

1. *an emphasis on national implementing measures being taken by the states parties;*
2. *the creation of international supervisory mechanisms to review compliance by states parties;*
3. *simplified procedures to enable rapid modification of the treaties;*
4. *the use of action plans for further measures;*
5. *the creation of new institutions or the utilization of already existing ones to promote continuous cooperation;*
6. *the use of framework agreements; and*
7. *interrelated or cross-referenced provisions from other environmental instruments.*

Types of International Agreements

Armed with these definitions and interpretations, we can now turn to the heart of our legislative inquiry—international environmental agreements—which fall under two headings:

- bilateral treaties, which involve agreements by two countries; and
- multilateral treaties, which involve agreements by three or more countries and perhaps one or several international organizations.

1. Bilateral treaties

Some of the oldest environmental treaties have been bilateral and have dealt with water and birds. The Convention of May 21, 1906, between Mexico and the US, deals with the irrigation of the Juarez Valley. A 1916 Convention between the United States and Great Britain on behalf of Canada protects migratory birds.

2. Multilateral treaties

Perhaps the most significant MEA in support of sustainable development is the UN Framework Convention on Climate Change, a treaty that has been signed by more than 175 nations and for which the total number of ratifications/accessions/acceptances is 120 throughout the world. The first sentence of paragraph 4 of Article 3 of this UN Convention states, "The Parties have a right to, and should, promote sustainable development." It further provides in paragraph 1(d) of Article 4 that Parties to this Convention must "Promote sustainable management, and promote and cooperate in the conservation and enhancement, as appropriate, of sinks and reservoirs of all greenhouse gases not controlled by the Montreal Protocol, including biomass, forests and oceans as well as other terrestrial, coastal and marine ecosystems." Thus, the concepts of sustainable development as well as sustainable management have a firm foundation in a treaty with almost universal acceptance.

Problems Associated with MEAs

1. Governance

Since the Stockholm Conference of 1972, MEAs have been at the center of discussion of international environmental problems and the need for reform (see Box 7-7 on Governance). One of these problems arises from the large number of MEAs. Professor Daniel Esty and Maria Ivanova, Director of the Global Environmental Governance Project at Yale, indicate (2002, p. 182) that there are "more than 500 multilateral environmental agreements ... more than a dozen international agencies share environmental responsibilities, and yet environmental conditions are not improving across a number of critical dimensions."

Box 7-7. Governance

Robert Keohane and Joseph Nye Jr. (2000, p. 12) define governance:

> By governance, we mean the processes and institutions, both formal and informal, that guide and restrain the collective activities of a group. Government is the subset that acts with authority and creates formal obligations. Governance need not necessarily be conducted exclusively by governments and the international organizations to which they delegate authority. Private firms, associations of firms, nongovernmental organizations (NGOs), and associations of NGOs all engage in it, often in association with governmental bodies, to create governance, sometimes without governmental authority.

Esty and Invanova point out (2002, p. 183) that "The haphazard development of international environmental laws and agencies has left three important institutional gaps in the existing global environmental governance system: (1) a jurisdictional gap, (2) an information gap, and (3) an implementation gap."

They also explain (2002, p. 186) that the jurisdictional gap arises from the perception held by national legislatures that their role does not include "addressing worldwide transboundary harms, while global bodies often do not have the capacity or the authority to address them." The information gap, they add (ibid.) arises from the "little coordination among data collection efforts" of international and other organizations and "poor ... comparability across jurisdictions."

Esty and Ivanova also suggest (2002, p. 187) that the "implementation gap" may be the "biggest single obstacle to environmental progress at the global scale" and that this gap is caused by "the lack of an action orientation." They also indicate (ibid.) that the implementation gap arises in part from the "existing financial mechanisms ... scattered across the Global Environment Facility, UNEP, the World Bank, and separate treaty-based funds such as the Montreal Protocol Finance Mechanism." They also explain (ibid.) that "few international environmental agreements contain serious enforcement provisions."

2. Ratification and implementation

Such problems related to the implementation of environmental agreements were addressed at the Global Judges Symposium on Sustainable Development and the Role of Law held in Johannesburg, South Africa, August 18-20, 2002. A 2002 UNEP publication, entitled "Status of Ratification of Selected Multilateral Environmental Agreements," distributed at the symposium, identifies (2002, p. 1) key conventions and protocols that should be given "top priority in the environmental agenda" so that they will be ratified and implemented "through domestic legislation." "To help in achieving the objectives of those agreements," the UNEP publication indicates (*ibid.*) that UNEP is committed to promote and support their ratification "and to assist countries in implementing those agreements under the Programme for the Development and Periodic Review of Environmental Law for the First Decade of the Twenty-first Century (Montevideo Programme III)." Of these, two treaties have yet to be ratified, as shown in Box 7-8.

Box 7-8. Two Yet-to-Be Ratified MEAs

Two yet-to-be ratified MEAs listed in 2002 in "Status of Ratification of Selected Multilateral Environmental Agreements Published on the Occasion of the Global Judges Symposium on Sustainable Development and the Role of Law held in Johannesburg, South Africa":
- Amendment to the Basel Convention on the Control of Transboundary Movements of Hazardous Wastes and Their Disposal
- Basel Protocol on Liability and Compensation for Damage Resulting from Transboundary Movements of Hazardous Wastes and Their Disposal

Source: Global Judges Symposium

The Stockholm Convention on Persistent Organic Pollutants and the Rotterdam Convention on the Prior Informed Consent Procedure for Certain Hazardous Chemicals and Pesticides in International Trade, both originally listed among the yet-to-be ratified MEAs, were ratified in 2004.

This same UNEP publication identified 14 MEAs that had been ratified but needed assistance in implementation, as shown in Box 7-9. Since this UNEP publication, one of these 14, the Kyoto Protocol to the United Nations Framework Convention on Climate Change, was ratified in 2005.

3. US treaty ratification

Beyond the insights offered by Esty and Ivanova, what are some of the other current problems from the legal point of view in implementing MEAs? Let us begin with the process of ratification in the US. From the perspective of US constitutional law, as pointed out by Assistant Legal Adviser for Treaty Affairs Robert E. Dalton (1999, p. 190):

> ...a treaty is an international agreement (regardless of title, designation, or form) whose entry into force with respect to the United States takes place only after the Senate has given its advice and consent pursuant to Article II, section 2, clause 2, of the Constitution and the President has signed the instrument of ratification or accession on behalf of the United States.

Box 7-9. Fourteen MEAs in Need of Assistance in Implementation

Fourteen MEAs in need of assistance of implementation, listed in "States of Ratification of Selected Multilateral Environmental Agreements Published on the Occasion of the Global Judges Symposium on Sustainable Development and the Role of Law held in Johannesburg, South Africa" (2002)
- Convention on the Conservation of Migratory Species of Wild Animals
- Convention on International Trade in Endangered Species of Wild Fauna and Flora
- Convention on Biological Diversity
- Cartagena Protocol on Biosafety to the Convention on Biological Diversity
- Basel Convention on the Control of Transboundary Movements of Hazardous Wastes and Their Disposal
- Vienna Convention for the Protection of the Ozone Layer
- Montreal Protocol on Substances That Deplete the Ozone Layer
- United Nations Framework Convention on Climate Change
- UN Convention to Combat Desertification in Those Countries Experiencing Serious Drought and/ or Desertification, Particularly in Africa
- UN Convention on the Law of the Sea
- Convention for the Protection of the World Cultural and Natural Heritage
- Convention on Wetlands of International Importance Especially as Waterfowl Habitat
- Convention on Access to Information, Public Participation in Decision-Making and Access to Justice in Environmental Matters
- Rotterdam Convention on the Prior Informed Consent Procedure for Certain Hazardous Chemicals and Pesticides in International Trade

Source: Global Judges Symposium

Article VI of the US Constitution provides that "all Treaties made, or which shall be made, under the Authority of the United States, shall be the supreme Law of the Land." As Dalton points out (1999, p. 207), if the text of a particular agreement is given legislative approval, that legislation will generally include any necessary implementing provisions. For example, when the US became a party to the Environmental Protocol to the Antarctic Treaty, the US Administration proposed implementing legislation; "in the course of drafting new legislation... the Administration found existing legislation that permitted the executive branch to implement other obligations." (1999, p. 208.)

4. Ratification of treaties by other countries

Other countries have other processes for ratification. Some have a two-step procedure by which a treaty may become binding and implemented in part under international law, even though years may pass before appropriate domestic implementing legislation is enacted. The case of Nepal provides an example. As environmental law Professor Amber Pant of the Tribhuvan University Faculty of Law notes in a September 2003 e-mail message, Nepal enacted an Environmental Protection Act in 1997 and adopted accompanying rules that same year.

Furthermore, Nepal has more than 100 legislative acts that bear on the environmental sector. However, more than 20 environmental treaties to which Nepal has become a party do not have legislation that fully implements treaty provisions by designating appropriate institutions and authorities and taking other necessary steps. Pant points out, "It would be wrong to say that we have legislation for every treaty to which Nepal is a party." He goes on to state that "this would not be possible unless we ... suggest to the Government that they draft legislation. ..." Pant closes by suggesting that there is a lack of funds to engage "experts to...prepare draft legislation for the consideration of governmental authorities."

As a result of this two-step procedure, some treaties are called "paper tigers"; even though they have been ratified for the purposes of international law; since they have no implementing domestic legislation, they have no teeth. This creates an imbalance for countries like the US, which often proceeds slowly over many years before ratifying treaties, while some other countries ratify treaties relatively quickly and then enact implementing legislation a few years later. Concerning these other countries, note that Article 18 of the Vienna Convention on the Law of Treaties provides a "good faith" obligation for treaties signed but not ratified—"[an] obligation not to defeat the object and purpose of a treaty prior to its entry into force."

5. Different legal traditions

Another problem arises from the great differences in the legal traditions of the countries of the world. Take the Philippines, which is far ahead of many Asian countries in terms of environmental law. Professor Antonio A. Oposa of the School of Law at the University of the Philippines recently published a 792-page treatise, entitled *A Legal Arsenal for the Philippine Environment* (2002), reproducing and describing the nation's more than 200 environmental laws and 20 international environmental agreements. Significantly, the book (2002, p. v) opens with a quip: "To Filipinos, may we learn to make less laws; Instead, may we learn to make them work just a little bit more. ..." In this regard it is noteworthy that in 2003 only a half dozen of the Philippines' 91 law schools taught environmental law, but that in 2005 about two dozen of them did.

Many law schools in developing countries have inadequate libraries and do not have a single computer devoted to legal research and scholarship. Furthermore, the schools may teach environmental law, but the facilities, the traditions, and the training are not the same as those found in developed countries. As a result, some developing countries lack lawyers, judges, and administrators with in-depth knowledge of environmental law.

6. Availability of financial resources

The disparity in availability of funds among the various international environmental organizations can also be a problem. The Global Environment Facility (GEF), with headquarters in Washington, D.C., is well funded, with a tranche of $2.92 billion. The GEF focuses on just a few treaties such as biodiversity, climate change, international waters, ozone, the Stockholm Convention on Persistent Organic Pollutants, and desertification. Despite the short list of MEAs, the GEF has quite enough to do. On the other hand, UNEP, which was founded in 1975 with headquarters in Nairobi, Kenya, expends in any one year less than $100 million on the entire range of international environmental issues, including drafting MEAs, capacity building, and global judges' symposia.

7. Political will and the need for capacity building

If the public does not support a program, politicians are not likely to implement it. Also, on a worldwide basis, we lack legislators, administrators, lawyers, judges, entrepreneurs, and others who are sufficiently informed or have the resources to implement sustainable development within the many constraints that confront them. Many key decision makers did not have the opportunity to study environmental law when they were students, and they often lack the opportunity to attend workshops on relevant environmental topics now. Judges are poorly paid, as shown in Box 7-10. Perhaps because of these two aspects, many countries lack necessary environmental legislation and implementation.

Box 7-10. Judicial Remuneration

As indicated in an ADB publication prepared by the Asia Foundation (2003, p. 19), the
importance of adequate judicial remuneration and fiscal resources for court administration was summed up by Singapore's President Lee Kuan Yew, who remarked, "You pay peanuts, you get monkeys." The disparities in judicial remuneration among the countries in this publication are striking. Moreover, in most countries in South and Southeast Asia...judicial salaries are not simply low but seriously inadequate. In some countries they are not even at subsistence levels. ...In Thailand, as in the Philippines, judges are paid relatively well in comparison to judges in Lao PDR, Cambodia, and Viet Nam. Still, the average judicial salary is approximately US $3,000 per month, or US$36,000 per year. Likewise, in Pakistan, Nepal, and Bangladesh, judges receive inadequate compensation, though relatively higher salaries than judges in Southeast Asia. High court judges in Pakistan, for instance, receive only US$1,400 per month, or about US$16,800 per year, plus certain benefits, and other superior court judges earn slightly less.

Source: The Asia Foundation, *Judicial Independence Overview and Country-Level Summaries*, ADB, 2003

When the people are aroused by a threatening situation, things do get done. Thailand has made enormous progress in controlling air pollution. There came a point when the people said they would not put up with dangerous, unbreathable air anymore. In a single year, Thailand practically eliminated the two-cylinder gasoline engine, which was a key pollutant. With the air cleaned up, the Thais are now turning their attention to cleaning Bangkok's polluted canals.

The PRC has very comprehensive environmental legislation and a leadership that increasingly emphasizes the importance of dealing with environmental issues. The country is on the way to improving and expanding that legislation. However, it needs to improve the implementation of its environmental legislation at the local level.

The major work to be done relates to policy dialogue, finance, workshops, and publications, which together might be referred to as capacity building. Here the World Bank, the GEF, the regional banks, NGOs, universities, and think tanks will likely play a very significant role. An example of how international organizations and many others can work together for capacity building is provided by an ADB grant of $600,000 to the Commission on Environmental Law of the IUCN and UNEP to train law professors from 15 countries spanning the region from Pakistan to the Fiji Islands, and to produce a book dealing with capacity building. Sixty-three law professors were trained at the Asia-Pacific Center for Environmental Law, located in the Faculty of Law of the National University of Singapore. The resultant book in two volumes, *Capacity Building for Environmental Law in the Asian and Pacific Region: Approaches and Resources*, was edited by three IUCN Commission on Environmental Law members, law professors Donna G. Craig, Nicholas A. Robinson, and Koh Kheng-Lian (2003), in conjunction with staff of ADB and about 200 other contributors. Thousands of copies of this book and an accompanying CD-ROM have been made available to professors, students, judges, and administrators.

8. Improving law schools and judicial academies

While public awareness is crucial for supporting new environmental legislation, we also need better law schools and judicial academies to formulate and implement the legislation. Clearly, the role of UNEP needs to be expanded. If the GEF is spending almost $3 billion annually on about a dozen areas of concern, and UNEP has only about $100 million per year to handle everything else, there are bound to be problems. Simply put, UNEP is underfunded. It can approach many issues and do many things that the GEF cannot, because UNEP has a worldwide mandate. It can approach the judiciary, playing an important role in building capacity in the judicial branches of governments throughout the world. UNEP can also undertake capacity building in educational institutions in ways that other organizations cannot or will not.

9. World Trade Organization, agricultural subsidies, and trade barriers

Among the 14 agreements cited in Box 7-9, there is no mention of WTO.

Yet the treaty establishing WTO is likely one of the most important multilateral "environmental" agreements in the world, because it deals with a great many environmental issues under the heading of trade. For example, there is legislation in the US about net fishing, enacted to save the dolphin, the sea turtle, and other endangered marine species. However, these laws can be construed as a restriction on trade. If Mexico ships fish to the US that were caught in violation of US legislation, someone can appear before the relevant bodies of WTO, which might decide the case in a manner not pleasing to environmental advocates (Hunter, Salzman, Zaelke, 2002, pp. 1169-1180). See Box 7-11 concerning trade disputes and protection of endangered species.

In this regard it is of interest to note that in cases involving net fishing for tuna that resulted in catches of dolphins, recent WTO decisions have recognized the role of NGOs in advancing rules implementing international law. In these WTO cases, the US sought to require Thailand and others to certify that techniques for catching tuna were safe for dolphins. WTO allowed US environmental groups to submit amicus briefs, even though Thailand and others objected by suggesting that US NGOs represent the position of the US Government.

Box 7-11. Trade Disputes and Protection of Endangered Species

Professor L. Damrosch et al. (2001, pp. 1534-1535) describe the role of WTO in resolving the tuna/dolphin dispute as follows:

Environmental issues have arisen in a number of international trade disputes before the World Trade Organization. In the so-called Tuna/Dolphin dispute, the United States banned the import of tuna caught by Mexican fisherman without proper regard for dolphins. In 1991, this ban was ruled incompatible with the GATT [General Agreement on Tariff and Trade]. See Dispute Settlement Panel Report on United Nations Restrictions on Imports of Tuna, 4 World Trade Materials 20 (1992), 30 I.L.M. 1594 (1991). In the Shrimp Turtle case seven years later, a W.T.O. Panel came to the same result with regard to the U.S. import ban of shrimp from India, Malaysia, Pakistan and Thailand. ... On the appeal by the United States, this decision was partially overturned by the Appellate Body. ... In its decision of October 12, 1998, the Appellate Body made reference to major international environmental conventions, especially to the Convention on Trade in Endangered Species and the Convention on the Conservation of Migratory Species of Wild Animals, and held that the trade restraints imposed by the U.S. regime served a legitimate environmental objective and were not incompatible with the GATT. However, the Appellate Body found that, while the environmentally based trade restraints were not themselves contrary to the GATT, the United States had contravened the GATT by applying those restraints unilaterally in a discriminatory manner. The Appellate Body accepted the amicus curiae briefs of three groups of non-governmental organizations from the U.S. submission. ... Concluding its decision the Appellate Body underlined (paras. 185-186):

...We have not decided that the sovereign nations that are Members of the WTO cannot adopt effective measures to protect endangered species, such as sea turtles. Clearly they can and should. And we have not decided that sovereign states should not act together bilaterally, plurilaterally or multilaterally, either within the WTO or in other international fora, to protect endangered species or to otherwise protect the environment. Clearly they should and do.

What we have decided in this appeal is simply this: although the measure of the United States in dispute in this appeal serves an environmental objective that is recognized as legitimate under paragraph (g) of Article XX of the GATT 1994, this measure has been applied by the United States in a manner which constitutes arbitrary and unjustifiable discrimination between Members of the WTO, contrary to the requirements of the chapeau [hat] of Article XX. ...

For an example of how the Cartagena Protocol regulates trade in genetically modified organisms, see Box 7-12.

A second example relates to the rules permitting agricultural subsidies and the creation of trade barriers. These rules can have a profound effect on the environment. For example, subsidies can often result in wasteful overproduction of goods and services that unnecessarily deplete natural resources in the country providing such subsidies. Similar problems may arise from trade barriers, which can prevent the sale of economically and environmentally sound goods and services originating in countries outside of such trade barriers. (See http://www.ewg.org/farm/home.php.)

Box 7-12. Genetically Modified Organisms

Professors Lori Fisler Damrosch, Louis Henkin, Richard Crawford Pugh, Oscar Schachter, and Hans Smit describe the treatment of genetically modified organisms under the Cartagena Protocol as follows (2001, pp. 1536-1537):

Whether biotechnology involving the release of genetically modified organisms (GMOs) threatens the environment has become an issue for governments and international organizations. A Protocol on Biosafety, the first global regime regulating trade in GMOs, was adopted on January 29, 2000 and is to enter into force after ratification by 50 states. As the negotiations began in Cartagena, Colombia, the protocol is referred to as the Cartagena Protocol. The biosafety regime is a protocol to the 1992 Convention on Biological Diversity. Consequently a state that has not become a party to the Convention (for example the United States) cannot become a party to the Protocol. Nevertheless, a state not party to the Protocol will have to comply with its provisions when exporting to states parties to the Protocol.

The Biosafety Protocol allows its member states to bar imports of genetically altered seeds, microbes, animals and crops they regard as a threat to their environment. But the Protocol provides no requirement that shipments of genetically altered products identify the specific variety, a provision proposed by Europeans. The United States and Canada refused to agree to that requirement, claiming it would harm international trade in safe foods. In the last years, European resistance to American food products (about half the soybeans and one-third of the corn grown in the U.S. in 1999 contained foreign genes, making the crops resistant to herbicides or insects) has caused significant U.S. export losses. See "130 Nations Agree on Safety Rules for Biotech Food," N.Y. Times, Jan. 30, 2000, at 1, 8.

The Protocol requires exporting states to apply for advance permission from the importing country before shipping of a particular living GMO (seeds, living fish for example) meant for release into the environment. Such advance permission is not required for exports of agricultural commodities meant for eating or processing, hence not released into the environment. After a crop has been approved for commercial use in one country, that country is obliged to send information about it to an Internet-based biosafety clearinghouse. Other countries are then free to decide whether or not they are willing to accept the imports. The aim is to ensure that recipient countries have both the opportunity and the capacity to assess risks involving the products of genetic modification. This may be viewed as an application of the precautionary principle allowing a state to take action to protect itself even if there is no scientific certainty that the (barred) import of a GMO would be dangerous. The Protocol does not apply to human pharmaceuticals.

Treaty Roles for Nongovernment Organizations

It is also possible that NGOs might be the wave of the future in dealing with some of these problems. NGOs have the capability to approach people on a one-on-one basis. Rather than dealing with problems from afar, NGO personnel are in the villages, on the farms, and in the forests, applying hands-on solutions. As a result, NGOs can accomplish many important things that governments have a difficult time doing. It is also worth noting that some international NGOs like IUCN (see Box 7-13) have annual budgets and a cadre of employee roles equal to the budgets and employee cadres of UNEP.

Box 7-13. The World Conservation Union (IUCN)

Following an international conference in Fontainebleau, France, the International Union for the Protection of Nature (IUPN) was founded on October 5, 1948 (W.M. Adams, 2001, p. 91). In 1956, the organization changed its name to the International Union for Conservation of Nature and Natural Resources (IUCN). In 1990, its name was shortened to IUCN—The World Conservation Union.

A recent example of an IUCN contribution to international environmental law is the Convention on Biological Diversity, one of the key products of UNCED in Rio de Janeiro in 1992. According to W.M. Adams (2001, p. 91), IUCN, in conjunction with other international organizations (including the WWF, UNEP, the World Resources Institute, and the World Bank), prepared a draft convention on biodiversity in the mid-1980s. Kiss and Shelton describe (2000, p. 103) IUCN in similar terms by stating that it "has played an essential role in the elaboration of some half dozen major international conventions relating to the conservation of nature and natural resources, including the 1968 African Convention, the 1973 Washington Convention on Trade in Endangered Species (CITES), and the 1979 Bonn Convention on Migratory Species."

Some 140 countries contribute members, including over 70 states, 100 government agencies, and more than 750 NGOs. Today IUCN has 1,000 staff members in offices located throughout the world working on some 500 projects. IUCN also has many volunteers, including more than 10,000 internationally recognized scientists and experts from more than 180 countries serving on its six global commissions. For example, some 800 members of the IUCN Commission on Environmental Law seek to advance environmental law both by developing new legal concepts and instruments and by building the capacity of societies to employ environmental law in support of the IUCN mission.

To respond to requests to build environmental law capacity in developing countries and economies in transition, in November 2003, the Commission on Environmental Law of IUCN launched a new scholarly network of environmental law faculties and professors: the IUCN Academy of Environmental Law, a consortium of specialized research centers in university law faculties throughout the world.

See <http://www.iucn.org/themes/law/>

SOME EARLY CONTRIBUTIONS TO ENVIRONMENTAL LAW AND SUSTAINABLE DEVELOPMENT BY LAWYERS, SCHOLARS, AND JUDGES

Thomas Jefferson, a very capable lawyer known for his contributions to the US Declaration of Independence, summarized the concept of sustainable development in eight words (Talbot Page, 1997, p. 580): "The earth belongs in usufruct to the living." In layman's terms, "usufruct" means "you may use the fruit." There is, of course, a more precise definition of "usufruct" (a word used by the Romans more than 2,000 years ago). In Black's Law Dictionary (1999, p. 1542), it is defined as the "right to use another's property for a time without damaging or diminishing it, although the property might naturally deteriorate over time."

Adam Smith, a contemporary of Jefferson, noted the importance of the social dimensions of development in his book, *The Wealth of Nations*, published in 1776 (1976, p. 88):

> *But what improves the circumstances of the greater part can never be regarded as an inconveniency to the whole. No society can surely be flourishing and happy, of which the far greater part of the members are poor and miserable.*

Pacific Fur Seals Case

From the legal point of view, the concept of sustainable development began more than 100 years ago with the Behring Sea fur seals fisheries case, decided in international arbitration. According to Philippe Sands (2003, p. 306):

> *Indeed, the inherent features of the concept have been an aspect of international legal relations since at least 1893, when the United States asserted a right to protect Pacific fur seals, for the benefit of mankind, from wanton destruction, in opposition to the assertion by Great Britain that its nationals were entitled to exploit these resources for their own developmental purposes."* [footnote omitted]

First Treaty Reference to Sustainable Development Prior to Brundtland

According to Sands (2003, p. 307), the first formal treaty to refer to sustainable development was a 1985 ASEAN Agreement on the Conservation of Nature and Natural Resources. Two years later the Brundtland Commission Report (1987, Vol. I, p. 90), which helped bring together the fields of study in development and environment, gave us the leading definition of sustainable development: "development that meets the needs of the present without compromising the ability of future generations to meet their own needs."

Sands' review of the development of the concept of sustainable development in international agreements such as this 1985 ASEAN Agreement indicates (2003, p. 254) that:

> *[f]our recurring elements appear to compromise the legal elements of the concept of "sustainable development," as reflected in international agreements:*
> 1. *the need to preserve natural resources for the benefit of future generations (principle of intergenerational equity);*
> 2. *the aim of exploiting natural resources in a manner which is "sustainable," or "prudent," or "rational," or "wise or appropriate" (the principle of sustainable use);*
> 3. *the "equitable" use of natural resources, which implies that use by one state must take account of the needs of other states (the principle of equitable use, or intragenerational equity); and*
> 4. *the need to ensure that environmental considerations are integrated into economic and other development plans, programmes and projects, and that development needs are taken into account in applying environmental objectives (the principle of integration).*

Sands subsequently points out (2003, p. 266) that "[i]nternational law recognizes a principle (or concept) of sustainable development, which includes 'the acceptance, on environmental protection grounds, of limits placed upon the use and exploitation of natural resources,' as reflected in international agreements."

Ethics and Environmental Law

In his article on "The 'Ascent of Man': Legal Systems and the Discovery of an Environmental Ethic," Nicholas Robinson (1998, reprinted 2003, Vol. I, p. 101), IUCN Legal Advisor and Chairman of the IUCN Commission on Environmental Law, begins by pointing out that ethics played a crucial role in the evolution of environmental law, which he traces from Ralph Waldo Emerson's "seminal essay, 'Nature,' [written] in 1836," through Aldo Leopold, Albert Schweitzer, and Rachel Carson in 1962. Robinson describes this evolution in part as follows (*ibid.*):

> Leopold would have us extend our human ethics that permit civilized behavior among people, to embrace the living systems of the land as a part of our community of interdependent parts. ... Albert Schweitzer had found the same truth in the tropical nature of Africa: "Ethics is nothing else than reverence for life." When we neglect this ethic and choose to destroy agricultural "pests" with pesticides that also widely kill or harm other life forms and impair the relationships which exist among these, we may well end up destroying our song birds, and more, and bringing cancers to ourselves as Rachel Carson described in Silent Spring.

Robinson continues (1998, reprinted 2003, Vol. I, p. 103) by describing how "laws...harmonize human conduct with...science...human health and ecological systems":

> Most of our environmental laws today seek to harmonize human conduct with what we have found science telling us about how best to sustain human health and ecological systems. We identify and contain externalities that our economic markets disregard. We seek to safeguard species threatened or endangered with extinction through the Endangered Species Act or the Convention on the International Trade in Endangered Species (CITES). ... We detect acid snow and rain, perceive how they interrupt the food chain and reproductive systems of biota, and in turn, seek to use the Clean Air Act to eliminate the precursors of water vapor pollution.

One of the most recent contributions to ethics and environmental law is the Earth Charter, which is described on its website (see <http://www.earthcharter.org/>) as "an authoritative synthesis of values, principles, and aspirations that are widely shared by growing numbers of men and women in all regions of the world." The Earth Charter was formulated by the "Earth

Charter Commission, which began work in early 1997 to oversee consultations and drafting processes and to approve a final version of the Charter, which was released in March 2000, following a Commission meeting in Paris at the UNESCO headquarters."

Johannesburg Principles on the Role of Law and Sustainable Development

On August 20, 2002, judges representing 59 countries at the Global Judges Symposium on Sustainable Development and the Role of Law adopted the Johannesburg Principles on the Role of Law and Sustainable Development. The second page of the Principles emphasizes (2002, p. 12) the concept of sustainable development, including reducing poverty, for the present and succeeding generations:

> We emphasize that the fragile state of the global environment requires the Judiciary as the guardian of the Rule of Law, to boldly and fearlessly implement and enforce applicable international and national laws, which in the field of environment and sustainable development will assist in alleviating poverty and sustaining an enduring civilization, and ensuring that the present generation will enjoy and improve the quality of life of all peoples, while also ensuring that the inherent rights and interests of succeeding generations are not compromised.

Accordingly, these judges agreed with the third page of the Principles on the need for guidance for the judiciary, including "full commitment to contributing towards the realization of the goals of sustainable development through the judicial mandate to implement, develop and enforce the law, and to uphold the Rule of Law and the democratic process." The agreed upon program of work, included on page 14, calls for "strengthening of environmental law education in schools and universities, including research and analysis as essential to realizing sustainable development" as well as the "achievement of sustained improvement in compliance with and enforcement and development of environmental law."

CONCLUSION

The roots of environmental legislation, international law, MEAs, and sustainable development reach back into ancient times. Some might even suggest that the notion that we can stop our neighbor from polluting our backyard comes from such philosophers as Confucius, who in his lifetime from 551 to 479 B.C. wrote: "What you do not want done to yourself, do not do to others." (*Bartlett's*, 2002, p. 62.)

Just as ethics has played a key role in the modern development of sustainable development, so have Greek and Roman law. In about 347 B. C., Plato formulated a law concerning water pollution, as described in Box 7-14.

Box 7-14. Plato on Water Pollution Law in about 347 B.C.

And let this be the law:--If any one intentionally pollutes the water of another, whether the water of a spring, or collected in reservoirs, either by poisonous substances, or by digging, or by theft, let the injured party bring the cause before the wardens of the city, and claim in writing the value of the loss; if the accused be found guilty of injuring the water by deleterious substances, let him not only pay damages, but purify the stream or the cistern which contains the water, in such manner as the laws...order the purification to be made by the offender in each case. (Plato, 1982, p. 740)

Box 7-15. Criticism of International Law

In a classic article dealing with such questions as "whether there is such a thing as international law" and "how efficient is international law?" John H.E. Fried (1998, edited by Ku and Diehl, pp. 25, 26, 29, 32, 42, 45) lists under four headings some criticisms of international law:

1)*"International law is so weak and defenseless...that only dreamers would put any reliance on it."* 2) *"International law is so vague ... that, with some juggling and legalistic gymnastics it can be made to serve virtually every policy."* 3) *"... Its basic weakness is the absence ... of a reliable, powerful, impartial enforcement machinery. ..."* 4) *"International law is unfortunately still in its infancy. ... [n]ot too much reliance can unfortunately be bestowed on international law. ..."*

In response, Fried replies in part that an international law expert like "Leo Gross has pointed out, not only that ' states by and large obey international law' but that this fact of fairly general obedience 'is commonly accepted' [footnote omitted.]" Fried continues by quoting another expert, who describes the general applicability of the problem of enforcement:

The enforcement of law is a troublesome matter. Even in well developed countries like the United States the number of thefts that go unpunished, or the breaches of contract that bring no recompense to the wronged parties, make shocking figures.

Concerning enforcement difficulties, Fried also points out that international law confronts the same problem as constitutional law:

Much of the constitutional law of individual countries wrestles with the same problem as does much of international law: viz., how to regulate the behavior of large collectives. ... Whereas the reliability of the policeman's arresting the thief is so often held up as a reproach to international law, the actual frailty and frequent unenforceability of the highest level of domestic law, namely, constitutional law, is hardly ever mentioned in this connection.

Fried concludes in part by arguing "a remarkable superiority of international over domestic law":

...the basic tenets of international law are more stable and reliable, more resilient and less destructible than are the allegedly firm, but actually often fragile, basic laws of constitutions of nations.

One of the strongest international law foundations for sustainable development is the UN Framework Convention on Climate Change, a multilateral environmental agreement ratified by an overwhelming majority of the planet's countries, which incorporates the phrase "sustainable development," effectively giving that phrase legal sanctity throughout the world. Though some might suggest that international law is weak, vague, unreliable, and still in its infancy, as described in Box 7-15, such international treaties are part of the "supreme Law of the Land" as specified in the US Constitution and have similar status in the constitutions of most other countries.

Kiss suggests (2003, p. 9) that "sustainable development should be considered as a concept," with the content for this concept provided for in the following duty and six basic principles of the Declaration of the International Law Association during its conference in New Delhi in April 2002. These are the principles of international law in the field of sustainable development that "have been proposed to establish its concrete content":

1. The duty of the States to ensure sustainable use of natural resources.
2. The principle of equity and the eradication of poverty.
3. The principle of common but differentiated responsibilities.
4. The principle of the precautionary approach to fields such as health, natural resources and ecosystems.
5. The principle of public participation and access to information and justice.
6. The principle of good governance.
7. The principle of integration and interrelationship, in particular in relation to human rights and social, economic and environmental objectives.

As Kiss points out, these principles must be implemented through policies dealing with such matters as land-use planning, energy, soil protection, education, and capacity building. Kiss further points out (2003, pp. 14-15) that implementation of each such policy involves legal measures, good institutions, and good norms, and that among these legal measures are international conventions, constitutional provisions, statutes providing basic services such as water, statutes protecting the environment, relevant regulations, and judicial decisions.

To achieve all of this, much will need to be done, particularly with respect to awareness raising, education, training, and capacity building. From the legal perspective, each person will need to contribute both individually and through participation with others to the formulation of sustainable development policies, and then to the conversion of these policies into enforceable laws. Significant support will likely be required for such international organizations as UNEP, for development banks, for governments, and for schools and universities. The lack of support for such basic institutions as judicial academies and law schools as well as insufficient salaries for judges constitute two of the leading problems in the worldwide effort to achieve sustainable development.

CHAPTER 8

SOCIAL DIMENSIONS AND POLICIES

The social dimension is sometimes referred to as the third dimension of sustainable development (the others being the economic and environmental dimensions).[1] The world's GDP has been growing at a robust rate. In Asia, GDP trebled from 1975 to 2000. Even South Asia, which is the poorest part of the region, doubled its GDP growth within the same period. However, despite a healthy growth rate in GDP, one in every five persons in this world, including a significant majority of women and girls, is living below the poverty line (income of less than $1 per day) and one of every two lives on less than $2 per day. As a consequence, the third dimension of sustainable development, the social dimension, gained prominence in the late 1980s. It was also because people became aware of the fact that they should be able to participate in the developmental decisions made on their behalf either by the government or by some external agency (Box 8-1).

Box 8-1. Cake of Culture

The social domain—society—is best understood as a complex set of interacting cultural and institutional systems that vary from one place to another. All have bodies of knowledge for adapting to the physical environment; modes of producing and exchanging goods and services; systems for finding partners, raising children, and inheriting property; arrangements for public decision making and conflict management; bodies of belief and related rituals; and systems of prestige or ranking, and aesthetics. From the outside the complexity and dynamism of these interacting systems are mind boggling. Viewed from the inside by the people who constitute a society, they fit together in a sensible and seamless way, and individuals' attitudes and behaviors reflect the values and pressures that they have internalized while growing up. This holds true whether people live as hunters and gatherers, nomads, agriculturalists, or in complex urban centers, and it applies equally under socialist or capitalist regimes. Social development is about helping people, whatever their circumstances, to overcome poverty by learning new skills, securing access to legal and other rights, developing new ways of organizing and managing their societies, and exercising responsibility for continuing change processes.

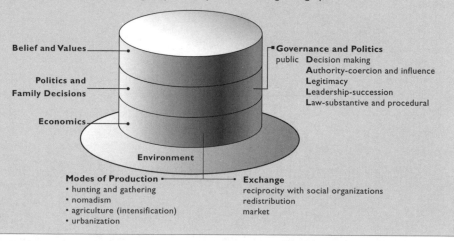

Source: Based on a lecture by Jay Palmore

[1] The authors thank Anne Sweetser and Eugenia McGill for their insightful contributions to this chapter.

This chapter discusses ten social dimensions of sustainable development:

- poverty reduction
- participatory development
- consensus building
- nongovernment organizations
- gender and development
- involuntary resettlement
- indigenous peoples
- social exclusion
- social analysis
- social development indicators

ERADICATION OF POVERTY

Poverty is the most significant socioeconomic dimension of sustainable development. The most obvious aspect of poverty is physical: hunger, disease, long hours of work, unhealthy work environments, substandard housing, the lack of basic necessities, and inadequate income. However, there is a legal aspect: of all people, the poor have the greatest difficulty in claiming rights to services and accessing justice. There is also an emotional aspect of poverty: the humiliation of dependency, powerlessness, and shame because of social exclusion. Finally, for the poor, there is a moral issue as well: having to make painful decisions based upon budgetary constraints: Should limited funds be devoted to buying more food, sending the children to school, or attending to the medical needs of a family member who is critically ill? Because the poor have limited choices, they are often targets for unscrupulous merchants. In the City of Manila in the Philippines, poor people have no option but to buy their water from street venders, to whom they pay on average three times the price that middle- and upper-class households do to buy piped water from the water authorities.

Poverty, as defined by UNDP, takes into consideration the lack of essential human capabilities, notably literacy and nutrition. UNDP also created a human poverty index, which is basically a measure of deprivation and basic human development determined by three factors: the percentage of people who are expected to die by the age of 40; the percentage of adults who are illiterate; and the overall economic provisioning, which is the GDP per capita.

World Bank Study

If poverty is so painful, why is it not being addressed? To get an answer to this question, the World Bank financed a major study in 1999 called "Consultations with the Poor," featuring 81 participatory exercises. Some 60,000 poor men and women from 50 developing countries were asked what they thought about their plight. The study concluded that keys to overcoming poverty are security (from violence as well as hunger and physical deprivation), opportunity (to enjoy good health, go to school, and obtain decent work), and empowerment (for engaging in both personal and public decision making). The World Development Report 2001 (World Bank, 2001), which was based on this study, drew five major conclusions about poverty.

1. Poverty is multidimensional.

Six elements feature prominently in how the poor define poverty. First is lack of income and assets. Second is hunger and lack of food. Third is lack of access to basic infrastructure such as shelter, clean water, energy, and transportation. Fourth is lack of access to education, which the poor cannot afford, though it is crucial, and is their only escape from the cycle of poverty. Fifth is poor health and illness, which are also indicators of poverty. Sixth is social exclusion, whereby the poor see themselves as voiceless and not a part of the society making decisions.

2. The state has been largely ineffective in reaching the poor.

It is generally recognized that national, regional, and local governments need to reach out to the poor. However, the respondents felt that their lives remained unchanged due to government interventions or lack thereof. The poor report extensive government corruption in those areas that most affect their lives: health services, education, relief assistance, and employment.

To be fair, the poor admit that there are some state officials and politicians who are good, honest, and incorruptible; but they also say that the number is so small that they cannot make any significant changes in their lives.

The poor also report that law enforcement agencies are more brutal and corrupt in their neighborhoods than elsewhere, and feel safer without such agencies in their communities. They further feel that gender discrimination is prevalent, despite official slogans about gender equality.

3. The poor have mixed impressions about the efficacy of NGOs.

Many poor people feel that the role of NGOs in their lives is limited. Although they complain to a much lesser extent about NGOs than the state, they report that NGOs in many instances are self-serving, corrupt, poor listeners, and largely irrelevant to their communities. So in another example of resilience, the poor rely more on informal trust-based networks within their communities, or with similar outside groups with access to power—than on either NGOs or the government.

4. Many households are disintegrating.

This happens when men fail to earn enough to feed their families, due either to ill health or to harsh economic conditions. Women, on the other hand, may take any job, no matter how demeaning, dangerous, or illegal, as long as it puts food on the table. Hopelessness, shame, and degradation in the quality of life are known to be the prime correlates of alcoholism and domestic violence among the poor. This is especially true in some societies where women are compelled to become the sole wage earners, further undercutting men's self-esteem. That women are capable breadwinners in a modern economy as well as in many traditional societies can be gleaned from the figures presented by the microfinance banks. Ninety-four percent of the clients at the Grameen Bank are women taking out loans to start up and later expand home- or village-based cottage industries.

5. The social fabric in poor communities is unraveling.

The pressures of poverty gnaw at the family structure and eventually corrode its integrity. From the perspective of the poor, given the failure of both the government and NGOs to improve their condition, their only insurance is their dependence on each other. But with perpetuating poverty and a sense of hopelessness, even these bonds of trust and reciprocity—the heart of social capital—are strained or disappearing.

ADB Study

Just about the same time as the World Bank published its findings, ADB published a report entitled "Reducing Poverty: Major Findings and Implications" (Asian Development Bank, 1999). While the World Bank study covered 50 countries and was limited to interviewing only the poor, the ADB study restricted itself to just 10 countries and involved not only the poor but also other stakeholders, including NGOs, other civil society groups (such as universities, business foundations, professional associations, labor unions, and religious organizations), the government, and the financial institutions that are trying to reduce poverty.

The purpose of the ADB study was different. It was trying to determine the major issues surrounding poverty and to create a plan of action with its stakeholders that would reduce poverty. ADB also redefined poverty as the amount of money that a person needs to meet minimum consumption requirements.

The ADB study tried to build a framework for poverty reduction entailing three factors: economic growth, population growth, and distributional effectiveness. The latter is to be determined by the percentage of GDP growth that is devoted to government projects designed to create employment and assets in overpopulated, underdeveloped, poverty-stricken areas. In relation to each of these three factors, there are three sets of criteria that need to be defined for poverty reduction: the policy environment, institutional factors, and the program focus (Table 8-1). The following section presents general criteria and guidelines for reducing poverty through economic growth, distributional effectiveness, and population growth.

Economic Growth

1. Policy environment

Growth must be stimulated in poverty-stricken areas through the allocation of resources. Economic growth must be market friendly, generally demand-driven and not supply-driven; but since poverty is often locality-specific, economic growth to reduce poverty can depend on such supply-side services as access to information, training, and education, plus access to health services, land, credit, and an effective judicial system.

Table 8-1. Elements of a Poverty Reduction Strategy

POLICY ENVIRONMENT	INSTITUTIONAL FACTORS	PROGRAM FOCUS
A. Economic Growth		
• Market friendly • Sound fiscal policies • Unsound public enterprises divested • Inflation-controlled • Sound use of subsidies • Sound labor market • Environmental sustainability • Limited government borrowing	• Free of political distortions • Efficient • Accountable • Eliminate corruption • Performance-rewarding • Demand-based • Transparent	• Financial sector stability • Established capital market • Stable government policies • Essential infrastructure
B. Distributional Effectiveness		

• Labor-intensive growth
• Universal education
• Pro-poor government subsidies
• Effective, broad-based tax collection
• Needs-based resource allocation
• Efficient/equitable social safety nets
• Minimum labor standards in place
• Land tenancy titling reform
• Accessible courts
	• Effective participation of poorer communities
	• Effective participation of women
	• Effective participatory planning
	• Minimum political distortion
	• Accessible labor markets
	• Mobile labor force
	• Client-focused government agencies
	• Program transparency/accountability
	• Pro-poor judicial system
	• Social capital strengthened
		• Targeted programs for:
		  –impoverished areas/sectors
		  –empowered ethnic groups
		  –women
		• Basic health care
		• Basic education
		• Basic infrastructure

C. Population Growth		
• Reproductive health access for men and women • Universal education for girls	• Gender-sensitive institutions/staff • Effective mother/child health centers • Significant number of female teachers/health workers	• Targeted economic growth in areas of high population growth • Female education and empowerment

Source: ADB (1999)

222

Sound fiscal management is one of the criteria for a good policy environment that will reduce poverty. Nonfunctioning public enterprises, on the other hand, are counterproductive and should be eliminated or turned over to the private sector. Many public enterprises in developing countries simply do not work. For example, in India, the sugar industry and public sector/government-run manufacturing plants would be more effective if they were turned over to the private sector.

The use of subsidies has become a controversial issue, but the sound use of subsidies can be a means of reducing poverty, if the subsidies benefit primarily the poor and not the rich. Subsidizing large farms can undercut farmers with small plots and have a negative effect on poverty reduction. However, in some instances, a subsidy can be effective in helping the poor. For example, the water rates in many cities are based on a step-by-step approach. The price of the first few cubic meters of water consumed is low; then the tariff increases as consumption increases. The minimum subsidized rate fulfills the basic needs of the poor.

Effective public investment is another means of reducing poverty. The word "effective" here means that public investment will be designed to serve the purposes of the poor and that it is not driven primarily by inappropriate, short-term political maneuvers to buy votes.

Environmental sustainability is a significant factor under policy environment. It means, among other things, stopping illegal logging and upstream pollution, and careful management of common property resources.

2. Institutional factors

In discussing poverty reduction, economic growth decisions should be free from political manipulation. Project proponents should be efficient and accountable. The government must promote transparency and work to eliminate corruption of all kinds and at all levels. Finally, economic growth should be demand-based and reward performance by providing incentives to do well.

3. Program focus

Economic growth should be based on sustainable development principles, meaning that any project or program implemented must be equitable, economically viable, environmentally sound, and socially inclusive. Program focus should also consider basic infrastructure, stability of the financial sector, and national development programs. These should be designed for the majority of the people, preferably following priorities they have articulated, not for a small, influential group that wants a project in its area.

Financial sector stability is important because it influences the global economy. The financial meltdown in Asia in 1997-1998 affected not only the economies of that region but also the economies of the entire world.

Distributional Effectiveness

Economic growth is not a sufficient condition for poverty reduction. Equitable distribution of economic growth, or at least more equitably than we have seen, can be equally important. Therefore, we have to look at distributional effectiveness, and here there are different concerns under policy environment, institutional factors, and program focus. These are overlapping, because, after all, economic growth also has to take into account basic needs.

1. Policy environment

The policy environment that would distribute income better would include labor-intensive growth and minimum labor standards in terms of minimum wage, health, and occupational safety. Universal education is an important ingredient under policy environment in promoting better distribution. It is like the parable of the fish and the fishing net: Give someone a fish and he or she will be hungry again the next day. Give him or her a net, and he or she may never be hungry again. Give the poor an education and appropriate job training and they will be able to develop marketable skills.

Pro-poor government subsidies; needs-based resource allocation, financial and human; and efficient and equitable social safety nets are all essential elements of reducing poverty through better distribution of income. Some suitable subsidies would be social protection funds, food coupons, a subsidized health-care system, and subsidized housing for the people in abject poverty.

Land tenancy is important and should be available to both men and women, with husbands' and wives' names listed on deeds. The goal of joint titling is broad: to ensure that both husband and wife consent to any sale or mortgaging of their land; if the husband migrates for work, the wife will be a recognized owner of the property in the event of a land dispute; if the husband divorces the wife, she has a legal claim to the land; and if the husband predeceases the wife, she will not be dispossessed by other relatives. The deed to land tenancy inspires responsibility for a resource. Without it, the poor, in many cases, inadvertently degrade the environment, thus contributing to the perpetuation of a vicious cycle of poverty: A degraded environment causes poverty, and poverty causes a degraded environment.

Accessible courts are important. In many cases—whether involving environmental degradation, injustice, or violence—there may be laws in the country to address the problem. But as much as the poor wish to apply a law or enforce a regulation, they cannot, because they lack access to either the law, the legal framework, or the courts. It is often beyond the capacity of poor people, particularly women, to take a case to court. Even if they do, and they win, it is almost impossible for them to enforce the judgment.

Many governments are not client-focused. Yet poverty reduction requires client-focused government agencies. Program transparency, ongoing capacity development, a pro-poor judicial system linked with accessible courts, support for networks of association or social capital, and social strengthening all fall under the policy environment.

2. Institutional factors

Effective participation of poorer communities is important for distributional effectiveness, an improvement in the participation of women, and minimum political distortion.

Well managed decentralization—creation of opportunities for local and regional governments to take increasingly more responsibility for planning and implementing development activities and devolution or allocation of responsibility for managing the resources involved—may contribute to capacity development throughout a society. However, there is a risk that local elites may "capture" the devolved responsibilities and resources.

Transportation is also a relevant institutional factor. A mobile labor force is important, because often the poor cannot reach employment even when it is available and cannot get their products to market even though markets exist and poor citizens have knowledge of these.

3. Program focus

Better distribution of income means targeted programs for impoverished areas, sectors, and groups. Such program focus should be on basic health care and education, water supply and sanitation, and basic infrastructure.

Population Growth

1. Policy environment

There should be access to reproductive health care for both men and women; to primary and secondary education, particularly for girls; and to effective family and population planning. In fact, many Asian countries have population policies and programs, and there has been remarkable progress in expanding access to contraceptives and lowering fertility rates over the past 30 years, even in rural areas. Attitudes are also changing.

2. Institutional factors

Institutional factors include gender-sensitive institutions. What is the percentage of women who hold government jobs? Even though some women in Asia are holding positions of political leadership, the percentage of females staffing government positions, particularly high level ones, in proportion to the total female population, is still very low. Attention might be given to the roots of limited public roles for women in age- and gender-governed patterns of decision making and control of resources within households and in communities.

3. Program Focus

In areas with high population, targeted economic growth should stress education and empowerment of women as program goals.

Reducing Poverty: Practical Means

The first of the eight MDGs is to reduce by half the proportion of people earning less than $1 per day by 2015 and by half the proportion of people suffering from hunger, also by 2015. To achieve this first goal, countries and communities must set their policy environment, institutions, and program focus along the lines just described under economic growth, population planning, and better distribution of income.

ADB has suggested some generic guidelines for poverty reduction: invest in social infrastructure, health, education, water supply, and sanitation; establish special programs like microfinance savings and lending to reduce the dependence of the poor on the natural resource base; and improve the physical linkages between rural communities and market centers so that the poor can get a fair price for their goods. Too often the poor are forced to sell to entrepreneurs who do little more than transport goods that they then sell at steep markups. Good roads and inexpensive public transportation would eliminate price distortions introduced by these people.

Enhancing accessibility to modern agricultural inputs is one way of reducing poverty. Although governments are distributing high-quality seeds, fertilizers, and pesticides, or introducing organic methods and building irrigation canals, the beneficiaries are usually the large farmers, who, because of their wealth and influence, have access to the government and therefore can capture or control these inputs. Even worse, is the fact that rich farmers have access to government information, so they know what future inputs the government will provide and where. They then convince the small farmers to sell their land at a low price before the modern inputs are introduced.

Promotion of good local governance can reduce poverty. One of the findings of the ADB study on poverty reduction is that often decentralization of authority and resources, in the absence of good local governance, increases poverty. Decentralization is not a panacea for solving the problem of poverty, unless the capacity of people in the local and regional governments to manage and implement a pro-poor policy in an honest manner is developed.

Enhanced international financing for poverty reduction is another key element. It is possible to augment the financial resources available to developing countries through fair international trade, attracting private sector investment in key sectors, and increased overseas development assistance (ODA) flow. Total ODA has increased in the last several years, mainly as a result of the large commitments of funds to fight HIV/AIDS. Several G-7 members have recently committed to substantially increase their ODA levels over the next 10 years. A pilot project of the International Finance Facility for Immunizations and other financing proposals are described in the latest IMF/World Bank reports to the Development Committee (see the World Bank website—list of documents from spring 2005 meetings).

Unless innovative ways of augmenting the available financing for poverty reduction are found, it will be very difficult to reduce poverty just by population control, economic growth, and distributional effectiveness. There must be income before it can be distributed. International collaboration on financing poverty reduction in the developing countries is essèntial. Several international fora have discussed the issue of financing sustainable development by way of raising "Tobin Tax," "bit tax," etc. and reducing military expenditure. However, so far, no significant progress has been made. This issue also did not make much headway at the WSSD in 2002.

Poor People Classified According to Settlement Areas

There is no single measure to reduce poverty. The task is a multistep process. First, we have to identify who the poor are and determine their aspirations and needs. Only then is it possible to design a program to reduce poverty. Depending upon the settlement area, four categories of poor people are described below. For each of the categories, projects should be designed to respond to people's actual needs, focusing on at least three specific issues: (i) a holistic view of resource management, incorporating gender equity, improving management skills, developing institutional capacity, and disseminating information; (ii) development and transfer of appropriate technology; and (iii) building on indigenous knowledge in the fields of low-cost urban water supply and sanitation, water management, sustainable pest management, mangrove management, composting, and clean rural industry.

I. Poor people who are dependent on fragile land

Today many regions of the world are affected by desertification, and other areas are heading in that direction. The PRC, Mongolia, Spain, and Sub-Saharan Africa are just some examples. People living on arid land need good common-property managers who can introduce irrigation systems that nurture crops and conserve water. In drip irrigation, for example, water is introduced into the fields through a perforated pipe whose holes exactly match up with each plant. This way water is not spread everywhere but delivered just to the root system.

Sand dune stabilization is another important need for dry communities. Some of the deserts in India have been planted with a fast-growing shrub species imported from Israel that prevents the dunes from moving into the irrigated fields.

There is need for rodent control and special grazing techniques in desert areas. Goats, for instance, when left unchecked, can destroy an entire field down to the root system.

2. Poor people who live in areas with good agricultural potential

Even in the areas with good precipitation, there are poor people because they do not have access to modern farming techniques and so eventually become tenants on large farms. The needs of such people often include water resource control technology and access to high-yielding seeds, fertilizers, and pesticides. There is also need for land redistribution through agrarian reform, which is a difficult and sensitive issue in most developing countries.

3. Poor people who live in urban areas

The needs of the poor who live in cities are environmental health and sanitation, shelter, safe drinking water, and enhanced livelihood possibilities.

4. Poor people who live in coastal areas

A single natural disaster in a coastal area such as a typhoon or tsunami (tidal wave) can kill several hundred thousand people, as in Bangladesh (1970), Sri Lanka (2004), Indonesia (2004/2005), and Thailand, Maldives, and India (2005). The basic needs, therefore, are protecting the mangrove forests (nature's first line of defense against tsunamis), creating early warning systems, building cyclone shelters, and improving sustainable fishing mechanisms and skills—all in the interest of achieving sustained livelihood for people living in coastal belts.

Overcoming Structural Barriers

For each of the above groups of poor people, projects should be designed to respond to specific needs and aspirations to reduce poverty. Economic growth is a necessary (but not sufficient) condition for reducing poverty. According to an estimate made by UNDP (2003), if income distribution is held constant at the present value, the poverty rate will decline by 2% for every 1% increase in income per capita. At this elasticity of 2, if poverty is to be halved between 1990 and 2015, a constant GDP growth rate of 2.9% will be needed during the period. Such a growth rate is quite achievable in developing countries, assuming that reasonably favorable conditions (e.g., law and order situation, pro-poor growth policy) prevail. In fact, many countries have attained higher rates than such growth which are the minimum required to attain the goal of poverty reduction in accordance with the MDG. This is a hopeful and positive indication that the world may be able to achieve and may even exceed the target by the year 2015 to reduce the 1990 poverty level by half.

PARTICIPATORY DEVELOPMENT

The second social dimension of sustainable development is participatory development—the process through which stakeholders influence or share control over development initiatives, decisions, resources, and outcomes. In the absence of political will and public awareness, it is difficult to implement participatory development in a country or a region.

Benefits of Participation

Participation enhances sustainability. If a project is designed in consultation with the stakeholders, there is a better chance it will be sustained. When people are involved in making decisions, such as planning a water supply system, they develop a sense of (psychological) ownership of the endeavor and feel motivated to sustain it. This is especially true if they are empowered to monitor and manage the system and can obtain appropriate support when needed. It is also important that there be a clear understanding of who makes the capital investment, who will pay for the project's operation and maintenance, and what rights and responsibilities the beneficiaries have. Though additional time is required at the front end for the consultation or more engaged participatory process, implementation is usually smoother because there is shared understanding and agreement on steps to be undertaken to achieve certain goals. When a project is started without consultation, delays due to subsequent public protest are not uncommon. Development finance institutions (DFIs) such as the World Bank and ADB have witnessed many projects that had to be totally abandoned because of NGO protests or difficulties encountered by the stakeholders (ADB, 2003).

Participatory development is demand responsive rather than supply responsive. It strengthens local ownership and the commitment of the people consulted. It also makes cost sharing easier. In many developing countries, people believe that if the government initiates a project it will also maintain the infrastructure. They feel that if a government-built pump breaks down, the government should supply the parts and repair it. That is because there was little preplanning at the start of the project, and therefore there is little sense of ownership or shared responsibility among the beneficiaries of the project. Participatory development also enhances social capital by bringing groups together, and both technical and management capacity of people is enhanced through experiential learning. As a power group, a farmers' cooperative can help the entire community get the modern agricultural inputs it needs.

Critics are quick to cite the "risks" of participation. They point out that it is (or rather can be) time and resource consuming, and logistically and organizationally troublesome. In the process of participation, some groups may not be represented, conflicts may be aggravated, and expectations may be raised. Careful planning of the participatory process based on stakeholder capacity, and context analysis can minimize these problems. Critics should realize that the gains far outweigh the "risks" when managed in this manner.

Conflicts may be aggravated by participation, but skilled facilitators can employ conflict management techniques to address these. For example, holding a series of workshops with individual stakeholder groups prior to a large consultation meeting may avert misunderstanding by disseminating information and helping participants to clarify their concerns and preferences and prepare to discuss their differences more constructively. Project proponents must be scrupulously honest about realistic expectations to avoid implying excessive benefits. To do otherwise is unfair to people and contributes to project delays and other serious problems.

Categories of Stakeholders

There are four categories of stakeholders in development. Their roles vary according to the demands of a project. For example, the central government might be crucial at the beginning, as well as citizens and local NGOs who can assume great importance as planning of a project begins in a given locality.

- The primary stakeholders are those expected to benefit directly from the project. Included are the poor, women, indigenous peoples, and vulnerable groups such as the elderly and disabled.
- The secondary stakeholders are those with expertise, public interest, and/or linkages to the primary stakeholders. These are the NGOs, intermediary organizations of government, civil society, the private sector, and technical and professional bodies that are indirectly affected by the project.
- The third group of stakeholders consists of the governments or private sectors raising/ borrowing money to finance that project.
- The fourth category is the lender—the financial stakeholder such as the World Bank, ADB, government or a private bank. Private investors have become active in developing countries, particularly in soft sectors such as water supply and agriculture. Private investment is expanding in both sectors (e.g., subcontracting of urban water and sanitation management to private companies; commercial food processors contracting with farmer cooperatives). They are also interested in building infrastructure in middle- to high-income countries, where the risk is lower.

Facilitating Stakeholder Participation

There are four mechanisms to facilitate participation among stakeholders. These form a continuum from shallow to deep engagement among stakeholders. Facilitators employ a range of methods or tools suitable to specific stakeholder groups. Some organizations include consensus building as a middle step in this list of participatory mechanisms.

1. Information sharing

This is generally a one-way flow of information. Either citizens share information by responding to questionnaires or a project proponent, whether government or the private sector, reveals its plan to the affected people at an early stage. If necessary, the information is translated into the local language, but then there is the problem of low literacy rates. A case in point is India, where there are many regional and local languages, and most of the primary stakeholders do not speak English, in which the original proposal was most likely made. Once the plan is translated into the vernacular, one can disseminate written materials, post signs, conduct seminars, make presentations, and hold public meetings regarding the project. Information campaigns using mainstream media, as on Severe Acute Respiratory Syndrome (SARS), good nutrition, or sanitation, are other examples.

2. Consultation

Consultation is a limited two-way flow of information comprising meetings with the stakeholders, making field visits, conducting interviews at various stages of work, and listening to the stakeholders regarding their aspirations and needs. "Experts" analyze the information they gather and then make decisions, so little authority is shared with the public. They may think that it would be unnecessary to share results with stakeholders who took part in planning an activity. Overreliance on poorly planned consultations have left many feeling frustrated that their views are not heard or taken into consideration. This is known as "consultation fatigue."

3. Collaborative decision making

In collaborative decision making, some power to influence the process and outcome is shared between outsiders and local stakeholders. The issues and questions that are raised may include topics that external experts consider to be relatively unimportant but that matter to local citizens. One method that has been employed by ADB and others to facilitate collaboration is the "write shop" approach. Stakeholders from government and NGOs have worked together with some ADB staff members for one week to draft and redraft the text of ADB's NGO strategy. Other examples include participatory planning exercises with representatives of local and district governments and civil society organizations as project implementation starts in their area.

4. Facilitating empowerment

The fourth and deepest mechanism promoting participation is facilitating empowerment. Empowerment has a variety of meanings. It may refer to an individual gaining a sense of "agency," a sense that he or she is capable of taking action to bring about change in his or her own life or community. For Nobel economist Amartya Sen, this is the essence of development. Empowerment also refers to devolution of authority to citizens or to local organizations. In Bangalore, India, and the Philippines, citizens have had the opportunity to rank various government agencies on a "report card." The results have motivated some agencies to strive much harder to provide adequate services. In many countries, authority (over both decisions and resources) has been devolved to those directly responsible in regional and local government. As stated earlier, decentralization in the absence of good local governance can be counterproductive. Delegation of authority for decision making often requires capacity building among stakeholders.

A key to sustained results, capacity development involves not only transfer of job-related knowledge but experience-based learning about management to implement new skills effectively within changing organizations. When those who will receive training are asked to analyze through a participatory process the structure and function of their organizations and identify necessary changes and the additional skills required to implement them, their motivation is great, and learning is maximized. This should be financed as an integral part of the project.

In addition to self-help initiatives, participatory monitoring is key to empowering communities or members of organizations to manage their own development. For example, prior to releasing funds for building a water system, a project could require that a neighborhood prepare a plan for monitoring it. This would involve selection of a number of indicators of success they hope to achieve and delineation of the roles and responsibilities of members of a committee that will conduct inspections on a certain schedule, meet periodically to review progress, and call public meetings to discuss issues that arise. Within any organization a similar exercise could be undertaken, with members identifying new behaviors they must adopt to accomplish particular goals and planning periodic reviews of their compliance.

Empowerment also means strengthening the financial and legal status of stakeholder organizations and transferring responsibility for project maintenance and management to them. The capital cost is borne by the project proponent, but the proponent must inform the stakeholders what it is going to cost them in maintenance and management once they assume responsibility for the project. The stakeholders must also understand that they are the only group that can properly maintain and manage the project, since it involves their livelihood and the quality of their lives.

Consensus Building

Conflict can emerge at any time. If there are conflicting views between two or more groups, the process has to move on to a consensus-building phase.

Consensus building is defined as the process of seeking unanimous agreement of a group of stakeholders, with the goal of meeting the interests of all. When there is a conflict, it is probably impossible to reach a 100% satisfaction level, but it should be possible to find some middle ground that the various conflicting groups can live with.

Consensus building has its own vocabulary. The *convener* is the person who organizes the meeting, knows all the stakeholders, and is accepted by all of them. The *assessor* is the person who is given all the relevant documents and makes an assessment of what the conflict is all about, who are involved, and what is the view of each of the parties. The *facilitator* conducts the consensus-building meeting. The *assessor* is independent of the facilitator and has the job of reviewing the documents. The *recorder* functions as a secretary, not only taking notes but also setting the agenda and ground rules and evaluating computer-based communication options. The job of a *mediator* is to sit with groups of participants holding differing views and to try to narrow down the gaps in their viewpoints. Conflict resolution is usually a long-term process carried out in five steps as follows:

1. Convening

A discussion of whether or not to have a consensus-building dialogue is initiated. It might be that there is no point in having such a dialogue, because the conflict is so acute that a review of the case would only determine that a resolution cannot be reached. If it is determined that a discussion is warranted, a *convener* is appointed who is in a position to bring the stakeholders together and who is respected and considered neutral. Before a meeting is convened an independent *assessor* should be entrusted with the responsibility of preparing a conflict assessment document. There should be a contract between the *convener* of the discussion and the *assessor* for the conflict assessment document. The *assessor* must identify appropriate representatives of the conflicting parties and secure the necessary funding. Once the funding source(s) and the participants are identified, the *convener* will organize a meeting of all the parties, including the ones who are known as missing actors, meaning those who are not present.

2. Clarifying responsibilities

In the second step, the roles and the responsibilities of the *facilitator* and the *mediator* should be determined. During this phase an agenda and the ground rules for the consensus-building meeting should be established, and a list of participants and a computer-based communication system should be prepared.

3. Deliberation

At this stage, the actual deliberations are held for consensus building. It is necessary to pursue the debate in a constructive fashion, create subcommittees (if necessary and appropriate), and seek expert advice in order to produce a single written report. According to *The Consensus Building Handbook* (Susskind et al., 1999), it is vital to have one draft only, because it will be difficult to come to a consensus if there are several different drafts on the table. The single draft can always be modified. Another important task is to determine whether the conflict resolution will be public or held behind closed doors. If it is to be public, then there must be ground rules for observers. Will it be an open forum or can observers participate only at the request of the mediator? And while talking is important, listening is vital. If the participants listen only to themselves, consensus may well be difficult. Ad hominem arguments must be avoided. They rarely strengthen a position and will most likely be counterproductive. There is already a conflict, but if the disagreement involves personal rancor, consensus will not be reached. Participants must learn to disagree politely. If one wants to disagree, one should simply say: "I respect your opinion, but this is the way I feel and that is what I want to go into the record."

4. Decision

The fourth step is coming to a decision by trying to maximize joint gains and by keeping a record of whatever is decided. Once the decision is announced, especially if there is a lack of unanimity, the opponent(s) should be asked whether they can live with the outcome, rather than simply disagreeing. If they cannot, their views should be recorded.

5. Signing

Once an agreement has been reached, stakeholder ratification is sought by signing the document. The document should acknowledge that the outcome has been a joint decision and that it is going to be implemented and monitored. Ongoing evaluations will keep track of adherence and progress.

NONGOVERNMENT ORGANIZATIONS (NGOs)

The role of NGOs is the fourth social dimension of sustainable development. The term NGO refers to a nonprofit organization that is not based in government. In this respect, NGOs may be defined more by what they are not than by what they are.

While NGOs are supposedly nonprofit organizations (which means that after internal and external expenses are paid, no profit should be made), they still need money to operate. Many are self-financing. They collect funds from their members, governments, corporations, and individuals through fund-raising drives. Other NGOs receive funds from financial institutions such as ADB and the World Bank by way of assisting them in providing an enhanced quality of service to their clients. Some of the smaller NGOs in the south are funded by international NGOs in the north.

NGO Classification

NGOs are categorized based on their theme, nature of operations, or level of operation. Thematic NGOs deal with specific issues such as the environment, rural development, health, or women's empowerment. NGOs can also be classified on the basis of their operations such as advocacy, research, or training. The third possible classification might be based on their level of operation, i.e., they can be international, national, or local.

Role of NGOs

According to OECD, there are some 4,000 NGOs in developed countries investing $3 billion per year in activities that affect the lives of 100 million people (Coninck, 1995). As impressive as this number sounds, one must remember that there are 1.3 billion people in the world who are living in abject poverty (earning less than $1 per day). Because NGOs are sometimes seen to be acting in their own interest rather than primarily for the poor, the World Bank study revealed that the perception of many of the world's poor is that NGOs have not made a difference in their lives. Nevertheless, some credible, well-functioning NGOs have the potential for making significant contributions to the sustainable development of the world. Especially with close knowledge of local communities, NGOs can identify new approaches and create new models for specific developmental activities. Local knowledge also allows NGOs to guide development projects so that they are implemented in ways that respond to local needs. NGOs can also serve as bridges between project authorities and affected communities, as well as facilitate participatory processes, including local decision making and consensus building where there are not too many opposing views.

An NGO can provide a stable link between a project implementer and the community. All too often the personnel roster for a project changes, and a problem of continuity arises. The new people are unaware of local conditions and problems, causing delays and work stoppages. A local NGO is often needed to put a project back on track.

Finally, NGOs are becoming key players in the development process. The advocacy-oriented NGOs can create significant public awareness.

Policy on Cooperation with NGOs

NGOs can create capabilities and comparative advantages, particularly at the grassroots level. Not many of the staff of DFIs can make time to go to the villages and communities to conceive and implement projects. Some staff may not be fully aware of specific local situations, customs, and culture. Therefore it is an advantage to have a collaborating NGO that does possess that type of knowledge to provide guidance.

According to its Policy on Cooperation between ADB and NGOs (1998), ADB "will seek to cooperate with competent NGOs that have substantial knowledge in their areas of focus and with which cooperation would be appropriate and mutually beneficial. Such cooperation, whether in project, programming, or policy activities, would relate to the type of NGO, the issue or interest being addressed, and country-specific considerations." If ADB is looking for a partner to collaborate on a water supply project in India, then it will look for an NGO that not only has substantial knowledge in that area but also acknowledges accountability for the project. Furthermore, according to the 1998 policy, ADB "will continue to explore innovative approaches to cooperation with NGOs."

While it sounds like ADB's policy of cooperation with NGOs is qualified, it is actually a positive stance for overall development. To strengthen its cooperative stance with NGOs, ADB has over the last decade strengthened its internal capacity. Sometime ago some ADB staff members working in project-related departments may not have known how to best employ an NGO's expertise when they visited a project site. Merely sharing information, or even consulting, meaning a two-way flow of information, is not enough. There must be collaborative decision making and empowerment of stakeholders.

Has the ADB policy of cooperation been effective? A report on collaboration with NGOs from 1990 to 2000 identifies which NGO was involved in which project, what the results were, and if it was a successful collaboration. For the most part, collaboration proved both positive and productive.

Still, some NGOs are not happy with the current policies and criticize ADB-financed projects. One major criticism is that ADB, as sole arbiter, determines which NGOs are competent. This is a criticism that ADB takes in stride, saying: "We are involving you in improving the quality of service that ADB provides to its clients, so we decide whether in our judgment you are qualified."

GENDER AND DEVELOPMENT

An important social dimension of development is gender, which refers to the social norms that define the roles, rights, responsibilities, and obligations of men and women in a society. Promoting gender equality in development is not only a moral or a human rights issue. It is also recognized as fundamental to poverty reduction, sustainable development, and environmental conservation (*Engendering Development Through Gender Equality in Rights, Resources and Voice*, World Bank 2001; *Women and the Environment*, UNEP and WEDO, 2004). Yet women and girls have systematically had poorer access than men and boys to a range of resources, including human resources (education, health care), social capital, physical and financial capital, and employment and earnings. Women's contribution to the sustainable use of natural resources is also not fully appreciated.

Gender–Related Trends

As global statistics show, there have been tremendous advances in reducing gender inequality throughout the world. In just three decades (1960-1990), gender equality in primary and secondary education significantly improved. In 1990, 86 girls were enrolled in primary school for every 100 boys, compared with 67 for every 100 boys in 1960. Similarly, 75 females per 100 males were enrolled in secondary schools in 1990, compared with 53 in 1960. The average six-year-old girl now goes to school for 8.4 years, compared with 7.3 years in 1980, which means that today a six-year-old girl will be in school until she is 14.4 years old. Previously she would leave school at 13.3 years. In general, however, a poor girl is less likely to be able to attend school than one from a nonpoor family.

Since the 1950s, the official female labor force in developing countries has grown at twice the rate of the male labor force, so that in 1990, 30% of women over 15 years were in the formal work force. In 2004, the percentage of women in the labor force in developing countries was estimated to be 40%. Women as a percentage of the labor force in Southeast Asia went from 21% to 35.8% between 1970 and 1995. Although most of these women were working in garment factories and cottage industries, which traditionally employ more women than men, there has been tremendous gender progress in other sectors also. For example, Asia is known for its important female political leaders, including presidents and prime ministers who have come to power in Bangladesh, India, Indonesia, Pakistan, the Philippines, and Sri Lanka.

Unfortunately, alongside this progress exist persistent gender inequalities. Even now, of the 900 million illiterate people in the world, women outnumber men by 2 to 1. Of the 1.3 billion people who are living below the poverty line, 70% are women. At least half a million women die each year from complications due to pregnancy. Soon one in four women (and one in five men) may be infected with HIV/AIDS in countries where the pandemic is spreading rapidly.

In developing countries, women's wages are 30% to 40% lower than those of men for comparable work; however, similar percentages can be found in many developed countries. In developing economies, women's and men's employment also tends to be highly segregated, with women generally performing lower-skilled tasks for lower wages, often in the informal sector. In rural areas, women are generally active in agriculture, but they have little direct access to extension services, credit, or other agricultural inputs, and their access to land is likely to be through their husbands or male relatives. In most developing countries, women's representation in the civil service, elected bodies, the judiciary, and local governments is low, and women's participation in community-level decision making is likely to be limited by social norms.

Women in ethnic minority, low caste, or other marginalized groups, as well as widows and elderly women heading households face a particularly high risk of being poor throughout the world. This is because they are less likely to be educated, to have access to quality health care, to have productive assets or strong property rights, or to have a pension. As the world population ages in the twenty first century, larger numbers of poor elderly women will need social services.

Legal and Policy Measurements to Promote Gender Equality

Since the 1970s, a number of actions have been taken to promote gender equality and the empowerment of women at the international and national levels. Although the United Nations Charter affirms the equal rights of women and men, an international consensus emerged that there was need for a separate convention addressing women's rights. The United Nations Convention on the Elimination of All Forms of Discrimination Against Women was adopted in 1979 and came into force in 1981. As of May 2005, a total of 180 nations had ratified it. Women's legal rights appear to have improved in many countries as a result of this convention. Furthermore, the activism of women's organizations has been enhanced: some nations have included gender equality in their constitutions and others have amended their laws to remove discriminatory provisions relating to such matters as citizenship, marriage, contracts, land and other property, inheritance, and employment. Several countries have also amended their criminal laws or adopted new laws to address domestic violence and human trafficking.

Since 1975, there have been four world conferences on women sponsored by the UN, in which governments and international organizations have reviewed their progress toward gender equality and have made policy commitments to further reduce gender gaps and improve women's opportunities and rights. The Fourth World Conference on Women held in Beijing in 1995 identified 12 critical areas of concern among the world's women: poverty, health, education, violence, armed conflict, the economy, decision making, human rights, media, the environment, the girl-child, and the national and international machinery. Since 1975, most national governments have established policies and action plans to promote gender equality, and have set up mechanisms to implement these policies and plans, including separate ministries or departments, government-wide commissions and networks of gender focal points. Most development agencies and development banks have also adopted policies on gender and development. For example, the ADB originally adopted a policy on the role of women in development in 1985, which was updated and replaced in 1998 by a policy on gender and development.

Some of the common elements in the gender and development policies of governments and development finance institutions (DFIs):

- Gender sensitivity: to observe how programs and projects affect women and men, and to take into account women's needs and perspectives in planning operations;
- Gender analysis: to assess systematically the impact of a program or project on men and women, and on the economic and social relationships between them;
- Gender planning: to formulate specific strategies that aim to bring about equal opportunities for men and women;
- Mainstreaming: to consider gender issues in all areas of activity, accompanied by efforts to encourage women's participation in the decision-making process;
- Agenda setting: to formulate strategies (or assist governments in formulating their strategies) to reduce gender disparities and in developing plans and targets for women's and girls' education, health, legal rights, employment, and income-earning opportunities;
- Gender budgeting: to analyze national expenditure frameworks and budgets, sector budgets and project budgets in terms of their alignment with gender goals and their likely impact on women and men.

Gender, Environment, and Sustainable Development

As the majority of the world's poor, women play decisive roles in managing and preserving biodiversity, water, land, and other natural resources, yet their centrality is often ignored or exploited (*Women and the Environment,* UNEP and WEDO, 2004, p. 3). The contributions of women and women's organizations are particularly noticeable in three environmental areas:

1. Biodiversity

Because of their traditional roles in gathering forest and bush products for food, medicine, religious, and other uses, many rural women have in-depth knowledge of their natural environments, especially in indigenous communities. Women farmers in many agrarian societies are also responsible for the selection and saving of seeds, and they manage home gardens including a diversity of species. However, researchers and extension workers often fail to take women's traditional knowledge of plant varieties into account, and a number of forces are eroding or undermining this rich knowledge base.

2. Water resource management

Women and men generally have distinct roles related to water and water systems, and therefore tend to have different stakes in water use. For example, in rural areas women and girls generally collect water for household use, and also for raising small livestock, for home gardens and for microenterprise activities. Although men generally manage irrigation facilities, women often contribute to the operation and maintenance of these facilities. Despite their important roles in water use, women have not traditionally been included in national or local decision making related to water management. However, in response to advocacy by women's organizations and networks, a number of countries have recently integrated a gender perspective in their water laws and policies.

3. Desertification

In dryland ecosystems, women as well as men have developed essential skills and practices to survive under challenging conditions. Environmental degradation places an extra burden on women, who must walk farther and farther to collect water, food, and fuel. Women also have to take on additional responsibilities when their husbands migrate for work. Yet women in many dryland societies have low status and limited rights, and this subordination is further reinforced by land conservation and development programs that exclude them (*ibid.*, pp. 30-71).

Over the past 20 years, women's roles in environmental protection and sustainable development have increasingly been recognized. The Third World Conference on Women in Nairobi in 1985 specifically noted women's role in environmental conservation and management, and the Platform for Action adopted at the Fourth World Conference on Women in Beijing in 1995 included women and environment as one of its critical areas of concern. In the run-up to UNCED, the Women's Environment and Development Organization organized the First Women's World Congress for a Healthy Planet in 1991, which developed a platform known as the "Women's Action Agenda 21." UNCED itself recognized women as a "major group" in sustainable development, as reflected in Rio Principle 20, Chapter 24 of Agenda 21 ("Global Action for Women Towards Sustainable and Equitable Development") and references to women in other chapters of Agenda 21. The Johannesburg Declaration adopted at the WSSD in 2002 reaffirmed governments' commitments "to ensuring that women's empowerment, emancipation and gender equality are integrated in all the activities encompassed within Agenda 21, the Millennium Development Goals and the Plan of Implementation of the Summit."

Consistent with their general policies on gender and development, national governments and international organizations have taken various steps to "mainstream" gender concerns in their environmental work. For example, UNEP has committed in its 2004-2005 program of work to make gender a cross-cutting priority in all of its programs with an emphasis on:
- empowerment of women in environmental decision making,
- active participation of women,
- technical assistance to women's networks,
- focus on women in reports on environmental links to ill health,
- development of education and training materials,
- organization of workshops, and
- gender balance in meetings (*ibid.*, Box 1, p. 6).

Despite these efforts, much more needs to be done to translate international and national commitments to gender equality into concrete actions. The key ingredients include political will and accountability at all levels; and coherent, gender-responsive institutions, including the participation of civil society groups and women in particular. In the area of environment and sustainable development, gender-responsive solutions must also draw on traditional knowledge systems and be adapted to local conditions and social structures (*ibid.*, p. 103).

INVOLUNTARY RESETTLEMENT

Involuntary resettlement, the sixth social dimension of sustainable development, is a process that assists people who are displaced or temporarily disadvantaged because of a private or public project, and helps them rebuild their lives in a new environment. One key test of successful involuntary resettlement is whether the project-affected people are better off with the project than without the project.

General Principles

A number of general principles of involuntary resettlement are followed in any resettlement policy. The first is that involuntary resettlement should be avoided whenever possible. But sometimes it is necessary in the broader interest of the community or the nation. That brings us to the second principle: When population displacement is unavoidable, it should be minimized by exploring all viable options. For example, with a highway project, there are two other options: one is not to build the road; the other is to consider alternative routes to the highway that will displace a smaller number of people.

Once a decision has been made and people either have to be displaced or suffer short-term economic hardship, they should be compensated and assisted so that their economic and social future will be generally as favorable as it would have been in the absence of the project. In many countries, particularly in developing ones, when communities have to be involuntarily displaced, the government or the project proponent merely gives each household some form of compensation and expects them to move out. Those instances, where there is no consultation and no redress, are not successful resettlements. A workable resettlement policy must include full compensation and assistance. Attention should also be paid to the communities into which displaced peoples will move to minimize conflict and promote successful integration of the newcomers.

What form should this assistance take? In the case of vulnerable groups such as women, children, the disabled, or the aged, help is needed in physically moving their belongings. Many, not just those categorized as vulnerable, will need skill development. For example, the movement of a community located along a coast to an inland site calls for new skills. The community is likely to be made up of fisherfolk, who will have to learn a new occupation such as upland farming or will need assistance in finding employment opportunities in their new habitat. It is also important to assist communities to reconstitute their internal communication and support networks, and link these with networks in their new location. All of these services must be extended to them in addition to compensation.

People about to be displaced should be fully consulted. Just informing them that they have to move or suffer temporary economic problems is not enough. They should be consulted on the planned resettlement and on their compensation options, and an agreement should be reached. If an agreement cannot be reached, the people should not be forced out. It must also be remembered that in any resettlement process three parties are involved: the project proponents, the people who are to be displaced, and the community that is being asked to accept them.

In conducting these consultations, it is best to employ the services of the existing social and cultural institutions in both communities. A social design study or a resettlement planning study should be carried out to determine what social and cultural institutions exist in the communities and how to make use of them. These institutions may have the best knowledge of the local culture and of the needs and aspirations of the people.

Those being resettled should be integrated economically and socially into host communities. There have been cases where civil disorders erupted due to the resettlement of people. In Assam, India, some time ago, several hundred resettlers were massacred because those already living there were under ecological stress and did not accept additional people moving in.

In many developing countries, project proponents claim that the people about to be ejected are squatters who have no formal title to the land they occupy and therefore are not entitled to any resettlement compensation. This is a sensitive issue, but ADB, in reformulating its policy on involuntary resettlement, decided that the absence of a legal title to the land should not preclude people from getting compensation. The Resettlement Policy of ADB "specifies that a lack of formal legal title to land is not a bar to compensation and other assistance. This may apply to a range of people affected, e.g., informal dwellers, land users with traditional or customary rights, squatters or those with adverse possession rights but no formal legal title to land and assets. (see http://www.adb. org, at paragraph 34, p. vii.) Everybody must be compensated and resettled, whether possessing legal title to the land or not. This is especially germane if the affected households are headed by women or other vulnerable groups such as indigenous people and ethnic minorities. This was a reversal of an earlier policy, which said if people could not show legal title to the land, or demonstrate that they were legally settled there, they would not receive compensation when displaced.

As far as possible, plans for resettlement should be laid out and executed as an integral part of any project at the conceptual stage, in terms of both its budget and planning. In many cases, a project was started and the issue of resettlement came up later.

When is a full resettlement program needed? The MDBs, particularly the World Bank and ADB, have set the figure at 200; that is, if 200 or more people are to be displaced, then a resettlement plan must be prepared. However, if indigenous or vulnerable groups of people are involved, then 50 is the threshold number, and a full resettlement plan becomes mandatory.

Resettlement Costs

There are four components of resettlement costs: (1) resettlement preparation and compensation for those who are temporarily affected as well as those who must move, (2) relocation and transfer, (3) income restoration and social integration, and (4) administrative costs to pay for the other three components.

The full cost and benefits of resettlement and compensation should be included in the presentation of project costs and benefits. In many resettlement plans, the project proponent lists only the cash compensation as the cost of resettlement. That is inaccurate. The full cost of a successful resettlement includes not only cash compensation, but also the cost of reconstructing buildings, replacing damaged equipment, moving people physically from their original habitat to the new area, and providing training and livelihood skills that they need to get a job in the new habitat.

In many instances, the project proponent, whether a government or a community, underestimates the resettlement cost, so that the project stands a greater chance of approval. However, such a project is also more likely to run into difficulty at a later stage of implementation, because its budget does not include the full cost of resettlement. Therefore, the full cost of resettlement and compensation should be included in the overall financing plan for the project. If the lending agency is one of the DFIs that has made a resettlement policy mandatory, it should not have a problem in financing the full cost of resettlement. Too often the government assures the lending agency that it will take care of resettlement and compensation. But what actually happens in many cases is that, once the financing is approved, the compensation paid by the government to resettlers is less than what is required in accordance with the policy of the DFI.

Adherence to Policy

Unquestionably, strict adherence to a resettlement policy creates problems for the project proponent, which is usually the government. But on the other side of the coin, if the DFIs do not follow their resettlement policies, they are shirking an ethical duty and are bound to be criticized.

For example, one development bank not so long ago faced such a situation concerning a highway project in a particular country. Conforming to its policy, the bank asked for a resettlement plan. The government refused to provide the analysis and threatened to get funding from other sources such as private banks or to finance the project from domestic resources. The government indicated that it had sufficient financial resources to build the road even without the assistance of DFIs (though the country was still classified as a developing country). The relevant staff of the bank failed to resolve this issue in conformity with the bank's resettlement policy, in this particular case becasue of its strict adherence to its policy on involuntary resettlement.

Resettlement Planning

Not all sectors and not all project components require the same degree of resettlement effort. Only certain sectors, and certain components of those sectors, require resettlement planning. For instance, the transport sector may require resettlement in cases involving terminals, bridges, airports, seaports, and river ports. In the power and energy sector, laying transmission lines that pass through lands where people live requires a resettlement plan. Hydroelectric power, one of the most important components of the power and energy sector, almost always requires resettlement, as dams inundate huge tracts of land. In the case of solid waste projects, examples are transfer stations and landfill sites. Within water supply projects, pipelines, pumping stations, water treatment sites, and reservoirs usually require relocation. In urban-renewal projects, education, and the health-care sector, resettlement may or may not be required. If it is not, then resettlement planning is unnecessary. Comparatively simple road repair projects may damage sections of many people's fields and crops, block access to shops, or necessitate movement of buildings when widening the right of way; in this case resettlement planning may be needed.

INDIGENOUS PEOPLES (IPs)

One topic of concern that is coming to the forefront regarding resettlement planning is moving indigenous peoples (IPs) off their ancestral lands. This has become an issue in the last 15-20 years, because development planners have exhausted most of the potential sites for development and are moving into remote areas in search of new project sites.

The definition of IPs is subject to both national and international law. It is perhaps helpful to review some history of the development of this term under international law.

In 1957, the International Labour Organization (ILO) organized the Convention Concerning the Protection and Integration of Indigenous and Other Tribal and Semi-Tribal Populations in Independent Countries. In 1957, the phrase was "indigenous and other tribal and semi-tribal populations," not "indigenous peoples," which is used today. This convention, known as Convention 107, reflected the prevailing view that indigenous populations, "should be assimilated into national society."

In 1989, ILO Convention 169 (Concerning Indigenous and Tribal Peoples in Independent Countries) supplanted Convention 107 and rejected its assimilationist ideology. Moreover, Convention 169 substituted the word "peoples" for "populations" in referring to IPs. This change, representing an important gain concerning the language of self-determination, was brought into international law. The ILO change of terminology thus helped indigenous peoples to assert their right of self-determination. However, Convention 169 does not itself recognize this right of indigenous peoples. Indeed, it explicitly disavows it.

In many Southeast Asian countries, the term "tribal peoples" is used instead of IPs. "Natives" is sometimes used in the US. "Aboriginals" has been used in Australia. The UN uses the generic term "indigenous peoples" in all its documents, and instead of trying to define this term more elaborately, has identified a set of unique characteristics that are associated with IPs.

Characteristics of Indigenous Peoples

The first characteristic of IPs is that they have descended from population groups that were present in a given area before the existence of modern states or territories. These are the so-called early settlers. A second characteristic is that they maintain cultural and social identities that are different from the mainstream society, including a distinct institutional or legal framework, meaning that mainstream institutions, laws, and social mechanics are not applicable in their areas. For example, in an IP community, a number of loosely associated villages may be headed by tribal chiefs who decide, using tribal law, on matters of concern to their society.

Another important characteristic is self-identification and identification by others as being part of a distinct, ancient cultural group. Linguistic identity differs from that of the dominant society. In the Chittagong area of Bangladesh, the tribal people speak a dialect not spoken anywhere else in the country. IPs have unique ties to traditional habitats and ancestral domains, which is often where difficulties arise. It is very hard to prepare an involuntary resettlement plan for them, because they often will not accept any kind of compensation for giving up their ancestral domain.

Yet another characteristic of IPs is that they live in remote areas, although those are not that remote anymore. Development planners are moving toward ancestral lands, and very soon one of every four or five projects that governments finance will be in tribal areas. That will create unique and possibly terrible problems in terms of resettlement planning.

Protecting Indigenous Peoples' Rights

A number of important international law declarations and agreements help protect the rights of IPs. As early as 1948, the UN, in its Universal Declaration of Human Rights, proclaimed the importance of the economic, social, and cultural rights of various sectors of the world's population. The declaration covered IPs, although they were not specifically mentioned. However, this was where their legal protection began. The first international convention that specifically addressed the rights of IPs was ILO Convention 107 in 1957. It noted the rights of IPs to pursue their material well-being and spiritual development. In 1989, ILO adopted Convention 169, which was more specific about the right of IPs to participate in development projects that may affect their lives. However, some critics (Maiyan Clech Lam, 2000) contend that Convention 169 undermines indigenous aspirations by emphasizing "participation" or "consultation" rather than "self-determination."

In 1992, Agenda 21 recognized the actual and potential contribution of IPs to sustainable development. Although not a treaty, a convention, or even legally binding, Agenda 21 still manages to provide a comprehensive program of national and international action for sustainable development in the twenty-first century, which many nations are now implementing. Chapter 26 of Agenda 21, entitled "Recognizing and Strengthening of the Role of Indigenous Peoples and Their Communities," recommends that measures be undertaken, including the establishment of a process to empower IPs and their communities; recognition that the lands of IPs and their communities should be protected from activities that are environmentally unsound or ones that IPs consider to be socially and culturally inappropriate; respect for traditional values, knowledge, and resource management practices with a view to promoting environmentally sound and sustainable development; and instituting capacity building for indigenous communities, based on the adaptation and exchange of traditional experience. The Convention on Biodiversity adopted a series of resolutions in 1992 that direct contracting parties to harness biodiversity with respect to traditional knowledge of IPs for preservation of biodiversity and its sustainable use. Finally, the Vienna Declaration and Programme of Action, adopted by the World Conference on Human Rights on June 25, 1993, was developed with the participation of IPs for the first time in the history of UN. The Vienna Declaration addresses issues such as the right of IPs to direct their own developmental priorities, to decide upon the use of ancestral territories and resources, and to sell them. The World Conference on Human Rights recommended in part that UN "organs and agencies related to human rights consider ways and means for the full implementation ... of the commendations contained in the present Declaration." (See http://www.unhchr.ch/huridocda/ huridoca.nsf/(Symbol)/A.CONF.157.23.En? OpenDocument.)

The UN General Assembly declared 1993 as the International Year of the World Indigenous Populations. A UN working group on indigenous populations prepared a draft, the Universal Declaration of the Rights of Indigenous Peoples, which was more or less in line with the Vienna Declaration. Part II of the Universal Declaration deals with several key issues, including sacred places and burial sites. One of the key elements of the draft, found in Part III, calls for restitution of cultural, intellectual, religious, and spiritual property taken from IPs without their free and informed consent or in violation of their laws, traditions, and customs. The Vienna Declaration is considered to be a "soft law," which means that it is important for its persuasive effect, not because it is a hard law with legal obligations.

An example of IPs exercising their rights happened in Chiapas, Mexico. In 1999, the US government agreed to finance a $2.5 million project for biological prospecting, specifically for new medicinal plants. The IPs of Chiapas, led by Dr. Antonio Perez Mendez, strongly objected to the project. They insisted on a moratorium on all biopiracy projects in Mexico so that the affected IP could discuss, understand, and propose their own alternative approaches to using their resources and knowledge. Furthermore, they wanted assurance that no one could patent these resources and that the benefits of the resources would be shared by all the IPs. The project was cancelled in November 2001.

Resettlement Policy for Indigenous Peoples

A successful resettlement policy for IPs must be consistent with their needs and aspirations. It should also be compatible in substance and structure with affected groups and with their cultural and socioeconomic institutions. To write an IP policy, some of the essential elements should be conceived, planned, and implemented with the informed participation of the affected communities. It should be equitable in terms of developmental efforts and impacts, and it should not impose negative effects of development without appropriate and acceptable compensation.

It is important to note that some developmental efforts have greater negative impacts on IPs while having little negative impact, if any, on mainstream society. This should also be considered as part of the involuntary resettlement policy for IPs, even though it is more difficult to implement, since the IPs do not place a cash value on their culture and ancestral lands.

ADB's Development Plan for Indigenous Peoples

In 1999, ADB published a developmental plan for IPs containing the following elements:
- preparation, during project design, of a development plan that takes into full account the desires and preferred options of IPs affected by the project;
- studies to identify potential adverse effects on IPs that will be induced by the project and to identify measures to avoid, mitigate, or compensate for these adverse effects;
- measures to strengthen capacity (social, legal, and technical) of the government institutions dealing with IPs;

- involvement of appropriate existing institutions, local organizations, and NGOs with expertise in matters relating to IPs;
- consideration in project design of local patterns of cultural belief and use of ancestral territory and resources;
- support for viable and sustainable production systems that are adapted to the needs of local environments and circumstances of IPs;
- avoidance of creating dependency of IPs on project entities and instead promoting self-reliance among these peoples;
- capacity building for indigenous communities and organizations to facilitate and support effective participation in development processes; and
- adequate lead time and arrangements for extending follow-ups, especially in dealings with IPs in remote or neglected areas where little previous experience is available.

SOCIAL EXCLUSION

Social exclusion, the eighth element of the social dimensions of sustainable development, needs some explanation as to its origin, meaning, and implications. The French philosopher Rene Lenoir used the term "social exclusion" for the first time in 1974. It referred to the tenth of France's population who were mentally and physically handicapped, suicidal, aged, abused children, substance abusers, delinquents, single parents, dysfunctional households, marginal people, and other social "misfits."

Although Lenoir coined the term, the idea is not new. The Greek philosopher Aristotle and the Scottish political economist and philosopher Adam Smith explored some of the concepts contained in social exclusion. Both of these thinkers linked exclusion to a lack of individual choice or freedom to make choices. For Aristotle, the richness of human life was explicitly linked to the necessity of first ascertaining the function of man, followed by exploring "life in the sense of activity." In his view, an impoverished life is one without the freedom to undertake important activities of choice. Smith defined the freedom to live a nonimpoverished life as "the ability to appear in public without shame." As an example he cited that "custom has rendered leather shoes a necessary [sic] of life in England. The poorest creditable person of either sex would be ashamed to appear in public without them."

Smith's focus on deprivation, which revolved around not "being able to appear in public without shame," is a good example of a capability deprivation that takes the form of social exclusion. This relates to the importance of taking part in the life of the community and, ultimately, to the Aristotelian understanding that the individual lives an inescapably "social" life. Smith's point is that the inability to interact freely with others is an important deprivation in itself (like being undernourished or homeless), and has the implication that some types of social exclusion must be seen as a constitutive component of poverty, if not a core component. For example, being excluded from employment or being unable to secure credit often leads to economic impoverishment, which in turn leads to other deprivations such as malnourishment or homelessness. Social exclusion can thus constitutively be a part of capability deprivation as well as instrumentally a cause of diverse capability failures. The case for seeing social exclusion as an approach to poverty is easy enough to establish within the general perspective of poverty as capability failure.

Two Categories of Social Exclusion

Nobel Prize winner Amartya Sen did a study, "Social Exclusion: Concept, Application and Scrutiny in 2000" for ADB. Sen identifies two major categories of social exclusion:

- *Active social exclusion—something promulgated by law or by pronouncement, such as not allowing a group of people, because of ethnicity or some other defining reason, to participate in a political process. Malaysia's Constitution, for example, excludes certain groups of people from holding high positions in the government or owning land. It is an elite form of exclusion, since those being excluded are not poor or in other ways disadvantaged. In another example, when a group of immigrants or refugees are not accorded a political status, they are automatically deprived from many social and economic benefits by way of active social exclusion (Ogata, 1998).*

- *Passive social exclusion—something that comes about through social (as opposed to legal) processes such as poverty or isolation. No one may be excluding a person from buying food or from participating in some social activity, but because of a sluggish economy or financial crisis, he or she may not be able to afford it and, therefore, be excluded. In 1997, all of Southeast Asia, but mainly Thailand, Malaysia, Indonesia, and the Philippines, faced a serious financial crisis. Currency values went down drastically, and one million people in that region became known as the "transitional poor." Another example of passive social exclusion was revealed by the Boston Food Bank in November 2001. Called "Hunger in America 2001," the study covers a four-year period when the US economy was rather strong. According to the study, 40% of the people served by the Boston Food Bank had to choose between eating and paying their rent or mortgage; 29% said their children were not eating enough; and 22% were employed and still could not afford to put food on the table. The study also indicated that poverty cut across racial lines. More than 54% of the people served by the Boston Food Bank were Caucasian, 30% were African-American, and 9% were Hispanic.*

Active and Passive Social Exclusion—More Examples

The ADB guidelines set out six examples of both active and passive exclusion:

- *Poverty. The inability to purchase basic necessities and/or required luxuries (e.g., leather shoes) leads to social exclusion. (passive)*

- *Exclusion from the labor market. By closing off the labor market (low end) or some professions (high end), groups of people are effectively excluded from earning a livelihood. (active)*

- *Credit market exclusions. The far-reaching impact of denying access to credit and other financial services to poorer people can be seen as a common example of social exclusion. (active)*

- *Gender-related exclusions. Women's interests have been consistently neglected, especially in Asia. Women have been routinely excluded from employment opportunities, basic education, land ownership, and access to the law. Depending upon the country, it could be either active or passive exclusion. Afghanistan, for instance, actively keeps women out of school. However, in other countries that boast of universal educational systems, women may be kept out of school by custom or poverty, which may be a passive form of exclusion.*

- *Health care. The exclusion of large sections of a population from public health services has been a matter of considerable discussion in recent years. It is an extensive problem in many developing regions. For example, the world is facing an AIDS pandemic, and many of those affected cannot be treated because the drugs, although now available, are too expensive. Some social scientists have proposed making this a separate category, "international exclusion," to delineate the inability of poorer nations to afford modern life-saving and -sustaining medical techniques and medicines. (passive)*
- *Food market and poverty. Some countries have no food shortages in the market but host a large malnourished population. These are people who are passively excluded from buying the available food due to lack of purchasing power. However, some form of active exclusion could cause their predicament. In this case, the cost of food may be high because of high transportation and distribution costs.*

A final point could be the sum of the previous ones—the exclusion of participation. Many people, because of poverty, disability, sickness, or being from the lower classes of the community, are excluded from participation in various social and economic spheres.

When dealing with social exclusion, it is important to note how people are socially excluded. Are they excluded because of some pronouncement, some law? Or are they excluded because of poverty? If it is because of poverty, their exclusion could be either active or passive or both. Health insurance is an excellent example. A person may not have health insurance because he or she cannot afford it, which is passive exclusion. But if the government does not provide health insurance for a given section of the public, it is active exclusion.

SOCIAL ANALYSIS

Similar to the EIA, social analysis is conducted for projects having significant social impacts. Also, similar to what is done in an EIA, projects are classified on the basis of their social impact as A, B, or C—although their significances are different.

Project Categories

Category A projects are expected to have a direct positive social impact on specific sectors such as agriculture and the social sectors. For example, social infrastructure projects such as irrigation, water supply, or sanitation are expected to have, first, a direct social impact, and, second, a positive impact because they create facilities for poverty reduction and the social good.

Category B projects rarely have any immediate direct positive or negative social impacts. Projects in the energy, transport, and industry sectors do not have direct linkages with poverty reduction or participation. They are usually designed without the participation of the affected community. A telecommunications project developing cell phones may not need popular participation beyond information gathering by market researchers and later a publicity campaign. It essentially involves telecommunication experts who do research, develop a product, and then market it.

Category C projects are large dams, highways, or mines that have a potential for direct negative impact on the lives of many people. A social analysis might propose abandonment of the proposed project and a search for alternatives; thus a detailed social assessment is required for such projects.

Three Types of Social Analyses

1. Rapid social assessment (RSA)

An RSA is comparable to an IEE. It is a checklist for projects with minimal social impact to see if any of the components will cause problems. If there are some problematic elements in the project or if significant social impacts are identified, a detailed social design study should be conducted.

2. Environmental impact assessment

An EIA is a systematic identification and evaluation of potential impact of a project or program on the environment. (See Chapter 5 for further discussion.) In relation to this chapter, the EIA is a vital tool in collaborative decision making, a part of participatory development.

There is an ongoing debate between environmentalists and social scientists as to who should conduct the participation exercises. Should it be part of the social assessment or the EIA? Environmentalists claim that participation has been an integral part of the EIA for years.

Social assessment procedures, as separate from an EIA, are recent. The policies in many social development issues, such as gender, participation, and the rights of indigenous people, have come into being in just the last 5–10 years. Formerly they were part of EIA, but not carried out in depth and often relegated to the summary. Today social scientists are doing a thorough job on each of these social dimensions, although they are still part of EIA.

3. Social design study (SDS)

An SDS is done for all Category C projects and perhaps for Category B projects, but probably not for Category A projects. To determine the need for an SDS, an RSA should be conducted first to determine if the project has a negative social impact and high level of need or demand, and if the community where the project will be located has a high absorptive capacity. Only if these factors are in the affirmative will an SDS be required.

Take the case of a Category B project where the RSA has found that there are limitations in need or demand. In this case, it is necessary to determine the reasons why some people do not want the project. Perhaps there is a deficiency in the absorptive capacity of the community. The people may not understand what benefits this project is expected to bring. Or perhaps there are some potential negative impacts on a subpopulation, whether it is tribal people, small farmers, or large landowners. In any of these situations, an SDS is required. It is necessary to find out why there is a limitation in the need or demand and then create a demand through certain social mitigation measures. If there is a defect in absorptive capacity, it is necessary to know what it is and how it can be improved. If there are potential negative impacts for some of the subpopulations, it is necessary to determine who is predicting these impacts and on what grounds, and then to take measures to minimize them. All of these elements are part of an SDS.

In Category C projects, which are likely to have highly significant negative social impacts, it may be necessary to undertake an SDS. However, if the RSA results show that the chances of implementing the project are nil, an SDS is not necessary. What is needed is to reformulate the project, consider another project, or consider doing nothing.

Preparing an RSA Report

Using a hydropower project as a hypothetical example, it is necessary first to identify the subpopulations and list them down as a column (see Table 8-2). IPs, subsistence farmers, small marginal farmers, and/or large farmers may inhabit the project area. In another column the percentage of each subgroup occupying the area can be listed. Other columns may record the level of development, needs, demands, absorptive capacity, percentage of population, and specific weaknesses and strengths of each subgroup of population. In this hypothetical example, it is found that, in the case of IPs, which make up 15% of the population, there is a low level of development, a high to low level of need or demand exists, and the subpopulation forms a close-knit but passive community. The level of need/ demand here requires some clarification. Some IPs may have a high demand for a hydro project because they farm the highlands, so they need water for irrigation. But the lowland indigenous groups are afraid that if irrigation comes in the absence of land leveling, their land is going to be flooded; so in their case, the demand is low. Because they are working on somebody else's land, subsistence farmers have a medium demand and very low level of organization and morale. They do not have much ambition to get irrigated water, high-yielding varieties of seed, and fertilizer. Small farmers have a high demand, but they are disorganized. Large farmers have a poor history of repayment. This is a typical RSA report from which one can then determine the need for SDS.

Table 8-2. Typical RSA Report Form: A Hypothetical Example

Sub-population	Level of Development	Level of Need/ Demand	Level of Absorptive Capacity	Percent of Target Population	Specific Strengths/Weaknesses
Tribals	Low	High/low	Medium	15	Close-knit, but passive community
Subsistence farmers	Low	Medium	Low	40	Very low level of organization and morale
Small/ marginal farmers	Medium	High/medium	Medium	30	Keen but disorganized
Large farmers	High	Medium/low	High	15	Poor history of repayments

Source: ADB (1991)

The objectives of an SDS are to optimize the project design by integrating the target group's preferences and priorities, then developing appropriate project implementation strategies, providing a detailed social justification for the project, and identifying major social risks that may affect implementation.

Importance of Well-Drafted RSAs and SDSs

A well-researched RSA should provide detailed drafts of any conditions and covenants, indicating those steps that need to be taken to offset risks. These conditions and covenants should be attached to the report. By ensuring compliance with such conditions and covenants, success of the project will be more likely, as will cost recovery for the loan repayment. If there is a default in cost recovery, the internal rate of return of the project will likely be such that the project cannot be financed, as it will not be bankable.

An RSA is a necessary part of the social dimensions of sustainable development. However, since the techniques of social design studies are new, the question is, who are qualified to undertake these assessments? A DFI may lack the trained personnel for the job. Such an institution may fund as many as 100 new projects a year, many of which need an RSA—and perhaps more than the institution can handle in-house. Thus the DFI will have to outsource these studies to experts and consulting companies. Unfortunately, many of the companies that are awarded such work are more familiar with engineering and environmental assessments than social assessments.

There is therefore a need for a new breed of consultants with expertise not only in economic and environmental assessment but also in social design, who have the knowledge and facilities to conduct RSAs and SDSs.

How Social Development Policies Work

Despite the shortage of social development experts, the responsibility for implementing resettlement and social design policies lies with project proponents assisted by finance institutions. A lot of time is spent on this process. For example, even though the RSAs may be done by outside consultants, the social development experts of ADB spend a great deal of their time dealing with these issues. A built-in procedure at ADB requires a project to be reviewed by both staff and management before it is submitted to the Board of Directors for approval. After the project design is completed, the social development experts look at it to ascertain if it is in accordance with the approved guidelines.

Once the social development experts approve a study, it goes to the management of the DFI for final approval. The top officials will then meet with the heads of the involved departments to clear the project before it goes to the board. If there is a question on the social assessment, the EIA, or the economic and financial viability of the project, it is generally returned to the initiating office for further work.

After approval of a project by the board, and once the loan is extended, staff of the DFI are assigned to monitor the progress of implementation. If the loan conditions or covenants designed to minimize the risks identified in the RSA are not being complied with, a financial institution might hold back the unreleased tranche of the loan until the loan conditions are satisfied. Finally, DFIs have postevaluation offices, whose job is to evaluate the performance of a project as originally intended, once it is completed. The objective of this exercise is to provide feedback of lessons learned into the project cycle so that mistakes are avoided and good lessons are repeated in future project design and implementation.

SOCIAL DEVELOPMENT INDICATORS (SDIs)

Social development indicators (SDIs) comprise the final element of the social dimensions of sustainable development.

Selecting the Parameters

Although there has been some discussion on environmental indicators, the literature on SDIs is relatively new. One has to choose some critical social development parameters such as longevity, income per capita, gross primary enrollment (which reflects the state of education), and basic needs satisfaction (such as the percentage of people who have access to a safe water supply) and monitor their progress in a country. This is essentially the concept embedded in UNDP's HDI. On the basis of the HDI, countries are ranked as high (55 countries), medium (86 countries), or low (34 countries). HDI values vary from 0 to 1. High values range from 1.000 to 0.800, medium values from 0.799 to 0.500, and low values from 0.499 to 0.000.

In 1994, the World Bank published a series of social development diamonds (see Chapter 4) using the parameters of life expectancy, school enrollment, GNP per capita, and access to safe water. Development diamonds can be created for any given country using these four indicators (Figure 8-1). This method allows comparison of the degree of social development as measured by these parameters in given countries or regions.

Social Development Elasticity

The concept of social development elasticity (SDE) is derived from the concept of environmental elasticity. SDE is defined as the percentage change in the ratios of income distribution (as measured by the ratio of income of the richest 20% of the population to the poorest 20%, divided by the aggregate percentage of change in the economy, which is measured by GDP growth). The concept is also derived from the Gini Coefficient, which is a measure of aggregate inequality of income (see Box 8-2). The coefficients for developed countries lie between 0.50 and 0.70, whereas for developing countries they vary in the range of 0.20-0.35 (Box 8-2).

Figure 8-1. Social Developmental Diamonds

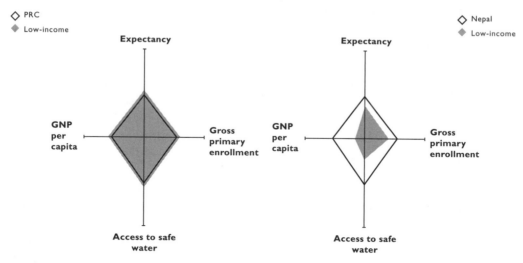

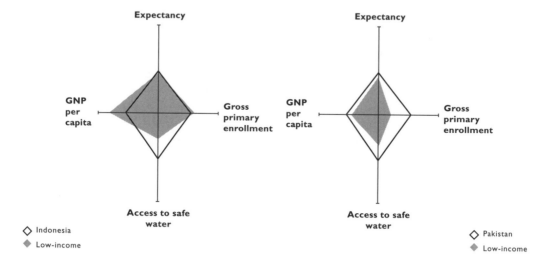

Source: P. Rogers et al. (1977)

Box 8-2. Calculating SDE

In calculating SDE, one has to find the answer to the following question: For every percentage growth of GDP per capita, what has been the percentage decrease of the ratio of the income of the richest 20% to the poorest 20% of the population in a country? If this ratio of income decreases with the increase in GDP per capita, it indicates positive elasticity and is a sign of improved income distribution. Economists have drawn elasticity curves in the form of a Lorenz Curve, but it was recognized as an income distribution curve at best. What is significant in the elasticity concept is that such improvement of income distribution with increasing GDP per capita in a country is a positive indication of implementation of pro-poor economic and social development policies.

As a hypothetical example, take the data given in Table 8-3. In 1990, Q5/ Q1 was equal to 30.1. In 2000, the same ratio was 25. The social elasticity is:

$$\text{SDE} = \frac{\text{Percentage decrease in ratio of } Q_5/Q_1}{\text{Percentage increase of GDP}} = \frac{(30-25.0)/30}{(500-400)/400} = \frac{16.6}{25.0} = +0.664$$

Table 8-3. Hypothetical Data for SDE Calculation in Box 8-1

Q5 equals the income of the richest 20% of the population. Q1 represents the income of poorest 20% of the population

	1990	2000
Q5/Q1	30.1	25.0
GDP/Cap	$400	$500

Figure 8-2. Population Groups by Income

Population Groups by Income

Richest (20%)	Q_5
High Income (20%)	Q_4
Middle Income (20%)	Q_3
Low Income (20%)	Q_2
Poorest (20%)	Q_1

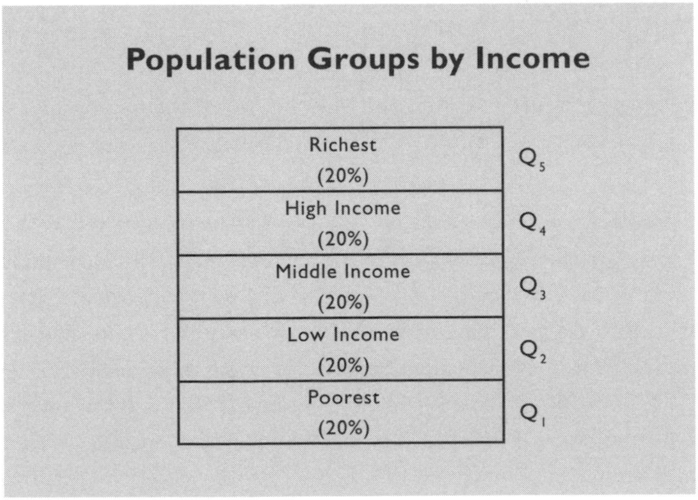

Q5 = Income of richest 20% of the population
Q1 = Income of poorest 20% of the population

These SDE measurements, which are based only on income, are dynamic. They use two points of time, for instance, 1990 and 2000. What was the ratio of income distribution of the richest 20% to the poorest 20% within the given time frame? (See Figure 8-3.) Has it decreased or increased? A decrease means income distribution is naturally improving. An increase means income distribution is growing further apart as GDP changes.

The Four Quadrants

A typical social elasticity graph consists of four quadrants: positive income distribution with negative growth, positive income distribution with positive growth, negative income distribution with negative growth, and negative income distribution with positive growth (Figure 8-3).

Figure 8-3. Map of Social Development Elasticity

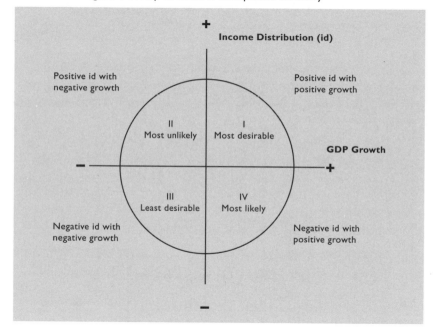

Positive income distribution means that the ratio of the income of the richest 20% to the poorest 20% is decreasing; negative distribution means it is increasing. The most desirable quadrant is the one where the income distribution is positive and growth is positive. That means, if the ratio of the richest 20% to the poorest 20% in 1990 was ten, and if it was nine in 2000, income distribution improved. The most likely situation, however, in which most developing Asian countries lie, is where GDP is growing but income distribution is getting worse. If the ratio of the income of the richest 20% to the poorest 20% was ten in 1990, and then in 2000 it became 20, GDP increased but income inequity also increased.

There is another, albeit unlikely, scenario, but one that could occur, where income distribution is improving but GDP's decreasing (Quadrant II). This means that the rich and poor are coming closer but the country is getting poorer. And of course, the least desirable situation is when both income distribution and growth are negative (Quadrant III).

Some experts believe that even if the GDP per capita grows, the income gap between the richest 20% (Quantile 5) and the poorest 20% (Quantile 1) may not improve and in fact may even widen (See Table 8-9). They say this is probably because the flow of income does not go from the richest to the poorest. There may, however, be a trickle-down effect between the high-income group and the middle- and low-income groups. The poorest 20% are not affected, because they may be so poor that they cannot or do not want to take part in development activities. They may not be able to work because they are disabled or they do not possess marketable skills.

If we take the ratio of the high-income group (Quantile 4) and divide it by that of the low-income group (Quantile 2), we get a better measure of income distribution (SDE 1) than if we divide the ratio of income of the richest 20% by that of the poorest 20% (SDE 2). That is why we do not see much improvement in terms of equity between the richest and the poorest (see Chapter 2).

It should be noted, though, that data can be interpreted differently. SDE1 is the social elasticity when we take the ratio of the richest 20% to the poorest 20% and monitor whether they are increasing or decreasing (Figure 8-5). SDE2 is also social elasticity, but instead of comparing the income of the richest to the poorest, SDE2 compares the income of the high-income to low-income group. The income distribution pattern is expected to be better than from the richest to the poorest.

Figure 8-4. Social Development Elasticity I for the PRC and India, 1989-1992

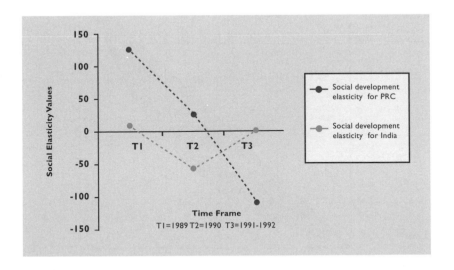

Nevertheless, SDE, as a yardstick for social development, shows promise because it concentrates on the most critical issue relevant to social justice—income distribution as measured by the income gap between the rich and the poor.

Measuring Income Distribution

How do we measure the distribution of income? Let us take a hypothetical country. The first thing is to break down the population into five quintiles, from the richest 20% to the poorest 20%, to see what percentage of the national income each group receives. For our hypothetical country, let us assume the income of the richest 20% to poorest 20% is 40%, 28%, 18%, 10%, and 4% as shown in Table 8-4.

Table 8-4. Income Distribution among the Five Quintiles

Quintile	In a given time
Q5	40%
Q4	28%
Q3	18%
Q2	10%
Q1	4%

Next, we will plot a Lorenz Curve (Figure 8-5), which is a graphical way to look at income distribution.

Figure 8-5. Lorenz Curve

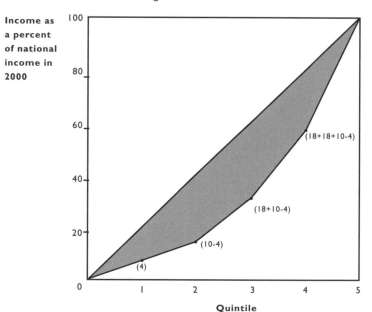

The Lorenz Curve is closely related to and can be derived from the Gini Coefficient (see Box 8-3).

Box 8-3. Gini Coefficient

The Gini Coefficient was developed by the Italian statistician Corrado Gini. It is a measure of the income inequality in a society.

The Gini Coefficient is a number between 0 and 1, where 0 means perfect equality (everyone has the same income) and 1 means perfect inequality (one person has all the income; everyone else earns nothing).

While the Gini Coefficient is used mostly to measure income inequality [see Figure 8-2 and Table 8-4], it can be also used to measure wealth inequality.

The Gini Coefficient can be further understood using areas on the Lorenz Curve diagram. If the area between the line of perfect equality and the Lorenz Curve is A, and the area underneath the Lorenz Curve is B, the Gini Coefficient is A/(A+B). This is expressed as a percentage or as the numerical equivalent of that percentage, which is always between 0 and 1 [See Figure 8-5].

Source: Wikipedia, the free encyclopedia

Income as a percentage of the national income lies on the X axis, and the quintiles make up the Y axis. The curve runs from zero (no population, no wealth) to 100 percent of the population owning 100 percent of the wealth. In our case, Q1 holds 4 percent. The plotting is cumulative. The next quintile holds 10 percent plus 4 percent. What would a Lorenz Curve look like if income were evenly distributed? It would be a straight line. Our graph has a distinct bow, so income is not evenly distributed in our hypothetical country.

Taking another set of figures for time $t + \Delta t$. One can calculate the shift of the Lorenz Curve to see if the distribution of income has improved or worsened. SDE precisely demonstrates the same measurement to indicate the shift of the Lorenz Curve to the right (worsening income distribution) as to the left (improving income distribution).

CONCLUSION

An increasingly important dimension of sustainable development is the social dimension – the others being the economic and environmental. Primarily, two factors governed the emergence of social dimension: (i) despite robust economic growth, one out of five people on earth remained poor; and (ii) increasing awareness and recognition of the need for people to participate in the development process that affects their lives. It is universally recognized that eradication of poverty is the most important factor governing the sustainability of development. The core of a conceptual framework for eradication of poverty lies in identifying the right kind of policy environment, institutional set-up, and program focus for promoting economic growth, population growth, and distributional effectiveness. Distributional effectiveness is determined by the percentage of GDP growth allocated to projects designed to create employment and assets in poverty stricken areas. On the other hand, the practical steps to eradicate poverty is to identify the poor on the basis of their geographic location, their needs, and their aspirations. Programs and projects should then be designed and implemented to meet those needs and aspirations. Other social dimensions of sustainable development are: participation (NGOs, civil society, and private sector), gender equity, needs of the indigenous people, involuntary resettlement, social exclusion, and social assessment.

CHAPTER 9

THE ECONOMICS OF SUSTAINABILITY

EVOLUTION OF ECONOMIC THINKING ABOUT THE ENVIRONMENT AND THE ROLE OF ECONOMIC FACTORS

The economics of sustainability[1] deals with natural, human-made, and human capital. It is thus more than environmental economics, because it includes the development of an economy and society, not just management of environmental issues. Economics in general deals with the production and distribution of wealth and is sometimes defined as the science dealing with the use of, or allocation of, scarce resources.

To achieve sustainable development, people often talk about the triple bottom line—economic efficiency, equity, and environmental sustainability, in short, the three E's (See Chapter 1). There are even companies that put a triple bottom line on their balance sheets, to indicate how they are doing economically, how they are doing with regard to the social issues, and how they are doing with regard to the environment (*The Economist*, January 2005). This is not a new idea; it is simply thinking conceptually about the three E's and indicating how well the components meet these goals. In this chapter we focus on economics, the first of the triple bottom line. To understand sustainable development, we have to understand that the concepts often used in economics provide a very important part of the tools needed.

Land, Labor, and Capital: Adam Smith and David Ricardo

The great economic philosopher Adam Smith, in his treatise *The Wealth of Nations*, published in 1776, and the English economist David Ricardo, who published his *Principles of Political Economy and Taxation* in 1817 (*Cambridge Biographical Encyclopedia*, 2000, p. 789), were concerned with the economic valuation of what they considered to be the three most important factors of production: land and the natural environment; capital, by which they meant the development of the land and nature; and labor, through which land is transformed into real assets. Smith may have arrived at his conclusions based on his view of the world from eighteenth-century Edinburgh, Scotland. The economy then was largely based on an agrarian society.

Labor and Capital: Karl Marx

After the industrial revolution in Britain, which began in the second half of the eighteenth century, Karl Marx focused on the key factors of labor and capital in *Das Kapital*, published in three volumes in 1867, 1884, and 1894, respectively (*Cambridge Biographical Encyclopedia*, 2000, p. 625). For Marx, the proletariat and capitalists were the key factors. Land did not matter. Capital and labor were all that was needed to produce results. Marx described how the capitalists took the people out of the countryside and put them into Blake's "dark, satanic mills" and factories to produce manufactured products. The natural environment seemed to have been dropped from the economic equation. The reason was that natural environmental factors were not viewed as being scarce at

---

[1] The authors thank John Dixon for his insightful contributions to this chapter.

that time. During Marx's time, many millions of people moved away from the land to the newly industrialized cities, taking for granted that the land would always be there. Colonization and the establishment of global empires further reinforced that view. If a resource in one country was destroyed or degraded, industrialized countries simply appropriated other countries' resources and imported them under the guise of colonialism.

Marxism in the twentieth century was the extreme version of this earlier concept. The focus was just on capital—capital accumulation and capital creation—and on labor, but only as an input into the process of capital accumulation. The leaders of the Soviet Union thought they could solve all of their problems by building megalithic projects. Capital investment was the way to development, an ironic approach coming from avowed anticapitalists.

John Maynard Keynes

The Global Depression of the 1930s challenged all previous economic assumptions. The English economist John Maynard Keynes brought labor back into the equation. He noted that the people's demand for goods and services really mattered and that the lack of consumer demand was a major contributing cause of the depression. Many big mills, docks, and factories had been built, but people were not buying the products of these facilities. So Keynes focused on expanding the demand for the products, and thus on capital and labor. He argued that the government should step in and augment the demand of the private sector in order to increase the level of aggregate demand.

Keynes was not particularly concerned with the environment, and he did not bring environmental considerations into his broadened discussion of the economy. The environment was taken as given, and environmental issues were not subject to policy discussion.

Capital, Labor, and Land

It was not until after World War II, sometime in the early 1950s, that land rejoined capital and labor to form a complete economic picture. Its entry marked the birth of modern environmental economics, which reemphasizes the importance of land as an economic factor. By land, today's environmental economists mean ecosystems. This is a fairly recent definition; previously, the term "land" was used in a general sense.

In a sense, we have gone full circle (Table 9-1). We started out with land as an economic factor in the eighteenth century, forgot about it for about 100 years, then put it back into the equation in the middle of the twentieth century. It was not because reality changed, but rather because the perception of reality changed. In the early part of the twentieth century, a company would issue stock certificates beautifully engraved with factories billowing black smoke into the air from giant chimneys to show how modern and progressive it was. Now, of course, it is just the opposite. So, again, perceptions have changed, but the effects, for good or ill, have remained the same.

Table 9-1. Evolution of Economic Thinking

Land	Labor		Malthus
Land	Labor	Capital	Adam Smith, David Ricardo
Labor	Capital		19th century Industrial Revolution, Karl Marx
Capital			Marxism in 20th century USSR
Capital	Labor		John Maynard Keynes
Capital	Labor	Land	Modern environmental economics

Source: Based on John Dixon (personal communication, November 2002)

CONCEPTS OF WELFARE

Utility Maximization and Vilfredo Pareto's Frontier

According to the *Oxford English Reference Dictionary*, the philosophers Jeremy Bentham (1748-1832) and John Stuart Mill (1806-1873), together with "an important antecedent" provided by David Hume (1722-1776), "advanced utilitarianism," the "theory that an action is right insofar as it promotes happiness, and that the guiding principle of conduct should be to achieve the greatest happiness or benefit of the greatest number." Under utilitarianism, utility should be maximized in order to promote welfare, which is defined as "well-being, happiness; health and prosperity (of a person or a community)."

Figure 9-1. Utility Maximization

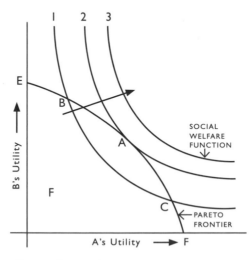

Broad Utility Criterion (Pareto Frontier)

Sharp Utility Criterion (Social welfare function with intersection at Pareto frontier)

Source: Based on *Economics of the Environment: Selected Readings*, R. Dorfman and N.S. Dorfman, eds. (1972)

Figure 9-1 attempts to indicate how a person or a group of people, designated as A, and another person or group of people, designated as B, can maximize their utility.

Each seeks its own preferences without making interpersonal comparisons. In a world in which resources are limited, as A maximizes its utility, B's utility becomes limited, and vice versa. Under normal circumstances, there is a trade-off on the frontier between the utility of the two. By plotting what happens to the decrease in A's utility as the utility of B increases, one can create a line called the Pareto frontier.

The Pareto frontier is named after Vilfredo Pareto, who was an "economist and sociologist" who first worked as an "engineer, and directed a railway company in Italy (*Cambridge Biographical Encyclopedia*, 2000, p. 721)." The Pareto frontier is a very helpful concept that suggests that, along this frontier, stretching from point E on the vertical ordinate to point F on the abscissa (horizontal ordinate), there are many solutions to the welfare of A and B. Furthermore, it suggests that both A and B can be better off by moving in a northeast direction from any point such as point F interior to this frontier.

There could also be some parties demanding to be in the area to the northeast, beyond the Pareto frontier. But the problem is that such an outcome is not feasible, because it is physically and technically impossible to move outside of the frontier. The Pareto frontier is formed by joining a series of joint outcomes that cannot be exceeded without making the other party worse off. A Pareto frontier can be generalized to many conflicting groups or individuals.

What we would like to do is find a place on that frontier where both A and B can be happy. If we have some sort of social welfare function, shown by curves 1, 2, and 3 in Figure 9-1, we will be able to show the combined welfare of A and B for each point on the curve (there are a lot of logical reasons why they would take the shape shown in the figure). If the welfare functions exist, then where the Pareto frontier just touches a social welfare function curve would be the optimum solution.

The Pareto frontier is a useful concept, but it is very hard to put actual numbers on the axis showing the utility of A or B, or to put numbers on the social welfare function lines. Notice there is no scale marked on the axes. The real problem is that we do not know how to define utility functions or social welfare functions in terms other than their broad shapes, but the concept illustrated in the figure provides us a useful entrée into thinking about the concept of welfare, even though it is hard to accomplish in fact. People are assumed to have a utility function, based upon all the goods and services that they consume. It is assumed that each person's utility is improved by consuming more goods and services. One's utility function can be visualized as a vector function based on a person's wish for goods and services. Generally, most people with normal behavior would maximize their utility by consuming more goods and services.

These goods and services can include environmental quality, which may not be among the usual sorts of goods and services that people seek. One person might seek an expensive automobile and expensive vacations and things like that, but another person might wish to consume other things, like listening to popular music or opera. Without explicit functions it is hard to maximize utility. However, using this definition and some plausible assumptions about individual economic behavior, concepts and data that have been developed for GDP, we can operationalize the maximization of utility by use of actual data and the generation of competitive market solutions.

GDP as a Proxy for Utility

1. Trade-offs between city inhabitants and farmers

Suppose a big water project is to be built, and some people want water for recreational purposes, while others want water for irrigation. Figure 9-2 illustrates the benefits attainable by each of the groups. Suppose further that recreation expressed in person-days is shown on one of the axes, and irrigation expressed in hectares of land is shown on another axis. Those seeking recreation, primarily city inhabitants, and those seeking irrigation, primarily farmers, will have to make some trade-offs. If their demand for irrigation and recreation can be plotted, the possibilities of all feasible combinations of recreation and irrigation as a curve creates a proxy for the Pareto frontier called the Production Transformation Curve in this context. The analysis focuses on maximizing the utility in terms of persons identified as A, who want water for irrigation, and persons identified as B, who want water for recreational purposes. Based upon this analysis it is still not possible to identify the locus of the point on the curve at which total welfare is maximized. To do so we need some additional information about the relative values of irrigation and recreation; and this comes from prices.

Figure 9-2. GDP as a Proxy for Utility

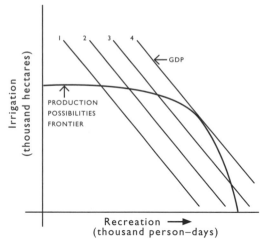

Broad Productivity Criterion (Production Transformation Curve)
Sharp Productivity Criterion (GDP) (Intersection of GDP and Production Transformation Curve)

Source: Based on Dorfman anf Dorfman (1972)

2. GDP as an indicator of welfare

If, however, prices can be associated with each of the two commodities, a line can be drawn showing the trade-offs between the utilities of A and B. This is sketched as lines 1 through 4 in the figure. The GDP, or the relative contributions of irrigation and recreation to GDP, can now serve as a proxy for utility, or as an estimate for the welfare function. Indeed, GDP is often used as a proxy for the welfare of nations. Some critics are unhappy with such a use of GDP, though most people use GDP as a proxy. In fact, GDP is one of the most important indicators that people use when they are describing how well countries are doing. As such, GDP is a powerful indicator of welfare. Other indicators are given in Chapter 11.

Economic Efficiency and Pareto Optimality

Economic efficiency can be defined as the organization of production and consumption such that all possibilities for increasing economic well-being have been exhausted.

Pareto optimality consists of the "allocation of resources such that no further reallocation is possible which would provide gains in production or consumer satisfaction to some firms or individuals without simultaneously imposing losses on others." Pareto optimality can be expressed simply as as attainment of economic efficiency in production of goods and services; economic efficiency in distribution of goods and services; and resource allocation consistent with consumer preferences. If Pareto optimality is achieved, then economic efficiency is achieved.

Pareto reasoning depends on at least four value judgments. First, since individual preferences count, the economic welfare of a society is based upon the welfare of individual citizens, which is a reasonable assumption. Second, the individual is the best judge of his/her own well-being. Third, a change that makes everybody better off with no one being worse off constitutes a positive change in welfare. Fourth, if the gainers could compensate the losers and still be better off, the change is judged an improvement.

The foundation for a great deal of environmental work focuses on the need to talk to people and to get them to participate in the decisions about how the environment is managed, because individual preferences are vital in expressing the welfare of society. Since individual welfare is best judged by an individual's well-being, not by a national, authoritarian entity, everybody is better off knowing how to achieve a positive change in welfare. This means finding the Pareto frontier, and moving along the frontier until the social welfare function is maximized, as shown in Box 9-1.

Box 9-1. Production Approach

- ...an organization of production and consumption such that all unambiguous possibilities for increasing economic well-being have been exhausted.
- ...an allocation of resources such that no further reallocation is possible which would provide gains in production or consumer satisfaction to some firms or individuals without simultaneously impossing losses on others (Pareto Optimality).
- ...Pareto Optimality can be expressed simply as attainment of economic efficiency in distribution of goods services, and resource allocation consistent with consumer preferences.

Source: John Dixon (personal communication, November 2002)

Some Macroeconomic Concepts

1. Production approach

Why does a loaf of bread cost so much? In a competitive economy, every person who has something to do with the manufacturing process adds his or her own cost or value *added* before passing the product on to the next consumer. This accumulates down the production line, from the farmer to the grocer.

The cycle begins with capital. If one owns capital and uses it, one gets paid for it. The farmer starts out with his capital, consisting of land, irrigation water, and farm implements. He then adds the value of his own labor to these components for producing wheat. When the miller buys wheat from the farmer and with his equipment, his capital, turns the wheat into flour, he also adds value on top of the farmer's value added. The baker does the same thing after he turns flour into bread, as does the grocer who sells the bread to the consumer, who pays for the actual retail value of the bread.

This is the production approach (see Figure 9-3), which measures GDP by summing the value added by each firm or "economic agent," in the economy.

Figure 9-3. Production Approach

Measuring GDP by summing the value added of each firm in the economy

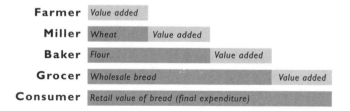

2. Gross national product (GNP)

GNP is the market value of all the final goods and services produced by the economy in a given year. All goods and services involved in public and private transactions are included in GNP. Private goods and services are valued at cost. Certain components of GNP are imputed. These include the rental value of owner-occupied houses, and the value of goods produced and consumed by farms. Certain kinds of services are not counted, however. Since there is no reliable way of evaluating the services of housewives, for example, they are not part of GNP. Voluntary community service are also excluded for the same reason.

This definition raises the issue about goods and "bads." "Bad" things can increase the value of GNP. More prisons mean a larger GNP, because of the goods and services traded. More wars chalk up the same results. The buying and selling of military hardware and paraphernalia are profitable activities from the point of view of GNP; more automobile accidents also increase it.

3. Gross domestic product (GDP)

GDP is the sum of total value of final goods produced and services provided in a country in one year. This includes the value of products that are produced in a country for local consumption or for export, but does not include imports from other countries.

GDP is calculated by adding private and public spending, investments, and exports, minus imports, and minus value generated by foreign-owned companies. Thus the *Oxford English Reference Dictionary* (1996), defines GDP as "the total value of goods produced and services provided in a country in one year." GDP is probably a better measure of welfare than GNP, because GNP includes foreign trade and exchange rates, which are not always directly related to welfare within a country. GDP, on the other hand, correlates well with such aspects of welfare as life expectation at birth.

This is why the World Bank and the UN often rely on GDP per capita to evaluate development in countries. Part of the problem is that people value things differently in different societies. The World Bank and the UN try to solve this by using purchasing power parity (PPP) as a yardstick. PPP is especially important in valuing nontraded goods and services. A haircut, for example may cost 50 cents in Bangladesh and $15 in the US, yet is essentially the same "commodity." PPP takes into account these adjustments and commodity-measured income for the poorest countries and measured income for the richest countries (e.g., Switzerland's GDP measured in PPP is reduced by 6%). They ask how much a similar basket of goods would cost in Bangladesh as compared with the US. It is a way of trying to evaluate GDP fairly, because GDP per capita is so low in some countries like Bangladesh that it would appear that nobody could earn enough to survive.

Some Microeconomic Concepts

1. Price for gasoline and mineral water

The price of gasoline is price responsive. Demand and supply curves can be used to demonstrate how such a responsive price is established. Typically a demand curve slopes downward (Figure 9-4), while a supply curve slopes upward. The supply curve shows the marginal cost of the producers, so it may be calculated from the production costs. The demand curve for a given product represents the total quantity of that product that people will want to buy at a given price. It is the sum of the total demand of all individuals in that society. Demand is a behavioral aspect of consumers, while supply is the technical response of producers.

Supply and demand curves can be important in suggesting when buyers will "clear" a market of certain goods. They also indicate the technical options available, since supply curves are based largely on technology and what is possible within a resource base. They determine how much it costs to supply a certain amount of a commodity, while activating the behavioral characteristics of the market, since consumers act with respect to the price of the commodity.

Normal goods have downward sloping demand curves, depending on what the goods are and how price elastic they are. If they are not price elastic, then they are quite steep. For example, mineral water is more price elastic than gasoline. Price changes greatly affect our consumption of mineral water; if the price is very high, then we simply buy something else, because we can do without it. But

Figure 9-4. Change in Price

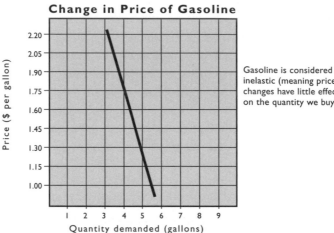

Change in Price of Gasoline

Price ($ per gallon)

Quantity demanded (gallons)

Gasoline is considered inelastic (meaning price changes have little effect on the quantity we buy)

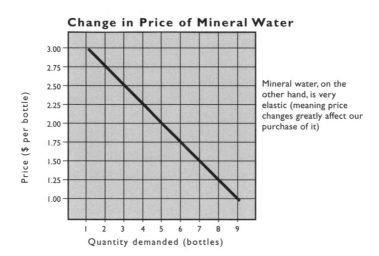

Change in Price of Mineral Water

Price ($ per bottle)

Quantity demanded (bottles)

Mineral water, on the other hand, is very elastic (meaning price changes greatly affect our purchase of it)

price changes in gasoline, a more basic commodity, have little effect in the short run on the quantity we buy. Demand curves relate to consumer behavior everywhere, from Kansas to Kathmandu. As the price goes up, people consume less; as the price goes down, people consume more.

Demand is a purely behavioral trait, and it is not constant. The slope is different depending upon how wealthy one is and how valuable other resources are. See Figure 9-4. Where does a supply curve come from? How would we figure out the gasoline supply curve? Well, we would ask an engineer to estimate it for us, since engineers are good at figuring out what it costs to produce a certain quantity of goods. Engineers design a system, with the cheapest items being produced first. Then the next cheapest option is used, and the next cheapest, so we get increasing costs. The supply curve is a technical calculation based on the availability of resources and technology. It has little to do with human behavior and a lot to do with science and engineering.

2. Supply, demand, and willingness-to-pay

If we plot the supply curve and the demand curve on the same piece of paper (Figure 9-5,) the point where the supply curve and the demand curve intersect indicates the optimal allocation of resources. It shows how much we should buy, how much we should use, and at what price. The price here is the market-clearing price, presuming, *ceteris paribus* (all other things being equal), a free market economy.

Based on Figure 9-5, if the price is greater than C, then we will underconsume; if the price is less than C, then we will overconsume the commodity. If a supplier does not set the price right, for example below C, then the clients will consume more of this good. The supplier does not have to worry about being above or below the market-clearing price in a competitive market, because he or she will be put out of business; but the supplier does have to worry about over- or underconsumption in a market caused, for example, by government-set prices.

For instance, water in most parts of the world is underpriced, so people consume too much of it. If water is priced correctly, that is at the market-clearing price, people will consume the amount indicated by A. If we want to economize on the use of a product, we might raise the price higher to limit consumption and avoid supply problems in the future.

Thus prices provide very important signals. What is the price for irrigation water in Egypt where there is no free market for water? Since the price is close to zero, Egyptian farmers use a lot of water, and it is virtually impossible to get the Egyptian government to actually raise the price of water, because the government is supplying the water and paying for all of the goods and services used at the water facilities. Taxpayers are actually paying for the use of all of the resources, but for political or social reasons, the government does not want to charge for water. So with a price of zero or close to it, we are not surprised if people are using as much water as they can get.

The issue is how to persuade people to reduce demand to some reasonable level. This case has nothing to do with market clearing and a free economy. The issue is how to ration water resources by changing the price. However, many Egyptians would suggest that rationing of water could be accomplished using signals other than higher prices (such as enforced rationing). However, there are almost no effective alternatives to changing the price in this case.

The Libyans have constructed a large artificial river at a cost of about $30 billion. This river has tunnels that run from an aquifer under the Sahara to the coast. Double-decker buses could run through these large tunnels. It is an expensive way of getting water. How much do people pay for water in Libya? Very little! That may be considered wonderful by consumers, but it is a questionable price. The government imposed a tax levy 20 years ago when construction of the facility began. It is argued by Libyan taxpayers that nobody should be asked to pay for water now, because the construction has already been paid for by the taxpayers. Unfortunately, this will do little to curb current demand for the unpriced water.

Economists are right when they advocate pricing for a resource, even if the exact price is not known. Zero is never a good price, because people behave like drunken sailors when they get things free. The price for delivering water has to be greater than zero. This type of analysis tells us something about consumer surplus, which is represented by the area CBE in Figure 9-5. Note that a discriminating monopolist could actually extract a higher price at a lesser quantity than where the supply curve intersects the demand curve, because people are willing to buy a lesser quantity of water at a higher price along the demand curve until it reaches point E, where it crosses the axis representing the price line. While the producer is getting paid the optimal price at the intersection of the supply curve and the demand curve, he could get paid a higher price by producing smaller amounts if he were a monopolist.

Figure 9-5. Supply, Demand, and Willingness-To-Pay

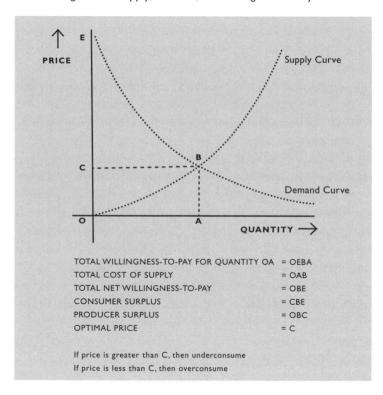

The demand curve tells us that the consumer would have been willing to pay a price of E, but paid only C. Hence, the consumer has a benefit with each succeeding unit of consumption until he ends up paying C per unit.

The consumer surplus is shown as the area between points C, B, and E; its parallel on the producer's side, the producer surplus, is shown in the area between O, B, and C. Total willingness to pay for a quantity represented by A on the horizontal axis is the area OABE; it provides an estimate of the consumption benefit from investments to produce the goods and services sold at price C in the figure.

A government may choose to permit people to consume a certain amount of water at zero price. To accomplish this objective, it may need armed guards at various locations to check the amount of water to be drawn by the people. Thus such distribution of water would be undertaken by fiat, or command and control. This is typically a very difficult way of doing things, and there are many ways to get around it. For example, in this case, who will take most of the water? It is the people who are at the head end of the canals. Since they are not paying for the water, they take all they want and more. People at the other end of the canal do not receive as much, if any, water, even if they are supposed to receive a designated amount under the command and control approach.

Why is this so? It may be that the guards who were sent to guarantee the distribution of water at a price of zero get paid less than the farmers are willing to pay for the water. The guards and farmers set a price for the water distributed, and payment goes directly from the farmer to the guard. Corruption is spawned. This is obviously a bad way of pricing a commodity.

In relatively well-organized societies like the US, there are still water utilities that do not use volumetric pricing. New York City has only recently started to install water meters; the UK does not have water meters in most residences. Droughts occur occasionally in New York. What is to be done about water shortages during such droughts? If people do not understand that they have to pay for a resource, including the cost of the pipes and other goods and services to bring that resource to their homes, they are not likely to worry about drought until it occurs, when it may be too late.

Rent

The English economist David Ricardo is closely associated with the economic concept of rent. He observed that the quality of the land determines its price. Simply put, naturally fertile land is more valuable because it is more productive regardless of the level of other inputs (labor, seed, fertilizer). This extra benefit that comes from the natural state of the land and goes to the landowner when he/she rents it out to farmers is called "rent" in economics.

Rent is a fundamental concept. Many of the problems in analyzing and managing the environment arise because different resources in the environment have different inate or natural values, depending on their productivity and how people value them. A lot of this extra value is called Ricardian rent. The attempt to capture some of these rents, particularly in natural resources, is known as rent-seeking behavior.

The environment contains different rents deriving from various agricultural activities such as fisheries, forestry, and use of water and soil. There can also be aesthetic rents such as scenic landscapes, which command a premium price. In Hawaii, for instance, a beachfront house is worth many times more than an identical house located inland.

Cleaner environments also produce more valuable rents. Part of the challenge in environmental economics is measuring rents that arise from having a clean environment. To do this we ask this question: If we manage the environment more sustainably, what is the magnitude of these extra benefits?

It should be emphasized that rent arises from the fact that it is difficult to find substitutes for some desirable factors or attributes, and people are thus willing to pay a premium for them.

This can be demonstrated with a demand curve that is highly inelastic. An environmental example would be beachfront property, which is scarce, and a good substitute is hard to find. Therefore it goes with a high price, and rent is generated. A non-environmental example would be rock stars, who do not have close substitutes, so they can demand high fees.

The benefit we receive above and beyond what we pay for a good or service is called *consumer surplus* (area CBE in Figure 9-5). It can be an important concept in environmental economics, because if we are fortunate enough to obtain or use something at low or zero cost, our consumer surplus could be large, particularly if we are willing to pay a high price for the product or service. We could say that we are the beneficiaries of rent.

The concept of consumer surplus can also be used as an argument for a clean environment and livability. That "something" might not actually belong to us. In a rural setting, it could be walking in nearby woods, or in an urban setting, going for a walk in a public park. If the pleasure derived is more than the cost of admission, the extra benefit that we do not pay for is the consumer surplus. It is a rent that we can partake of and is produced by the environment.

Similarly, when resources are degraded or when the air or water is polluted, we lose some of these benefits and surpluses. Many problems in environmental economics arise precisely because of the existence of these nonpriced, and often nonmarketed values. Sometimes we can market the rent, such as beachfront property, but other rents are much harder to capture, because they are public goods.

PUBLIC GOODS, COMMON PROPERTY, AND PRIVATE GOODS

To develop resources, much hinges on property rights—who owns the property rights, and what are the roles of the property owners? There are three types of property:

- public goods: non-excludable, nonrival consumption (e.g., lighthouse, flood control);
- common property: non-excludable, rival consumption (e.g., fisheries, flowing streams); and
- private goods: excludable, and rival consumption (e.g., food, consumer goods).

Public Goods

Many classical economists claim that all we have to do is establish property rights, devolve these rights to the people so that everybody has property, and then the market will take care of everything after that. This may work fine when we are able to privatize the goods, but not if we have public goods or goods that look like public goods or close to them, or common property resources, since they do not fit in nicely with property rights, which can be used in a market setting.

Many people think natural resources are public goods just because they are available to the public. To qualify as a public good, two strong requirements need to be satisfied: (i) no one can be excluded from the consumption of public goods, and (ii) there is no rivalry in the consumption of public goods. A lighthouse is a good example of a public good, because it is hard to stop anyone on a nearby boat from navigating after seeing a lighthouse, and such use of a lighthouse by one person has no effect on its use by another person. Use of a lighthouse is non-excludable and has nonrival consumption.

Some public goods are less "pure" public goods; a flood control system is such an example. If we provide flood control, everybody within the area benefits. It appears that there is no rival consumption, but in fact we can exclude some people from using a flood control system by building embankments at different places, so it could be excludable.

With pure public goods, it may be difficult to rely on markets to pay for their costs. However, in the early 1700s there were, indeed, privately financed lighthouses on the US east coast. People then were willing to pay for lighthouses even though "free riders" used them, because they did not want to run aground on the rocky shores. That kind of lighthouse presents a sort of anachronism. Generally speaking, public goods, like flood control systems, are difficult to finance from private funds. That is why the US Federal Government typically pays for flood control on large projects. If there is a multipurpose water project involving irrigation, water supply, hydropower, and flood control, the US Federal Government usually pays for the project component containing the flood control system, because that is deemed a public good.

Common Property

Common property involves non-excludable goods or services, but which allow rival consumption. A classic example is the Boston Commons, which was once considered common property, but due to the rival consumption of cattle, a few landlords appropriated the grazing rights. Not too many cattle are seen on Boston Commons these days, but there may still be families in Boston who have the right to graze cattle there.

The same is true of fisheries, because they typically involve non-excludable use of a common property. Today we have the Law of the Sea, which establishes exclusive 300-kilometer zones, creating a sort of established property right for some fisherfolk. Open ocean fish are common property, since people cannot be excluded from fishing in the open ocean, but there is rival consumption.

Private Goods

Private goods are goods that are excludable and have rival consumption. Persons who own property, be it land or water, can keep other people off that property. For example, in parts of the US people can have water rights that permit them to own quantities of flowing water in perpetuity.

It is important to bear in mind what is a public good, what is common property, and what is private property. These things merge in some cases, and they generate a lot of heat when they do. Thus "privatizing" has become a bad word in the international community. For example, NGOs and citizen groups talk negatively about privatization of water companies that sell water to some and not others, especially the poor, who cannot afford to buy water.

SUMMARY

This short chapter serves to introduce a few economic concepts that potentially have great relevance to the issues of sustainability. We note, however, that the history of environmental economics has been developed only within the past three decades and that it is grappling with important issues usually ignored by the neoclassical economic tradition. Concepts of wealth and utility are fundamental to all human endeavors; only the economists have been bold enough to provide computable indices of concepts. These concepts, together with Pareto's notion of efficiency and optimality, provide a rich palette for the development of sustainability economics. This chapter provides the useful macro-and microeconomic concepts to complete the economic paradigm. Chapter 10 discusses the problems of market and government failures that cast doubt on the simple applicability of the powerful economic concepts to the study of sustainability. Chapter 10 attempts to provide the necessary fixes to the theory that make it more sustainability friendly.

SUSTAINABILITY: EXTERNALITIES, VALUATION, AND TIME EXTERNALITIES

A n externality can be defined as something that affects people, for good or for evil, over which they have no hand in the decision-making process. (See Box 10-1.) The key element here is the recognition that those involved did not play a role in determining the amount sold or the price paid for the commodity. As a result, the amount and the quality of the goods or services sold in the market might not maximize the welfare of society.[1]

In environmental terms, we generally think that externalities are bad things, but in fact externalities can be very positive. If we build a dam on a river, many people would say that is bad (unless, perhaps, the dam will provide them with vital amounts of water). Dams are good, however, for producing hydropower or water for irrigation; but they are often bad for the fish and the estuary downstream. Much depends on how we operate the dam.

Another aspect of an externality is that, by its very nature, it cannot be accounted for in a normal budgeting framework. The price of a loaf of bread in the supermarket does not necessarily take into account the soil erosion (an externality) caused by growing grain; it does factor in the fertilizers used (a non-externality), but does not include the eutrophication in rivers due to the fertilizer use. When we start looking at the life cycle of a product's manufacturing process, like a simple $1.98 loaf of bread, we might find that, when we calculate the externalities, its actual cost to society may be many times larger.

A simple example can help in explaining what is, and what is not, an externality (personal communication from John Dixon, November 2002). You are driving a car and the person sitting next to you lights up a cigarette. The windows of the car are closed. Is this an externality or not? It is. You were never asked about your health or comfort, and you have to inhale the secondary smoke, which is harmful. In a second case, and this is more realistic, if the person asked permission to smoke and you were to give it to him provided he rolls the window down, does this constitute an externality? No, it does not. Giving him permission makes you part of the decision-making process. The externality has been internalized. Even though it still affects you, you are now part of

Box 10-1. Making Externalities Sustainable

There are three ways externalities can be incorporated or not into any project. If we begin a project without consulting the people who will be affected by it, then the externalities will not be incorporated. If we do ask, and they say yes, then there is a willingness to accept the burden. But it might still be considered an externality if the educational status or the socioeconomic status of those affected is such that they do not understand the project's impacts. The externality only disappears when the transaction becomes a two-way street, i.e., those affected by the project and those undertaking the project both understand the scope of the impact of the proposed project and discuss compensation when necessary.

Source: John Dixon (personal communiction, November 2002)

---

[1] The authors wish to thank John Dixon for his important contributions to this chapter.

the decision-making process and, assuming you are informed and know the benefits and costs, you made a decision to allow the passenger to smoke.

A third example involves the same car and the same cigarette. But now when your passenger asks if he can smoke, you tell him yes, but it will cost him $1. Are you now affected by an externality? No, because if he does not smoke, you are not affected, and if he does smoke, you have set the price for compensation for your willingness to accept any risk to your health. So a compensation principle is at work.

By understanding this technical definition of an externality, we can understand why environmental economists try to identify first what the externalities are over space and over time, and then try to assign a value to them.

VALUATION

Looking back at the cigarette example, the driver might decide that cigarette smoking is annoying but he will put up with the risks and annoyances for a large compensatory amount. Hypothetically, the driver might not accept any amount of money, because the annoyance and the risks are too great. Realistically, there is probably some price that will induce the driver to put up with the smoker.

Generally in quantitative terms, the driver might decide to be indifferent between not smoking and the $1 compensation for smoking. By doing this the driver has established a market, and the externality has been internalized. When we internalize an externality, it goes away.

Ronald Coase and Internalization

In both examples given above, you are part of the decision-making process, and the externalities are being internalized. This is basically the Coase theorem (Coase, 1960, pp. 1-44). He says, when people are engaged in an issue and they enjoy well-established property rights, then in fact just by negotiating and by being part of the decision-making process, they can internalize the externalities, and thus solve the problem.

According to Coase, it does not matter who owns the initial property rights; if rights can be bought and traded, one can still end up at a superior solution. In a case involving a natural resource dispute between resort owners, a fleet of boats owned by fishing companies, and a logging company, the resort owners and fishing companies can combine resources and either reform the logging company's practices or buy it out.

The trouble with such Coasian solutions is that they do not work very well if the groups have large differences in numbers of members, political power, discount rates, and/or time horizons. For example, if logging has to be stopped, then the company has to be bought out, and it will at least need to be compensated for lost revenues. Restoring a degraded forest and compensating for related social costs arising to local inhabitants from logging of timber resources will likely cost more than buying out the timber company.

Note that such a Coasian solution through internalization of externalities may not work if there are 60,000 people impacted by one smoking factory chimney, and if all the impacted people get together and try to negotiate a solution. The transaction costs of such negotiations will be too high. But if there are two or three groups, or appropriate representatives of groups are involved, then it might work. Such considerations are part of the argument for participation in environmental negotiations. This is a way to try to internalize externalities by negotiation so that people can agree on how to deal with or eliminate externalities, perhaps by providing compensation, like someone who wants to smoke a cigarette paying $1.

Policy Making and Policy Response in the Face of Externalities

How do we respond to problems that we observe in the environment? First, we need to identify the externalities, the costs, and the benefits. Then we must decide the kind of responses likely to bring a society from a less efficient to a more efficient outcome, one where the total social welfare is increased. Externalities are thus very important when we are considering the meaning of "sustainability" in the phrase "economic sustainability."

Policy making requires looking at the externalities, trying to identify those who are or are not affected, and finding some way to bring those concerned into the decision-making process. It can be done by a government setting taxes or fees, or directly through consultation and other measures.

There may be externalities when resources are exploited, but this does not mean that such resources cannot be used. If the externalities are considered in the decision-making process, a much more informed decision can be made. And that is really the challenge. Economists concerned with sustainable development are trying to help make better decisions that result in a sustainable environment over time, that benefit various affected segments of society, and that recognize that ecosystems are linked. One must look at the whole picture in order not to miss any important parts of the equation.

Sources of Market Failure

The inability to make good decisions using classical economic methods is considered part of market failure, and often the reasons for this failure arise because we are dealing with public goods and externalities, which means that

- they involve non-excludable, nonrival consumption;
- they are common property resources; and
- they involve externalities.

Public goods have these three characteristics that are inconsistent with the assumptions of the classical economic model, which excludes external effects.

Unpriced Assets and Missing Markets

There may be no market for a particular good. Some things do not have a price, such as rainbows, and, of course, market clearing can take place only when we have prices on things. Where there is no market for particular commodities, they do not show up in the marketplace, they are self-consumed, or they are traded without a direct market.

Shadow Pricing

Shadow pricing refers to assigning of prices to nontraded goods, or adjusting the value of traded goods to account for market failures. When people have trouble estimating prices precisely, they look for values associated with the use of the resource. Typically, for nontraded commodities, where questions arise about the applicability of prices, we may have to establish shadow prices for the commodities in question. Cow dung, for instance, is a commodity that in many societies is not traded; but it is a valuable commodity and its shadow price can be computed. How can a shadow price for cow dung be established? For example, it can be used as a fuel. The alternative to using cow dung as a fuel is to buy fuel, such as firewood or kerosene. Or we can use cow dung as a fertilizer, and now we find an interesting issue. Is the shadow pricing for fertilizer more valuable than the shadow pricing for fuel? The arguments go up and down on both sides of these questions. These are serious attempts to put values on commodities that are not traded. Actually cow dung is traded in many parts of the world. The delivery system for cow dung can involve sticking it on a wall, and when it dries and falls off, sellers put it on top of their heads in big stacks and deliver it to the consumers. How about cow urine? That is a valuable product because cow urine contains many valuable nutrients: nitrogen, phosphorus, and potassium (NPK). If we can figure out what it costs to buy fertilizer, then we can estimate the shadow price of NPK in urine.

This is what shadow pricing is about: it deals with best estimates of important things that are not part of normally traded goods. If we do only a superficial economic analysis based upon traded commodities, we will ignore valuable resources such as the NPK in urine. To bring such items into the analysis, we have to be able to put prices on them. We have to be able to take them into account to have a complete GDP, since they generate income, and thus some values can be attributed to them.

Lack of Property Rights

Lack of property rights presents a classic problem in many areas. If we do not have property rights, then either we use too much of what is freely available, or we may not have access to the resource that may be used up by others before we have an opportunity to use it. We see that all over the world with resources like water. Where people do not have a clear title to the resource, they may use as much as they can, particularly if they do not have to pay for it.

Transaction costs can be high. A classic example concerning use of water relates to monitoring and measuring flows of water for irrigation and rural uses even with clear property rights. There are no low-cost, foolproof meters for such purposes. To measure such goods and services, great amounts of high-quality time and highly motivated government servants are required.

Irreversibility

There is also the issue of irreversibility. Textbook economic theory is often based on mythological items such as "widgets." One widget looks like another widget, and we keep on making widgets forever. We cannot do that with resources, such as land, water, air, climate, and species of plants and animals. We are in an area in which simple economic models will not provide accurate guidance.

Ignorance and Uncertainty

Ignorance and uncertainty can lead decision makers to make inappropriate decisions. Indeed, a lot of ignorance stems from uncertainty, and there is a lot of uncertainty in dealing with the environment. For example, did anyone really expect Florida to be hit by six hurricanes in 2004 and 2005. They were highly unlikely. Since the nineteenth century, there were few hurricane seasons with so many hurricanes coming ashore. Is it going to stay this way? How often are they going to come? The answers to these questions are very, very uncertain, but they will make a big difference in planning for the future.

Sources of Government (Policy) Failure

Market distortions occur when market prices do not reflect the "true" cost of providing something. One cause of market distortions is government subsidies, and many major governments, including the governments of the US and Europe, provide such subsidies. Market distortions can also arise from the lack of good governance. A competitive free market usually works well when there is a strong government behind it, and when there is good governance. There must be contracts, contract laws, and enforcement of contracts; and other institutions, such as courts, must also be in place.

If the government does not provide for these aspects, problems can arise, including market failure, which should be distinguished from a government or policy failure. However, the failure to correct a distortion in a market is often considered a government or policy failure.

Subsidies, nonsustainable resource uses, polluters, inappropriate tax incentives and credits, overregulation, underregulation, and conflicting regulatory regimes; all of these exist in the US and elsewhere and result in government failure. For example, the number of pages in the US Federal Register dealing with water regulation is unknown, but one estimate suggests that there are 55,000 such pages. Those pages deal with federal regulations, not regulations by the states or local governments. This might be overregulation, or underregulation, but it certainly gives rise to some conflicting regulatory regimes. The US Federal Endangered Species Act conflicts with much of the other environmentally relevant legislation. For example, some people have recognized water rights, yet some of these water rights are, or appear to be, in conflict with more recent legislation, particularly the Endangered Species Act.

Externalities and Valuation

Externalities may be both spatial and temporal. Spatial externalities are obvious: for example, picture smoke from a factory blowing over a city. Temporal externalities have an impact in the future. Climate change is an example of a temporal externality, as many of the effects will be felt much later.

Valuation, both qualitative and quantitative, is another important issue. Consider the decision-making issues related to the value and location of goods and services arising from a mangrove forest.

There are marketed and nonmarketed goods, while the location of goods and services may be on-site or off-site (see Figure 10-1). The box in the top left corner indicates that on-site and marketed goods and services usually are included in economic analysis. Such products of a mangrove forest as poles, charcoal, wood chips, mangroves, and crabs are all marketed, and if they are marketed, they have prices. So those are priced commodities. Other goods and services, shown in the upper right box for off-site and marketed goods and services, are priced off-site and may include fish or shellfish that were nurtured in the mangrove forest but caught in adjacent waters. Mangrove forest goods and services on-site but nonmarketed, shown in the lower left box, are seldom included in decision making, but can include such valuable goods and services as medicinal products, domestic fuelwood, food in times of famine, nursery areas for juvenile fish, feeding grounds for estuarine fish and shrimp, and opportunities for viewing and studying wildlife. Off-site and nonmarketed goods and services of a mangrove forest, shown in the lower right corner, include such items as nutrient flows to estuaries and buffering against storm damage, all of which are often ignored.

Figure 10-1. How Externalities and Valuation Affect Decision Making
(an Example from a Mangrove Forest)

		Location of Goods and Services	
		On-Site	Off-Site
Valuation of Goods and Services	Marketed	1 **Usually included in an economic analysis** (e.g., poles, charcoal, wood chips, mangroves, crabs)	2 **May be included** (e.g., fish or shellfish caught in adjacent waters)
	Nonmarketed	3 **Seldom included** (e.g., medicinal uses of mangrove, domestic fuelwood, food in times of famine, nursery area for juvenile fish, fishing ground for estuarine fish and shrimp, viewing and studying wildlife)	4 **Usually ignored** (e.g., nutrient flows to estuaries, buffer to storm damage)

Source. John Dixon (personal communication, November 2002)

All of these economic goods and activities are generated by a mangrove forest and would be lost if the mangrove ceased to exist. The problem is that most analyses focus only on on-site, marketed goods and services, because people are familiar with on-site prices and can estimate what the resulting benefits would be.

APPROACHES TO VALUATION

How do we place economic values on goods or services that often do not pass through markets? There is a rich menu of approaches that can be used to place monetary, economic values on different parts of the environment that are being used for economic purposes. These approaches include changes in production, hedonic approaches, survey techniques, and surrogate markets (Figure 10-2).

Figure 10-2. Approaches to Valuation

Changes in production	Survey Techniques
• Crops, fisheries, water • Health • Opportunity cost	• Contingent valuation market
Hedonic Approaches	Surrogate Markets
• Property value • Land values • Wage differential	• Travel cost

Source: John Dixon (personal communication, November 2002)

Changes in Production

With tangible products like crops, fisheries, and water, it is fairly easy to determine values. When we have a real product, we often have a market price, and therefore it is fairly easy to measure the impact of increasing or decreasing production. But, as we just saw in the case of a mangrove forest, if fish caught off-site were not recognized as being dependent on the mangrove, that value could be overlooked by the landowner of the mangrove forest. The landowner might ignore it in making a decision as to the value of the mangrove. Thus in this case, a simple change in production approach could not be used.

Hedonic Approaches

What other approaches to valuation may be used in places where we do not have prices? Hedonic approaches, from the Greek *hedone*, meaning "pleasure," deal with those environmental attributes that give pleasure, such as scenic surroundings, an office with a view, and so on. We can often measure the benefits received from unpriced environmental attributes through what people are willing to pay for them. Recall the example of the house on the beach versus the same house inland. Housing prices, especially different prices between comparable dwellings in different locations with different environmental attributes provide an example of hedonic pricing.

Property values and land values can provide important information on how people value different attributes of the environment, and we can use that information to estimate monetary values. We can value nonmarketable attributes, such as an ocean view, by seeing how much an individual is willing to pay for the beach house or how a community sets its real estate taxes for ocean front versus inland properties.

Wage differentials can also be explained by a hedonic approach: sometimes people are willing to work for less money if the job is more attractive or is in a more attractive environment. A comparison of wages for traffic policemen who work outdoors with policemen who work in tunnels where there is a lot of air pollution might give some sense of wage differential for an environmentally unfriendly occupation.

People with identical qualifications and jobs will be paid less in Hawaii than in any less attractive location, because they want to be in Hawaii for other, nonwork-related reasons. For example, many places in Alaska must pay premium wages to attract workers, because many people tend to go there solely for monetary reasons.

Survey Techniques, Including the Contingent Valuation Method

Survey techniques or contingent valuation methods rely on asking people literally how much they are willing to pay for a cleaner environment or some attribute of the environment. These techniques also focus on how much people are willing to accept in compensation for decreasing environmental quality. Going back to our earlier example, when the car driver told the passenger he could smoke but it would cost him $1, the driver was setting a price for his willingness to accept any risk to his health. The smoker, on the other hand, had yet to make a choice whether he should pay the driver compensation or refrain from smoking.

Admittedly, while the sampling is small—the driver and the smoker—the example is basically a survey. Surveys can be very important and are commonly used when markets do not exist or when we cannot look at property values or other indices. Ideally a fairly large sample would be required to provide a reliable result.

One, however, has to be wary when relying on a survey. We are gathering information, but we have to be careful in determining what the answers mean. There are many examples of surveys that are meaningless because the questions were drawn up incompetently or the answers were misinterpreted. Sample size is one of the ways of improving reliability, as is improving the randomness of the sample.

Surrogate Markets

The last set of techniques is called surrogate markets. Here again, the basic idea behind the surrogate market is that environmental economists are interested in determining a value of some nonmarketable attribute of the environment. It might be a recreational destination, a national park, or a cultural monument. We want to observe how people value it. The problem is that often the entrance fee is zero or small.

Economists approach this problem by looking at tangential aspects such as the time and money people spend in traveling to a site. We can actually use that information—when a lot of people come from different distances to visit a place—to create a demand curve. The data are the cost and time of travel and a series of steps are required to estimate demand. The basic underlying idea is that those visitors who live near a site have a lot of consumer surplus, while the most distant visitor has basically no consumer surplus. We can use this information to get estimates of the value added per visitor per day for different types of recreational destinations.

All of these techniques are being used to place monetary values on things that are not easily bought or sold. Sometimes by using a hedonic approach we can determine a price, although not for the commodity of interest per se but for something else that is embodied in the commodity. That is to suggest that, through a hedonic approach, we can establish the value of a home with a view of the ocean, but not necessarily the cost of building and maintaining such a home.

Total Economic Value

A final concept, which puts all of these approaches in context, is total economic value (see Figure10-3). The basic idea is to combine use values and non-use values. People are generally confused at this point and ask, what exactly are non-use values? Before answering that question let us consider an easier concept—use values.

Use values are concrete, such as the value we get from the production of goods; establishing fisheries, forests, and water resources; building dams; and so on. Use values can be broken down into two separate categories, which we call direct and indirect use.

Figure 10-3. The Concept of Total Economic Value

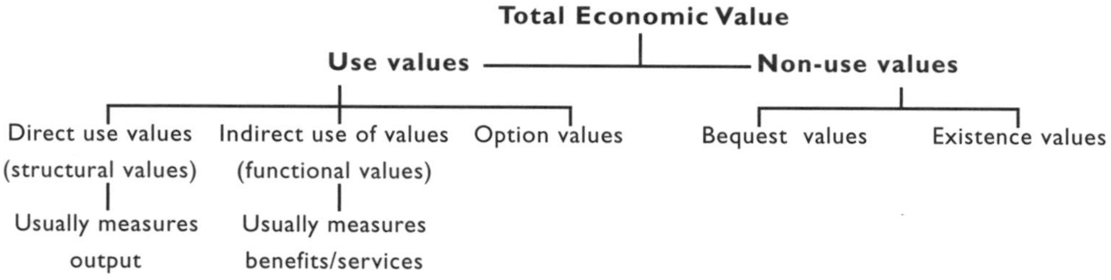

Total Economic Value

Use values ———————— Non-use values

Direct use values	Indirect use of values	Option values	Bequest values	Existence values
(structural values)	(functional values)			
Usually measures output	Usually measures benefits/services			

Source: John Dixon (personal communication, November 2002)

Direct and Indirect Use Values

A direct use value occurs when we directly use something or consume something so that we must produce more of it, such as fish. There can also be nonconsumptive direct use, as when we go SCUBA diving in the same marine area that produces the fish. The diver is using the same resource but not consuming it. It is obvious that nonconsumptive use is usually more sustainable. A hundred years ago, the East African game parks were hunting grounds. With no regulation, the animals were hunted almost into extinction. Today visitors to these parks come with cameras instead of guns. Discounting poaching, the animal population is recovering. Hunting turned out to be nonsustainable.

However, some restrictions on hunting, when appropriately enforced, can result in a sustainable result. For example, it is still possible to hunt animals in certain countries, but one must pay a large fee (about $10,000 to take down a wildebeest), and the hunting is strictly controlled. This is a way to manage game and at the same time extract some economic rent. Over time, we sometimes see big shifts from consumptive to nonconsumptive uses of the same resource and then back again to a sustainable equilibrium.

Indirect use values are usually measures of benefits or services—ecosystem services, water purification in wetlands, and greenbelts around cities that help reduce pollution in the air and water. There are a lot of ecosystem services that we benefit from directly or indirectly whether we consume them or not, but they are a little harder to measure.

For instance, if we take water out of the river for irrigation or for drinking, that would be for a direct use of the water. Indirect use would involve, for instance, use of water for aesthetic values associated with looking at the water. Water for fisheries, water used by wildlife, and water for the ecosystem may involve both direct and indirect use values.

We can estimate values and prices for such uses. The indirect use values, which are often ignored, are often very important. Studies conducted on the use of water in the Charles River in the mid-1970s focused on the value of rental properties on the river, both facing the river and facing away from the river. These properties consisted of identical-sized apartments with identical amenities; the only difference was that some people had a view of the Charles River and some people had a view of the Back Bay. The properties with a view of the river commanded several hundred dollars more in the monthly rental. This extra rental is an amenity value, which arises primarily from viewing, not consuming, the water in the Charles River. This is an example of the Hedonic valuation method.

The irony is that the Charles River was at that time actually in terrible shape, and could not be used in the sense of a direct use. Today wind surfers and sailors enjoy contact uses of the river, which are direct uses; others enjoy walking along the banks of the river, which is a use of the river without actually consuming it, for which people are willing to pay. In the good old days, when the Charles was pretty smelly, particularly during the summer, Harvard University bought millions of gallons of water from the Metropolitan water authority to augment the river flow and thus reduce the smell during commencement week ceremonies. That is an example of an indirect use value based on what the river looks like and smells like, and this indirect use value was certainly worth a lot of money. It is thus possible to monetize non-use values with actual dollar figures, or to think of good proxy values for them.

Option Values

Another use value is what is called an "option value" or an "option demand." It is an economic or environmental value that is deferred. It is a value where people might say of a recreational area: "I may not want to go there now, but I am willing to pay something to maintain that resource in case I decide to go later." Or it could be that society as a whole may decide that it wants to maintain resources so that future generations can use them. Many NGOs around the world are very effective in raising money from people who are willing to pay something to maintain a habitat or to protect endangered species for future use or enjoyment. Thus we can measure option and existence values by looking at donations.

For example, perhaps we do not want any more dams on the Colorado River. We may not be keen about going down the Colorado River on a raft, because we could fall overboard and be injured, but on the other hand we would like to keep open the option to go there and experience the wild river. How do we express value for that? Perhaps by sending a donation to an NGO trying to preserve the Colorado River. We may want this option for ourselves or for our grandchildren.

In Maryland one can pay an extra $20 to buy a "Protect Chesapeake Bay" license plate for a car. The money goes to a special fund to protect the bay. People who buy the plate may never go to the bay area, but they value it enough to pay for its protection and for ensuring that it will still be there in case they do go. They may also want to protect this environment for future generations.

Non-use Values

Non-use values consist of existence values and bequest values. Option values, which appear under "use values," have a different time horizon than non-use values. It is important to distinguish between option values and non-use values. Bequest values, which appear under "non-use" values, are technically the same as option values except that bequest values have a longer time frame. Both are usually estimated using the contingent valuation method.

1. Bequest values

A direct equivalent of an option value is a bequest value—something held for the next generation. For example, even though we may not plan to go to a particular wildlife park, we may want our children to have the option to do so. We are willing to pay something to ensure that option, and such payments for the continuing maintenance of a particular wildlife park constitute the bequest value of the resource. It is amazing the amount of money that is generated worldwide from people who contribute to various NGOs such as Greenpeace, Conservation International, and the WWF precisely for these types of benefits. For instance, Basso (2005, p. 7) reports that in 2003 the annual revenue at the top 30 US environmental organizations exceeded $2.1 billion. While bequest values may appear a bit murky, we can quantify them, and the numbers tend to be quite large, because a large number of people are involved.

2. Existence values

Existence values, which fall under non-use values, are pure benefit—knowing that something exists for the very value of its existence, like whales or mountains. It is the least tangible of these types of values. When we move from direct use to indirect use to option to bequest to existence, and actually try to estimate value, the evaluation techniques become less and less tangible. When evaluating use values we can look at things such as prices and quantities. We can even do this for some indirect use values. However, when we try to measure existence values we always end up relying on survey-based approaches and contingent evaluations (the latter phrase relates to whether something, such as a forest, will indeed exist when the time of the proposed use, such as a camping trip, occurs).

Non-use Values: The Global Warming Example

Let us try to evaluate something that is of concern to everyone: global warming. Global warming would probably fall under non-use values, sub-indexed as an existence or bequest value. While the present generation is presumably safe, we worry about what kind of world we will leave for our children. There are things that can be done now, but when we deal with a global phenomenon, it becomes much more difficult. We have externalities dealing not just with space and time but also with cultures and political jurisdictions. Global warming, if it does occur at a significant level as predicted by many scientists, is something that is very likely a long way off in the future. How do we measure the value of protecting against something that might occur in the distant future like global warming or a possible collision of the earth with a big meteor? People generally do not value the future nearly as much as they do the present, and so the challenge is to convince society that the future is something to be concerned about and to not discount too much the likelihood of its occurrence.

In sum, there are different evaluation approaches that can be used for each type of effect. As in many other things in economic analysis, it depends on the data we have, the time available to do the analysis, and the resources to do a study.

ECONOMIC ASSESSMENT OF SUSTAINABLE PROJECTS

The meaning of sustainable is not clear in the context of public and private investment appraisal. Sustainability implies taking into account the factors affecting an investment not well reflected in market prices and financial profits. This has been attempted since the late 1950s by benefit-cost analysis (BCA), which adds social evaluation to financial appraisal. Private investors are concerned mainly with profit and financial return based on prices of inputs and outputs associated with a project. BCA attempts to base an assessment on social prices, which are estimates of prices that would obtain in a truly free market with no distortion by government or other institutions. The purpose is to calculate the benefit of a project to the nation state as a whole. It could be applied equally to public and private investment. In practice it is costly, requires highly skilled practitioners, and is ultimately arbitrary with regard to the estimation of social prices. It has not been used widely except by the World Bank and the regional development banks. For example, these banks would price unskilled labor at zero, because it comes from the ranks of the unemployed, or perhaps from the farm sector, where the only cost is the extra food that laborers consume while working. In recent years there has been more emphasis on financial internal rate of return (FIRR), which uses market prices and values, rather than economic internal rate of return (EIRR) based upon shadow prices.

Social considerations are given effect by subprojects to cater to the welfare of those directly affected by a project, perhaps those displaced by a dam. This gives rise to a paradox. Sustainability is directed at the actions intended to improve or preserve the environment as a whole. It does not mean every project must survive forever. A mine is a good example, whereas a renewable resource like a fishery or a forest would be conserved. Sustainability is given effect at the project level by emphasis on economics, environment, and equity—the three Es or triple bottom line.

Methods used to assess the sustainability of a project are different in the public and private sectors, but first we will discuss the common aspects of the methodology, of which accounting for time is of paramount concern.

How to Discount the Future

The discount rate is used to compare money available at different points in time. Consider a preference for $100 today compared with $100 after one year. Everyone has a personal discount rate, albeit subliminal. Most would prefer $100 today; invested at low risk, it might earn 4% per year. Correcting for inflation at 2%, it will still be worth 4% minus 2%, or 2% per year. There is also a time preference for money that varies with every individual. Consider how much you would want in a year to be equal to $100 today. Frequently students will say this is $130, meaning their personal simple discount rate is 30%!

Private investors and companies also have discount rates that they apply to all projects. There is some debate on this, because the rate should reflect the cost to the company of borrowing money—the so-called risk-free rate—plus an allowance for risk, which may be different for each investment. If the cost of borrowing capital were 4% and the risk assessed were at 5%, the company discount rate would be 9%. This is known as the $[r+ r`]$ expression. If the corporate tax rate were 50%, then the rate becomes $2[r+ r`]$ or 18%. No investment that yields less than 18% would be acceptable. In practice, rates of borrowing differ between companies and states, as does intuitive assessment of risk, so thresholds of expected discount differ widely. Companies frequently operate on a 10% to 15% FIRR. Development banks usually specify 10% as an acceptable EIRR. Private companies and public sector enterprises will calculate cash flow—annual income and expenses— for each project. That discount rate, that makes an annual income stream equal to an annual stream of expenses is a measure of return or profit. Alternatively, that discount rate that makes the stream of net income—or net present value—equal to zero is called the internal rate of return (IRR). This approach is known as discounted cash flow. If income flow is measured in market prices, it is known as a financial assessment. If social prices are used, the approach is known as social benefit-cost analysis. So the discount rate is used to compare projects with different annual (or even monthly) cash profiles over 10 or 20 years. Note that using a 15% discount rate means the present value of income in years beyond 10 becomes essentially zero. Before the discounted cash flow was used and even now, companies will sometimes want their money back in three years, say for investments abroad, implying a much higher discount rate.

Market Rates of Discount

If one has a mortgage at 4.8% for 30 years on a house, we can calculate to the nearest penny what will be the interest paid each year or each month. There is no ambiguity in that. However, we do not typically make public investment decisions using the private market rate of discount. If one were in a decision-making role in government, and dealing with investments in environmental facilities or investments that will influence what happens in the future, then one would use the social rate of discount. What is the social rate of discount, and what actual rate should it be?

Social Rates of Discount

The social rate deals with how we as a society view the future. Political considerations are very important in setting the social rate of discount. In the US the social rate of discount is set every year by the US Congress, so it tells agencies, for instance the Corps of Engineers, what rate to use to discount future benefits and the future costs associated with federal water projects. It is not an interest rate that the market generates, but what the social and political system agrees on. Historically in the US, it was 3.5% or 4% for a long period of time, and now is it is quite low (3% on June 14, 2005). It has varied between 7.5% and 2.5% over the past 200 years. It is part of our view of how we ought to treat the future in a public sense. If we use a high discount rate, the present value of future costs or benefits after 10 or 15 years is very insignificant. Of course many people ask, what has the future ever done for us? And that is actually a good question, because if we look at the history of the industrialized countries, every succeeding generation seems to be better off than the previous one. And so we can ask, why are we saving money, why are we worrying about the social future of these people? They are going to be vastly wealthier than we are. We should consume now.

Hence, it is very hard to figure out what the right number for the social rate of discount should be. But certainly it ought to be the same across the governmental investment sectors. In developing countries both private and social discount rates are influenced by the availability of capital. There are different niches, and different people can borrow at these different rates. Clearly, if the capital market has a very high discount rate, then this information should be used by the politicians who establish social rates of discount as an indication that maybe they should go slowly on raising social rates of discount on future investments. International agencies like the World Bank and ADB pick a proxy for the social rate of discount. Years ago, it used to be about 10%. Currently it is about 7%. And when they do a project evaluation, they accept the project as a good one or a bad one depending upon the discount rate that they use. The World Bank's historical yield on its bonds was in the region of 6%, and they lent out money at 7% for infrastructure and social programs. Nowadays, because of the concern about the environment and due to the power of international NGOs, it is very hard to actually build environmentally intrusive projects such as dams with multilateral or bilateral official funding. The international private banks, however, are happy to lend money for dams at private rates of interest. So we find some developing countries borrowing money at higher rates from sources that let them cut corners environmentally. The Three Gorges Dam in the PRC, which is the biggest dam in the world, was built entirely with the country's own resources and with some loans from private banks.

Pure Time Preference

Another aspect of discounting is pure time preference. This confuses the concept of the social rate of discount. People and institutions have a preference for consumption in the present: we do not know what it is, maybe 2%, maybe 3%. Pure time preference can be added to the inflation rate to arrive at an estimate of the appropriate social rate of discount.

Problems with Discounting

With large-consequence events that may happen a long time in the future like global warming, which may cause serious damage in 100 years, when applying any of the discounting rates, even a social rate of discount as low as 2% to 3%, future damages are miniscule in present value terms. The actual bad consequences are so small when discounted back to the present that it is hard to justify spending hundreds of billions of dollars in the near term. Some suggestions involve spending major amounts in the next few years on switching from fossil fuels and sequestering CO_2. There are many options, but they are all expensive, and because we rely on discounting that emphasizes relatively short-term effects, we have difficulty in dealing with intergenerational problems.

CATEGORIES OF COSTS

To carry out discounting, we must be able to specify the benefits and costs in monetary terms. As in all human endeavors, costs are much easier to assess than benefits. So much of the literature on discounting focuses upon things like capital costs, operation and maintenance costs, variable costs and fixed costs, and salvage value.

Capital Costs

The capital cost is easily understandable. For example, when buying a house in Cambridge for X-million dollars, one could put the X-million dollars into the seller's bank account. More typically one would arrange for a loan from the Cambridge Trust Bank, and take that X-million dollars from their depositors and give it to the seller. That is a capital transfer, and it tends to happen in big lumpy payments.

Many of the investment costs are not paid all on the first day. We spread them out. Little investments (like buying a house) are still lumpy, but they are not exactly like $20 billion for the Three Gorges Dam. There are some subtleties involved in the capital markets, too. But certainly, the capital costs that we are dealing with in investment projects for development in any country in the world are unique, because typically the front-end cost is large.

Variable and Fixed Costs

Once the project is up and running, operation and maintenance costs accrue, which are usually relatively small in comparison with the capital costs. They are maybe 2% or 3% of the capital costs, or maybe even less. For example, for a coal-fired power plant, which produces only one thirteenth the energy output (kwh) of the Three Gorges Dam in the PRC, there are large variable costs, and also large fixed costs such as operation costs, including buying, shipping, and storing coal in addition to the fixed costs of labor and management.

Salvage Value

Salvage value raises interesting issues, because in public investment analysis, salvage value is very rarely used. For example, what is the salvage value of the Aswan High Dam? That is hard to figure out, because if it fell apart, or if it became filled with silt, or if it were no longer needed by the Egyptian government, we cannot send a trailer truck and take it away. It is hard to imagine what the salvage value is.

Think about a nuclear power plant. Nuclear power plants are examples of projects that, when they have finished their useful life, have large dismantling and storage costs to be met. So the salvage value is negative even though there is a big secondary market for the turbines, generating sets, and similar items. People buy and sell them and take them away after they have been used.

ECONOMIC LIFE OF A PROJECT

When discussing sustainability it is important to ask: How long should we expect things to last? How do we define the life of the project? Here is a hint: some dams in Spain and in North Africa built by the Romans are still in use. That is a long time—2,000 years. There are also irrigation projects in the PRC that have run continuously for 2,000 years. There is a physical life, clearly; physical life is how long the thing lasts. But there is an economic life, which says, at some point, the operation and maintenance costs may overtake the value the project is supposed to provide.

This works very nicely when a discount rate is used, because if we are using a discount rate of about 8% to 10%, future benefits that occur after 20 or 40 years contribute little in present value terms. Thus, it does not matter about the end of the project, because by the time we have discounted it to the present, all the benefits and all the costs in the future have disappeared; they are not affecting our decision right now. So in a sense, it is a moot point. In most public works projects, people have not bothered about salvage value. The discount rate will take care of it.

There is an interesting question as to the sustainable life of equipment that arises when considering the shoals off the Massachusetts coast, where wind generators are proposed; if we make the investment now, would it preclude other investments in the future for more efficient machines? That is not so hard to address, because the assumption would be that the proposers of these windmills have taken into account their economic life. Windmills are things that do have a salvage value. Wind generators also have operation and maintenance costs, which increase over time. So as they age, the cost of maintaining them goes up, and at some point even if the windmills are still working, the economic life is reached, because the expected benefits less the costs will become negative.

How and what do we know about the costs of sustainable investments? *The Engineering News Record Cost Index* is a construction cost index, started in 1908, which has been normalized to 100 in 1913. It is based upon a basket of goods including 200 hours of common labor, plus 25 hundred-weight of standard structural steel shapes at the mill price, plus 1.128 tons of Portland cement, plus 1,088 board feet of two-by-four lumber. In 1913, it was 100 and it was at 6,581 by 2003, a 65-fold increase!

The Engineering News Record Cost Index is published quarterly, but it is not the only price index. The EPA has its own price index; there is a Department of Commerce consumer price index (CPI), plus many other price indices. It is important to figure out what they are based upon to be able to go back and forth between the present level and historical times. For instance in 1967, the CPI was 33.4 (based upon a 1982-84 average of 100). Now it is more than 190. Salaries in major educational institutions in Cambridge, Massachusetts, have gone up at least 6.5 times over the same time period. But these are not really wage increases; rather they have been just keeping up with the CPI. However, the price of a house in Cambridge has increased considerably, by more than 15 times in that time period, or more than twice the CPI.

Whatever happened to the 10-cent cigar? We can look it up in these types of indices and find that 10-cent cigars are actually just about the right price now. Gasoline, however, still costs less than it did in 1973, when it was considered to be outrageously expensive. So a gallon of gasoline now priced at about $3 a gallon is still less than it was in deflated dollars in the early 1970s when deflated using the CPI.

ECONOMIC ASSESSMENT OF SUSTAINABLE PLANS AND PROJECTS

In an excellent review article, McFarquhar (2001) shows graphically (Table 10-1) the relationships among the various economic accounting methods and their implications for economic sustainability.

Table 10-1. Relationships Among Net Present Value,
Benefit-Cost Ratio, and Economic Internal Rate of Return

NPV	BCR		EIRR
If > 0 then	> 1	and	> r [cost of capital]
If < 0 then	< 1	and	< r
If = 0 then	1		= r

EIRR   economic internal rate of return
BCR   benefit cost ratio
NPV   net present value

Source: McFarquhar, http://www-pam.usc.edu/volume4/v4i1a3s1.html (2001)

Table 10-2. Financial Internal Rate of Return versus Weighted Average Cost of Capital

FIRR > WACC	Project covers cost and yields profit
FIRR = WACC	No private profit
FIRR < WACC	Project requires subsidy
FIRR = ZERO	Project covers costs except cost of finance
FIRR < ZERO	Cost recovery not possible

FIRR   financial internal rate of return
WACC   weighted average cost of capital

Source: McFarquhar, http://www-pam.usc.edu/volume4/v4i1a3s1.html (2001)

In Table 10-2 he shows the relationships that must hold for a project to be financially sustainable by comparing the FIRR with the weighted average cost of capital (WACC). This analysis helps reveal the subsidy requirements of projects that are deemed socially desirable but do not cover costs.

Against this background, how are sustainable projects to be assessed? The current approach in the MDBs is to do conventional FIRR and EIRR analyses of projects to reflect their financial and economic benefits. The essence of sustainability is that major factors such as energy and environment should be taken into account, and local people affected by the project should not be disadvantaged by it. So specific subprojects can be designed to address these factors with their own net income stream. These are then included in the project assessments. Perhaps a project may provide an alternative site for frogs whose habitat is destroyed by a dam. Or it may provide compensation in the form of retraining for displaced farmers. Emphasis on women may involve projects for their education and training. Energy may involve economy in the use of fossil fuels. The benefits of these projects are measured qualitatively. Compensation is provided to those who stand to lose from a project

In the private sector, corporate social responsibility rules. This means that companies are exhorted to make sacrifices in the interest of sustainability by observing good practice above that required by law. This may involve pollution control, reducing energy per unit of output, paying equal wages to women with privileges for child minding, flexible hours of work, holiday privileges, or whatever.

Some may argue that this has no cost, as it will make companies more attractive to investors. To some extent companies are probably doing these costless things anyway.

It has always been in the interest of a company to consider employees, consumers, and other stakeholders as a way of increasing shareholder returns. But more likely a politically correct image on energy, environment, and reverse discrimination does have costs. These are borne by the taxpayer and the shareholders. The taxpayer, represented by government, is unlikely to resist companies assisting in the burden of welfare provision. How far the shareholder will tolerate reduced profit before shifting investment to less hostile climes, most likely overseas, remains to be seen. For example German unemployment is at a very high level, and German companies are unable to compete because of high welfare wages. This is probably unsustainable in the long run.

ECONOMIC ASSESSMENT OF INVESTMENTS IN CLIMATE CHANGE MITIGATION

Climate change mitigation presents an interesting series of questions associated with it. Figure 10-4 shows the market interest rates of US long-term government bonds from 1790 to 1999. This is an approximation of what might be considered a proxy for the social rate of discount. The nice thing about these data is that we have a consistent time series. Over these 210 years, the interest rate was fairly constant between 2% and 6%, although there were some jumps during the 1970s, during the presidency of Jimmy Carter. Subsequently there has been a steady decline; the interest rates were high in the past, and they have come down. If we are looking to the past for clues for discounting the future, these data are very suggestive of what may happen.

Figure 10-4. Long-Term Market Interest Rates from 1790 to 1999

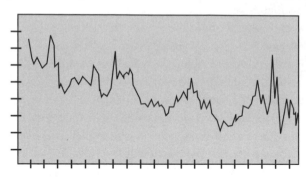

Market Interest Rates, US Long-Term Government
Bonds, 1790-1999 (adjusted for inflation)
Source: Newell and Pizer (2002), p. 17

Richard Newell and William Pizer (2002) from *Resources for the Future* authored an interesting article examining potential algorithms for discounting the long-term intergenerational future. The second column of the Table 10-3 shows the value today of $100 in the future. At year zero (now), $100 is worth $100; if you have $100 in your pocket, you have $100. If someone offers you $100 in 20 years time, you would be willing to offer him or her only $45.64 if the discount rate is 4%. This is the time value of money. One hundred and sixty years in the future, $100 will be worth only $0.19 right now. This says that the future does not really amount to much. After 100 years you would not worry a lot about what is happening. If you are going to spend a lot of money now to attempt to control climate change in the future, the benefits are going to come in 100 years, and those benefits will be worth only $4 for every $100 spent now. We have to think about trading off a $150 billion investment now to control climate change against the value of those effects in the future.

In Table 10-3, Newell and Pizer show the values using a 4% discount rate (column 2). In column 3, they calculate the discount factor averaging between 1% and 7%. This interest rate range is between where it has been historically. The present value of $100 in column 3 is actually worth a little bit more after 60 years than with the straight 4% discounting; it is worth $10 or twice as much using a discount factor averaging between 1% and 7% even though the average rate is still 4%.

So the Newell and Pizer argument is that perhaps we should discount not based on the constant, which is the way it is usually done. Almost all practitioners are dedicated to constant interest rates or variable ones that are written into contracts. But the future is worth a little bit more with this averaging between 1% and 7%.

Now the fourth column on Table 10-3 is methodologically very interesting; it is a random walk. Random walks are a way of taking stochastic events and simulating them. Column 4 is based upon thousands of random walks, between 1% and 7% averaged out. Now we find that the future is worth a lot more; after 60 years $100 has a present worth of $12.

If we are planning to curb future global warming, what discount rate should we use? Four percent is a low figure, and may be close to what most experts would propose, and it is close to a proxy for the social rate of discount, which is historically the average of US federal bonds.

So what we need is some way now where people can say if we use a zero discount rate, or negative discount rates, the future counts more than the present. Countries like Japan were close to having a negative interest rate for a while because their interest rates on bank deposits were so low. When we take out the inflationary aspects, possibly it would have been negative. This is a conundrum that we cannot resolve right now, but it is very important in any discussion of long-term changes in the environment, since sustainability is what we are talking about. If we were talking about 400 years in the future, at 4% the benefits would be zero. They would still exist under column 3—not very strongly, but certainly, we could still argue for present day action if the benefits were huge. The damage, as portrayed in the movie *The Day After*, would be so colossal as to be close to infinite. If we have an infinite value there, then it is going be infinite if we discount it back to the present. Some people believe climate warming is going to be the end of human life on earth; for *Homo sapiens* that could be considered close to infinite damage! Fortunately, few observers believe that the damage is going be infinite.

Table 10-3. Value Today of $100 in the Future Under Different Discounting Paradigms

Years in future		Discounted rate model		Value relative to constant discounting	
	Constant 4%	Mean reverting	Random walk	Mean reverting	Random walk
0	$100.00	$100.00	$100.00	1	1
20	45.64	46.17	46.24	1	1
40	20.83	21.90	22.88	1	1
60	9.51	10.61	12.54	1	1
80	4.34	5.23	7.63	1	2
100	1.98	2.61	5.09	1	3
120	0.90	1.33	3.64	1	4
140	0.41	0.68	2.77	2	7
160	0.19	0.36	2.20	2	12
180	0.09	0.19	1.81	2	21
200	0.04	0.10	1.5	3	39
220	0.02	0.06	1.33	3	75
240	0.01	0.03	1.18	4	145
260	00.0	0.02	1.06	5	285
280	00.0	0.01	0.97	7	568
300	00.0	0.01	0.89	11	1,147
320	00.0	0.01	0.83	16	2,336
340	00.0	0.00	0.78	26	4,796
360	00.0	0.00	0.73	43	9,915
380	00.0	0.00	0.69	74	20,618
400	00.0	0.00	0.66	131	43,102

Source: Newell and Pizer (2002), p. 19

For instance, using Newell and Pizer's (2002) calculations in Table 10-4, assessing the damage value of a ton of carbon introduced into the atmosphere as CO_2 at $20, one finds that at a 2% discount rate the BCR is always greater than 1. At the higher discount rates the BCR never reaches 1. This implies that it may be better to wait before engaging in large climate modification projects now. If we discount using constant 4%, the expected benefit is $5.74; using 2% the expected benefit is $21.73. To the question of what is the expected discounted value of climate mitigation benefits per ton of carbon, there is no one answer, as it depends on the selection of the social rate of discount! However, based upon 210 years of US experience, it suggest that not investing now is the best strategy.

Table 10-4. Expected Discounted Value of Mitigation Benefits

Government bond rate		Benefits from 1 ton of carbon mitigation	Relative to constant rate
4%	Constant	$5.74	
	Random walk	$10.44	82%
	Mean reverting	$6.52	14%
2%	Constant	$21.73	
	Random walk	$33.84	56%
	Mean reverting	$23.32	7%
7%	Constant	$1.48	
	Random walk	$2.88	95%
	Mean reverting	$1.79	21%

Source: Newell and Pizer (2002), p. 19

Box 10-2. Contrary Views

Many economists challenge the usefulness of the "economics of sustainability" on the following grounds:
1. It is difficult to make estimates of social prices and environmental values.
   a. In practice it is costly and ultimately arbitrary to estimate prices of social considerations. For example, social considerations are given effect by subprojects that cater to the welfare of people affected by the project, such as women, IPs, and the like. There is little agreement on how such subprojects should be planned, and estimating the costs of such subprojects is costly and difficult. In fact the private sector often makes no such estimates unless required to do so by law.

      b. Environmental values are hard to measure in practice. Surrogate and simulated markets are subject to criticism. Estimates of the value of biodiversity may not be consistent with what people are actually willing to pay for it. The cost of research to provide contestable estimates of costs and benefits is very large and impractical for most projects. Again, the private sector often makes no such estimates unless required to do so.

      c. Bureaucratic elites, often under pressure from lobbies, try to estimate values for social and environmental considerations when such values should be determined by individuals through competition in markets.

2. Environmental costs and benefits should be included in the cost and benefit stream of any project, ideally measured at prices appropriate for the time and value preferences of society.

3. Each person or entity has a different discount rate, so how can project costs and benefits be discounted over generations?

      a. A student may demand $130 before investing $100 for one year, while a salaried individual may demand $115 before investing $100 for one year. Companies frequently seek 10% to 15% return on an investment, while development banks usually specify 10%, though less may be accepted for projects involving benefits for women or IPs. A private investment abroad may not be feasible if it does not return all investment costs within three years.

      b. There is no agreement on how to distribute benefits over time and between generations even within the disciplines of environmentalists, social scientists, or economists. Should economists maximize total utility or utility per head by averaging?

      c. Discounting, a widespread practice in most of the world to compare returns on investments, cannot be done between generations; then it is not in the interest of current or future generations to attempt such comparisons.

4. The private sector often ignores externalities such as environmental damage, pollution, and effects on others not reflected in the markets, unless legislation or judicial precedent requires the private sector to take into account such externalities.

5. Corporate social responsibility (the triple bottom line) means that companies are exhorted to pay for practices in the interest of sustainability above the level of practices required by law. Such practices may include pollution controls or energy constraints not required by law. Such practices have costs, which are borne by the customer and the shareholder. Will shareholders tolerate reduced profits or will they shift their investments to other jurisdictions overseas? Is corporate responsibility sustainable?

6. Sustainability is directed at actions intended to improve or preserve the environment, such as a renewable resource like a fishery or forest. Sustainability is a difficult concept to apply to a private sector project like a gold mine, which has limited duration.

SUMMARY

This chapter covers a wide terrain of applied economics ranging from how to define and deal with externalities, valuation (including shadow pricing), resolving intertemporal conflicts over resource use by discounting, assessment of costs, and the application of social benefit-cost analysis. The chapter concludes with a simple example using these concepts to suggest how one may assess the choice to act on global warming now or later.

Box 10-2 gives a litany of complaints about the economics of sustainability that we hope to have, at least partially, addressed in Chapters 9 and 10. We believe that Pareto and Coase have addressed the major critiques of points 1a in the Box; 1b and 1c are addressed in our lengthy discussion of valuation; the section on social benefit-cost analysis and shadow pricing respond to point 2; the long section on discounting addresses points 3a, b, and c; the section on externalities comprehensively deals with point 4; and point 5 is raised by the chapter as a question that must be addressed. Point 6 in the Box is not a criticism of the sustainability economic approach, but rather a comment on the inherent difficulties in operationalizing the concept of sustainability itself. We are not claiming that we have all the answers to these criticisms, but rather that we provide a coherent framework within which these and other critiques can be addressed.

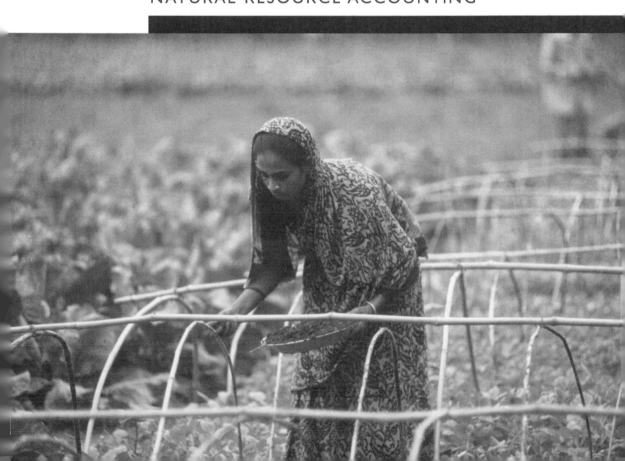

Sustainability accounting is an important approach to understanding how sustainable an economy might be.[1] The approaches used in national economic accounting, suitably adjusted, can be very helpful. The genuine progress indicator (GPI), UNDP's HDI, and the World Bank's measures of Genuine Saving and National Wealth rely on these national economic accounts. The new measures provide insights into the "sustainability" of the environment and social systems in a country and thus assist in the decision-making process. To explore the usefulness of these newer measures we need to show their grounding in measures of national accounting.

NATIONAL INCOME: DEFINITIONS AND LIMITATIONS

First, let us define and discuss the terms of gross national product and gross domestic product. GNP and GDP both quantify aspects of the state of a nation's economy; but they do not always reveal the same picture. For example, GDP is GNP with the values of net exports and imports removed. For an economy like the US, the difference between the two is very small and hence of little interest to sustainability policies; but in many other countries of the world, GNP fluctuates widely as a result of currency devaluations and other fiscal and trade issues that may be less relevant to sustainable environmental development in the country. Therefore, we suggest that GDP is the most relevant economic accounting index to use for developing countries.

Gross Domestic Product

GDP as noted in Chapter 9 is the market value of all the final goods and services produced by the economy in a given year. Other widely cited economic indicators are:

- **Net national product**, GDP *minus* the cost of capital goods "used up" during the accounting period. For purposes of measurement, depreciation charges and any other allowances for the consumption of durable capital goods are used to estimate the amount of capital "used up" in the production of a given volume of output.
- **National income**, the aggregate earnings of labor and property during the accounting period. It is an estimate of *total cost* of all factors of production during a given year.
- **Personal income**, a measure of the current income received by *all* "persons" from *all* sources. For accounting purposes, nonprofit institutions, private trust funds, and private health or welfare funds are classified as "persons." Personal income is measured before taxes.
- **Disposable personal income**, the income held by persons after the deduction of all personal taxes and other payments to general government. It is the amount of income available during a given year either for spending on consumption or for saving.

When economists talk about depreciation in the economy they are referring to the depreciation of capital goods. Unfortunately, net national product does not include the depreciation

---

[1] The authors thank John Dixon for his significant contributions to this chapter.

of environmental goods and ecosystem services, which are of course the major sustainability issues. We can have a robust economy while consuming all of our natural resources and would never be warned by the increasing GDP that at some point they will all be used up. This suggests that the conventional measure of net national product overstates the true level of economic activity by neglecting the depreciation of environmental goods.

In 2004, total expenditures in the US amounted to $8,214 billion in private consumption, $1,927 billion in gross private domestic investment, a deficit of $1,173 billion in exports of goods and services, plus government purchases of goods and services totaling $2,216 billion (Table 11-1). The sum of these items equals a GDP of $11,733 billion, quite a large figure. What is interesting is that the largest numbers are personal consumption expenditures and government purchases of goods and services. To paint a healthy economic picture of a rising GDP in the US, ever-larger personal consumption and government expenditures are needed even if a true picture of the economy, after taking into account environmental degradation, is not so healthy. Thus, we can ask whether GDP (or GDP/capita) presents an accurate picture or provides an appropriate measure. It is a serious question. The point is, since GDP ignores environmental depreciation and many social issues, it does not represent an accurate and appropriate picture of aggregate economic activity upon which to base sustainability decisions.

According to Table 11-1, US GDP was $91.3 billion in 1930; in 2004 it was $11,733 billion. This appears to imply that the US is much better off in 2004, as GDP increased by a factor of more than 100 compared with 1930. Personal consumption expenditures in 1930 were $70.2 billion. In 2004, they rose to $8,214 billion, with government expenditures reaching $2,216 billion. Again, on the face of it we seem to be dealing with large increases. But in 1930, $100 was worth more than what $1000 was worth in 2004. We need to put these numbers on a constant basis by adjusting for price changes.

Using the Consumer Price Index (CPI), which is published monthly by the US Department of Commerce, it is easy to evaluate the change in value of money from year to year. The index gives the consumer prices every year, so we can go back and forth between years. After making adjustments to reflect price changes, we see that real personal consumption expenditure did increase substantially by more than a factor of ten to $767.4 billion (in 1930s dollars) since the 1930s, but even so this indicated improvement in living standards might be overstated if environmental depreciation and reduced quality of life were to be taken into account.

Green Accounting

The UN has been interested in green accounting for some time (UN, 1993) largely based on a version of Leontief's input-output method (Leontief, 1986). The EU has also taken a lead in green accounting (OECD, 1994), and there is a whole series of World Bank reports on green accounting as well (Lutz, 1993; Hamilton and Lutz, 1996). Green accounting is a way of addressing issues that are typically ignored in the conventional economic accounting literature. The conventional accounts must be modified to consider environmental and social externalities caused by production and consumption activities.

Table 11-1. Gross Domestic Product or Expenditure, 1930-2004 (in billions of current dollars)

	1930	1940	1950	1960	1970	1980	1990	1995	1999	2000	2004
Gross domestic product	$91.3	$101.3	$294.3	$527.4	$1,039.7	$2,795.6	$5,803.2	$7,400.5	$9,268.6	$9,872.9	$11,733
Personal consumption expenditures	70.2	71.2	192.7	332.2	648.9	1,762.7	3,831.5	4,969.0	6,250.2	6.728.4	8,214
Gross private domestic investment	10.8	13.6	54.1	75.7	150.4	484.2	847.2	1,110.7	1,636.7	1,767.5	1,927
Exports of goods and services	4.4	4.8	12.3	25.3	57.0	278.9	557.2	818.6	989.8	1,102.9	1,173
Imports of goods and services	4.1	3.4	11.6	22.8	55.8	293.8	628.6	902.8	1,240.6	1,466.9	1,793
Government	10.0	15.1	46.9	113.8	237.1	569.7	1,181.4	1,372.0	1,632.5	1,741.0	2,216

Numbers may not add up due to rounding
GDP=sum of personal consumption expenditures, plus gross private domestic investment, plus net of exports minus imports, plus government expenditures
Source: www.bea.gov, US Department of Commerce, 2005

Limitations of GDP as a Measure of Economic Welfare

For a long time economists have pointed out that neither GNP nor GDP is an ideal measurement of national development; they are too limited and often lead to erroneous conclusions. What are the limitations of GDP as a measure of economic welfare? Only market activities are included in GDP, which places no value on leisure; it does not reflect improvements in quality of life, nor deterioration of environmental quality, nor depletion of the stock of natural resources. In fact, using conventional accounting, environmental damage improves GDP—the more that has to be spent on maintaining the environment and treating pollution, the more road accidents, the more people put into prison, etc., the higher the GDP. If we take that argument to its logical extreme, we would have to say that by totally destroying the environment and being forced to spend a great deal of money repairing it, GDP would soar. But would we be better off? Clearly, there is something wrong with this type of argument. GDP should be replaced with some other indicator when we are considering sustainable development. A number of alternatives have been proposed; we refer to just three of them here.

GENUINE PROGRESS INDICATOR (GPI)

One such alternative to GDP that incorporates both "green" thinking and other factors is the GPI, which the creators (Cobb et al., 1995) believe reflects the true state of the economy more accurately than GDP (see Box 11-1).

Box 11-1. The Genuine Progress Indicator

GPI starts with GDP, to which we add value for positive items such as education, research and development, and natural capital while subtracting items such as mineral exploitation, depletion of energy resources, depletion of capital, and population growth. It is designed to give a more realistic understanding of how a nation's macroeconomic policies are working in an economic index.

See http://www.redefiningprogress.org/projects/gpi/

To calculate GPI, the personal consumption item from GDP is used as a base and various adjustments are made to reflect the corrections needed to compensate for the defects of GDP. In addition to environmental factors, it is important to consider the distribution of income in evaluating the accuracy and appropriateness of GDP. In GDP, income is not distributed equally across the population, so Cobb et al. (1995) used the Gini coefficient, which takes into account differences in percentage of population and percentage of income. For the US, income distribution is getting worse, so they adjusted the figures proportionately to reflect a deteriorating income distribution, and they made other adjustments (shown in Box 11-2) such as the value of housework and parenting, which are not included in GDP.

GDP also assigns homemakers' work a value of zero, unless they receive welfare payments while they are actually out of a job, since welfare payments are measured in GDP. GPI includes housework and parenting, assigning it a wage, and assessing the number of people involved in those activities, which increases GPI.

Capital improvements made to highways and streets are shown only as investment costs in GDP, but in fact highways and streets provide additional services that are not accounted for. In GPI, those services are valued positively. Other goods and services not counted in the standard GDP but accounted for in GPI include volunteerism, costs of household pollution abatement, and the cost of noise pollution. Box 11-2 shows conceptually how some of these corrections may be made. In fact, most of the items either ignored or subtracted from GDP are positive values in GPI. Box 11-3 shows the actual calculations based upon year 2000 data.

Figure 11-1 shows the relative performance of GDP and GPI from 1950 to 2000. The result shows a slight growth in GPI over 50 years, as compared with an approximate threefold increase in GDP over the same half century, even though there was a significant difference in the annual growth rates of GDP and GPI during each decade during this half century.

In 2000, while US GDP measured $33,497 per capita, GPI had increased to just around $9,500 per capita (Figure 11-1). Although there is a huge difference between these indicators, GDP is still growing;

Box 11-2. Examples of the Valuation Method for Some GPI Components

GPI CONTRIBUTORS	CALCULATION METHOD
Personal consumption	component of GDP (68% in 1998)
Income distribution	Gini coefficient of distribution of income among households used as index number
Weighted personal consumption	consumption divided by income distribution index
Value of housework and parenting	estimated number of hours per year times fixed dollar amount
Value of volunteer work	estimated number of hours per year times fixed dollar amount
Services of consumer durables	stocks of cars, furniture, etc. times fixed percentage
Cost of crime	direct cost to households plus effective expenditures to avoid crime
Cost of family breakdown	divorce costs (lawyers plus effect on children) plus imputed cost of TV watching
Loss of leisure time	difference between hours of leisure in 1969 and in other years times $11.20 per hour of labor force
Cost of unemployment	members of labor force working fewer hours than they want times the number of "constrained hours" per year they are not working times $11.20
Cost of consumer durables	spending on cars, furniture, etc. (offset services of consumer durables)
Cost of commuting	out-of-pocket costs plus value of time spent commuting
Cost of household pollution abatement	spending by households on pollution abatement—mostly for vehicles
Cost of automotive accidents	vehicle damage and hospital costs
Cost of water pollution	loss of water quality plus siltation
Cost of air pollution	damage to vegetation; structures, and aesthetics; soiling of cloth materials; acid rain; loss of urban property values (net health or mortality costs)
Cost of noise pollution	reduced quality of human environment
Loss of wetlands	annualized value of cumulative loss of services (purification, flood control, wildlife habitat) with value increasing exponentiially as a result of scarcity value
Loss of farmland	annualized value of cumulative loss of soil productivity based on assumption that inherent soil fertility will have greater value in the future as fertilizer and other inputs become more costly (soil erosion, soil compaction, urbanization)
Depletion of nonrenewable resources	annualized value of cumulative loss of potential services of resources that have been permanently lost (measured as increasing cost of what could be required to replace the cumulative quantity of energy resources produced domestically)
Cost of long-term environmental damage	present value of cumulative expected costs of future damage from climate change and nuclear waste managemet (fossil fuel and nuclear energy consumption times fixed dollar value per unit)
Cost of ozone depletion	cumulative world production of CFC-11 and CFC-12 times fixed dollar amount per unit
Loss of old-growth forests	cumulative value of the loss of ecological services from old-growth forests plus damage from forest roads
Net capital investment	change in stock of fixed capital minus change in stock of capital required for new workers equals net additional stock available for all workers (swings modified by use of rolling average)
Net foreign lending or borrowing	change in the net international position (corresponds to change in current trade balance) smoothed by using a five-year rolling average

Source: See http://www.redefiningprogress.org/projects/gpi/

Box 11-3. Adjustments to 2000 GDP to Estimate GPI ($ billion)

Economic costs	
Adjustment for unequal income distribution	-959
Net foreign lending or borrowing	-324
Cost of consumer durables	-896
Social costs (such as the cost of divorce, household cost of crime,	
and loss of leisure time)	
Cost of crime	-30
Cost of automobile accidents	-158
Cost of commuting	-455
Cost of family breakdown	-63
Loss of leisure time	-336
Cost of underemployment	-115
Environment costs (such as the cost of pollution and depletion of our	
stock of natural resources)	
Cost of household pollution abatement	-14
Cost of water pollution	-53
Cost of air pollution	-39
Cost of noise pollution	-16
Loss of wetlands	-412
Loss of farmlands	-171
Depletion of nonrenewable resources	-1,497
Cost of long-term environmental damage	-1,179
Cost of ozone depletion	-313
Loss of old-growth forests	-90
BENEFITS IGNORED BY GDP THAT ARE ADDED TO GPI	
Value of housework and parenting	2,079
Value of volunteer work	97
Services of consumer durables	744
Services of highways and streets	96
Net capital investment	476
TOTAL: THE GENUINE PROGRESS INDICATOR	**2,630**

(Per capita GPI in 2000 was $9,550. Per capita GDP in 2000 was $33,497.)

Source: See http://www.redefiningprogress.org/publications/2001/2000_gpi_update.pdf

its growth rate is almost always positive (except during a recession). While figures indicate that US GDP per capita grew at about 2% per annum between 1965 and 2000, GPI grew at a much lower rate.

Figure 11-1. US per Capita GPI and GDP for 1950-2000

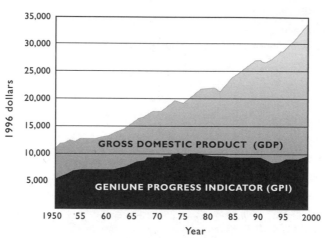

Source: Website for Gross Progress Indicator

Figure 11-2. GPI per Capita for Burlington, Chittenden County,
the State of Vermont, and the US, 1950-2000

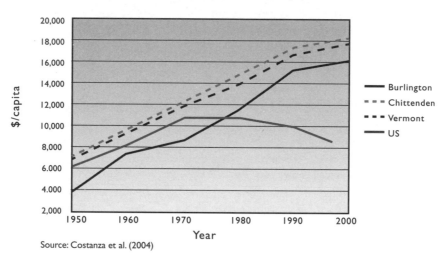

Source: Costanza et al. (2004)

GPI also has important implications for subnational sustainability accounting. One of the best examples is Costanza et al.'s (2004) application to Burlington, Vermont, over the period from 1950 to 2000. Figure 11-2 shows how GPI changed from 1950 to 2000 for the US, which peaked in

1970; for the State of Vermont and Chittenden County, both of which continued to grow at the same levels and rate; and for the City of Burlington, which started at a lower level than them but continued to grow at about the same rate. If we believe the central hypothesis of GPI, then we can conclude that Vermont, Chittenden County, and Burlington all showed genuine progress over the 50-year period, but not the US as a whole.

HUMAN DEVELOPMENT INDEX

Another approach to assessing environmental and social development is the annual UNDP Human Development Index (HDI) as discussed previously. Refer to Chapter 4 for an extended discussion on the HDI.

WORLD BANK'S WEALTH OF NATIONS

The World Bank (1997) established norms for measuring national wealth to include natural capital such as minerals and fossil fuels, timber, nontimber benefits of forests, cropland, pasture land, and protected areas. Human resources are also counted as wealth and are measured by the present value of future income streams. There are countries with virtually no natural resources that do extremely well, like Singapore, and those with relatively few natural resources, such as Japan and the UK. These are countries that have invested heavily in human resources.

The balance between natural and human resources will depend upon each country's endowment. The problem is that we have difficulty measuring the value of human resources. As a result, there is a tendency to ignore them when making estimates of national wealth. That is all right if it is a small line item, but when it is the biggest item on the account sheet, it seems that we really ought to try to estimate the value of the human resources. However, we need to remember that GDP is a flow of income that arises from the use of the wealth that a country has accumulated. Capital is also required in order for labor to be productive. So there are difficulties measuring the wealth embedded in the labor force.

In *Where Is the Wealth of Nations?* (2006), the World Bank posited the existence of three accounts that measure a nation's wealth and should be part of an overall assessment of improving sustainability. The accounts are
- natural capital,
- produced capital plus urban land, and
- human and social capital (now referred to as intangible capital).

The World Bank document shows how to estimate the values of these accounts in sensible numerical terms. Figure 11-3 shows schematically how the component parts of wealth estimates relate to each other. The intangible (human and social) capital is computed as a residual between total wealth, estimated as the net present value of the stream of future consumption, and the sum of the two other capital accounts, which are estimated directly.

Using this methodology, the World Bank estimated the three capital contributions of wealth for 150 countries and summarized them by income group in Table 11-2, and for the top ten countries in Table 11-3.

Table 11-2. Wealth per Capita by Region and Income Group, 2000

GROUP	Dollars per Capita				Percent Share of Total Wealth		
	Total Wealth	Natural Capital	Produced Capital	Intangible capital	Natural Capital	Produced Capital	Intangible capital
Latin America and the Carib.	67,955	8,059	10,830	49,066	12%	16%	72%
Sub-Saharan Africa	10,730	2,535	1,449	6,746	24%	13%	63%
South Asia	6,906	1,749	1,115	4,043	25%	16%	59%
East Asia and the Pacific	11,958	2,511	3,189	6,258	21%	27%	52%
Middle East and North Africa	22,186	7,989	4,448	9,749	36%	20%	44%
Europe and Central Asia	40,209	11,031	12,299	16,880	27%	31%	42%
Low Income	7,216	2,075	1,150	3,991	29%	16%	55%
Lower Middle Income	23,612	4,398	4,962	14,253	19%	21%	60%
Upper Middle Income	72,897	10,921	16,481	45,495	15%	23%	62%
High Income OECD	439,063	9,531	76,193	353,339	2%	17%	80%
World	90,210	4,681	16,160	69,369	5%	18%	77%

Notes: the data in this table include oil-exporting countries. All dollars at nominal exchange rates.

Source: Based on *Where Is the Wealth of Nations?* World Bank (2006), p. 26

Table 11-3. Total Wealth: Top 10 Countries, 2000

Country	Wealth per Capita	Natural Capital	Produced Capital	Intangible Capital
Switzerland	648,241	1%	15%	84%
Denmark	575,138	2%	14%	84%
Sweden	513,424	2%	11%	87%
United States	512,612	3%	16%	82%
Germany	496,447	1%	14%	85%
Japan	493,241	0%	30%	69%
Austria	493,080	1%	15%	84%
Norway	473,708	12%	25%	63%
France	468,024	1%	12%	86%
Belgium-Luxembourg	451,714	1%	13%	86%

Source: Based on *Where Is the Wealth of Nations?* World Bank (2006), p. 22

Figure 11-3. Estimating the Components of Wealth

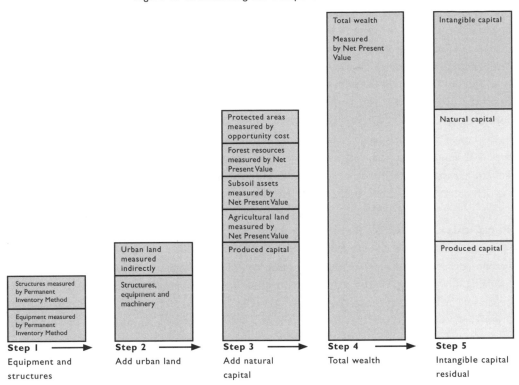

Source: Based on *Where Is the Wealth of Nations?* World Bank (2006), p. 22

Human Resources

In the World Bank wealth indicators, knowledge-based products are not mixed in with the category of natural capital or produced assets such as cars or computers. A country like the US has a huge amount of natural capital that is not being exploited. As markets have been working, taking into account policy constraints (for example, political and environmental constraints on exploitation of Alaskan oil), greater emphasis has been put on knowledge-intensive activities. For example, the US does extremely well in modern telecommunications, but the actual physical components it uses come mostly from places like the PRC.

Human resources of developing nations were valued at 59%, while high-income countries posted a human resource component at 80% of total wealth. Thus we see that the largest resource base for countries like the US is its educated people. Even countries with a high investment in social programs get into trouble when they become major exporters of primary products. The Netherlands faced a major crisis when it discovered large gas fields in the North Sea. Using export revenues, it built a huge welfare system and now finds it almost too expensive to maintain. Social malaise has crept in, and many people lost the incentive to work. (If one receives almost as much money when unemployed as when employed, why bother to work?) The UK faces a similar problem. The British welfare system, which was in bad shape, got a huge boost from the discovery of oil and gas in the North Sea. Both the Netherlands and the UK may not have invested the gas revenues wisely. By contrast, Norway, which also discovered huge amounts of petroleum, placed its oil revenues in long-term investments. It is one of the few oil-exporting nations that coupled its windfall with rational development; the natural temptation for countries is to enjoy a bonanza and then face financial hardship.

The best investments appear to be durable human resources and produced assets. Produced assets, however, can be tricky because of systemic failures resulting from resource depletion. The former Soviet Union invested heavily in produced assets while squandering its extensive natural resources in a way that has not led to long-term development. This concept of the durability of wealth is important. In fact, countries in the Middle East that do not have oil like Lebanon, Jordan, and, to a lesser extent, Turkey, do a lot better in terms of investment in human resources than do oil-rich countries like Saudi Arabia.

Per Capita Wealth by Region

The wealth of the US was $513,000 per capita in 2000 (Table 11-3). Of that, 82% came from human resources and other nontangible resources. This raises the question about the value of investing in education. Unfortunately, the World Bank did not report the oil-exporting countries separately in its 2000 estimates, but it did in the 1995 estimates. At that time the Middle East had a per capita wealth of $150,000; but, of that, only 43% was attributable to human resources. The bulk of its wealth was in natural capital. What will happen when the oil runs out?

Libya apparently thought about that question when it started the irrigation project, noted in Chapter 9, financed by oil revenues, to bring water from the Sahara to the coastal cities via an enormous pipeline. One would think this a wise investment of the revenue from natural capital, but even here there are many questions. Critics point out that Libya would probably have been better off investing more of its oil earnings in education and training. They claim that the pipeline is "nonsustainable" in the long run because there is a limited amount of renewable groundwater under the Sahara.

GENUINE SAVINGS

Another important sustainability indicator for a country is the amount and rate of savings as a percentage of GDP. Saving allows for investment in all aspects of development infrastructure. Unfortunately, there is a need to distinguish between the conventional views of savings in national economic accounting and calculated "genuine savings" rates, which take social and environmental issues into consideration. Simon Dietz, Eric Neumayer, and Indra De Soysa have this to say:

> Genuine saving is an established indicator of weak sustainable development that measures the net level of investment a country makes in produced, natural, and human capital less depreciation. Maintaining this net level of investment above zero is a necessary condition for sustainable development. However, data demonstrate that resource-rich

countries are systematically failing to make this investment. Alongside the familiar resource curse on economic growth, resource abundance has a negative effect on genuine saving. In fact, the two are closely related insofar as future consumption growth is restricted by insufficient genuine saving now.
(see http://papers.ssrn.com/sol3/papers.cfm?abstract_id=545502)

In Figure 11-4, the World Bank shows schematically how estimates of genuine savings can be made, and in Figure 11-5 gives an example of how the components fit together for Bolivia based upon 2003 data.

The World Bank has suggested that countries ought to be realistic about their measurements of savings. The problem is, government economists use these statistics to demonstrate that the nation is doing well and are loathe to tell the whole story. From the 123 countries for which the World Bank calculated genuine savings, 30 show negative savings rates, with a low of −52.7% for Azerbaijan; 93 show positive genuine savings rates, with the highest being Singapore with 35.2%. Clearly, if we have an estimate of the wealth of a country and of its genuine savings rate over recent periods, we could be able to provide an intelligent assessment of the sustainability of government policies governing sustainable development. From the World Bank's study, the political system in Singapore is doing an excellent job despite its paucity of natural resources.

Figure 11-4. Estimating Genuine Savings

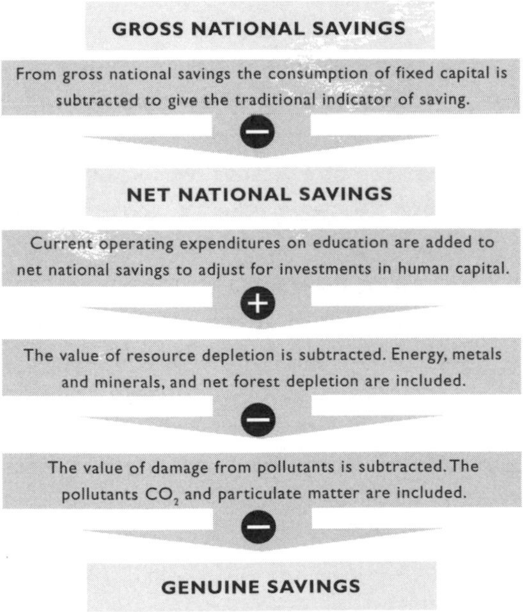

GROSS NATIONAL SAVINGS

From gross national savings the consumption of fixed capital is subtracted to give the traditional indicator of saving.

⊖

NET NATIONAL SAVINGS

Current operating expenditures on education are added to net national savings to adjust for investments in human capital.

⊕

The value of resource depletion is subtracted. Energy, metals and minerals, and net forest depletion are included.

⊖

The value of damage from pollutants is subtracted. The pollutants CO_2 and particulate matter are included.

⊖

GENUINE SAVINGS

Source: Based on *Where Is the Wealth of Nations?* World Bank (2006), p. 37

Figure 11-5. Adjustments in the Genuine Savings Calculation for Bolivia (2003)

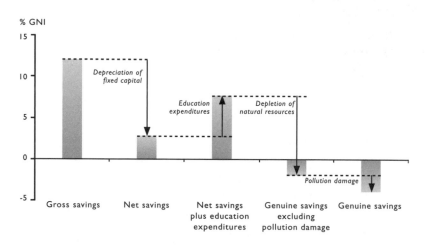

Source: Based on *Where Is the Wealth of Nations?* World Bank (2006), p. 40

SUMMARY OF NATIONAL SUSTAINABILITY ACCOUNTING

Each of these approaches requires massive amounts of data and computation, and that is a problem. In addition, all methods of sustainability accounting suffer from serious deficiencies, either conceptually or in implementation. Conceptually, there are problems with fixed coefficients in the input-output relationships. Some of the definitions of how to assess the value of human resources are fairly suspect, and there is the issue of evaluating the relative importance of those factors. Costanza et al. (1997), referred to in Chapter 4, value the ecosystem's services at 1.8 times the current world GNP; this is a fascinating, but highly suspect, figure. There are some better methods; for example, GPI seems to work well for the US. The World Bank's expanding measure of wealth is also attractive, even though there are some serious conceptual and data problems. UNDP's HDI (see Chapter 4) is now becoming widely used as an indicator of improvement of social, economic, and environmental conditions around the world. There is clearly a need for better ways of articulating overall states of the environment with an eye towards "sustainability." Despite many flaws, the approaches discussed here are becoming useful for assessing sustainability and nudging policy choices toward the goals of sustainability.

CHAPTER 12
THE ROLE OF INTERNATIONAL
FINANCIAL INSTITUTIONS

Multilateral Development Banks (MDBs), including the World Bank, African Development Bank, Asian Development Bank, European Bank for Reconstruction and Development, Inter-American Development Bank, and International Fund for Agricultural
Development, have made the environment a part of their approach to development.
Regrettably, some officers in these institutions sometimes fail to perceive the environment
as a holistic ingredient of a development path. For this reason, they still have a long way to go in
regarding the environment not as a burden but as a benefit.

A review of all the MDBs could easily be the subject of an entire book. Where pertinent, the
work and contribution of MDBs are discussed in various other chapters of this book. This chapter,
however, concentrates on the World Bank (WB), as this global organization provides an excellent
example of how an international financial institution can help realize sustainable development
objectives.[1]

DEVELOPMENT AND ENVIRONMENT AT THE WORLD BANK

The WB was established in 1944, before the end of the Second World War, to help reconstruct
countries devastated by the war. Its first loans were made to the European countries and to Japan.
Most people, including most Japanese, are not aware that the WB financed Japan's famous bullet
train. In Europe, Finland received the first loan. For quite a long time, the WB's clients were
countries that today are considered wealthy.

In the 1950s, the WB's emphasis was growth and development. In the 1960s, it was rural
development; and in the 1970s, economic reform. In the 1980s, there was a major shift in the WB's
policies toward human development and assistance to developing countries. In the 1990s and
2000s, the WB has been focusing on poverty reduction.

When James D. Wolfensohn was president of the WB from 1995 until mid-2005, he placed the
issues and needs of the developing countries, especially the poorest ones, on the global agenda. Yet
the role the WB would play was not clear. One area it was sure about was that, as a financial source,
it could fund and guide environmentally friendly programs. The WB began looking for projects that
would improve the environment and make it a resource to improve people's lives.

Today the WB is owned by 184 member countries. It lends about $20 billion annually and has about
10,000 staff, of whom about 400 have multidisciplinary training in social and environmental areas.

Types of World Bank Assistance

The WB has three types of instruments (Figure 12-1): lending, nonlending, and grants. There
are three types of lending instruments: investment loans that fund actual projects like road building;
adjustment loans, the WB's most controversial activity, through which it funds nations that wish
to make changes in their policies; and financial intermediary loans or funds funneled through a
country's financial system for agreed-upon objectives.

---

[1] The authors thank Kristalina Georgieva and Warren Evans for their significant contributions to this chapter.

Figure 12-1. Types of World Bank Instruments

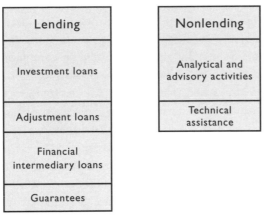

Source: Based on World Bank data

The WB also provides loan guarantees to high-risk projects.

As part of their vision of helping developing nations help themselves, the WB also undertakes nonlending analytical work and offers technical assistance. Its analytical work focuses on long-term development issues, of which the environment is a major one.

The WB has an annual $150 million development grant facility (Figure 12-2). The biggest beneficiary of this facility is agricultural research in developing countries.

Figure 12-2. Grant Resources: Channeling Funds for Environmental Improvements

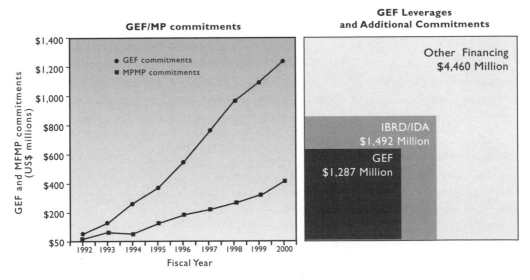

Source: Based on World Bank data

The World Bank's Environmental History

The WB's environmental history has gone through several stages. The first WB environmental adviser was appointed in 1969 (Box 12-1). For 10 years it was a one-person department. A Developmental Committee was set up in 1987 to begin a discussion on how the environment impacts on development and what the role of the WB should be. Up to this time, the environmental aspect was not fully defined; the WB had been primarily interested in development.

Why did the Development Committee suddenly realize that the environment should be part of the development agenda? Because the WB had miscalculated the environmental impact of several projects, and the world community reacted by telling the WB that it could not simply sign off on development projects without an environmental assessment. In response, in July 1987, the WB established a central Environment Department, and, in October 1989, four regional environmental divisions. An operational directive on environmental assessment was adopted at that time. This meant that from then on every single operation of the WB would have to go through a screening process for environmental impacts. Later, a process for evaluating social impacts was added (Box 12-2) to what became known as "Do No Harm" policies. The credo of these policies is to do no harm to the environment or to people unnecessarily, and, if harm is done, to mitigate it.

Box 12-1. Phase I: 1969-1989

- 1969: first World Bank environmental advisor appointed
- 1970: Office of Environmental Affairs created
- May 1987: first Development Committee discussion on environment and development held
- July 1987: central Environment Department and four regional environmental divisions established
- October 1989: first operational directive on environmental assessment adopted

Source: Based on World Bank data

Box 12-2. "Do No Harm" Policies

Safeguard Policies and Guidelines

Environmental Policies
- Environmental Assessment
- Natural Habitats
- Forestry
- Pest Management
- Safety of Dams
- Physical Cultural Resources

Social Policies
- Involuntary Resettlement
- Indigenous Peoples

Legal Policies
- Disputed Areas
- International Waterways

Guidelines and Related Policies
- Pollution Prevention and Abatement Handbook
- Environmental Assessment Sourcebook (and updates)
- Involuntary Settlement Tool Kit
- Disclosure of Operations Information

Source: Based on World Bank data

From 1990 to 2000, the WB went through a second stage. It raised its principle of "Do No Harm" to a higher level by actively addressing environmental problems (Box 12-3). In 1990, it instituted the GEF. The most important benchmark was the Rio Summit on Sustainable Development in 1992, which had tremendous implications for the whole world in terms of putting environmental issues on the map. The Summit prodded the WB's client countries to set up ministries of the environment, regardless of how weak they were. These ministries are now a legitimate part of governance structure.

Box 12-3. Second Stage of "Do No Harm"

Phase II: 1990-2000
- 1990: Global Environment Facility
- 1992: Rio Summit and World Development Report on Environment and Development
- September 1993: first annual World Bank Conference on Environmentally Sustainable Development
- Rapid growth of environment portfolio (from less than $200 million in 1989 to more than $5 billion in 2000)

Phase III: 2001 to present
- July 2001: New World Bank environmental strategy
  - Integrate environment into poverty reduction and development strategies and actions (mainstreaming) and explicitly target health, sustainable livelihoods, and vulnerability reduction impacts
  - Create conditions for the private sector to become the driver of sustainable economic growth
  - Help find equitable solutions to regional and global environmental challenges
- Millennium Development Goals
- Environmental portfolio was about 12% of WB portfolio in 2004

Source: Based on World Bank data

The Rio Summit also helped countries to build up environmental management capabilities, set environmental policies, and appoint people who would enforce those policies. It did the same for the WB.

In September 1993, the first annual World Bank Conference on Environmentally Sustainable Development was held. In many countries the WB worked with the government and concerned NGOs, taking up environmental priorities through national environmental action plans and strategies. The WB also significantly and rapidly increased the size of its environmental portfolio, including projects that have tackled hot-spot pollution problems, natural resource management, biodiversity protection, and other environmental problems. In July 2001, the WB adopted its current environment objectives (Box 12-4) to integrate the environment into poverty reduction and development strategies and actions, create conditions for the private sector to become the driver of sustainable economic growth, and help find equitable solutions to regional and global environmental challenges. To accomplish these objectives, the World Bank has adopted seven new instruments:

- environmental and social safeguards
- information disclosure
- compliance mechanisms (Indigenous Peoples, Compliance Advisor/Ombudsman Office)
- poverty reduction strategies (Participation and Civic Engagement in Poverty Reduction Strategy)
- debt relief for heavily indebted countries – 27 countries benefiting from $52 billion debt relief over time
- community-driven development (10% portfolio)
- empowerment agenda

Box 12-4. Three Current World Bank Environmental Objectives

- Improve the quality of life by
  - reducing environmental health risks and supporting better health,
  - enhancing people's livelihoods, and
  - reducing vulnerability to environmental change.
- Improve the quality of growth by
  - supporting reforms to improve incentives and encourage efficient use of natural resources,
  - promoting environmentally sustainable urban and rural development,
  - assisting clients to strengthen their environmental management capabilities, and
  - supporting sustainable private sector management.
- Protect the quality of regional and global commons by
  - convening stakeholders' meetings on collective solutions to transboundary problems,
  - maximizing the overlap between local and regional/global benefits, and
  - applying WB skills and experience as an executing agency under international conventions with specific mandates and funds.

Source: Based on World Bank data

INTEGRATING ENVIRONMENT AND POVERTY REDUCTION

In the development community today the WB has the most comprehensive set of policies and procedures on social and environmental issues. It has a set of policies for environmental assessment, natural habitats, forestry, pest management, safety of dams, physical and cultural resources, involuntary resettlement, and indigenous people. It has two legal policies on projects in disputed areas and international waterways. The WB produces a library of literature, primarily for its staff, but also for outside economists and environmentalists. Its publication list contains guidelines and related policy guides regarding pollution prevention, environmental impact sourcebooks, and involuntary resettlement tool kits. Again, what puts these policies into one package is their most important feature: "Do No Harm."

Box 12-5. Learning from Past Experience

- Safeguards: improved project design, but weak supervision and borrower capacity, and inconsistencies in implementation
- Environment portfolio: performance is close to World Bank average, but weak in institutional impact
- Mainstreaming: increased environmental lending in key sectors, less success in mainstreaming at the policy level
- Global issues: progress made, but links with local priorities need to be strengthened

Source: Based on World Bank data

By the end of 2004, the WB had invested more than $14 billion in environmental projects and objectives (Figure 12-3). Of this, about $4.4 billion financed self-standing environment projects; the balance, about $10 billion, was earmarked for environmental components or objectives in nonenvironmental projects.

Figure 12-3. Lending: Improved Environment and Natural Resources Management (ENRM)
Lending by Sector

(at end of FY2004 3rd quarter)

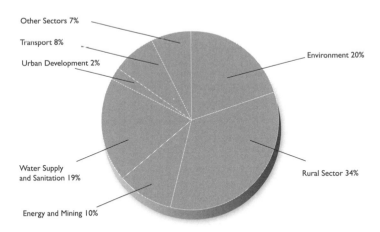

Percentages are based on commitment amounts.
- 80% of ENRM lending is managed by other sectors
- 40% of ENRM lending is managed by infrastructure sectors
  (Water and Sanitation, Energy and Mining, Transport, and Urban Development)

Source: Based on World Bank data

The core challenge at the WB over the next 30, 40, or 50 years is to provide productive work and a good quality of life for the existing 2.8 billion people now living on under $2 per day while absorbing the two to three billion people who will be added to the world's population in the next 30-50 years. Thus, we will need substantial growth in output and productivity in developing countries, and improvement in the ecosystems and the socio-fabric on which development depends. Indeed environmental factors are critical to poverty reduction (Box 12-6).

Box 12-6. Environment Is Critical for Poverty Reduction

- Environmental factors cause significant damage to health
  - About 20% of the burden of disease in developing countries is caused by environmental factors—lack of access to safe water and sanitation, indoor and outdoor air pollution, exposure to agrochemicals
- Natural resources degradation threatens livelihoods
  - Land and soil degradation, water scarcity, deforestation, and biodiversity loss deprive people of their resource base
  - Poor people are highly dependent on natural resources and often live in fragile ecosystems
- Poor people are most vulnerable to natural disasters and environmental change
  - Limited coping mechanisms
- Children are most vulnerable of all

Source: Based on World Bank data

Is this realistic? If history is a guide, then the answer is yes. In the last 30 years we have absorbed an additional two billion people on the planet. And despite this increase in population, average per capita income has increased quite substantially. Some of the key indicators for development—like infant mortality rate, literacy, and improvements in environmental conditions—have also gone up. The following are some achievements to date:

- Despite the increase in population, average per capita income (population weighted in 1995 dollars) rose from $989 in 1980 to $1,354 in 2000.
- The infant mortality rate fell from 107 per 1,000 live births in 1970 to 58 in 1999.
- The adult illiteracy rate fell from 47% in 1970 to 25% in 2000.
- There have been some successes on the environment front (e.g., phasing out ozone-depleting substances and eliminating lead as an additive to gasoline).
- From 1990 to 2000, access to sanitation rose from 44% to 52%.

This is a growth path with achievements that we sometimes do not really appreciate. Overall, however, the growth path has been costly.

Because of high cost, this development path is unlikely to be sustainable for a number of reasons. First, while the countries have managed to raise average incomes, the income disparity in the world has increased substantially. The ratio of the 20 richest countries to the 20 poorest has doubled in the last 30 years, and it has doubled not so much because the rich countries got richer, but because the poorest countries have not experienced any growth. In fact, the growth rate in these poorest countries has been minus 1%. They have lost ground. Where we stand today from the social perspective can be highlighted under a few headings (based on World Bank data):

- Income ratio: wealthiest 20/poorest 20 countries
  - Double the ratio of 1970
  - Primarily due to the lack of growth in the poorest countries (-1% in the last decade)
- Absolute number of poor people remains high
  - While it has declined since its peak in 1993, it remains above one billion
  - Number is similar to independent statistics on those undernourished and underweight
- 17 of poorest 33 countries in conflict since 1990
  - Destroys past development gains
  - Leaves a corrosive legacy of mistrust impeding future gains

In sum, there has been low growth, high conflict, and inequality, which taken together have undermined development gains.

Lack of opportunities in the poorest countries is what keeps them at the bottom. The number of poor people remains unacceptably high. Even if income is discounted as an accurate indicator of well-being, other measurements, such as malnutrition, or children under the age of five that are underweight, confirm the number of the poor—about 900 million people, close to the 1.2 billion that now earn $1 a day. What is even more alarming is that, of the 33 poorest countries, 17 have been engaged either in civil, ethnic, or border wars since 1990. Such military conflicts, of course, bring down development benefits and corrode social structure. Thus, we have a group of countries that are under stress, are falling behind socially and economically, and yet have not been at the center of global public attention.

ENVIRONMENT AND GROWTH

That environmental degradation is an impediment to growth is one of the issues that concern the WB.

How is the environment doing today?

Pollution, Water, and Soil Productivity

Developing countries are in a sorry state. Negative environmental trends have neither been reversed nor even arrested. Where we are today from the environmental point of view can be quickly summarized under three key headings:

- *Air:* Choking—Pollution levels (particulate matter less than 10 microns in diameter, PM10) in many cities are multiples of WHO standards; emissions from fossil fuels have breached the biosphere's CO_2 absorptive capacity.
- *Water:* Scarce for many—33% of the global population live in countries experiencing moderate to high water shortages, and this percentage is increasing.
- *Soil:* Degrading—23% of agricultural land (cropland, pasture, and woodland) worldwide has been degraded—39% lightly, 46% moderately, and 16% severely.

These patterns of degrading environmental stocks cannot be repeated. The sorry state is especially true in the lower income countries with high population densities. Some five million people are dying from pollution factors in developing countries.

Biodiversity, Fisheries, and Forestry

Both developed and, especially, developing countries, are losing soil productivity at a rate that, if combined with population increase, is both worrisome and problematic, as summarized below (based on World Bank data):

- *Biodiversity:* Disappearing—33% of terrestrial biodiversity, covering 1.4% of the earth's surface, is at risk.
- *Fisheries:* Declining—70% of world fisheries are fully overexploited; 58% of coral reefs are destroyed, critical, or threatened.
- *Forests:* Shrinking—20% of tropical forests have been cleared since 1960.

The world is losing biodiversity, not just the intangible beauty of the planet, but also the ecological services that biodiversity provides, from health benefits to sustaining watersheds.

Fisheries are declining dangerously. All of these impacts impede growth (Box 12-7).

Box 12-7. Environmental Degradation is an Impediment to Growth

- Economic costs: Environmental damage ranges from 4% to 8% of GDP annually in many developing countries.
- Investment climate: Competitiveness of developing nations is negatively affected by inefficient resource use and low environmental quality.
- Productivity: Water scarcity, land degradation, loss of biodiversity, and decline in ecosystem's health undermine food security in developing countries.
- Wealth: The "genuine" savings rate, which factors in a country's natural as well as human and produced capital, is negative in nearly 30 developing countries, and declining in 20 more.

Source: Based on World Bank data

We are losing our forests. A forest the size of Greece is disappearing every year. (We usually use Greece as an indicator, because it does not have much forested land. If we used a country that has forests, some people from such a country would always declare that they are not the worst offenders.)

However, in the next half century, there are some trends, which, if managed well, could provide opportunities.

Science and technology are very important drivers for positive change, although they cannot solve everything. Also, income growth generates larger markets, allows people greater mobility, and also generates billions of dollars of investments in long-term assets. But there are two transitions that will most likely happen on this planet, one in our lifetime, and one in the lifetime of our planet itself. The first is the demographic transition from a growing population to one that is stable; the second is a population transfer from primarily rural to primarily urban areas.

Projections for 2030 and 2050 show an increase of about 80-90 million people living in more developed nations. The figure is based on actual births and not on immigration. In developing countries, there will be constant growth until 2050; then the world population will likely stabilize at eight to nine billion (Figure 12-4).

Figure 12-4. Projected Population

Developing and Transition Countries (DTC) and OECD Countries

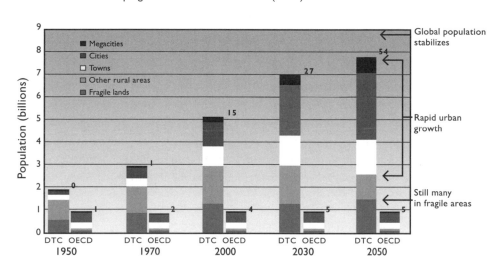

Source: Based on World Bank data

What is surprising about these predictions is that there is constant population growth in fragile lands and high biodiversity areas (Figure 12-5).

Conventional wisdom says this should not happen. David Ricardo, an early nineteenth-century political economist in the tradition of Adam Smith, postulated that people would move from an area with diminishing capacity to an area with higher productivity or from an area with diminishing opportunity to an area with higher opportunity. But this is not happening for two reasons: opportunities are not growing that fast elsewhere, and population growth elsewhere is also very high. It seems that there is no easy way out for people who live in fragile ecosystems.

Another surprise in these projections is the rapid rise of megacities. The number of megacities in OECD member countries is projected to increase from four to five between 2000 and 2050 and in developing countries from 15 to 54 over the same period. Considering the challenges facing those 15 megacities today, imagine the scale of urban infrastructure necessary when the number climbs to 54.

Figure 12-5. Complementary Indicators

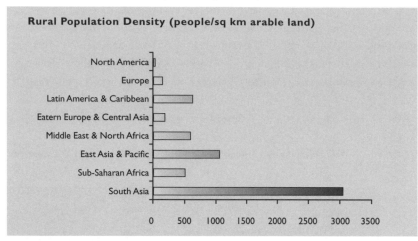

Source: Based on World Bank data

We clearly have to keep an eye on these projections, which are a combination of urban and demographic transitions. If we take seriously the commitment that was made at the Millennium Summit to create a world free from poverty, and if we are true to our word of having, by 2050, a world where no one will be poor, what will that require in terms of economic growth in developing countries (Box 12-8)?

Box 12-8. The Next 50 Years: The Goal of Prosperity for All

In 2050 we can predict a world economy of $100-$130 trillion (three to four times its current size).
• To ensure the current middle-income level of $6,300 in developing countries, they need continuous growth at an average of 3%-4% per year.
• To maintain prosperity and dynamic economies in current OECD members, they need to grow at an average 1%-2% per year.

Source: Based on World Bank data

Historical and Potential World Product to 2050

The answer is to ensure that the current middle-income levels, which are about $6,300 per capita in developing countries, grow at 3% to 4% per year (some economists and environmentalists believe the growth rate must be 4% to 6% per year). Furthermore, to maintain prosperity and dynamic economies as current OECD members, the countries need to grow at an average of 1% to 2% per year. So, to free the world of poverty will require incredible growth and productivity in the developing countries, some of which are currently posting negative figures.

This is what has to happen to bring this world to a more prosperous status, and one in which we have more social equality. Yet there are two big dangers: either it will not happen, or we will actually manage to raise income levels but at a cost that basically undermines sustainable development. Obviously, we have to figure out how to avoid this.

MILLENNIUM DEVELOPMENT GOALS AND THE WORLD BANK

Why is the year 2015 significant? It is the threshold year for meeting the MDGs. Our goals are to
- eradicate extreme poverty and hunger;
- have universal primary education;
- have gender equality and women's empowerment;
- reduce child mortality;
- improve maternal health;
- combat HIV, malaria, other diseases;
- ensure environmental sustainability; and
- develop a global partnership for development.

The MDGs are an ambitious agenda for reducing poverty and improving lives that world leaders agreed on at the Millennium Summit in September 2000. For each goal, one or more targets have been set, most for 2015, using 1990 figures as a benchmark. Sometimes the MDGs are referred to as International Goals. Whichever name is used, the primary target is to reduce world poverty by 50% by 2015.

The only way this can happen in current time standards (the goal was set in 1990) is if one assumes constant growth. That actually is one of the flaws of this system, because it is dependent on economic climates and political stability. For many regions, these cannot be assumed. For example, think of what has been happening in Eastern Europe in the last decade, or of the collapse of the Soviet Union. To assume constant growth there is extremely naïve.

Today 20% of the wealth of the world is in developing countries, while 80% is in the developed countries. In terms of population, it is exactly the reverse. WB projections for 2015 predict some improvements. In terms of the share of the wealth the developing world enjoys, the aim is to move 50% of the poor out of poverty. However, the other impoverished 50% will not appreciate the progress made so far. Many feel it is not ethical to leave the job half done. To complete the job, we need to generate a $140 trillion world economy, four times the current figure.

The Millennium Summit established a series of targets that were related to arresting and reversing the loss of biodiversity resources as well as improving urban environmental conditions. To ratify the commitment made at the Millennium Summit, a series of major international goals that focus on measurable improvements on a global scale must be realized. These goals came to be known as the Eight Millennium Development Goals.

There are ethical difficulties. Take the first MDG target, which is to reduce poverty by 50% by 2015. It seems obvious that if we want to show success in the number of people that policies have positively impacted, we would target the PRC, India, Indonesia, and Nigeria and focus our resources there. It is then likely we will reach the target number because these are very large countries, and the impact will be on a large scale. But when we select other targets, say, mortality rates for children under five or the use of traditional fuels, then we will perforce deal with smaller countries.

What the WB has done is to identify the worst offenders, the most severe problem cases in terms of each one of the indicators, and create "top 10" lists; or perhaps they should be called "bottom 10" lists, because these are the countries with the most severe performance vis-à-vis the targets under the MDGs (Table 12-1).

Table 12-1. Some "Top 10" Lists

Mortality Rate, Under Five (per 1,000 live births)	
Afghanistan	279
Sierra Leone	267
Niger	248
Mali	218
Guinea-Bissau	211
Angola	208
Burkina Faso	206
Rwanda	203
Mozambique	200
Somalia	195

Traditional Fuel Use (% of total energy use)	
Chad	98
Eritrea	96
Ethiopia	96
Burundi	94
Congo, Dem. Rep.	92
Côte d'Ivoire	92
Mozambique	91
Tanzania	91
Uganda	90
Nepal	90

Sanitation (% of population with access)	
Rwanda	8
Afghanistan	12
Eritrea	13
Ethiopia	15
Cambodia	18
Congo, Dem. Rep.	20
Niger	20
Gabon	21
Benin	23
Nepal	27

Improved Water Source (% of population without access)	
Afghanistan	13
Ethiopia	22
Somalia	29
Cambodia	34
Chad	34
Papua New Guinea	39
Mozambique	42
Lao PDR	43
Madagascar	45
Congo, Dem. Rep.	46

Source: Based on World Bank data

However, it is just not good enough to go only to the PRC, India, Indonesia, and Nigeria to secure showy results. In fact, this is something all the MDBs are warning against—not to get obsessed with numbers and hence forget about equality and fairness.

The use of traditional fuels such as wood and cow dung (Figure 12-6) is a big environmental concern. Burning these items is unhealthy, and in nations with a high population density, ultimately unsustainable. North America, Europe, the Middle East, and North Africa use very little of these traditional fuels. The Middle East and North Africa do not have much forest anyway. But in Sub-Saharan Africa and South Asia, the usage is tremendous. That is looking at the problem only by region. When we check traditional fuel usage by income, there are no surprises. Usually, the poorer the country is, the higher the percentage of use of traditional fuels (Figure 12-6).

Figure 12-6. Complementary Indicators: Traditional Fuel Use

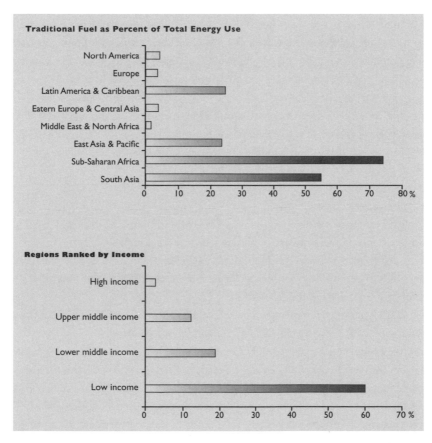

Source: United Nations

327

ATTACKING POVERTY THROUGH SUSTAINABLE DEVELOPMENT

The WSSD held in Johannesburg focused on the complexity of the problems of sustainable development. The theme of the Summit was "People, Planet, and Prosperity." More than 22,000 participants from 183 countries attended, 104 of them heads of state.

The goal of the Johannesburg Summit was to eradicate poverty through sustainable development. It was very different from the summit in Rio de Janeiro in 1992, where the goal was more focused on the environment. The World Summit came up with results never before seen at a global meeting: 220 partnerships were formed, saying in effect, we have to find a common ground among civil society, business, and government to accelerate and coordinate our efforts, because the challenges are too big for each one of us working alone.

One WSSD statistic stands out. For the first time since the Seattle meeting, a world conclave was able to gather without violence. It was probably because, unlike Seattle, this meeting was pro-poor.

The first thing it did was to make sustainable development, once a fuzzy concept, a bit more real. It integrated concepts found in the Millennium Summit, which was about the needs of the poor in developing countries. The second thing the WSSD achieved was to emphasize that sustainable development cannot be attained without growth in the developing world. It broke the perception that the environment can be protected only if we stop growth and development. Finally, the Summit was able to push the environment community to rise up to the challenge of becoming mainstream, of becoming part of the development agenda.

The WSSD expanded the MDGs so they now have additional targets linking them to health, growth, and poverty reduction (based on World Bank data):

- Reduce by half the number of people without access to sanitation by 2015.
- Reduce biodiversity loss by 2010.
- Restore fisheries stock by 2015.
- Establish a representative network of marine protected areas by 2012.
- Switch to production of chemicals that do not harm health and the environment by 2020.
- Support the New Partnership for Africa's Development objective of ensuring access to energy in Africa for at least 35% of the population.

And the WSSD was about implementation: replacing talk with action, with seeing how we can hold ourselves accountable to the MDGs in this development package.

One new, very important step was to add a sanitation target which was not in the original framework of the Millennium Summit (Figure 12-7). Omitting a sanitation target would not have made any sense. In a water-scarce country, where perhaps only 8% of the population has access to sanitation, what is going to happen to the limited amount of water over time as the population continues to grow?

A target was set to reduce biodiversity loss by 2010. But that presented a problem. We do not have a baseline for this, so how do we measure it? If we do not have good data as to where we are today, how can we know how to reverse this loss? The same question crops up regarding the restoration of fishery stocks. But at least here the numbers in some parts of the world appear to be better known, because there is a commercial interest in gathering data.

Figure 12-7. Significance of New Targets: Access to Water and Sanitation

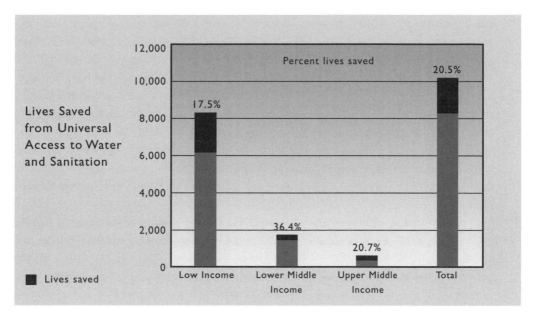

Source: Based on World Bank data

Other targets were to switch to chemicals that do not harm our health or the environment by 2020, and one regional objective for Africa—to increase access to energy for at least 35% of the population.

There were also some commitments without targets that were equally important (based on World Bank data):

- Actively promote corporate social responsibility.
- Recognize that opening access to markets is critical to development.
- Support the phase-out of export subsidies.
- Provide incentives for investment in cleaner production through loans, venture capital, and technical assistance.
- Enhance cooperation to reduce air pollution.
- Improve rural disaster preparedness and response.
- Mobilize resources to address challenges presented by climate change in Africa, small island-states, Latin America, and Asia, particularly adaptation to the adverse impacts of climate change, as well as mitigation issues. WB adaptation projects include those designed to address problems arising from drought. Its mitigation projects include promoting energy sector reform, renewable energy, waste management, reduction of greenhouse gas emissions, and carbon sequestration through land management activities.

- Assist in the prevention of invasive alien species (certain animals or plants transported to a new environment, where they take over that environment), the second greatest threat to global biodiversity and the number one threat for small islands. Invasive alien species are a new development issue resulting in part from increased trade and tourism as well as poor land and water management. (See http://www.cbd.int/programmes/cross-cutting/alien/default.asp.)

- Protect coral reefs from sediments emanating from poor land use, deforestation, dredging, nutrient and chemical pollution, overfishing and global market pressure to harvest fish and invertebrates beyond sustainable yields, coral bleaching caused by elevated sea surface temperatures due to global climate change, rising levels of CO_2 causing decreasing calcification rates in coral reef organisms, diseases and invasive alien species increasingly linked to human disturbances in the environment, rising poverty and alienation from the land, and lack of capacity and political will to manage coral reefs. (Based on World Bank data; also see Wilkinson, 2004.)

For the first time at a big international meeting, there was recognition that action is needed not only to reduce CO_2 emissions, but also to help countries that already suffer from increased vulnerability because of droughts, floods, and severe weather events.

Up to the time of the WSSD, national and corporate responsibility was an alien idea. Recently, a group of climate change experts met with staff of the WB. At the time the WB was developing its environmental strategies, and one of the issues was to address vulnerability to climate change. One of the experts, a climatologist, was aghast and refused to discuss the issue. It was not due to the debate on whether the North should be held accountable for the 80% of CO_2 emissions that it pumps into the atmosphere. Rather it was because that expert thought the WB was referring to the vulnerability of OPEC, which he believed should be compensated under the Kyoto Protocol because it will not be able to export that much oil anymore. This climatologist did not have any idea that the poor people in developing countries are already paying a very high price for the impact of CO_2 in the atmosphere.

WORLD BANK EXPERIENCE AND GOALS

The WB is learning from experience. Some things it does well; others need improvement.

Project Design

After careful analysis, the WB implements projects around the globe, and for the most part it is successful. Where it sometimes fails, it may be due to issues related to supervision. The WB establishes policies, but these are not always followed. These are instances where the stakeholders of projects can demand an investigation of the WB's failure to adhere to its own policies (called "inspection"). The WB is concerned with the capacity of developing countries to fully understand the nature of sustainability; they ultimately have to be able to deal with their own environmental problems. Yet the WB still see cases where a major problem gets minor attention, and a minor problem gets major attention. Developing nations will have to improve their analysis of real problems.

Achieving Objectives and Goals

The WB undertook a quite thorough review to see if its environment portfolio was performing as well as the rest of its portfolios in terms of achieving its goals. Unfortunately, the WB is not doing well in terms of sustainability, in both the areas of project impact and institutional impact. This is due partly to weak institutions and partly to being faced with a new set of problems. The conclusion is that environmental issues require a longer time frame than traditional sector problems like energy and infrastructure development. The WB project cycle has usually been four to six years. It is now apparent that this is not long enough. Some projects and programs need up to four times the traditional time frame. A WB project in Indonesia—protection of coral reefs—is running on a 15-year time frame; a program for Victoria Nyanza, the second largest freshwater lake in the world, covers 20 years; and a new project in the Nile basin is scheduled to run for 25 years. To be effective, the WB has to be in for the long haul.

Environmentally Sound Portfolios

A question the WB has been asking itself is, are its environmental scientists seeing to it that the WB's other portfolios are environmentally sound? In the energy, water, and sanitation sectors, the answer is yes. The WB on the whole is alert to the environment and its implications. Concerning energy lending, in 2001 and 2002, the share of projects and programs dealing with renewable sources and efficiency in the WB energy portfolio went up to 64%. That might not be a trend (two years is a very short period); still, 64% is an excellent number. With the exception of Iceland, there is not a nation in the world that has this kind of record.

Where the WB is weak is in its policy lending. Adjustment lending becomes difficult, because the environmental impact of policy changes is very often nonlinear and unpredictable. If an adjustment is made to improve and liberalize trade, it has environmental impacts, perhaps on forestry, because of increased logging. Right now, there are only two countries—the Netherlands and the PRC—where policies and programs are scrutinized by law for their environmental impact. But although these two nations are getting serious about their environmental resources, they still have a long way to go. Even the Dutch, who are traditionally more advanced in their thinking and policies on sustainable development, do not appear to have the skills and the capabilities to do a proper analysis of environmental implications. The WB and its member nations must regard policies holistically if they are to achieve sustainability.

Global Issues

The WB has made quite a lot of progress in this area, mainly because of the incentive provided by the GEF (Box 12-9). Through replenishment, the GEF operates on a $3 billion budget, pledged by 32 donor countries to fund operations between 2002 and 2006. With these funds, the GEF will promote interventions related to the global conventions on climate change, biodiversity, international waters, ozone, and the Montreal Protocol. Recently, two more conventions were added: persistent organic pollutants and desertification. Grants are being provided in these six areas to meet the incremental global costs associated with global benefits in developing countries. A side effect of the GEF programs is that they have helped the WB develop its environmental expertise, particularly in diversity and climate change.

Box 12-9. Global Environment Facility

The GEF, as indicated in its website, is an independent financial organization that provides grants to developing countries for projects that benefit the global environment and promote sustainable livelihoods in local communities.

Types of Projects
GEF projects address six complex global environmental issues:
• Biodiversity
• Climate Change
• International Waters
• Land Degradation
• The Ozone Layer
• Persistent Organic Pollutants

GEF Funding
Since 1991, the GEF has provided $4.5 billion in grants and has generated $14.5 billion in cofinancing from other partners for projects in developing countries and countries with economies in transition.
GEF funds are contributed by donor countries. In 2002, 32 donor countries pledged $3 billion to fund operations between 2002 and 2006.

Management of GEF Projects
GEF projects are managed by GEF implementing agencies:
• United Nations Environment Programme
• United Nations Development Programme
• World Bank

Seven other international organizations, known as GEF executing agencies, contribute to the management and execution of GEF projects. In May 1999, the GEF expanded opportunities for regional development banks to implement GEF projects.

Source: http://www.gefweb.org

Integrating Environment, Poverty Reduction, and Developmental Strategies

In July 2001, the WB's board of directors approved a new environmental strategy with very explicit targets concerning health, sustainable livelihoods, and vulnerability to environmental change.

The revised approach takes the environment into account as part of the investment climate and as a condition for private sector performers. It creates a level playing field in different countries in the context of globalization. For a viable global economy, it is important that the rules, including the environmental rules, are the same everywhere.

The new strategy has three objectives: to improve the quality of life; to improve the quality of growth in developing countries; and to protect the quality of the regional and global commons, meaning worldwide public goods or common resources impossible to deny to anyone, such as the oceans or the atmosphere.

The new 2001 WB strategy has the same framework as the Johannesburg Summit: people, planet, prosperity. The most important change that the WB helped create was a linkage between environmental protection and poverty. The new WB strategy has endeavored to change the myth, "When you grow up, you clean up." This myth is so entrenched that it even comes with a graph, the so-called Kuznets Curve, which says that when a country reaches $6,000 per capita per annum, then it can worry about the environment (see Chapter 1). Although there is some rationale behind first building up the economy so that it can actually afford to institute environmental policies, it is a risky proposition to wait until achieving $6,000 per capita per annum before taking action. Furthermore, there are many dimensions in which improving environmental conditions can actually contribute to making people's lives better and/or wealthier.

In the years 2000 and 2001, the WB published its "World Development Report," which challenged the traditional income-based poverty approach that had been used for many years. The Report indicated that poverty is not just the absence of money; it has many ugly faces—lack of opportunity, the lack of having a voice in decisions that impact one's life, and lack of security.

The WB tries to think of its environmental work through the triple lens of opportunity, security, and empowerment (Figure 12-8). Participation in the decision-making process and resource management are two critically important areas. Livelihood, health, vulnerability to environmental change, and full participation in decision making are identified as areas for environmental action that can directly improve people's lives. Then the WB formulates its priorities for natural resource management, access to water and sanitation, air quality, ecological fragility, natural disasters, property rights, and access to environmental information.

Figure 12-8. Integrating Environment and Poverty Reduction: Why Environment Matters

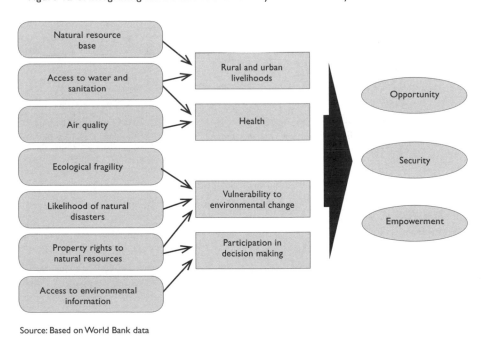

Source: Based on World Bank data

The WB is trying very hard to change people's attitudes vis-à-vis the Kuznets Curve, which implies that a good environment is a luxury that societies enjoy as they grow richer, not a necessity to be enjoyed as they industrialize (see Chapter 1).

A Ten-Point Plan of Action

As a strategy, the WB came up with a ten-point critical areas plan of action that it believes it should undertake in the next five years:

- First, mainstream environment into poverty reduction strategies.
- Second, improve WB upfront analytical work on environmental trends and capabilities of countries and conduct environmental assessment and country-level analyses. In this way, the WB helps leaders and administrators of developing countries to better understand how they can deal with these trends and how they can include the environment in their attempts to reduce poverty.
- Third, develop accurate accounting for development that captures the environment as a developmental factor ("natural resources accounting").
- Fourth, support effective policy approaches and institutions that establish the environment more at par with other development issues.
- Fifth, make markets work for the environment, not against it, by creating market incentives for environmental improvements, for example, by paying for ecological services.
- Sixth, promote good environmental management in the private sector.
- Seventh, build constituencies for positive change.
- Eighth, link local and global objectives (Box 12-10).
- Ninth, carry out institutional realignment.
- Tenth, set performance benchmarks.

Box 12-10. Progress in Building Synergy Between Local and Global Benefits

- Global Environmental Facility
  - Active portfolio consists of over 190 projects with IDA/IBRD cofinancing US$1.95 billion (as of January 2004).
- Montreal Protocol (MP)
  - Since its inception, over 122,000 ozone-depleting potential (ODP) tons (70% of the phaseout under the MP) were phased out at a cost of roughly US$600 million.
- Carbon Finance
  - More than $350 million is under management, and about $150 million is committed to carbon finance business projects.
  - The Community Development Carbon Fund, the BioCarbon Fund, and the OECD Country Funds are expanding the opportunities.

Source: Based on World Bank data

World Bank's Internal Environmental Performance

Unfortunately, the WB did not pay much attention to its own environmental performance as an institution until about 2001. However, things have changed since then. Today 6% of the energy the WB consumes comes from renewables like wind, and the target is to bring this figure up to 20%. It plans to cut down energy consumption by 5% per year. The WB has even reduced the amount of paper it consumes by working on both sides of a sheet. It sounds like a little thing until we think of how much paper such an institution uses, and then cutting consumption in half becomes meaningful. Even the coffee served is a shade-grown, organic, fair trade, certified variety. This might sound silly to some, but the WB finances projects in Central America promoting environmentally friendly coffee farming. In March 2003, the first report on this strategy was submitted to the WB Board of Directors and posted on its web page.

Challenging Conventional Measures of Wealth

The WB has found a way that, hopefully, will make sustainable development an easier goal to achieve. This approach features accurate accounting of development, use of valuation at the macro level, expansion of the measure of national savings into genuine savings (see Chapter 11), use of valuation at a micro level, and expansion of the marketplace by providing for payment of ecological services.

Under the heading of accurate accounting of development, the WB focuses on both the macro and micro levels. On the macro level, the question is, how can we get away from traditional GDP indicators that measure production and output but not environmental damage? The answer is, green accounting completes the measurement of income, savings, and wealth. Furthermore, costing environmental degradation will help in setting development priorities and environmental policy directions.

On the micro level, we need to realize that valuing the environment offers ways to decide on projects, to use valuation to expand the marketplace, and to internalize environmental externalities. For example, consider quantifying watershed benefits shown in Figure 12-9.

Upstream land uses affect the quantity, quality, and timing of water flows. Rural communities are being remunerated for conservation activities that benefit cities and water and power utilities downstream. Thus, those downstream who need the watershed protected are paying for it. These downstream beneficiaries include domestic water users, those engaged in irrigated agriculture, fisheries, and those who enjoy the downstream ecosystem for recreational purposes. It is a holistic system that is likely to prove sustainable. This watershed example suggests that expanding the marketplace raises three questions in the calculation of payments for ecological services:

- Who makes land-use decisions that affect watershed protection?
- How much would it cost them to change land uses?
- How can we channel payments from beneficiaries to these land users in ways that lead to sustainable land uses?

Figure 12-9. Quantifying Watershed Benefits

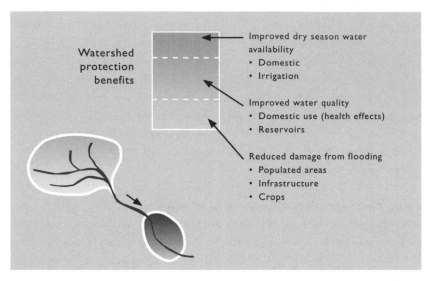

Source: Based on World Bank data

Payment for ecological services and expanding the marketplace also raises these three questions:
- Who benefits from watershed protection?
  - Downstream municipalities?
  - Irrigation systems?
  - Hydroelectricity producers?
  - Fishing?
  - Recreation?
- How much do they benefit?
- Are they willing to pay—and how much—for environmental services?

Using valuation to expand the marketplace can be accomplished through payment for ecological services and through carbon markets. Thus, use of valuation at the micro level can be accomplished through effective use of environmental impact assessments and integration of cost impacts. It also includes considering mitigation options and benefits as well as promotion of payment for ecological services. Doing this will make protection of the forest actually worthwhile.

In 1999, the WB introduced environmental indicators in its data on development. Among these indicators is genuine savings (Box 12-11), true savings, or real wealth, which adds an expanded measure to national savings, including depletion of the environment, investment in human capital, and population growth (see Figure 11-4).

Negative genuine savings per capita implies that an economy is not sustainable with its current policy mix.

Box 12-11. Policy Implications of Genuine Saving

Boosting saving rates requires
• sound macroeconomic policies,
• investment in human capital:
  – education,
  – health (including access to water supply and sanitation, clean fuels, proper drainage, etc.),
• efficient resource extraction and pollution control, and
• moderating population growth.

Source: Based on World Bank data

The concept of genuine savings helps the WB assess national savings, correcting for environmental depletion, investments in human capital, population, and population growth. When there are negative genuine savings, the economy is not sustainable, and the savings are not generating sustainable growth.

Not long ago, Costa Rica hosted a meeting on the Meso-American Biodiversity Corridor. The project was to build an ecological swath running from Mexico to Panama. Costa Rica is a leader in sustainable development. As an incentive to protect its forests, it pays its loggers an average of $52 per hectare for trees they do not cut down (Box 12-12).

Box 12-12. Costa Rica Ecomarkets Project

• Payments for forest conservation or reforestation
• Over 200,000 hectares of forest conserved
• Financed by
  – revenues from a fossil fuel sales tax
  – sales of certified tradable offsets of carbon
  – payments from private hydroelectric power generators
  – GEF grant
• Valuation used for
  – justifying need for project
  – comparing this approach to conservation with others
  – determining payments needed to ensure participation
  – identifying priority areas

Source: Based on World Bank data

Some of this money comes from the WB and some from the GEF, but much of it comes from fuel taxes and downstream water usage fees.

India registers $80 gross savings per person, which is not a bad rate of savings for a country with a per capita income of around $400 per annum. We then take the gross savings figure and begin adding in positive investments such as education, health, and research and development and then subtract depreciation of physical investments and the depletion of natural capital. Now from $80 we have $50 per capita; correcting for the population growth rate, we wind up with a wealth per capita in India of minus $24 (Figure 12-10). If the Indian economy continues along this path (1/3 of savings is lost because of environmental degradation), it is not moving on a sustainable basis.

Figure 12-10. Change in Wealth per Capita, India, 1997

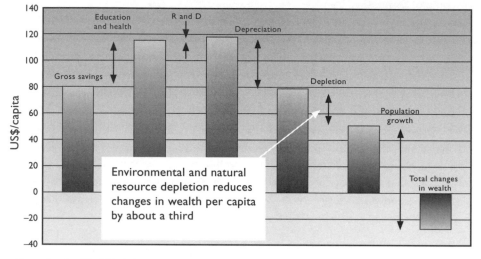

Source: Based on World Bank data

Saudi Arabia is an interesting case in terms of genuine savings. It is a very rich country but is very low on our scale of measurement because it is pumping out its natural capital at a nonsustainable rate. Another interesting country is the PRC, which is poor but has a positive genuine savings rate. One reason is that it has a very strict population growth policy. It is also getting better at preserving natural capital. It seems that in the mid-1990s, the PRC realized that it was growing at 8% per year and its environmental degradation costs were somewhere between 4% and 8% per year. The country's leaders realized they were on a downward treadmill and changed the way they did business.

Use of environmental evaluation at a micro level is also important, so that we can expand the marketplace while making sure the markets help protect the environment rather than hurt it.

World Bank Promotes Carbon Trade

Another area in which the WB is a global leader is in promoting the carbon trade. The carbon market is based on two key premises: First, the greenhouse gas effect is a global phenomenon, so the location of abatement of greenhouse gases is irrelevant; second, the marginal cost of abatement among developed countries such as OECD nations is $25-$150 per ton, versus less than $5 per ton in developing countries. The OECD private sector and governments invest in projects to reduce greenhouse gases in developing countries and receive credit for greenhouse gas ("carbon") emission reduction. At the same time, participating developing countries receive increased investment and cleaner technology. By making carbon a commodity, the WB hopes to bring down the overall costs involved in reducing CO_2 emissions in compliance with the Kyoto Protocol. (See Box 12-13.)

A second advantage to making carbon a commodity is that it becomes a vehicle for income generation and technology transfer for developing countries. The WB has created a fund called the Prototype Carbon Fund (PCF), designed to help set up environmental policies for developing countries and transitional economies beginning in the carbon trade (Figure 12-11). The purpose of the PCF is to help create a market for project-based carbon offsets under the Kyoto Protocol by

- demonstrating how the clean development mechanism and joint implementation trade can contribute to sustainable development,
- providing "learning by doing" experience for parties to the Kyoto Protocol on key policy issues (for example, defining and validating baselines), and
- building confidence that the trade can benefit both sellers and buyers.

Figure 12-11. The Prototype Carbon Fund: How Does It Work?

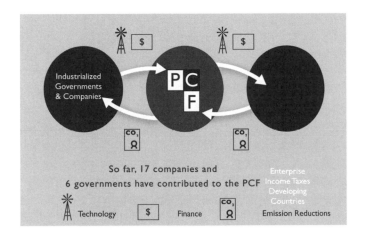

Source: Based on World Bank data

The mechanics of the PCF are relatively simple. Industrialized countries, either businesses or governments, put money in the fund. The fund then identifies projects that can bring down CO_2 emissions in a developing country. Then the CO_2 is sold back to the industrialized countries. Each sale is verified by the WB. The selling nation not only derives income, but gets new technologies, which also means more jobs.

In Johannesburg, the WB launched another new fund called the Community Development Carbon Fund (CDCF) (see http://carbonfinance.org/docs/CarbonFundweb.pdf). Its objective is to make the global carbon trade relevant to small users.

Box 12-13. The Kyoto Protocol

The Kyoto Protocol (KP) is an international environmental treaty that came into force on 16 February 2005 committing industrialized countries to reduce emissions of the six greenhouse gases: CO_2, methane, nitrous oxide, hydrofluorocarbons, perfluorocarbons, and SO_2. Each of these gases has distinct properties, and the overall emissions reduction targets for the six gases are weighted by the relative heat-trapping effect of each gas.

The KP specifies that both developed and developing countries have to take a number of steps, including designing and implementing climate change mitigation and adaptation measures; preparing national inventories of emissions removals by "carbon sinks"; implementing and cooperating in the development and transfer of climate-friendly technologies; and engaging in partnerships in research and observation of climate science, impacts, and response strategies. Developing countries are not legally bound to emissions reduction targets yet, because, historically, they have been responsible for only a small portion of the global greenhouse gas emissions.

Commitment Periods

The KP calls for each country to remain within its assigned emissions quota over a five-year period, from 2008 to 2012, the first commitment period. Under the KP, the overall emissions from industrialized countries are to be reduced 5% below 1990 levels during this period, and negotiations on reduction commitments for subsequent periods must begin no later than 2005.

Emissions Reduction Targets

The target amounts for each country are listed as a percentage of its base-year emissions (1990 for most countries), ranging from a reduction of 8% for most European countries to a 10% increase for Iceland.

A provision in the KP allows for a nation to meet its reduction quota by reducing emissions from power plants and automobiles; however, developed countries can also achieve their commitments by deducting the greenhouse gas emissions absorbed by carbon sinks (like forests) from their gross emissions in the commitment period. This provision includes emissions absorbed or emitted by certain land-use changes and forestry activities, such as reforestation.

Ratification

The ratification procedure required the signatures of 55 industrialized nations, accounting for at least 55% of the global greenhouse gas emissions from industrialized countries in 1990. Although the US signed the agreement on November 12, 1998, approval by a two thirds majority in the Senate has not been achieved. The text of the KP may be found at http://unfccc.int/resource/docs/convkp/kpeng.html. Article 6 of the KP defines Joint Implementation, which facilitates transfers of emission reduction units between Annex I parties, based on reductions achieved through projects. The Joint Implementation under Article 6 differs from the Clean Development Mechanism under Article 12 of the KP, since Clean Development Mechanism projects generate certified emissions reductions units, which represent a "new" unit. The KP also deals with land use and forestry activities.

Source: http://environment.about.com/library/weekly/aa090402a.htm

CORPORATE SOCIAL RESPONSIBILITY: THE TRIPLE BOTTOM LINE

Corporate social responsibility includes making an environmentally hazardous gas like CO_2 a commodity and getting businesses to fund projects that reduce that threat. The significance is in moving toward the triple bottom line, which indicates financial, social, and environmental performance (Figure 12-12).

Figure 12-12. Corporate Social Responsibility

The management of our physical facilities and liquid assets

Our Leadership

How we influence application of sustainable development to investment in emerging markets

Our "Footprint"

Our Business

Integrating sustainable development factors into our investment strategies and transactions

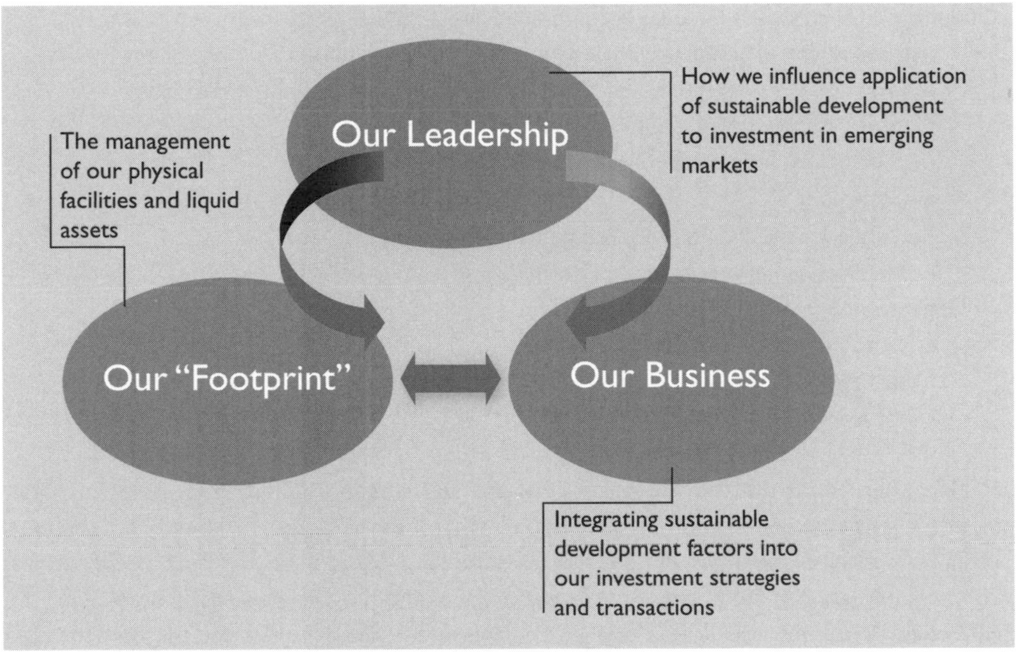

Source: Based on World Bank data

It is not well known, but socially responsible investing is actually growing both in the US and Canada ("The World According to CSR" [corporate social responsibility], *The Economist*, January 20, 2005). In Europegovernments have already created legislative incentives for companies that pay attention not only to their financial bottom line but also to their social and environmental performance, again constituting the triple bottom line.

Some of the legislation has just one line saying that long-term investors such as pension funds must report on the social and environmental performance of their assets. So if one buys, say, bonds, one has to know the social and environmental performance of the company that is issuing the bonds. This simply means that the company, in addition to reporting on its financial status, also has to report on its environmental performance. The WB now takes social responsibility very seriously, and its private sector arm (see http://www.ifc.org/) is conceptualizing and shifting its business toward this direction. To achieve sustainable development, everyone needs to consider the following when acting as consumer, investor, participant in trade, or active citizen:

- changing consumer behavior *(requiring certifications to buy, and/or willing to pay premiums)*,
- changing investor behavior *(growth of "green funds" and concern over governance-related risks)*,
- changing supply chain relationships *(what is not your fault can hurt you)*, and
- putting pressure on policies and regulations *(trade, subsidy removal, labeling, community relations, emissions, etc.)*.

Thus, to achieve sustainable development, we need to clarify what is valued and create an additional framework of tasks to be accomplished along the following lines:

- Management commitment and governance
  - Environmental management and social development commitment and capacity
  - Corporate governance
  - Accountability and transparency
- Environment
  - Process eco-efficiency and environmental footprint
  - Product/service environmental performance
- Socioeconomic development
  - Local economic growth and partnerships
  - Community development
  - Labor force health, safety, and welfare

The International Bank for Reconstruction and Development (IBRD) is fostering corporate social responsibility by influencing its member countries to adopt policies that are more sustainable. IBRD is one of five entities that constitute the World Bank Group. The other entities are the International Development Association, the International Finance Corporation, the Multilateral Investment Guarantee Agency, and the International Centre for the Settlement of Investment Disputes.

The WB's approach to Corporate Social Responsibility focuses on three areas: (i) improving the impacts of its physical facilities, including responsible procurement; (ii) enhancing the sustainability focus of WB products and services, including supporting clients on issues related to corporate social responsibility; and (iii) improving outreach to the global community on the relationship between sustainable development and corporate social responsibility.

Nations and businesses must go beyond complying with "Do No Harm" policies in a proactive way. Production and consumption patterns have to change, and this change has to start in the developed nations. It is just not possible to continue the consumption and production patterns in the wealthy countries and at the same time lift developing countries to a more comfortable level. The WWF says that if everybody consumed the way an average western consumer does, and if everybody continued current production practices, we would need four planets to sustain life.

DEVELOPED COUNTRIES AND SUSTAINABLE DEVELOPMENT

Overall, the development performance of the developed countries is insufficient in terms of providing incentives to achieve sustainable development through altered consumption and production patterns. Yet if these do not change, it is unlikely that sustainable development can be fully achieved. To protect the environment and to provide a better future for all people, everyone needs to lead by example. Developing countries are calling the WB hypocritical, asking it to do this and that while its shareholders are despoiling the planet. It all boils down to the "haves" telling the "have-nots" what they should or should not do, rather than showing them by example.

A Commitment to Change Consumption and Production

It is not all gloom, though. In Johannesburg there was a very promising change. The Western Europeans endorsed a commitment to a ten-year framework for changing consumption and production patterns. For the first time, a big international meeting put the "C-word," consumption, on the table. Hopefully, it will stay there. One also hopes for an increasing awareness of the problem in the US. Production patterns affect climate, and the US has had its share of severe droughts, floods, and hurricanes. To put it in terms of dollars and cents, due to the prevalence of severe natural disasters, insurance rates in the US are at an all-time high.

Sustainable Development and Population Growth and Control

A critical area of sustainability is population growth and control. However, this should not enjoy higher standing than changing production incentives, changing policy incentives, or changing consumption production patterns.

Population is a very sensitive issue. For instance, the WB has counseled India, which is receptive to reducing its fast-growing population. In some countries, the WB would like to foster educational programs for women. But some might say it is not culturally acceptable for women to go to school. In such cases the WB might begin a project that brings the school to the women through a neighborhood tutoring program. In some countries, a large population means security. These are places where having a lot of children ensures a more comfortable retirement, since having many children may equal a pension plan.

One point we have not touched upon is leadership. Many developing countries have governments that need to improve their performance by eliminating corruption. Their officials rob their own people and abuse their countries' resources to line their own pockets. Their greed denies future generations a secure life and a safe environment. This entails a multiplicity of problems. But positive changes come, albeit slowly.

CHAPTER 13

INTERNATIONAL COOPERATION

Sustainable development comprises various activities and dimensions such as concept, policy, operation, project design, implementation, capacity building, coordination, monitoring, financing, advocacy, and public awareness. These activities are all encompassing. They involve all stakeholders—citizens, enterprises, local governments, regional and national governmental organizations—as well as the various organizations and agencies of the UN, DFIs, and NGOs. The Interagency Committee on Sustainable Development established by the Secretary General of the UN is intended to coordinate the activities of all UN agencies and entities. However, each organization has its own structure and governing council that provides direct guidance to it in performing its respective role (Figure 13-1). In the past two decades, sustainable development has been treated as a global slogan and a bandwagon on which all of these agencies and organizations have been riding. Coordination among them is easier said than done, as many participants at the WSSD (2002) understood .

Figure 13-1. Global Sustainable Development Activities

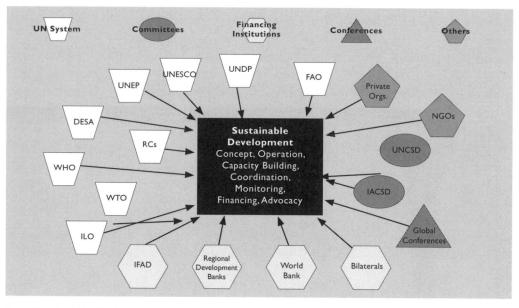

Source: Based on United Nations data

ORGANIZATIONS RESPONSIBLE FOR SUSTAINABLE DEVELOPMENT

Subsequent to the Brundtland Commission report, accepted by the UN General Assembly in 1989 (Resolution 44/228 of December 22, 1989), the Rio Declaration on Environment and Development was adopted at UNCED in 1992. That declaration articulated sustainable development principles with a focus on those responsible for sustainable development: human beings; states; national authorities; women; and others, including indigenous peoples.

The Rio Declaration begins with Principle 1: "Human beings are at the center of concerns for sustainable development. They are entitled to a healthy and productive life in harmony with nature." Principle 2 provides that "States have...the sovereign right to exploit ... resources," while Principle 3 restates the key Brundtland concept: "The right to development must be fulfilled so as to equitably meet developmental and environmental needs of present and future generations."

The Brundtland Report states that "Poverty is a major cause and effect of global environmental problems." In like manner, Principle 5 of the Rio Declaration responds with an overarching requirement: "All states and all people shall cooperate in the essential task of eradicating poverty as an indispensable requirement for sustainable development, in order to decrease the disparities in standards of living and better meet the needs of the majority of the world."

The other principles of the Rio Declaration deal with a wide range of concerns and suggest implied responsibilities under the heading of "sustainable development." For example, Principle 8 deals with such matters as reducing unsustainable patterns of production and consumption and promoting appropriate demographic policies. Principle 10 stresses the importance of participation and states that "Effective access to judicial and administrative proceedings, including redress and remedy, shall be provided." Principle 11 calls for enactment of effective environmental legislation. Principle 12 deals with economic growth and sustainable development as well as trade measures.

Principle 20 of the Rio Declaration states that "Women have a vital role in environmental management and development" and women are "therefore essential to achieve sustainable development." In like fashion, Principle 22 points out that indigenous people have a "vital role in environmental management and development." Principle 24 warns that "Warfare is inherently destructive of sustainable development."

At least five developments are noteworthy in the evolution of thinking about sustainable development subsequent to the 1987 Brundtland Report and UNCED in 1992, which adopted the 27 Principles that form the Rio Declaration, and Agenda 21, a nonbinding action plan for sustainable development. The first is the proliferation of entities concerned with sustainable development within the UN and other multinational organizations (Box 13-1).

The second development arises from the significant impact of globalization on trade and environment in the developing countries. This has become a major concern to those involved with sustainable development. It is perhaps an old issue, but with new dimensions not necessarily contemplated at the time the Brundtland Commission did its work.

A third change arose from the financial crisis of the late 1990s in Asia and Latin America, resulting in a significant devaluation of currencies, which in turn had a severe negative impact on the poor. The crisis created a new class called the "transitional poor," people who were not poor before but became poor due to the financial crisis and were trying to recover when the crisis was over.

A fourth change is the increasing influence and power of two particular categories of stakeholders: multinational corporations and NGOs. This change forms one of the thrusts of Chris Laszlo's book entitled *The Sustainable Company: How to Create Lasting Value Through Social and Environmental Performance* (2004, p. xiv). The book describes in part actions taken by "BP

Box 13-1. Organizations Promoting Sustainable Development

- United Nations
- United Nations Environment Programme (UNEP)
- United Nations Development Programme (UNDP)
- Food and Agriculture Organization (FAO)
- International Labor Organization (ILO)
- United Nations Education, Scientific and Cultural Organization (UNESCO)
- United Nations Conference on Trade and Development (UNCTAD)
- World Health Organization (WHO)
- World Meteorological Organization (WMO)
- International Atomic Energy Agency (IAEA)
- World Bank (WB)
- World Trade Organization (WTO)
- United Nations Department of Economic and Social Affairs (UN/DESA)
- United Nations Children's Fund (UNICEF)
- World Conservation Union (IUCN)
- World Wildlife Fund for Nature (WWF)
- United Nations Commission for Sustainable Development (UNCSD)
- Interagency Committee on Sustainable Development (IACSD)
- Others: Regional development banks (RDBs), International Fund for Agricultural Development (IFAD), bilateral agencies, NGOs, private foundations

Note: This is not an extensive list of organizations.

[British Petroleum], Shell, Dupont, Honda, GM [General Motors] and many others ... to preserve (and extend) open societies and markets that might be threatened by precipitous and calamitous environmental damage." NGOs have become more involved in development and social work, more articulate and more influential than ever before, as discussed in David Bornstein's *How to Change the World: Social Entrepreneurs and the Power of New Ideas* (2004).

The fifth change has been the increasing social and military conflicts throughout the world. Since the 1990s, ethnic rivalries, border disputes, and cross-border terrorism have engendered an environment of fear, a situation that seems to be getting worse. Despite the above problems, the concept of sustainable development has taken root in the international community and in leaders, in particular, of the UN, governments, and the private sector.

REFORM AND REVITALIZATION OF GLOBAL ORGANIZATIONS

To understand the complexity of the UN system, it is necessary to know that the entire system operates under the guidance of six principal organs. These are the General Assembly, Security Council, International Court of Justice, Economic and Social Council, Trusteeship Council, and Secretariat (see the UN organizational chart at http://www.un.org/aboutun/chart.html). There is a real need to revitalize these global organizations so that sustainable development becomes the focal responsibility of all (Box 13-2). At the same time, there is a need to delineate their responsibilities and strengthen their coordination mechanisms. So far, the discussion has ranged from changing the UN Charter and giving the primary responsibility for sustainable development to the Security Council or the Trusteeship Council of the UN to creating a new UN organization called the World Environment Organization (WEO).

At the WSSD in 2002, it was understood that sustainable development should be a principle of global governance. If this is to happen, some suggest that changes may have to be made in Article 22 of the UN Charter, which provides that the "General Assembly may establish such subsidiary organs as it deems necessary for the performance of its function." Also, a standing committee within the UN General Assembly may need to be established.

It is unlikely that the UN Charter will be amended soon. However, a proposal to establish a standing committee for sustainable development is under consideration by the UN General Assembly. If approved by the membership, what would be the advantages? Foremost, discussions concerning sustainable development would be held at a higher level than ministerial, as is currently the case. Second, the decisions and recommendations would have more weight, since the United Nations Commission on Sustainable Development (UNCSD) has representatives from only 53 member countries, while the General Assembly consists of the entire UN membership.

There was another proposal to put the sustainable development issue under the UN Trusteeship Council, since it is an issue involving the global commons. The Trusteeship Council, one of the six principal UN organs, was originally created to decolonize some of the trust territories and then assist in establishing them as independent, self-governing states. Since there are fewer colonies today, the Trusteeship Council has fewer functions to perform—an additional reason to consider it as an appropriate organ of the UN to deal with sustainable development. According to "Summary of Proposals in Reforming the United Nations," a 1995 report prepared by the Commission on Global Governance, because of this, the Secretary General had recommended that "the Trusteeship Council should be given a new mandate to exercise Trusteeship over the global commons." (Commission on Global Governance, 1995, p. 301.) The same report also says the specific functions of the Trusteeship Council could include administration of global treaties such as climate change, biodiversity protection, law of the sea, and the Basel Convention on Hazardous Waste. The Council could then refer appropriate economic, social, or security matters to the Economic and Social Council or the Security Council.

Critics say that this proposal is merely a survival argument for the Trusteeship Council. They feel that if sustainable development is about the economic, social, and ecological security of humanity, the responsibility should be given to the Security Council, which was established "to maintain international peace and security in accordance with the principles and purposes of the United Nations." (Charter of the United Nations, see www.un.org/aboutun/Charter/.) The World Resources Institute in Washington, D.C., a strong proponent of the plan, has argued that, if the Security Council is tasked to maintain ecological, economic, and social security in the world, its charter should be amended specifically to spell out this role (Dodds, 2000, p. 299). Furthermore, proponents of this plan point out that the global environment outlook report of UNEP for 2000

Box 13-2. United Nations System

PRINCIPAL ORGANS

Trusteeship Council	Security Council	General Assembly (GA)	Economic and Social Council	International Court of Justice	Secretariat

Subsidiary Bodies
Military Staff
Standing Committee and ad hoc agencies
International Criminal Tribunal for the Former Yugoslavia
UN Monitoring, Verification and Inspection Commission (Iraq)
United Nations Compensation Commission Peacekeeping Operations and Missions

Subsidiary Bodies
Main committees
Other sessional committees
Standing committees and ad hoc bodies
Other subsidiary programs

Functional Commissions
Commissions on
Human Rights
Narcotic Drugs
Crime Prevention and Criminal Justice
Science and Technology for Development
Sustainable Development
Status of Women
Population and Development
Commission for Social Developement
Statistical Commission

Specialized Agencies[6]
ILO
International Labor Organization
FAO
Food and Agriculture Organization of the United Nations
UNESCO
United Nations Educational, Scientific and Cultural Organization
WHO
World Health Organization
World Bank Group
IBRD
International Bank for Reconstruction and Development
IDA
International Development Association
IFC
International Finance Corporation
MIGA
Multilateral Investment Agency Guarantee
ICSID
International Centre for Settlement and Investments Disputes
IMF
International Monetary Fund
ICAO
International Civil Aviation Organization
IMO
International Maritime Organization
ITU
International Telecommunications Union
UPU
Universal Postal Union
WMO
World Meteorological Organziation
WIPO
World Intellectual Property Organization
IFAD
International Fund for Agricultural Development
UNIDO
United Nations Industrial Development Organization
WTO[3]
World Tourism Organization

Departments and Offices
OSG
Office of the Secretary-General
OIOS
Office of Internal Oversight Services
OLA
Office of Legal Affairs
DPA
Department of Political Affairs
DDA
Department for Disarmament Affairs
DPKO
Department of Peace-keeping Operations
OCHA
Office for the Coordination of Humanitarian Affairs
DESA
Department of Economic and Social Affairs
DGACM
Department of General Assembly and Conference Management
DPI
Department of Public Information
DM
Department of Management
OHRLLS
Office of the High Representative for the Least Developed Countries, Landlocked Developing Countries and Small Island Developing States
UNSECOORD
Office of the United Nations Security Coordinator
UNODC
United Nations Office on Drugs and Crime
UNOG
UN Office at Geneva
UNOV
UN Office at Vienna
UNON
UN Office at Nairobi

Programmes and Funds

UNCTAD
United Nations Conference on Trade and Development
ITC
International Trade Centre (UNCTAD/WTO)
UNDCP[1]
United Nations Drug Control Programme Organization
UNEP
United Nations Environment Programme
UNICEF
United Nations Children's Fund

UNDP
United Nations Development Programme
UNIFEM
United Nations Development Fund for Women
UNV
United Nations Volunteers
UNCDF
United Nations Capital Development Fund
UNFPA
United Nations Population Fund

UNHCR
United Nations High Commissioner for Refugees
WFP
World Food Programme
UNRWA[2]
United Nations Relief and Works Agency for Palestine Refugees in the Near East
UN-HABITAT
United Nations Human Settlement Program (UNHSP)

Regional Commissions
Economic Commission for Africa (ECA)
Economic Commission for Europe (ECE)
Economic Commission for Latin America and the Carribean (ECLAC)
Economic and Social Commission for Asia and the Pacific (ESCAP)
Economic and Social Commission for Western Asia (ESCWA)

Research and Training Institutes

UNICRI
United Nations Interregional Crime and Justice Research Institute
UNITAR
United Nations Institute for Training and Research

UNRISD
United Nations Research Institute for Social Development
UNIDIR[2]
United Nations Institute for Disarmament Reasearch

INSTRAW
International Research and Training Institute for the Advancement of Women

Other Bodies
Permanent Forum on Indigenous Issues (PFII)
United Nations Forums on Forests
Sessional and standing committees
Expert, ad hoc and related bodies

Other UN Entities

OHCHR
Office of the United Nations High Commissioner for Human Rights

UNOPS
United Nations Office for Project Services

UNU
United Nations University
UNSSC
United Nations System Staff College

UNAIDS
Joint United Nations Programme on HIV/AIDS

Related Organizations
WTO[3]
World Trade Organization
IAEA[4]
International Atomic Energy Agency
CTBTO PREP.COM[5]
PrepCom for the Nuclear-Test-Ban-Treaty Organization
OPCW[5]
Organization for the Prohibition of Chemical Weapons

NOTES: Solid lines from Principal Organ indicate a direct reporting relationship; dashes indicate a non-subsidiary relationship. 1) UNDCP is part of the UN Office on Drugs and Crime. 2) INSTRAW and UNIDIR report only to GA. 3) The World Trade Organization and World Tourism Organization use the same acronyme 4) IAEA reports to the Security Council and the GA. 5) CTBTO Prep.Com and OPCW report to the GA. 6) Specialized agencies are autonomous organizations working with the UN and each other through the coordinating machinery of the ECOSOC at the intergovernmental level and through the Chief Executives Board for coordination (CEB) at the inter-secretariat level.

Source: UN Department of Public Information

suggested that there are now more ecological refugees in this world (30 million) than political refugees. Therefore, if the Security Council deals with political refugees and political issues, should it not do the same with ecological refugees and ecological issues?

A World Environment Organization?

Another idea was to establish a World Environment Organization (WEO). UNEP was created after the 1972 Stockholm Conference, which focused primarily on environmental issues. But in 1992, the Earth Summit pointed out that the issue of environment was closely linked with trade, poverty, and finance issues. It was therefore felt that UNEP was not the organization to deal with sustainable development, and a new organization, the WEO, with a broader mandate, was needed. Some countries (notably, Germany, South Africa, Brazil, and Singapore) that supported the idea of creating a WEO brought it before the General Assembly in 1997 and wanted to raise the issue again at the Johannesburg Conference. They argued that such an organization, which could have a replenishing fund of $3 billion every three years, which is currently contributed by donors into the GEF, could also administer legal instruments such as international agreements dealing with climate change. The proposal was voted down by the General Assembly (Report on the General Assembly session, 1997) and was not seriously discussed at the Johannesburg Summit, since many delegations were against creating yet another UN entity to deal with sustainable development.

Role of WTO

Still another proposal was to turn sustainable development over to WTO (World Trade Organization), which was established on January 1, 1995 to foster trade liberalization for the benefit of all the world's nations, both developing and developed. Unfortunately, according to an analysis done by the United Nations Conference on Trade and Development, the benefits of WTO have been uneven (Andrew Simmons, 2000, pp. 160-165). The impacts on developing countries have been both positive and negative. Some of these are:

Positive Impacts
- increasing volume of trade
- increasing foreign investment
- increasing local employment
- integrating the economy and the environment by employing market-based instruments

Negative Impacts
- pollution exports from developed to developing countries
- trade barriers using an environmental argument
- loss of social and cultural traditions and values
- promoting illegal, transboundary flow of contraband (drugs and weapons), finances (currency racketeering), and human beings (immigrants, terrorists)

In the ten years since WTO was formed, developed countries have accounted for, and profited from, 70% of increased international trade. In its 2000 Annual Report, the WTO stated,

> It is ironic that the rich countries, whose policymakers urge poor countries to open their domestic markets and export their way to economic development, are responsible for denying these poor countries access. The United States earned $700 billion per year by maintaining trade barriers to their exports in low-tech industries alone. ...

Because of these policies, the former chief economist of the World Bank, Joseph Stiglitz (2004, p. 438), publicly declared that underdeveloped countries are left with "neither aid nor trade." With such performance, how could developing countries trust WTO to be fair to sustainable development and to the environment of poor developing countries? Thus the idea of making WTO the organization responsible for promoting sustainable development on the planet was abandoned.

Revitalizing International Financing Institutions

Some believe that international financing institutions could, perhaps under the leadership of the World Bank, take the lead for sustainable development, because they have both the financing capability and technical expertise. Some suggest that governments listen more readily to policy prescriptions and recommendations made by these institutions.

But critics believe that these institutions, particularly the World Bank, must also reform themselves in at least two ways. First, they should make poverty reduction their focus of action. And second, they should change their lending policies to favor programs that support pro-sustainable development.

Under the present circumstances, these institutions have a tendency to finance large infrastructure development projects in high- and middle-income countries, leaving insufficient funding for small, basic infrastructure projects in poor countries. Being in the business of banking, these institutions may naturally try to maximize their financial gains and minimize their transaction and technical assistance costs.

The focus of these organizations should not extend beyond making a profit through hard sector investments in high- or middle-income developing countries. Increasingly, their effort should be toward supporting basic infrastructure programs and social services in poor- to middle-income countries.

In fact, some critics say, middle- to high-income countries may not need development banks, because they can almost always approach the international capital market and the private sector to finance large infrastructure projects in such sectors as energy and transport.

The existence of international financing institutions can, therefore, be justified primarily if they support the development of low-income developing countries in both hard and soft sectors and the development of soft sectors (social infrastructure, agriculture, water, etc.) as well as growth in middle- to high-income countries.

Alternatives

As mentioned above, there are several alternatives to deal with the task of promoting global sustainable development. They are changing the UN charter, using the Trusteeship Council, passing the responsibility to the Security Council, creating a WEO, revitalizing WTO, reforming the international financing institutions, or simply working with what is in place but strengthening the coordination among existing organizations.

But which of these is the best? Would a charter change have enough teeth to be effective? What would be the driving force behind the words on a piece of paper? As discussed, placing global responsibility for sustainable development on each of the UN organs (General Assembly, Security Council, and Trusteeship Council) has its own merits and demerits. However, none of these organs has technical expertise on the subject and, therefore, this alternative might not work better than others.

Creating a WEO might work as long as it would have enough authority and power, including funding. The problem lies in its name. An environmental organization is usually regarded as lacking a mandate to deal with trade, finance, development, and, above all, poverty reduction.

So far, the benefits of WTO have been uneven. There have been some well publicized cases such as when Mexico brought a complaint against the US for the latter's unilateral actions under the US Marine Mammals Act, which forbids tuna importation if the tuna has been caught with nets that also catch and kill dolphins. A report of a WTO panel declared in part that the US could not impose legislative sanctions to protect dolphins outside of US jurisdictional limits. However, the report was not adopted "because Mexico and the US attempted to negotiate an environmental agreement to ensure proper dolphin protection." (Kiss and Shelton, 2000, p. 647; also see Chapter 7.) Other cases have involved the legal promotion of transboundary flows of goods, drugs, weapons, finances, currency racketeering, immigrants, terrorists, and so on. Even if the negative impacts of trade can be minimized and positive impacts maximized, there is some question as to whether WTO could lead the sustainable development initiative at the global level. It appears that, with the suggested reforms, the financial institutions led by the World Bank could be a possibility. In practice, however, what might happen is that the responsibility would continue to lie with various organs of the UN and with non-UN entities with strengthened coordination mechanisms, particularly with DFIs such as the World Bank and the regional development banks. evolving out of further discussion. This might also be the most cost-effective means of international cooperation on sustainable development (Willard, 2002, p. 4).

WORLD SUMMIT ON SUSTAINABLE DEVELOPMENT

From the previous discussions, several factors emerge as prerequisites for achieving sustainable development: reduce poverty, plan population growth, control pollution, rectify policy and market failures, establish good governance, and manage disasters. However, achieving these objectives in real world situations is not so easy. In August 2002, delegates from 191 of 195 countries, including 109 heads of state, attended the WSSD in Johannesburg organized by the UN. The official number of attendees was 21,000, with many more present but unregistered. The unofficial count of participants was as high as 60,000. Sources closely involved with the WSSD claim it was the most heavily attended conference in the history of the UN.

WSSD Agenda and Outcome

The Johannesburg WSSD agenda included discussions on health, biodiversity, ecosystems, agriculture, water and sanitation, and energy; cross-cutting issues included finance, trade, technology transfer, information, education, consumption patterns, and capacity building.

The WSSD had mixed results. According to UN officials, it was modestly successful. However, a number of NGO representatives attending the summit rated it between a qualified success and an outright failure, lacking any meaningful targets or commitments. Hugo Chavez, the President of Venezuela and then leader of developing countries, known as the Group of 77, chose to call it a "dialogue of the deaf, in which political leaders of the world have no real impact on the final outcome. ..." (See http://www.rio10. dk/upload/att/part1.pdf.)

Since the attending heads of state were not well positioned to discuss the technical details of sustainable development, their agenda—called "making it happen"—was limited to a broad discussion of implementation. Despite the vagueness of their agenda, it was considered very important, because the leaders' support and final declaration lent weight and urgency to the meeting.

In addition to the official agenda, there were many side events such as seminars, exhibitions, meetings, and panel discussions attended by representatives of NGOs, governments, and UN agencies. The subject matter of these events included water and sanitation, good governance, business, local government actions, trade and development, employment, private-public partnerships, and South-South cooperation (among developing countries). The Summit events took place over a two-week period. The first week was devoted to meetings among senior officials, while the second week was led basically by the heads of the governments. There were also many parallel unofficial events organized by UN agencies, NGOs, and the private sector.

There was agreement on the need for the private sector to operate within a transparent and regulatory environment reinforcing corporate responsibility. This was a high priority issue with the US policymakers. It was also stressed that there is a need for monitoring implementation of Agenda 21 of the Rio Conference; the MDGs, approved by the UN General Assembly; and the Johannesburg Commitment on Sustainable Development.

The heads of governments at the WSSD cited the importance of the need for monitoring implementation at a future conference, perhaps after five years. The idea would be for the governments to talk in a meaningful way about how they had fared in implementing WSSD recommendations. Although this may sound like "meeting begets meeting," some UN officials believe that this is one effective way of maintaining political pressure on governments and civil societies to ensure action.

One of the most important outcomes of the WSSD was the realization that sustainable development is only marginally successful on a global scale but highly successful when implemented region by region. Each region had its own perspective on the broad recommendations produced at the WSSD, and it should be up to them to monitor implementation of their own ideas. In fact, in some regions successes have been more visible at the national and local levels (Smith and Jalal, 2000).

Major Outcomes of the Summit

Two major products came out of the Summit: a political declaration, which has subsequently been adopted by all attending governments; and the Johannesburg Commitment on Sustainable Development, a technical document containing a set of recommendations, along with a plan of action, that the attending governments agreed to implement.

1. Political declaration

The political declaration reaffirms the commitment to sustainable development and attests that no nation should be denied the opportunity to benefit from development. There is a problem here, though. The declaration implies that if, for example, a country wants to develop a coal-fired power plant and has coal but does not have resources for environmental mitigation measures or for procurement of environmental technology, it should still proceed to do so. However, to resolve such problems, the international donor community has established the Global Environment Facility (GEF).

The political declaration further recognizes that poverty is the most pressing challenge in promoting sustainable development. Alongside this is the need for socioeconomic equality within and among the world's nations. The declaration also addresses the need to recognize the issue of good governance.

While the language of the declaration might sound like political rhetoric, it does show at least a commitment on some generic points upon which governments must act. Attending leaders agreed that democracy, the rule of law, respect for human rights and freedom, and achievement of peace and security are essential for sustainable development. They further agreed to combat terrorism, organized crime, and corruption. Another part of the document deals with political leadership, food security, water availability, sanitation, and health as items essential to human survival and sustainable development. The attending governments also committed themselves to an effort to reduce the damage caused by natural disasters by strengthening international cooperation and by developing sound technologies, including early warning systems.

2. Johannesburg commitment on sustainable development

The second result, the Johannesburg Commitment, is a plan for implementation. See Box 13-3. Four preparatory meetings were held three months prior to the WSSD to try to produce a document that all the participating governments would find acceptable. It was almost an impossible task. Whenever the people drafting the document could not get full agreement on a clause, the language was put in brackets. Of the 615 subparagraphs in the report, 156 were bracketed, indicating that delegates found problems with about a fourth of the document.

While achieving agreement among 191 countries on the remaining 75 percent on matters of great relevance does not seem too bad, the global community could not agree on globalization issues, with 93% of the paragraphs relating to this topic not agreed to. Developed countries upheld the benefits of globalization, while developing countries saw these only as an exploitation of resources, a diminishment of their cultural heritage, and a worsening of their environmental problems (such as the export of pollution).

Box 13-3. Important Commitments Made at the WSSD

On the positive side, some important commitments were made and initiatives implemented. For example, a commitment was made to reduce the proportion of people without access to sanitation by 50% by 2015. This is an old target that had already been approved by the UN General Assembly, and a "doable" one.

The US announced that it would invest $970 million over three years (2002-2005) in the area of water and sanitation. It also announced a commitment to spend $2.3 billion by 2005 on the health sector, mainly on research and development. Apparently a major part of this money was to be earmarked for AIDS research and medicines. But it was expected that those suffering from other diseases in the poorest of nations will benefit, too.

The EU announced a "water for life" initiative, which seeks to forge partnerships with others to meet established goals for water and sanitation. This initiative was to be taken primarily in Africa and Central Asia, where the water shortage is most acute. The EU has been at the forefront in implementing projects for sustainable development, but it is disappointing that it is not addressing the need to develop new sources of renewable energy. There was a commitment to increase access to modern energy services, increase energy efficiency, and increase the use of renewable energy. But even those commitments are vague. For this commitment there are no goals or targets, and no indication of how much money will be spent.

Another commitment now allows the GEF to combat desertification* in Africa. Initially, the GEF was used mainly in four areas: climate change, ozone depletion, international waters, and biodiversity conservation. Following the WSSD, the GEF became open to controlling desertification because of pressure from several African states.

The US also made a commitment to support some sustainable agricultural programs, and perhaps will also address agricultural subsidies to its own farmers, which are directly hurting potential income generation derived from agricultural exports among small Third World countries.

---

*"Desertification" is defined as a process that reduces the productivity of land and increases social distress (UNEP, 1977).

Source: UNEP (1977)

When it came to implementation, all agreed to paragraphs about reducing poverty, providing water, promoting sanitation, protecting human health, developing sustainable energy, and so on. The stumbling block here was money: A substantial majority of the delegations (89%) could not agree on how to finance mega projects; also, 85% could not agree on the issues concerning tariffs, trade barriers, and agricultural subsidies.

The document was finally approved, although it failed to fully address critical issues like globalization, finance, and trade. And although some of the bracketed subparagraphs had their brackets removed once the language was "cleansed," they were so diluted that they did not commit anyone to anything.

Positive Outcomes of the Summit

In hindsight, the Johannesburg Summit, even if it did not result in a concrete action plan backed by the necessary financial support, was a success for various reasons:

1. Entrenchment of the concept

In 1992, the Rio Conference focused on environment and development. The Johannesburg Summit, however, was the first to focus on implementing development and environment—recognizing that environmental management is not about managing the environment but about managing developmental activities within the assimilative capacity of the environment. Thus the concept of sustainable development was entrenched in the minds of the governments and others alike.

2. Improving global governance

The Johannesburg Summit also recognized sustainable development as a framework for global governance, a topic that would later be discussed at a UN General Assembly session.

3. Reiterating the political will of governments

Prior to Johannesburg, the UN had tried to create a new body called the World Environment Organization. The idea had been abandoned after participating governments pointed out that another layer of bureaucracy was not what they had in mind; instead, what was needed was improved coordination among existing organizations and the political will of governments. Even the vague political goals contained in the declaration, some of which were heard before at the Rio Conference, were significant.

4. Setting targets for technical and financial commitments

Finally, the WSSD provided an arena for setting targets for technical and financial commitments. Two types of agreements were reached:

- Type 1—an agreement between governments; and
- Type 2—an agreement between NGOs and the private sector or between two affiliates within the private sector.

For the first time in the history of UN-sponsored meetings, Type 2 agreements were forged and were considered to be significant. For example, several logging companies met with an investor insurance company at a private home in Johannesburg to discuss sustainable logging. The investors told the loggers that they can log, but it will be conditional upon ecological considerations such as achieving sustainable yields and using eco-labeling on wood products. Accordingly, a Type 2 agreement was reached. Usually issues of this kind cannot be discussed at a formal conference, because they open the governments, logging companies, and investors to criticism from NGOs and the media. Therefore, these type of agreements were regarded as innovative.

Regarding the many financial commitments made, it remains to be seen whether they are new, additional resources, and whether they will be used for the benefit of developing countries or primarily to benefit the countries that made them. All told, as the planners said, the outcome of this conference was a modest success. That the US is active in this area was underscored when Secretary of State Colin L. Powell led the American delegation at the Johannesburg Summit and presented a paper on "Making Sustainable Development Work."

Aside from the US government, various sustainable development initiatives have been taken by institutions at the local level. For example, the Harvard project for recycling wastes recovered a record 4,267 tons of recyclables in fiscal year 2002. This prevented the release of 2,336 metric tons of CO_2 into the atmosphere, the equivalent of taking 1,785 passenger cars off the road. There are many such success stories all over the world at the local level, even though sustainable development may not have succeeded at the national level (Smith and Jalal, 2000).

ROLE OF NON-STATE ACTORS
IN SUSTAINABLE DEVELOPMENT

There are other global organizations, not part of the UN system, that are very important to the achievement of sustainable development. Included among these are some international financial organizations such as ADB and NGOs such as IUCN and WWF. Also included are industrial NGOs such as the World Business Council for Sustainable Development, educational entities such as Cambridge University, and private foundations such as the Bill and Melinda Gates Foundation and the MacArthur Foundation.

How do non-UN organizations influence sustainable development? The World Business Council for Sustainable Development is a coalition of about 175 international companies from more than 35 countries and 20 major industrial sectors. Its members include Aventis, Aracus Celulos, Caterpillar, ChevronTexaco, Coca Cola, Deloitte Touche Tohmatsu, Dow Chemical, Dupont, ING Group, Johnson & Johnson, New York Times, Nokia, Shell Group, Toyota Motors, and Volkswagen. It is "committed to sustainable development via the three pillars of economic growth, ecological balance, and social progress." Its mission is to "provide business leadership" by promoting "eco-efficiency, innovation and corporate social responsibility." (See http://www.wbcsd.org; see also Box 13-4.)

Some companies in the private sector have become leaders in implementing the sustainable development concept. Robert Willard's book, The Sustainability Advantage: Seven Business Case Benefits of a Triple Bottom Line (2002, pp. 4-5), while discussing the World Business Council for Sustainable Development and "pressures on the environmental attributes of a business," (italics in the original) points out that, the environment is not going to disappear as an issue for business. Companies are, and will continue to remain, under pressure from customers, investors, employees, legislators, and, increasingly, from banks and insurance companies to be eco-efficient. After citing the definition of sustainable development employed in the Brundtland report, Willard, who once held a senior management position at IBM, describes (2002, p. 5) what sustainable development means for business:

Box 13-4. How Can International Companies within the World Business Council
Contribute to Sustainable Development?

According to the Council's recent publication, "Finding Capital for Sustainable Livelihoods Businesses: A Finance Guide for Business Managers," (2004, p. 39) the "Proctor & Gamble Health Sciences Institute has developed a water treatment product for home use. Each sachet purifies ten liters of water and retails at around $0.10 in countries including Guatemala, the Philippines, Morocco, and Pakistan. This is a simple, affordable way to provide safe drinking water to the one billion people who lack access to piped water.

This Council publication reports that this water treatment product will likely generate a profit and other benefits:

In markets where P&G sells through its own retail channels, this business is expected to be profitable long term. However, margins will be lower than in mature markets. These direct returns to P&G are enhanced by indirect benefits on the back of the social good achieved. These indirect benefits, such as a boost to employee morale, can help sell a business idea internally.

In economic language, it means we should live off the Earth's interest, not its capital. For a business, it means sustaining nature's resources as well as sustaining the company. Sustainable development is like a three-legged stool. Its legs are economic prosperity, environmental stewardship, and social responsibility. If one of the legs is missing, the stool is not going to work, so we need to be sure all three legs are in good shape.

A table entitled "Sustainable Development" immediately following in Willard's book includes the following concerning sustainable development:

Triple Bottom Line ... 3 Es, 3 Ps consist of

• Economy/Profit Sustainable Business;
• Environment/Planet Eco-Efficiency & Business;
• Equity/People Ethical Business, including Respect for human rights under the first subheading followed by "INTERNAL EMPLOYEES" and "Charitable contributions" as well as "Closing the gap between rich and poor" under the second and last subheading, "REST OF THE WORLD."

Willard continues (2002, p. 5) by specifying what companies must do with respect to the environment:

The environmental stewardship dimension of sustainable development not only requires companies to "do no harm" to the environment with their operations and products, but also stretches them to help restore the environment from harm already done. This requires reducing the amount of energy, water, and material consumed in the manufacture of products, reducing waste, and remediating contaminated sites.

Willard argues we need to achieve "eco-efficiency," a "contraction of ecological and economic efficiency—doing more with less over the full life cycle of a product. ..." Willard quotes (2002, p. 5)

> Stephan Schmidheiny, who along with 50 business leaders in the Business Council for Sustainable Development, elaborated ... what eco-efficient companies would look like:
> "Corporations that achieve ever more efficiency while preventing pollution through good housekeeping, materials substitution, cleaner technologies, and cleaner products and that strive for more efficient use and recovery of resources can be called 'eco-efficient' [footnote omitted]."

In the last three pages of his book (2002, pp. 151-153), Willard argues that

> [c]orporate leadership in sustainability will require active lobbying of national and international governments and agencies for more sustainable, friendly policies:
> Around the world, governments tax labor and investment while they subsidize the use of natural resources. The use of public land for grazing and logging, and public support for irrigation, agricultural subsidies, and fossil fuel infrastructure—all these programs work against sustainable development. Business leaders working for change can only go so far before they run into these barriers. At that point they can stop, or they can lobby for changes in public policy that will reward further investment in sustainable development. True leadership on this issue encompasses private investment decisions and public positions as well. [footnote omitted]

Willard outlines (2002, pp. 151–152) his "required five-step approach":
- Stop subsidizing the wrong things, and shift taxes from labor and profits to resource use and pollution.
- Pass tough regulations to support the right things.
- Ensure there are enough inspectors to catch violators.
- Prosecute the polluters.
- Publicize who is best and who is worst.

Willard also argues for the use of "environmental performance indicators" (2002, pp. 151-152):

> The adage "What gets measured gets managed" reminds us that a set of environmental performance indicators should be added to the measurement system of the business. Once sustainable development indicators are tracked within the same business cycle as other traditional measurements, change will magically happen.

On the next to last page of his book (2002, p. 152), Willard advocates using "worksheets in the Appendix [of his book] to help companies identify and quantify the financial benefits of seven potential benefit areas," including "reduced expenses at manufacturing and commercial sites" and "increased profit." In the last paragraph (2002, p. 153), he stresses that "[s]mart executives" will "take" the "benefits" of the sustainable development approach "before their competitors do" and that "[c]ompanies that lag will be history, trapped in the hoax of perpetual, unsustainable growth."

Another recent publication, *The Sustainable Company: How to Create Lasting Value Through Social and Environmental Performance* (2003), by Chris Laszlo, also discusses (p. 18) the relevance of the Brundtland Commission's definition of sustainability for "[p]lanetary ethics," which he describes as "operating within the earth's social and physical limits." Laszlo points out (p. 26) that "a growing cadre of executives argue that sustainable business is simply the ethical thing to do and that it will produce enduring shareholder value in the long run." In a quote from Auden Schendler in the June 2002 *Harvard Business Review* (2003, p. 26), Laszlo suggests the difficulties involved through the example of a company trying to retrofit "lighting in a hotel garage" which "showed a high payback" but which needed an ethical argument to gain approval:

> If the economic argument didn't work, what could I do? I needed another tool. In the end, I argued that the retrofit supported our corporate values . . . The bottom line: Corporate Sustainability won't occur without a company mandate that springs from ethics, not economics. Aristotle asked what it means to lead the moral life. Before business even approaches sustainability, that question will need to move from the classroom to the boardroom.

Laszlo then argues (pp. 26-27) that the "only sustainable business paradigm that will be both robust and compelling is one that combines shareholder value and stakeholder value." He discusses (p. 15) the importance of creating a "New Paradigm" of "Sustainable Value Creation" from the existing "Triple Bottom Line (separate tracks)" under the headings "Economic," "Environmental," and "Social." After chapters dealing with such topics as "What Gets Measured Gets Managed" and "Shareholder Value and Corporate Responsibility," Laszlo analyzes four companies, including the Atlantic Richfield Corporation (ARCO) (p. 65), that are the petroleum "industry's search for sustainable value."

Laszlo asserts (p. 46) that "[s]ustainability is a [w]orldview," which "starts with the belief that we are part of a larger system—a business ecology—and extends to a willingness to examine the larger socioeconomic system and how we impact it at the individual, community, and organizational levels, and eventually at the planetary level." He acknowledges (p. 46) that this worldview of sustainability

> challenges the prevailing belief articulated over 30 years ago by Milton Friedman, the Nobel Prize-winning economist, that "the only social responsibility of business is

to make profit," as well as [complying with] all the associated explicit and implicit rules that go along with that fundamental belief.

In conclusion, Laszlo stresses (pp. 121-122) that companies "must be skilled at ... discovering sustainable value opportunities and creating sustainable value." His "Sustainable Value Strategy," (p. 167) asks seven questions:

- *What is our sustainable value vision?*
- *How can we address social impacts, challenges, and future expectations while building business value?*
- *How should we identify and manage emerging issues?*
- *How should we measure success?*
- *What initiatives should we pursue?*
- *What capabilities do we need?*
- *How should we proceed?*

On the next to last page of his book (p. 173), Laszlo notes that even among the "20 companies seen as corporate responsibility leaders (such as Dow Chemical, Dupont, and Hewlett-Packard)," there is a "belief gap" among "financial managers." He also notes that

[a]mong managers answering the question "Who inside the company believes in the business value of corporate responsibility?" [o]ver 80 percent said that they believed in the business value but that less than 40 percent of the financial managers in the companies did.

An Appendix to Laszlo's book rates (p. 190) Standard and Poor's 500 companies on the basis of "total social impact," which includes evaluation of "principled business practices." Among the total social impact practices considered, as described in Laszlo's book (p. 192), is the following heading: "[t]he environment deserves protection and improvement through sustainable business practices," including measurements "focused on ... sustainability and life cycle impacts of products and services." Among the firms in the "Top Decile" of the total social impact companies are Ford Motor, General Motors, Dupont (E.I.), Dow Chemical, and Weyerhaeuser Corp. (pp. 194-195).

NGOs AND SOCIAL ENTREPRENEURS

In his book *How to Change the World: Social Entrepreneurs and the Power of New Ideas* (2004), David Bornstein describes (p. 4) how environmental organizations have grown significantly in number, size, and influence since about 1980:

> Twenty years ago...Indonesia had only one independent environmental organization. Today it has more than 2,000 [footnote omitted]. In Bangladesh, most of the country's development work is handled by 20,000 NGOs; almost all [of] them were established in the past twenty-five years...In France, during the 1990s, an average of 70,000 new citizen groups were established each year, quadruple the figure for the 1960s. In Canada, the number of registered citizen groups has grown by more than 50 percent since 1987, reaching close to 200,000. In Brazil, in the 1990s, the number of registered citizen organizations jumped from 250,000 to 400,000, a 60-percent increase. In the United States, between 1989 and 1998, the number of public service groups registered with the Internal Revenue Service jumped from 464,000 to 734,000, also a 60-percent increase...Finally, during the 1990s, the number of registered international citizen organizations increased from 6,000 to 26,000.

Bornstein describes (p. 2) the "social entrepreneur" as "play[ing] roles in education, health care, environmental protection, disability, and many other fields" analogous to the roles that Henry Ford and Steven Jobs played in "re-imagining cars and computers as mass-market goods." Bornstein quotes "the management expert Peter F. Drucker" as describing the social entrepreneur as one who "changes the performance capacity of society."

> According to ... Drucker, the term "entrepreneur" (from the French word, meaning "one who takes into hand") was introduced two centuries ago by the French economist Jean-Baptiste Say to characterize a special economic actor—not someone who simply opens a business, but someone who "shifts economic resources out of an area of lower and into an area of higher productivity and greater yield." [footnote omitted]

Bornstein describes (pp. 233-241) the "six qualities of successful social-entrepreneurs":
- *Willingness to Self-Correct*
- *Willingness to Share Credit*
- *Willingness to Break Free of Established Structures*
- *Willingness to Cross Disciplinary Boundaries*
- *Willingness to Work Quietly*
- *Strong Ethical Impetus*

Bornstein concludes his book (p. 279) by noting how the growth in significance of NGOs and social entrepreneurs can change the world:

> In 1990, there were a few dozen micro-credit programs in the world reaching less than 2 million clients. Today ... there are more than 2,500 reaching more than

41.6 million. Looking ahead to the next ten or fifteen years, I envision the same kind of growth in the field of social entrepreneurship—an explosion of activity. For those who seek to apply their talents to reshape a part of the world, the opportunities are endless—and they are just beginning to be seen.

Among these NGOs and social entrepreneurs are important scientific institutes, legal groups, indigenous communities, and the media (Sands, 2003, pp. 113-220). Individual scientists, teachers, doctors, lawyers, and other activists also pay significant roles.

FINANCING SUSTAINABLE DEVELOPMENT

How much money would the world need to achieve sustainable development? According to 1992 Earth Summit architects, to implement Agenda 21 the world would need $625 billion per year. Of that amount, $500 billion would have to come from domestic resources and $125 billion from external financing. Since the global GDP at that time was around $31 trillion, 2% of the global GDP would be needed to fight for sustainable development. A 1997 study (Rogers et al., 1997, pp. 83-112) revealed that to remedy environmental damage caused by past development activities, 1% to 7% of the GDP of developing countries in Asia would need to be devoted to remediation. An estimate for developed countries of Europe and North America puts this figure at around 2%.

How much financing is available for sustainable development? One figure comes from ODA, the external aid flow, which went down from $55 billion to $50 billion between 1990 and 2000. Domestic resource allocation for sustainable development in developing countries is also likely to remain static. There is thus, based on calculations, a resource gap of about $481 billion per year.

How do we then meet the resource requirements for promoting sustainable development? Some suggestions have come from various commentators, and conferences, including the 2002 Monterrey Conference on financing sustainable development prior to the WSSD in Johannesburg.

One suggestion is to close the financial gap through a special tax called the Tobin Tax. More than 20 years ago, Nobel Laureate James Tobin won the prize for his analysis of financial markets and their relations to expenditure decisions, employment, production, and prices. Earlier, in 1972, he argued that over $1.5 trillion is exchanged every day on the currency markets of the world, of which 95% of the transactions appear to consist of currency speculation. For example, if one thinks that the value of the yen will go up, one will sell dollars and buy yen. Tobin proposed that if 0.1% to 0.25% of this currency exchange value were imposed as a tax, it would generate about $150 billion per year.

The Canadian parliament approved the idea of a Tobin Tax in March 1999. However, worldwide political will to impose such a tax appears to be lacking.

Reduction of military expenditures by 10%, according to UNDP, could generate about $125 billion per year. Unfortunately, the study came at a time when global security was becoming an increasing problem. Whether it can and will be done is a decision that will be made by politicians and heads of governments.

Withdrawing subsidies on energy and water, which cause a lot of environmental damage and do not, in most cases, help the poor, could generate about $100 billion globally per year.

Domestic resource allocation, which is static at about 0.2%, could be increased to 0.3%. This alone would generate another $31 billion. Though this is a small figure, it would be important, because no donor nation wants to contribute funds if the developing countries are not doing their part.

The external aid flow could be increased from 0.2% to 0.7%, as specified in Chapter 33 of Agenda 21, which states in part that

> developed countries reaffirm their commitments to reach the accepted United Nations target of 0.7 percent of GNP for ODA and, to the extent that they have not yet achieved that target, agree to augment their aid programs in order to reach that target as soon as possible." (See Box 13-5.)

Box 13-5. Proposed New Deal on Finance

Needs Estimate
• Earth Summit/ Agenda 21 $625 billion/yr:
                                               $500 billion domestic
                                               $125 billion external

• Rationale
  – 2% of Global GDP needed
  – Asia: 1%-7% needed (Average 3%)
  – Global GDP 1999: $30,876 billion/yr

Source: UNCED, P. Rogers et al. (1997), WB's Green Data Book (2000)

It must be noted that at the UNCED in 1992 the US delegation stated that it would not be bound by this obligation and thus is not acting contrary to any obligation in this respect. To date, only the Netherlands, some Scandinavian countries, and a few other nations have increased their contributions.

In summary (see Table 13-1), financing sustainable development is a complex and difficult task. There is little possibility of matching demand (as estimated by the global community at the Earth Summit) with supply. With the current global situation, the ways to bridge the resource gap as suggested herein may not work – particularly reduction of military expenditure and increase of domestic resource allocation and ODA flow (which may stay static or increase incrementally for some time). Therefore, the global community has to reestimate the need downwards (assigning priorities within each priority) and to identify innovative methods of financing basic needs projects in developing countries with private sector and community financing.

Table 13-1. Ways to Bridge the Resource Gap

• Proposed Tobin Tax	$150 billion per year
• Reduction of military expenditure	125 billion per year
• Withdraw subsidy of energy and water	100 billion per year
• Increase domestic resource allocation by 0.3%	31 billion per year
• Increase ODA by 0.3%	75 billion per year
Total	$481 billion per year

Sources: Based on data from several sources, including UNDP, ODA, and OECD (2000)

In remarks entitled "A New Framework for Multilateral Development Policy", Larry Summers, then US Treasury Secretary and later President of Harvard University, said on March 20, 1999, that

> [e]conomic history has provided a clear, natural experiment regarding the efficacy of finance without conditions. Again and again, natural resources windfalls have financed presidential planes and palaces and entrenched official corruption, while producing very little in the way of lasting economic benefits.

Summers raised a very important issue: What would be the point of increasing the external aid flow and imposing the Tobin Tax if funds go to the developing countries or wherever the sustainable development problems are, only to see those funds used to finance either nonsustainable development activities or corruption? This has been emphasized again and again: Most of the DFIs today have adopted "anticorruption" and "good governance" policies that the borrowing member countries must follow in order for them to be eligible to borrow from these banks.

COOPERATION BETWEEN REGIONS

One of the most significant items in terms of promoting sustainable development is through North-South and South-South cooperation. ("North" generally refers to the developed countries or the members of OECD. It includes Australia and New Zealand, although these countries are geographically outside of the northern hemisphere. "South" generally refers to developing countries even if they are located north of the equator.) With decreasing flow of external aid, foreign investment, and ODA, the developing countries should get more involved in South-South cooperation, particularly in the flow of information and appropriate technology for sustainable development. Also with respect to key factors for promoting sustainable development, South-South cooperation could be significant.

Looking at poverty reduction often involves four key areas: increased financial flow, pro-poor economic programs, social justice, and good governance. What kind of economic growth should we promote? Should it be basic water supply, sanitation, and shelter? This may call more for South-South cooperation than North-South. Improving social justice and good governance can also often be assisted through cooperation among developing countries, though useful examples can be drawn from the developed world as well.

Similarly, pollution control has four primary components: urban environmental management, deforestation and desertification, technology transfer, and climate change. Urban environmental management often requires North-South cooperation. However, the problems of desertification and deforestation are often local in character, except to the extent that international market forces create incentives for harvesting and purchase of biodiversity, particularly forests, for sale abroad. Thus, desertification and deforestation often require cooperation among the affected countries in the South.

Regional cooperation on transboundary water issues has been a major area of discussion and negotiation among riparian countries in the respective basins of the regions. This type of cooperation would be mostly South-South in the case of river basins located in Asia, Africa, and Latin America. Funding for such cooperation could come partly from the GEF. The North could also join as possible funding/facilitating agencies with the agreement of all riparian countries.

Technology transfer is more dependent on the developed countries of the North. Dealing with climate change will also need North-South cooperation; and international trade and protectionism are, of course, very much a matter of North-South cooperation.

PEOPLES' EARTH CHARTER

The Peoples' Earth Charter, which was prepared by the Earth Council and approved and adopted by the Johannesburg Conference, is a people's manifesto. This is one way to promote understanding and cooperation on sustainable development among the citizens of a country. It is indeed a very effective means of promoting intraregional cooperation. The four principles of the charter, viz., (i) respect and care for the community of life; (ii) ecological integrity; (iii) social and economic justice; and (iv) democracy, nonviolence, and peace are unquestionable means for promoting global sustainable development.

Box 13-6. Peoples' Earth Charter: Principles

A. Respect and Care for the Community of Life
   1. Respect Earth and life in all its diversity.
   2. Care for the community of life with understanding, compassion, and love.
   3. Build democratic societies that are just, participatory, sustainable, and peaceful.
   4. Secure Earth's bounty and beauty for present and future generations.
B. Ecological Integrity
   5. Protect and restore the integrity of Earth's ecological systems, with special concern for biological diversity and the natural processes that sustain life.
   6. Prevent harm as the best method of environmental protection and, when knowledge is limited, apply a precautionary approach.

7. Adopt patterns of production, consumption, and reproduction that safeguard Earth's regenerative capacities, human rights, and community well-being.

8. Advance the study of ecological sustainability and promote open exchange and wide application of the knowledge acquired.

C. Social and Economic Justice

9. Eradicate poverty as a social and environmental imperative.

10. Ensure that economic activities and institutions at all levels promote human development in an equitable and sustainable manner.

11. Affirm gender equality and equity as prerequisites to sustainable development, and ensure universal access to education, health care, and economic opportunity.

12. Uphold the right of all, without discrimination, to a natural and social environment supportive of human dignity, bodily health, and spiritual well-being.

D. Democracy, Nonviolence, and Peace

13. Strengthen democratic institutions at all levels, and provide transparency and accountability in governance, inclusive participation in decision-making, and access to justice.

14. Integrate into formal education and life-long learning the knowledge, values, and skills needed for a sustainable way of life.

15. Treat all living beings with respect and consideration.

16. Promote a culture of tolerance, nonviolence, and peace.

Source: http://www.earthcharter.org/files/charter/charter.pdf

If all people accept and follow these four principles vigorously, the world will become a livable place for a great while (Box 13-6).

CONCLUSION

Sustainable development involves many global actions—from development of concepts, capacity, operational activity, and monitoring to financing for implementation of action plans. A large number of international organizations and entities are involved in these activities and coordination among them is difficult, to say the least. For more than a decade, the UN and its member governments have discussed various alternative models to reform and revitalize the UN system to implement a global program on sustainable development with limited success. An increasingly important role of nonstate actors (and in particular, the role of the private sector, NGOs, and civil society) has added further complexity to the problem. It appears that the best model for promoting international cooperation on sustainable development is yet to be built. Meanwhile, international organizations continue to do their best; and in some instances strengthen their roles in areas where they claim to have leading expertise. The UN Secretary-General continues to play his coordinating role in promoting sustainable development at the global level. This role is somewhat weakened by the fact that several international organizations and entities draw their mandate from their governing bodies on which the UN Secretary-General has limited control.

The big question remaining is, will the efforts by international organizations, business companies, NGOs, social entrepreneurs, and others be sufficient to meet the challenges waiting in the twenty-first century?[1]

CRISIS

The arrival of the new millennium has led to an outpouring of retrospectives on the twentieth century and prognoses for the twenty-first. Some of these are over 30 years old and already out of date. Some discuss the near future until 2020, others the entire next century, and still others the next millennium or even the next million years. There are scientific journals entirely devoted to futuristics, and dozens of books on methodology and actual predictions. Faced with this immense literature and with the difficulties associated with the uncertainty inherent in predictions, some authors such as Robert Heilbroner in *Visions of the Future* (1995) have steadfastly refused to make any predictions at all; and those who do, make predictions only of the most general form.

The approach taken in this chapter is based upon Heilbroner's vision of finding a secure terrestrial base for life. This will have to be achieved through wise husbanding of natural resources and minimizing negative environmental impacts. First, we look for generic processes such as eating, breathing, drinking, being transported, being safe, and being sheltered. These will remain constant throughout the twenty-first century. We can use these processes to help us estimate the demands placed upon natural resources and subsequently on the environment. In this analysis we have restricted ourselves to accommodating the population until the year 2050 on the supposition that, after that point, the global population will have stabilized or be nearly stable at 9.5 billion. We ask a series of questions:

- Will we have sufficient natural resources for the survival of our burgeoning populations throughout this century?
- Will we have enough resources to enable the growing populations to live a wealthier and healthier lifestyle?
- Even if we have sufficient basic resources, will we be able to survive the environmental consequences of their use?

An assumption, based upon the history of development of human communities and their perceptions of risks and the costs of action, leads us to believe that developed and less developed societies and nation states behave in a similar manner when faced with environmental and resource sustainability issues. For instance, the wealthy countries tolerated massive air and water pollution for decades before the perception and reality concerning the health and the damage being done to the ecosystem became intolerable. The major risks associated with polluted drinking water were dealt with first, followed by cleanup of particulates in urban air. Then concerns for the ambient aquatic system were expressed, followed by massive wastewater cleanups. Shortly thereafter, the

---

[1] P. Rogers, "Natural Resources in the 21st Century: Crisis, Conflict, and Compromise." Presented at "Erdpolitik: Programm für das 21 Jahrhundert," Rathaus, Zürich, October 1998.

oxides of sulfur in the air became of serious concern, leading to the introduction of low-sulfur fuels and sulfur scrubbers on smokestacks. Recently, the issue of automobile emissions, pollutants, and other volatile compounds in the air has become the target of increasingly stringent controls. Finally, the transboundary issues of long-range sulfur transport, ozone depletion, and CO_2 buildup in the stratosphere have become a major concern in every country, rich and poor alike.

This is exactly what we observe in the major developing countries, too: first a concern for drinking water quality, then for particulates in urban air, followed by concerns for ambient water quality to protect aquatic species, the removal of sulfur and other toxics from air, the improvement of air quality fouled by urban mobile sources, and finally a concern for the greenhouse gas problems caused by oxides of carbon and other gases. What is most interesting is the rapid rate at which the developing world is progressing through this sequence in comparison with how long it took the industrialized countries. All too often we are impatient with the slow rate of change in the Third World, but we should bear in mind the long distances developing nations have traveled in a span of a few decades rather than the many centuries the original industrialized countries took.

This progression basically constrains what is achievable on planet Earth: (i) We have to keep track of all material flows; (ii) we have to avoid unpleasant irreversible effects; and (iii) we can expect that all human societies, given time and sufficient wealth, will attempt to choose environmentally sustainable paths. The first two of these are immutable and not easily subverted by social and economic tinkering—in the long run the second law of thermodynamics guarantees the human species a heat death, although the speed with which we approach that final extinction is certainly a social choice. The rate, however, at which communities progress towards a sustainable path is entirely dependent upon social, political, and economic forces.

ROLE OF NATURAL RESOURCES AND THE ENVIRONMENT

An important question that must be addressed before proceeding is, *Why are natural resources so important in our musings about the twenty-first century?* Minerals, forests, land, air, and water grip our attention whenever we think about the future. Are we going to run out of natural resources? Is it possible to run out? Which are the more vulnerable? Which can we do without? These are the types of questions at the back of our minds as we fearfully trace the future of humankind on this tiny, vulnerable planet.

At a purely molecular level it may be reassuring that we cannot run out of anything, because matter is never destroyed but just transformed. In human time scale we like to make distinctions between renewable and nonrenewable resources, but these are rather arbitrary distinctions. Will we ever run out of mercury for example? Almost all of the mercury molecules that were present when the earth cooled down are still here, maybe in a different form or location, but nevertheless still here. If need be, that is if the willingness to pay were high enough, we could diligently refine all of these aberrant molecules back to their original form. This appears to be true for all of the mineral elements, except for fossil fuels. Fossil fuels will not run out because of the role that market forces, technology, and substitution of sources play in expanding or modifying the supply of a particular resource. As with most nonrenewable resources, there exists a *backstopping resource*, which in the case of all energy supplies is the sun—almost an infinite source of energy, at least for the next five billion years.

Stavins claims (1992) that the real resource limitation in the next decades will be in the renewable resources and not the nonrenewable resources. This is not because of resource availability, but rather because of impacts upon the environment based upon resource use. Pollution of water sources around the globe, and the threat of global warming due to the buildup of CO_2 in the atmosphere, are examples of adverse impacts on the environment. Of course, water and air are renewable resources, and both can be decontaminated at some cost. The backup resource for water is desalination of seawater, which, like the sun for fossil fuels, is an almost infinite source of supply. The CO_2 buildup is more complex, because the cost of mitigation appears to be an order of magnitude greater than the cost to remediate water and land contamination. Hence, a policy of avoidance rather than remediation may be indicated in this case.

Perils of Forecasting

A certain feature of any discussion about the future is the need to forecast changes in the socioeconomic parameters that influence all other aspects of resource use and technological change. While it is true that most of the males and females who will influence the size of the population in 2020 are alive now, there is still some uncertainty with respect to the expected size of the future population because of minor demographic changes such as the age of marriage, contraceptive practices, and desired family sizes. The range of uncertainty in the population forecasts is dwarfed, however, by the ranges expected in the forecasting of economic parameters, which in turn are dwarfed by the ranges of expected demands placed upon natural resources. How is it possible that we can go from fairly narrow bounds on population forecasts to such wide bounds on the demands for resources and subsequent environmental impacts? The reason is that, as time progresses and resources become scarce, several contradictory phenomena come into play on the demand side and on the supply side of the resource, all of which tend to limit the scarcity of the resource or shift the demands toward other, less constrained resources.

First, as a resource becomes scarce, the competition for it grows, and it increases in value; and, if politically possible, the price for it rises, which in turn leads to a stabilized or decreased demand for it. Second, because the resource is now more valuable, it becomes more economically attractive to exploit more expensive sources of it (for example, low-quality mineral ores now become economical), thus increasing its potential supply. Third, since the resource is now more expensive, it behooves the users to find more efficient ways of managing with less of it; hence, investments in technological improvements are made. Finally, as the resource becomes more expensive it becomes attractive to find substitute resources that will provide the same, or similar, services for the consumers. Of course, the above steps do not all take place at the same time, and there is a very wide range in the rates at which these come into play for different resources.

There is a large body of literature, starting with Malthus and Ricardo, that explains, or attempts to explain, the relative importance of the factors contributing to economic value: Malthus gave us a land theory of value; Marx gave us a labor theory; the early twentieth-century economists gave us a capital theory; and Charles Cobb and Paul Douglas (1928) provided a production function framework that allowed for substitutability and complementarity among these factors. *Work* by Arnulf Grübler (1997) has tended to focus on the role of innovation itself in improving the efficiency of resource use and, hence, expanding the supply. The experience of predicting technological innovations has, unfortunately, only a few successful examples.

A remarkable report of the US National Research Council in 1937 on Technological Trends and National Policy was based upon the results of a distinguished committee of scientific and engineering thinkers, who were asked to report on areas of technology that were going to be important in the US over the next decades. Apart from the importance of plant breeding, the development of synthetic rubber and gasoline (which Germany was already producing), and the possibility of improving the efficiency of electrical machinery, they missed every other important development of the next two decades—antibiotics, which were already being produced by Fleming, nuclear explosions, radar, rockets, space exploration, jet-engined aircraft, transistors, solid state electronics, computers, lasers, and biotechnology. It should be stressed that the committee was composed of experts, many of whom were working in similar or closely allied fields in which the great innovations were made.

One has only to look at predictions made 20 to 40 years ago to see how poorly the experts have done in predicting the future. One classic case in this regard is the Club of Rome's *Limits to Growth* (Meadows, et al., 1972). Making a fetish of the feedback and feed-forward concepts of electrical engineering, it built a classic Malthusian model that predicted "overshoot and collapse" as the mechanism by which the world would come to a sticky end early in the twenty-first century unless a series of draconian direct actions were not immediately planned and undertaken by national governments and the UN. Of course, those actions, stated in the most alarmist prose by the Club of Rome in the Commentary section of the book, were not taken, but decentralized types of actions, often relying on market or quasimarket solutions, have seen us through the end of the twentieth century without the collapse so ardently predicted. According to the estimates of the Club of Rome's Meadows et al., gold, silver, mercury, zinc, lead, petroleum, and natural gas were to have been thoroughly exhausted by 1998. Interestingly enough, the one feature of our present predicament that might possibly lead to collapse—global warming—was barely mentioned in the book, and little attention was paid to its potential for catastrophe. So much for the precision of even short-range forecasting!

Undaunted by the apparent lack of accuracy in their original predictions, Meadows et al. published *Beyond the Limits* (1992) after an interval of 20 years. The surprising thing about the second book is that it claimed that the first book's predictions had been more or less precise, and then made some minor adjustments to the original models and repredicted an equally gloomy next 50 years.

If the *Limits to Growth* team was prone to overestimate resource use and underestimate the reserves, the professionals in the oil and gas industry were only a little better in the opposite direction. For example, Daniel Yergin and Martin Hillenbrand (1982) underpredicted 1995 oil use by 10% to 30%, natural gas use by 50% to 70%, and coal use by 30% to 70%. They also predicted a

1995 oil price of $45 per barrel contrasted with the actual 1995 price of around $10. Being off by more than 100% and as much as 70% in consumption levels over such a short time horizon as 13 years should make us very cautious about making long-range forecasts.

Note as well, though, that in 2005 the per barrel price of oil is near $60, equivalent to about 47 1995 US dollars. Thus the prediction, even though quite wrong in 1995, seems to be fairly close to the actual 2005 price. This wide fluctuation in the petroleum markets confirms the difficulty of making long-range forecasts for resource demand and supply.

Tyranny of the Middle Classes

Nathan Keyfitz in a July 1976 article in the *Scientific American* entitled "World Resources and the World Middle Class," was the first to pinpoint the role of the worldwide rise of the middle classes in causing resource and environmental crises. In country after country, as disposable incomes rose, the demand for consumer goods rose more rapidly (an income elasticity of more than unity). With an increase of income comes an insatiable demand for nonfood commodities. The first steps are modest: a radio and a refrigerator; the later steps are rapacious: an automobile and a US lifestyle!

Keyfitz estimated that the globe could not afford to support more than two billion people consuming at Western European and US levels. However, even Keyfitz missed the potential for rapid technical and social change that may accompany the rapid rise in incomes of countries such as the PRC, leading to a much-increased per capita consumption. This seems to contradict the Kuznets Curve (see Chapter 1) hypothesis, but it does not, since large countries such as the PRC and India are on the left-hand side of the inverted U-curve. Hence, rapid increases in per capita consumption and resultant environmental consequences are observed. It is only when the countries start to become much more wealthy (maybe as high as $6,000 per capita income) that the consumption curve turns downwards, provided that property rights are not ill-defined, resource use is not subsidized, and externalities are internalized.

CONFLICT

How can conflicts arise from the conjunction of environment and resource crises? Conflicts will arise because of the inequalities of current and future resource endowments. There will be potential conflicts within nations and among nations as the demands placed upon domestic resources and the international commons grow. In many cases it will be the resources themselves that will cause problems. For example, over 50% of the world's population live within international river basins with large potential conflicts between upstream and downstream populations; polluted air masses travel over national boundaries; and each country contributes vastly different amounts of CO_2 to the atmosphere. The globalization of communications and the mass media will make comparisons of relative deprivation move away from local and regional considerations to global comparisons.

Table 14-1 shows the 1998 consumption of various goods and services by average inhabitants in each of the world's seven major regions. Values are given for land and crop areas, water and energy use, foodgrain production and consumption, CO_2 emissions, and motor vehicle ownership. Important asymmetries to note in this table are in cropped area, which varied from a low of 0.14 ha per capita in Asia to a high of 1.75 ha in Oceania—a more than twelvefold difference; total per capita energy use, which ranged from a low of 4.83 barrels of oil equivalent in Africa to a high of 49.09 barrels of oil equivalent in North America, a tenfold difference; water withdrawn for human use, which ranged from a low of 202 cubic meters per capita per year in Africa to 1,798 cubic meters in North America; and food grain (for humans and livestock) consumption, which ranged from a low of 226 kg per capita per year in Africa to a high of 891 kg per capita in North America.

The marked differences in lifestyles are dramatically illustrated by the data on motor vehicle ownership of 0.02 per capita in Africa to 0.72 per capita in North America, a 36-fold difference. Finally, as an example of the pollution of the global commons, CO_2 production in Africa was 0.96 tons per capita per year compared with 19.42 tons per capita for North America, an almost 20-fold difference. Table 14-2 gives 1998 estimates of the world total consumption of resources by region, and Table 14-3 shows the same data reported as percentages by region. We see that Asia, with with more than 60% of the population, had only 35% of the cropped area and 34% of the world's total energy use, whereas, North America, with 5% of the population, had 16% of the cropped land and used 25% of the total energy.

Table 14-1. 1998 Per Capita Resource Use

REGION	Population (thousand)	Area (ha)				Water (cubic m)		Energy (BOE)	CO$_2$ (ton)	Foodgrains (kg)		Motor Vehicles	Urban (%)
		Land	Crop	Pasture	Forest	Avail.	Used			Prod.	Cons.		
Africa	778,484	3.81	0.24	1.14	0.92	5,133	202	4.83	0.96	170.0	226.1	0.02	35
Asia	3,588,877	0.86	0.14	0.29	0.16	3,680	542	5.66	2.30	280.0	305.2	0.03	35
C. America	130,710	2.03	0.31	0.75	0.57	8,084	916	11.41	3.65	260.0	366.6	0.11	66
Europe	729,406	3.10	0.44	0.24	1.30	8,547	625	21.49	8.56	540.0	513	0.27	74
N. America	304,078	6.04	0.77	0.88	2.46	17,458	1,798	49.06	19.42	1,330.0	891.1	0.72	76
S. America	331,889	5.28	0.34	1.49	2.82	28,702	335	8.97	2.25	290.0	307.4	0.09	77
Oceania	29,460	28.82	1.75	14.60	6.80	54,795	591	47.51	10.95	1,240.0	545.6	0.43	70
World	5,892,904	2.20	0.25	0.58	0.70	6,918	645	10.21	3.83	354.5	351.2	0.10	47

BOE= barrel of oil equivalent
Numbers may not add up due to rounding
Source: P. Rogers, "Natural Resources in the 21st Century: Crisis, Conflict, and Compromise." Presented at "Endpolitik: Programm für das 21 Jahrhundert," Rathaus, Zürich, October 1998

Table 14-2. 1998 Total Resources Used by Region

REGION	Population (thousand)	Area (thousand ha)				Water (cubic km)		Energy (MBDOE)	CO_2 prod. (1000 tons)	Foodgrains (1000 tons)	Vehicles (1000)	Urban Pop. (1000s)
		Land	Crop	Pasture	Forest	Avail.	Used					
Africa	778,484	2,963,468	189,803	889,350	713,405	3,996	157	10.30	745,595	176,015	15,570	272,469
Asia	3,588,877	3,085,414	520,175	1,051,311	556,996	13,207	1,945	55.65	8,270,648	1,095,325	107,666	1,256,107
C. America	130,710	264,835	40,053	98,503	74,524	1,057	120	4.09	477,045	47,918	14,378	86,269
Europe	729,406	2,260,320	317,837	178,549	947,761	6,234	456	42.95	6,247,094	374,185	196,940	539,760
N. America	304,078	1,838,009	233,276	267,072	749,290	5,309	547	40.87	5,904,312	270,964	218,936	231,099
S. America	331,889	1,752,925	113,116	495,341	934,860	9,526	111	8.15	747,331	102,023	29,870	255,555
Oceania	29,460	849,135	51,553	430,077	200,252	1,614	17	3.83	322,535	16,073	12,668	20,622
World	5,892,904	10,344,106	1,465,813	3,410,203	4,177,088	40,943	3,353	165.84	22,714,560	2,082,503	596,028	2,661,881

MBDOE = million barrels per day oil equivalent
Numbers may not add up due to rounding
Source: P. Rogers (1998)

Table 14-3. Percentage Distribution of 1998 Resource Consumption by Region

REGION	Land	Crop	Pasture	Forest	Water	Energy	CO_2 Prod.	Foodgrains	Vehicles	Pop.
Africa	23%	13%	26%	17%	4.1%	6.2%	3.3%	8.5%	2.6%	13.2%
Asia	24%	35%	31%	13%	50.9%	33.6%	36.4%	52.6%	18.1%	60.9%
Central America	2%	3%	3%	2%	3.1%	2.5%	2.1%	2.3%	2.4%	2.2%
Europe	17%	22%	5%	23%	11.9%	25.9%	27.5%	18.0%	33.0%	12.4%
North America	14%	16%	8%	18%	14.3%	24.6%	26.0%	13.0%	36.7%	5.2%
South America	13%	8%	15%	22%	2.9%	4.9%	3.3%	4.9%	5.0%	5.6%
Oceania	7%	4%	13%	5%	0.5%	2.3%	1.4%	0.8%	2.1%	0.5%

Source: P. Rogers (1998)

To get some perspective on the question of "Will there be enough natural resources to go around?" we have made a simulation model of the future. The model is quite simple in that the demands are assumed to be income elastic but not price elastic. This means that increasing the scarcity of supply does not manifest itself in reduced demand through price effects. This assumption limits the predictive ability of the model, but makes it possible to exploit what few data we have. Much more complex models similar to those of William Nordhaus (1992) could be constructed if the data were available.

Case 1

Resource use in 2050 is predicted assuming that the population grows according to the UN medium fertility projection, and that the per capita use of resources remains at 1998 levels (shown in Table 14-2). The total world resource use by region in 2050 under these assumptions is shown in Table 14-4. The demand for foodgrains will rise by 983 million tons per year, or 47% over the period at a rate of 0.7% per annum. This is well below the 1970-1995 global annual growth rate of about 2.0%. Energy demands will rise by 61 million barrels daily oil equivalent (MBDOE), or 37% over the period at a rate of 0.6% per annum. The actual composition of supply will no doubt be quite different from the 39% oil, 26% coal, 22% gas, 7% nuclear, and 2% hydro of the current supplies, and, depending upon the actual policies pursued, each supply sector could be radically changed. The overall supply, however, looks likely to be fairly easily achievable by 2050. Water withdrawals will increase by 45% to 4,866 cubic kilometers, which is well within the 12,500 cubic kilometers that Gleick (1993) claims to be easily available, or the 9,500 cubic kilometers that Postel et al. (1996) claim to be available after allowances are made for pollution effects and ecological demands. The only serious problem appears to be the amount of CO_2 emitted, which would increase by 32%. This runs directly counter to the Kyoto Protocol, which came into force in 2005 and requires specified small increases from the 1990 levels for the most developed countries while permitting unspecified increases for developing countries.

Table 14-4. World Resource Use in 2050 Assuming 1998 per Capita Values

REGION	Energy (1000 BOE)	CO_2 Prod. (1000 tons)	Motor Vehicles (1000)	Foodgrains (cons.-1000)	Water (cubic km)	Urban Pop. (1000)	Population (1000)
Africa	27.08	1,959,946	40,928	462,691	413	716,240	2,046,401
Asia	84.40	12,542,518	163,277	1,661,071	2,950	1,904,898	5,442,567
C. America	7.21	840,969	25,347	84,474	211	152,081	230,425
Europe	37.55	5,460,681	172,148	327,081	398	471,813	637,585
N. America	51.63	7,457,214	276,519	342,231	691	291,881	384,054
S. America	12.87	1,179,417	47,950	163,776	175	403,309	532,778
Oceania	5.95	500,159	19,644	24,925	27	31,979	45,684
World Total	226.87	29,940,904	745,813	3,066,249	4,866	3,972,201	9,319,494

BOE= barrel of oil equivalent
Numbers may not add up due to rounding
Source: P. Rogers (1998)

Case II

The Keyfitz hypothesis of increasing middle-class standards in the formerly poor countries assumes that the standard of living in 2050 in each of the regions, except North America, will improve up to the 1998 level of the next group on the developmental echelon, that is, to the level of Europe for South and Central America; to the level of Central America for Asia and Africa; and to the level of North America for Europe and Oceania. Table 14-5 reports the results of this simulation. We can see some very interesting changes. Energy demands rise rapidly by 154% to 422 MBDOE at a rate of 1.8% per annum. This is, however, well within historical rates for energy growth. Foodgrain demand almost doubles to 4 billion tons, indicating an annual rate of 1.3%. This rate, while achievable, will require very careful attention to agricultural yield growth and preservation of croplands. The water demand is now right at the limit proposed by Postel et al. (1996), and CO_2 production more than doubles to 54 billion tons—clearly this is not a desirable outcome.

Table 14-5. World Resource Use in 2050 with Growth of Wealth in Developing Countries

REGION	Population (1000)	Energy (MBDOE)	CO_2 Prod. (1000 tons)	Foodgrains (1000 tons)	Water (cubic km)	Motor Vehicles (1000)	Urban Pop. (1000)
Africa	2,046,401	63.99	7,468,636	750,211	1,875	225,104	1,350,625
Asia	5,442,567	170.19	19,863,433	1,995,245	4,985	598,682	3,592,094
C. America	230,425	13.57	1,973,505	118,208	144	62,215	170,515
Europe	637,585	85.70	12,380,050	568,152	1,146	459,061	484,565
N. America	384,054	51.63	7,457,214	342,231	691	276,519	291,881
S. America	532,778	30.84	4,485,966	268,698	327	141,420	387,596
Oceania	45,684	6.14	887,051	40,709	82	32,892	34,720
World Total	9,319,494	422.06	54,515,855	4,083,454	9,250	1,795,893	6,311,996

MBOE= million barrels of oil equivalent
Numbers may not add up due to rounding.
Africa and Asia rise to level of Central America, Central and South America reach European levels, and Europe and Oceania reach North American levels.
Source: P. Rogers (1998)

This simple simulation helps address the resource availability questions, and a comparison of the results of Case I and Case II shows the impact of increasing middle-class consumption demands placed upon the world as distinct from simple population demands. Case I answers affirmatively the question about the availability of natural resources for sustaining a population of more than nine billion at the current levels of consumption. In terms of basic food, land, water, and energy, Case I also shows that there will not be too serious limitations on supply. For Case II, however, much more effort would have to be expended to reach the increased "middle-class" level of resource use.

Where the real conflicts appear to lie, however, are on the effluent side of the equations. It is hard to imagine a future with 1.8 billion motor vehicles on the earth, with the billions of tons of air pollutants they would emit and the billions of hours lost due to urban congestion. Also, will a water withdrawal of 9,250 cubic kilometers be possible by 2050? This would bring us close to the 9,500 cubic kilometers Postel et al. (1996) thought to be useable, and maybe just too close if we allow for the incremental water pollution associated with such large amounts of water diversions and for ecological flow requirements in streams and rivers (IUCN, 2003, and Postel et al., 1996). Also, if we examine the tremendous increases in the urban populations expected under both scenarios—3.9 billion for Case I and 6.3 billion for Case II (which is again the Keyfitz hypothesis of increasing middle-class standards in formerly poor countries), up from 2.8 billion in 1998—it is hard to imagine how the already overstressed urban environmental infrastructure would be able to cope with an additional 3.5 billion people. Just the cost of water supply, sewerage, and sanitation would far exceed current rates of expenditure. Similarly, the state of the watercourses could be maintained only with massive investments in water quality management, which have not been forthcoming in the recent past.

Even though the simulations have been simplistic, they are not unrealistic if the present system is allowed to progress at current rates. Obviously, there is a need for some form of compromise if we are to be able to match future demands and current realities.

If we make comparisons based upon regions, the potential crisis and conflict points stand out much more clearly. For example, the African region stands out as the one in which the most rapid increases would occur in food consumption, energy use, and water use on the resource input side, and the largest rate of increase in CO_2 production and motorization on the output side. South America is the second most stressed region in all cases except for motorization—this is probably due to its already relatively high level in 1998. While the required rates of annual growth in foodgrain consumption appear reasonable for the globe as a whole, the actual magnitude of the incremental annual production required in some regions to meet the predicted year 2050 demands seems unreasonably high. The tensions would also be greater within the individual states. For instance, in 2050, the Asian region, dominated by the PRC and India, would have an annual demand of foodgrains of almost 1 billion tons more than the 1 billion tons currently produced in the region. This amount would have to be produced largely domestically by increasing yield and by expanding the cropped area where possible. Probably less than one half could be supplied by international trade. This appears to be achievable, as described by Waggoner (1997), but will not happen without tremendous effort and possible major environmental degradation due to expanded irrigation systems and intensified agricultural chemical use. Rapid expansion of irrigation systems has a great potential for international conflicts due to the transboundary nature of river systems, particularly in sensitive regions such as the Middle East and North Africa, as described by Rogers (1998).

COMPROMISE

We can thus see essentially two conflicting concerns. The first is, Will we have sufficient natural resources for our burgeoning populations in the next century? and the second, and perhaps the more serious of the two, is, Even if we have enough, will we be able to survive the environmental consequences of their use? The paradox of having enough resources and having too many bad consequences of their use is one that needs our most serious attention as the new century unfolds. Based upon research, we believe that careful husbanding and wise use of water, land, atmosphere, and energy resources will ensure sufficient resources to be available for use by 9 to 11 billion inhabitants expected by the end of the twenty-first century. The big challenges are *Homo sapiens'* ability to deal collectively with the environmental impacts of this massive use of natural resources. Everyone, in both the wealthy and the poor countries, will have to take some responsibility for this effort.

For the sake of human solidarity, most people and governments are committed to a more equitable distribution of the consumption of resources in the future. As Keyfitz (1976) pointed out, however, this will inevitably lead to the worldwide rise of an immense middle class, with all of the consumption patterns associated with individual ownership of houses, automobiles, and energy-intensive appliances. This is where the major compromises have to be made. We are left with a series of subsidiary questions:

- Will the currently wealthy countries, and groups within them, be willing to reduce their consumption of the planet's resources and also be willing to reduce the environmental effects associated with the current use of resources?
- What are the political, social, and economic mechanisms that could be used to facilitate these compromises?
- Will these compromises have to be enforced by multilateral (UN) actions, or can they arise out of negotiated agreements among the wealthy countries themselves, or between the wealthy and the poor countries?
- What is to be expected of the poor countries? To what extent will their economic growth be reduced by the need to compromise on the environment?

The recent historical evidence on these compromises, based upon unilateral action by the wealthy nations, is quite encouraging. Despite being in its infancy, environmental diplomacy has recorded some major successes. The most notable has been the implementation of the 1989 Montreal Protocol on protecting the ozone layer. The 1997 Kyoto Agreement on reduction of greenhouse gas emissions, which entered into force in 2005, is notable for the compromises offered by most of the wealthy countries, with proposals of large reductions in greenhouse gas emissions. It remains to be seen, however, how the implementation of these agreements, particularly by the largest emitter of substances that deplete the ozone layer and of greenhouse gases, the US, will actually turn out. (The US has refused to ratify the treaty.)

Of course, technology may come to our aid and help us avoid hard decisions. However, one cannot count on it. For example, recent work by von Weisacker et al. (1995) and the Rocky Mountain Institute points to the strong possibility of reducing energy and material use by as much as a factor of four with little or no additional cost to society. The US EPA, along with most of its sister agencies in Europe, has strongly endorsed pollution prevention as the best way to avoid large environmental impacts of resource use. Research and case studies show that many low-cost options are available to industry for product modification and recycling that will avoid sending effluents into the air, water, and land. Some of these conservation, recycling, process, and product change options, however, will demand fairly radical rethinking of how resource use in society should be priced and regulated. These sociopolitical actions will be among the toughest compromises that the wealthy countries will have to face. Not only will the wealthy countries be faced with making these compromises, but as Tables 14-4 and 14-5 show, the bulk of the new pressures on resources and the environment will come from the rapidly developing poor countries themselves.

Unfortunately, all of the pollution-prevention technologies, except those that encourage energy conservation, are likely to continue to add to the greenhouse gas loads on the atmosphere. Take the case of the motor vehicle. It may have appeared to some to be a great energy and environment saver compared with horse and steam transportation when it was first introduced, but it has rapidly become a major menace to energy consumption and the environment in the crowded metropolises of the world. Unfortunately, fully 50 years after the developed world discovered that this was a bad technology choice due to the resource use, pollution, and congestion associated with motor vehicles, most Third World countries are supporting policies of rapid motorization. Despite its drawbacks, no other technology has appeared that is as flexible or has captured the hearts of so many people in the world. Aggressive pricing and regulatory policies in Singapore have made big impacts, but Singapore is not a good model upon which to base predictions of the general efficacy of policies. The PRC, which is aggressively pursuing a policy of motorization, is a much more likely role model for most developing countries. Unfortunately, all of the benefits of current technical advances such as smaller and more efficient engines, lighter cars, and better fuels are overwhelmed by the sheer rate of growth of demand.

Where does all of the above lead us? We can safely say that globally we have enough resources on the input side to sustain high population and income growth, but we must be much more pessimistic about our abilities to cope with the environmental externalities due to increased resource use. Locally, particularly in Africa and the Middle East, there are severe water, and hence food production, shortages. These local water shortages will exacerbate conflicts along the international rivers in the region. Major global conflicts are liable to develop long-range atmospheric sulfate and nitrate transport (acid rain), and greenhouse gas production as well. There will be a great need for research, innovation, and technical support to help the poorer countries deal with the internal and external impacts of resource use. There will also be a demand for investments in urban infrastructure—water, sewers, treatment plants, highways—on an unprecedented scale as countries desperately attempt to keep up with the burgeoning urban populations. The financing of these investments remains a question intimately connected with world trade regimes. Innovation and financial resource availability are the two major challenges that the wealthy countries should be ready to address as we progress into the twenty-first century.

SUMMARY

This rather lengthy book is drawing to a close, and the reader may ask why it has taken so long, since it has not had space to engage the current major sustainability issues on the world's agenda. For example, we know that population growth and urbanization, deforestation, food and water shortages and global warming are likely to call the sustainability of the planet into question. We have chosen, instead, to focus more upon the methodologies, institutions, and the policy frameworks than directly upon the substantive issues. One reason for this choice is that detailed analyses of these issues would require a set of volumes; not just one book, but more importantly we believe that the most serious missions for both civil society and nation states is to establish the best institutional, policy and governance frameworks that will enable societies to move forward on the contentious issues of global resource sharing. These are absolute prerequisites for moving the planet to a sustainable state by the end of the next century.

Box 14-1. Critics' View of Sustainable Development

Some critics of sustainable development argue as follows:

1. Future generations are likely to be much better off than the present generation. The well-known economist Wilfred Beckerman has predicted that in the year 2100, global average real per capita income is likely to be 4.43 times the current figure.* This is primarily the contribution of modern technology, which is rapidly increasing now and is likely to remain so during the twenty-first century. Beckerman therefore claims that we should not ask the present generation, including the 1.3 billion absolute poor, to make sacrifices for future generations since no moral credit can be gained by distributing income from the poor to the rich. The statement made in the literature that sustainability is mainly an issue of intergenerational equity is an illusion, at best. Critics therefore conclude that the greatest favor that the present generation can make to the future is to establish peace and security on earth and the principles of human rights and democracy.

2. When any natural resources, be they fossil fuels, water, or any others, become scarce, economic forces come into play; such scarcity is always related to a certain price, existing technological expertise, and substitutes. As an example, Beckerman has pointed out that past predictions of energy supplies from coal have proven to be wrong; although demand for coal has been increasing at a rate higher than predicted, known reserves of coal are estimated to last 1,000 years. On such grounds Beckerman and others (e.g., Lomborg**) claim the world will not run out of natural resources.

3. The real State of the World is much better and healthier than many environmentalists claim. Lomborg claims that environmentalists oftentimes show dramatic trends in negative environmental changes and make their points to invest more in the environment. For example, in 1998 the Worldwatch Institute was criticized for using short-term data to conclude that, "the world's forest has significantly declined in both the area and quantity in recent decades." However, Lomborg, quoting long-term FAO data, claims that the global cover actually increased slightly from 1950 to 1994 from 30.04% to 30.89%. Lomborg also criticized Ehrlich (1968) for his prediction of adverse impacts of the population explosion on global food security and starvation. In 1968, Ehrlich stated, "the world will experience starvation of tragic proportion—hundreds of millions will starve to death;" but Lomborg has revealed that, although the world population has doubled since 1961, the average calorie intake per capita has increased by 24% globally and 38% in developing countries.

4. Sustainable development can be damaging for the poor. Some critics believe that, on the pretext of promoting sustainable development and environmental protection, many rich countries are adapting protectionist policies by restricting imports of agriculture, forestry, fisheries, and other products from poor developing countries. They also claim that, in the absence of concrete scientific evidence, environmentalists are recommending adopting precautionary principles, thus incurring a very high cost to control climate change, ozone depletion, and sea-level rise, which may or may not be significant threats to mankind. They believe that resources released by not adopting such precautionary principles could otherwise be utilized to satisfy the basic needs of the poor in developing countries.

* Wilfred Beckerman (2003): A Poverty of Reason
** Bjorn Lomborg (2003): The Skeptical Environmentalist

In Box 14-1 we have compiled a set of widely aired criticisms of the concept of sustainable development and its utility as a policy tool. In our book we have addressed these criticisms in various places with varying levels of detail. With regard to the first comment, which is full of wishful thinking, we reply that in order to achieve peace and security as a platform for increasing prosperity for future generations we have to address the immense numbers of poor and very poor people now alive on the globe. This is not something that is going to happen based upon simply letting the markets work! We have seen the huge asymmetries in health and well-being that exist and are getting wider by the day due to the industrial and agricultural trade policies of the rich countries. By relying upon multilateral and bilateral agencies the world is attempting a huge experiment in poverty reduction via the Millennium Development Goals. This has been possible only through collective action driven by the specter of massive poverty, failed states, and terrorism.

Concerning point 2 of the Box, nowhere do we claim that resources will run out, but rather that scarcity will certainly drive up the prices as it currently has for oil. These increased prices are more likely to affect the poor and make their lives more difficult. We follow Ricardo, not Malthus, on the issues of resource depletion. Point 3 is a caricature of the Malthusians on one side and the Cornucopians on the other. While agreeing with Lomborg that the world is probably better off than is often presented, we do have to face a series of issues that, if not addressed, will cause severe problems sometime in the relatively near future; for example, agriculture has done remarkably well in the past decades but now faces some important turning points in the potential of food plants to keep up with the increasing demands for inputs of water, improved seeds, fossil fuel-based fertilizers, and available land. Each of these are by themselves solvable problems, but they will require a holistic viewpoint by institutions if the resources are to be mobilized.

The fourth and final point in the Box relates to sustainable development worsening the conditions of the poor. This is one of our great concerns, and we can see many manifestations of this already happening. For example, one of the best ways of overcoming declining productivity in food production is to move to new scientifically modified plant materials. In a false understanding of sustainability, some in the rich countries are banning GM foods and actively discouraging new developments in the field. Another example, could be excessive overinvestment in attempting to limit climate-related problems, which could drain valuable development resources away from the poor countries. In this context, for example, we need to have a much broader discussion of the Precautionary Principle in international fora, where genuine voices of third world scientists and civil society could help establish the parameters. We need to proceed with caution, but not to the extent that the world will be a much harsher place for the poor.

IS LIFE ON EARTH SUSTAINABLE?

I t is only fitting that this book, which began with Malthus, should end with him. What is so seductive about Malthus, and Malthusianism, is that he and his theory will ultimately be right—but only in the long run. The real mystery is, how can the globe avoid the Malthusian catastrophes for *Homo sapiens* predicted every decade from the 1780s up to the present, a time span during which the population has grown from just a few millions to more than six billion. Malthus' major example deals with the discrepancy between the rate of population growth and the rate of food production. Geometric growth meets arithmetic growth, and after a short while the world faces a major famine! Limited food supply will decimate the population.

Apart from a few great famines in the nineteenth and twentieth centuries, this global scenario has not happened. Ester Boserup (1965) formulated an entirely opposite hypothesis: increasing populations induce the food supply to increase! Over the 200-year span since Malthus, it looks as though Boserup has won.

The pro- and anti-Malthus debate has been raging in the US for more than 30 years. The Club of Rome opened the first salvo with its 1972 publication, *Limits to Growth* (Meadows et al., 1972). Coming at the time of the first oil embargo, it attracted many followers (including the president of the World Bank). It was a jeremiad that predicted disastrous consequences by the year 2000 unless drastic government actions were immediately undertaken. Fortunately, none of these came to pass despite the lack of any drastic, or even milder, government action. It did, however, legitimize a strain of US thinking that stressed that the globe and its inhabitants were running out of resources and dying of the consequences of pollution. In the 1980s, the scientists who had been concerned with the possibility of global cooling (Schneider, 1971) suddenly discovered the possibility of global warming based upon increasing CO_2 measurements in Hawaii (initiated by Roger Revelle and carried out by Keeling; see Scripps Institution of Oceanography, 1991).

The Malthus debate was enlivened in the late 1980s by Julian Simons' *The Ultimate Resource* (1981), which argued that human and intellectual resources, not physical resources, were limiting human development on this planet. Ehrlich (1968), Schneider (1971), and Holdren (1972) contested Simons' hypothesis, and a series of financial wagers were placed on the predictions of both sides about whether resources were declining or not. Even the outcomes of the wagers are still being disputed by the Malthusians, who apparently are on the losing side. However, one does get the feeling from Beckerman and Simon that everything is better than it was, and, if left to its own devices (usually a largely unrestricted capitalist market), will continue to improve. Our sense is that a careful integration of market approaches with diligent regulation of third party effects will indeed ultimately lead to improvements in the economy, the environment, and social equity. However, this will not come about by benign neglect; it will require utmost vigilance by all parties.

Throughout this book we have recounted the grim statistics of the human assaults on the environment and our resource base. They raise the question of what we, as a group, really believe is going to happen over the next 50 years. We could begin with the question, "Is life on earth sustainable?" The human population will rise from six billion to nine billion over the first half of the twenty-first century. In Chapter 14 we looked at a variety of areas of resource use and concluded that we can indeed survive until 2050 if we have a gentle and benign transition.

Even though we do not envisage the transition as being particularly hazardous, we have all the resources and technology available to us now to reach a sustainable 2050, provided that we exploit these in a sensible fashion. What in our perception are the events most likely to divert us from the sensible path of sustainability? We can think of at least four major events or outcomes that have such a potential. It should be clearly understood that we do not envisage these events happening, but they present potentialities, no matter how remote, that could lead us down a nonsustainable path. We have ranked them in the order of what we consider basic human needs: security, food, and a sustainable ecosystem.

- **Terrorism.** The worst-case scenario for terrorism is that terrorists may obtain nuclear weapons or other weapons of mass destruction. Nation-states are unlikely to use such weapons, but terrorist groups have no scruples. Apart from this dimension, terrorism will remain a nagging global problem, though unlikely to lead away from the general path of maintaining sustainability.

- **Climate change.** Climate change is a more complex issue because of the large uncertainties associated with potentially devastating outcomes. Its major outcomes, if they occur, will happen well outside our arbitrary 50-year time horizon for sustainability; hence, it is of less concern to us than events that are temporally more closely expected. There is always the possibility, however, that even within the 50-year time frame some climate events will initiate irreversible catastrophic processes that could have been dealt with only within the early periods.

- **The global food system.** Many would argue for "food first." We have ranked the global food system after two security issues, not because food is not a paramount human need, but because we see better prognoses for food than for the security issues. Loss of soil fertility is a major concern in countries such as the PRC that have been using large applications of chemical fertilizers for their agricultural production. There are at least five problems: First, after a certain level of application, decreasing returns set in, and additional yields cannot come from larger applications of fertilizer. Second, as chemical application of major nutrients increases, the micronutrients in the soil become increasingly depleted, leading to a diminution of yields. Third, as the world demand increases, the available supplies of inexpensive phosphate may be exhausted. Fourth, related to the third, is that soil erosion will remove precious topsoil and the nutrients adhering to it (notably phosphates); ultimately the soil and its appended nutrients will end up trapped in widely disbursed sediments under the ocean that are not easily recovered. And finally, due to excess demand, climate change, or pollution, the water needed for agriculture will not be available for producing the needed food.

- **Globalization.** Globalization is one event that has already happened, with many manifestations of unsustainable behavior. As envisaged, it is causing major impacts upon the environment. The cases mentioned earlier make it difficult for countries to use environmental sustainability as a criterion for restricting imports (e.g., the US-Mexico dispute on dolphin by-catch with tuna). Apparently, many polluting industries are moving offshore from those regions with strict environmental regulations to those with lesser standards. It does not have to be the factories and industries moving; it can merely be a shift from domestic production to importing from the less-regulated countries. We see this with leather tanning (from India to Bangladesh) and nonspecialty steel production (the US to the PRC). The potential for widespread environmental and ecosystem disruption is always present. There is, however, a more serious potential that deals with the global widening of incomes that may happen despite the fact that globalization via WTO and other trade organizations is designed to supposedly close the gap.

What Is the Canary in the Mine?

Canaries have a lower tolerance for carbon monoxide than humans, so when a canary dies in a coal mine, it is time to get out of there. Are there similar indicators for sustainability? Assuming that we are already on our journey to a survivable 2050, what particular items would indicate that we were losing our struggle to achieve a sustainable 2050? Some argue for climate change indicators. Is the sea level rising too fast? Are the glaciers and ice caps experiencing unusually high rates of retreat? Are African deserts expanding in area? Positive answers to these questions could immediately trigger remedial measures enforced by some world bodies. Others would argue that a rash of famine conditions around the world induced by climate or overpopulation would be the trigger.

In our opinion the most serious indicator of losing our way on the path to a sustainable 2050 would be an increase in absolute levels of poverty in the world, increasing gaps between the rich countries and the poor countries, and increasing gaps between specific countries. Recall that our definition for sustainable development requires social sustainability as well as economic and environmental sustainability. Increased polarization between the rich and the poor will lead to increased terrorist violence, failed states, further deterioration of the environment, and mass migrations for economic survival and environmental reasons.

Questions Concerning Sustainable Development in 2050

While we are taking steps towards the goal of sustainable development, we can ask the same question that came up at the WSSD. Where will we be in terms of sustainable development by 2050? Will it be a world without social justice and with environmental degradation, large inequities, and chaos? Or will it be a beautiful world with the entire social, economic, and environmental goals being pursued in an agreed upon manner?

Perhaps we will have a transformed world with fundamental changes in social values, cultural norms, and environmental considerations. Perhaps there will be a new coalition for power sharing, working from the grass roots up, and market forces will remain effective tools for economic growth. Perhaps economic, environmental, and social choices will be determined by people so as to promote and maintain solidarity, peace, and justice in the world. Those who favor this option think that such a transformed world is not only possible but is the only choice for all people, if we want to continue to thrive and not become extinct.

REFERENCES

Adams, William M. *Green Development: Environment and Sustainability in the Third World* (2nd ed.). New York: Routledge, an imprint of the Taylor & Francis Group, 2001.

Agenda 21, Rio Conference, 1992.

Amendment of Hazardous Wastes and Their Disposal, 1995.

ASEAN Agreement on the Conservation of Nature and Natural Resources, 1985.

Ayres, Robert U. *Technological Forecasting and Long Range Planning*. New York: McGraw Hill, 1969.

Barbier, Edward. "The Concept of Sustainable Development." *Environmental Conservation*, 14(2), 1987.

Bartlett's Familiar Quotations (15th ed.). Emily Morison Beck, ed. Boston/Toronto: Little Brown and Company, 1980.

Basel Convention on the Control of Transboundary Movements of Hazardous Wastes and Their Disposal, 1989.

Basel Protocol on Liability and Compensation for Damage Resulting from Transboundary Movements of Hazardous Wastes and Their Disposal, 1999.

Basso, Christopher J. *Environment, Inc.: From Grassroots to Beltway*. Lawrence, KS: University Press of Kansas, 2005.

Beckerman, Wilfred. *A Poverty of Reason: Sustainable Development and Economic Growth*. Oakland, CA: The Independent Institute, 2003.

_____. *Small Is Stupid: Blowing the Whistle on the Greens*. London: Duckworth, 1995.

Behring Sea Fur Seals Fisheries Arbitration, 1893.

Birdsall, Nancy and Juan Luis Londono. "Asset Inequality Matters: An Assessment of the World Bank's Approach to Poverty Reduction." *The American Economic Review*, 87(2), 1997.

Black's Law Dictionary (7th ed.). Bryan A. Garner, ed. Eagan, MN: West Group, 1999.

Bornstein, David. *How to Change the World: Social Entrepreneurs and the Power of New Ideas*. Oxford: Oxford University Press, 2004.

Boserup, Ester. *The Conditions of Agricultural Growth: The Economics of Agrarian Change Under Population Pressure*. London: Allen and Unwin, 1965.

_____. *Population and Technological Change: A Study of Long-Term Trends*. Chicago: University of Chicago Press, 1981.

Broecker, Wallace S. *How to Build a Habitable Planet*. Palisades, NY: Eldigio Press, 1985.

Brown, Lester R. "China Replacing the United States as World's Leading Consumer." *Eco-Economy Updates*, Earth Policy Institute, 16 February 2005.

Brown, Lester, Sandra Postel, and Christopher Flavin. "From Growth to Sustainable Development." In *Population, Technology, and Lifestyle: The Transition to Sustainability*. Robert Goodland, Herman E. Daly, and Salah El Serafy, eds. Washington, D.C.: Island Press, 1992.

Bryant, Dirk, Daniel Nielsen, and Laura Tangley. *The Last Frontier Forests: Ecosystems and Economies on the Edge*. Washington, D.C.: World Resources Institute, 1997.

Bulatao, Rodolfo A. "Mortality by Cause: 1970 to 2015." In *The Epidemiological Transition: Policy and Planning Implications for Developing Countries* (Policy research working papers). James N. Gribble and Samuel H. Preston, eds. Washington, D.C.: Committee on Population, National Research Council, National Academy of Science, 1993.

The Cambridge Biographical Encyclopedia (2nd ed.). David Crystal, ed. Cambridge: Cambridge University Press, 2000.

Canter, Larry. *Environmental Impact Assessment* (2nd ed.). New York: McGraw Hill, 1996.

Capacity Building for Environmental Law in the Asian and Pacific Region: Approaches and Resources, Vol. 1 (2nd ed.). Donna G. Craig, Nicholas A. Robinson, and Kheng-Lian Koh, eds. Manila: Asian Development Bank, 2003.

Carson, Rachel L. *Silent Spring*. New York: Houghton Mifflin, 1962.

Cartagena Protocol on Biosafety to the Convention on Biological Diversity, 2000.

"Charter of Economic Rights and Duties of State." United Nations General Assembly Resolution 3281, 1974.

Chinkin, Christine M. "The Challenge of Soft Law: Development and Change in International Law." *International and Comparative Law Quarterly*, 38(4), 1989.

Clean Air Act, United Nations Statutes, 1970.

Coase, Ronald H. "The Problem of Social Cost." *Journal of Law and Economics*, 3(1), October 1960.

Cobb, Charles W. and Paul H. Douglas. "A Theory of Production." *The American Economic Review*, 18(1), 1928.

Cobb, Clifford, Ted Halstead, and Jonathan Rowe. "If the GDP Is Up, Why Is America Down?" *The Atlantic Monthly*, October 1995.

"Coffee Connection." *Boston Sunday Globe*, July 29, 2001.

Confucius. "Analects." In *Bartlett's Familiar Quotations* (15th ed.). Emily Morison Beck, ed. Boston/Toronto: Little Brown and Company, 1980.

Convention Entered into by Mexico and the United States to Deal with the Delivery of Water for the Irrigation of Land in the Juarez Valley, May 21, 1906.

Convention for the Protection of the World Cultural and Natural Heritage, 1972.

Convention on Biological Diversity, 1992.

Convention on the Conservation of Migratory Species of Wild Animals, 1979.

Convention on International Trade in Endangered Species of Wild Fauna and Flora, 1975.

Convention on the Law of the Sea, 1982.

Convention on Wetlands of International Importance Especially as Waterfowl Habitat, 1971.

Convention to Combat Desertification in those Countries Experiencing Serious Drought and/or Desertification, Particularly in Africa, 1997.

Costanza, Robert. "The Ecological Economics of Sustainability: Investing in Natural Capital." In *Population, Technology, and Lifestyle: The Transition to Sustainability*. Robert Goodland, Herman E. Daly, and Salah El Serafy, eds. Washington, D.C.: Island Press, 1992.

Costanza, Robert, John H. Cumberland, Herman E. Daly, Robert Goodland and Richard B. Norgaard. *An Introduction to Ecological Economics*. Boca Raton, FL: St. Lucie Press, 1997.

Costanza, Robert, *et al*. "Estimates of the Genuine Progress Indicator (GPI) for Vermont, Chittenden County and Burlington, from 1950 to 2000." *Ecological Economics*, 51(1-2), 2004.

Costanza, Robert, Ralph d'Arge, Rudolf de Groot, Stephen Farber, Monica Grasso, Bruce Hannon, Karin Limburg, Shahid Naeem, Robert V. O'Neill, Jose Paruelo, Robert G. Raskin, Paul Sutton and Marjan van den Belt. "The Value of the World's Ecosystem Services and Natural Capital." *Nature*, 387, 15 May 1997.

"The Cost of Corruption." *Background Paper No. 3*. Tenth UN Congress on the Prevention of Crime and the Treatment of Offenders, 2000.

Dalton, Robert E. "National Treaty Law and Practice: United States." Chapter 6 in *National Treaty Law and Practice (Austria, Chile, Colombia, Japan, Netherlands, United States)*. Monroe Leigh, Merritt R. Blakeslee, and L. Benjamin Ederington, eds. Washington, D.C.: American Society of International Law, 1999.

Daly, Herman E. *Beyond Growth: The Economics of Sustainable Development*. Boston: Beacon Press, 1996.

_____. "The Economic Growth Debate: What Some Economists Have Learned But Many Have Not." *Journal of Environmental Economics and Management*, 14(4), 1987.

_____. "Summary of Introduction to the Steady-State Economy." In *A Survey of Ecological Economics*. Rajaram Krishanan, Jonathan Harris, and Neva Goodwin, eds. Washington, D.C.: Island Press, 1995.

Daly, Herman E. and John B. Cobb, Jr. *For the Common Good: Redirecting the Economy Toward Community, the Environment, and Sustainable Future*. Boston: Beacon Press, 1994.

Declaration of Principles of International Law Relating to Sustainable Development. The 70th Conference of the International Law Association held in New Delhi, April 2002.

Declaration on the Establishment of a New International Economic Order. United Nations General Assembly Resolution 3201, 1974.

Dernbach, John C. *Stumbling Toward Sustainability*. Washington, D.C.: Environmental Law Institute, 2002.

Desai, Bharat H. *Institutionalizing International Environmental Law*. Ardsley, NY: Transnational Publishers, 2004.

Diamond, Jared. *Collapse: How Societies Choose to Fail or Succeed*. New York: Viking/Penguin Group, 2005.

_____. *Guns, Germs, and Steel: The Fates of Human Societies*. New York: W. W. Norton, 1997.

Digest of United States Practice in International Law. John A. Boyd, ed. Washington, D.C.: Superindent of Documents, Department of State, 1978.

Dixon, John A. and Paul B. Sherman. *Economics of Protected Areas: A New Look at Benefits and Costs*. Washington, D.C.: Island Press, 1990.

Dodds, Felix, ed. *Earth Summit 2002: A New Deal*. London: Earthscan Publications, 2000.

Dower, Nigel. *World Ethics: The New Agenda*. Edinburgh: Edinburgh University Press, 1998.

Dowling, J. Malcolm and Ma. Rebecca Valenzuela. *Economic Development in Asia*. Singapore: Thomson Learning, 2004.

Dufournaud, Christian M. and Peter Rogers. "A Computable Index of Sustainability." *The Working Papers of the Study of Environmental Indicators and Indices*. Division of Applied Sciences, Harvard University, 1994.

Economics of the Environment: Selected Readings. Robert Dorfman and Nancy S. Dorfman, eds. New York: W. W. Norton, 1972.

Ehrlich, Paul R. *The Population Bomb*. New York: Ballentine Books, 1968.

Emerging Asia: Changes and Challenges. Manila: Asian Development Bank in cooperation with the Harvard Institute for International Development, 1997.

Emerson, Ralph Waldo. *Nature* (1836). A facsimile of the first edition with an introduction by Jaroslav Pelikan. Boston: Beacon Press, 1985.

Endangered Species Act. United States Statutes, 1973.

Engendering Development: Through Gender Equality in Rights, Resources and Voice. Washington, D.C.: World Bank, 2001.

Environment and Economics in Project Preparation: Ten Asian Cases. Piya Abeygunawardena, Bindu N. Lohani, Daniel W. Bromley, and Ricardo Carlos V. Barba, eds. Manila: Asian Development Bank, 1999.

The Environment Program: Past, Present and Future. Manila: Asian Development Bank, 1994.

Environmental Data Report 1989/1990. United Nations Environmental Programme. Oxford: Blackwell, 1989.

Environmental Protection Act, Nepal, 1997.

Esty, Daniel C. and Maria H. Ivanova, eds. *Global Environmental Governance: Options and Opportunities*. New Haven, CT: Yale School of Forestry and Environmental Studies, 2002.

Esty, Daniel C., Marc Levy, Tanja Srebotnjak, and Alexander de Sherbinin. *2005 Environmental Sustainability Index: Benchmarking National Environmental Stewardship*. New Haven, CT: Yale Center for Environmental Law and Policy, 2005.

European Convention on Civil Liability for Damage Resulting from Activities Dangerous to the Environment, 1993.

Expanding the Measures of Wealth: Indicators of Environmentally Sustainable Development. Washington, D.C.: World Bank, 1997.

FAO. *The State of Food and Agriculture 2003–2004: Agricultural Biotechnology Meeting the Needs of the Poor?* Rome: Food and Agricultural Organization, 2004.

Finding Capital for Sustainable Livelihoods Businesses: A Finance Guide for Business Managers. World Business Council for Sustainable Development, 2004.

Findley, Roger W. and Daniel A. Farber. *Environmental Law in a Nutshell* (5th ed.). St. Paul, MN: West Group, 2000.

Framework Convention on Climate Change. United Nations, 1992.

Fried, John H. E. "International Law—Neither Orphan nor Harlot, Neither Jailer nor Never-Never Land." In *International Law: Classic and Contemporary Readings*. Charlotte Ku and Paul F. Diehl, eds. Boulder, CO: Lynne Rienner Publishers, 1998.

Funk & Wagnalls. *Standard Dictionary of the English Language* (International Edition). New York: Funk & Wagnalls Publishing, 1973.

Funk, Karina and Ari Rabl. "Electric Versus Conventional Vehicles: Social Costs and Benefits in France." *Transportation Research Part D: Transport and Environment*, 4(6), 1999.

Geiser, Kenneth. *Materials Matter: Towards a Sustainable Materials Policy*. Cambridge, MA: MIT Press, 2001.

Gelber, Alexander and Peter Rogers. "The Environmental Snowflake and Social Choice." Division of Engineering and Applied Sciences, Working Paper, Harvard University, 2002.

"Global Environment Outlook 3 (GEO-3)." United Nations Environment Programme, 2002.

Goldsmith, Edward and Nicholas Hildyard. *The Social and Environmental Effects of Large Dams*. San Francisco: Sierra Club Books, 1984.

Governance in a Globalizing World. Joseph S. Nye and John D. Donahue, eds. Washington, D.C.: Brookings Institution Press, 2000.

Guidelines for the Economic Analysis of Projects. Manila: Asian Development Bank, 1997.

Guidelines for Social Analysis of Development Projects. Manila: Asian Development Bank, 1991.

Hamilton, Kirk and Ernst Lutz. *Green National Accounts: Policy Uses and Empirical Experience*. Washington D.C.: World Bank, 1996.

Handl, Günther. *Multilateral Development Banking: Environmental Principles and Concepts Reflecting General International Law and Public Policy*. The Hague, London and Boston: Kluwer Law and Asian Development Bank, 2001.

Hardin, Garrett. "The Tragedy of the Commons." *Ekistics*, 27, March 1969.

——————————. "The Tragedy of the Commons." In *Environmental Economics: A Reader*. Anil Markandya and Julie Richardson, eds. New York: St. Martin's Press, 1992.

——————————. "The Tragedy of the Commons." *Science*, 162(3859), 13 December 1968.

Harvard Business Review on Business and the Environment. Boston: Harvard Business School Publishing, 2000.

Hassan, Parvez. "Toward an International Covenant on the Environment and Development." *American Society of International Law Proceedings*, 87, 1993.

Hawken, Paul, Amory B. Lovins, and L. Hunter Lovins. *Natural Capitalism: Creating the Next Industrial Revolution*. Boston: Little Brown and Company, 1999.

Heilbroner, Robert. *Visions of the Future: The Distant Past, Yesterday, Today, and Tomorrow*. New York: Oxford University Press, 1995.

Hocking, Martin B. "Paper Versus Polystyrene: A Complex Choice." *Science*, 251(4993), 1 February 1991.

"How Many Planets? A Survey of the Global Environment." *The Economist*, July 6, 2002.

Human Development Report 2005. United Nations Development Programme. New York and Oxford: Oxford University Press, 2005.

Hunger in America 2001. The Greater Boston Food Bank, 2001.

ILO Convention (No. 169) Concerning Indigenous and Tribal Peoples in Independent Countries. *International Legal Materials,* 28, 1989.

Implementation Plan of the World Summit on Sustainable Development at Johannesburg. New York: United Nations, 2002.

Inhaber, Herbert. *Environmental Indices (Environmental Science & Technology Series).* New York: John Wiley & Sons, 1976.

Integrated Environmental and Economic Accounting: Interim Version. Studies in Methods, Handbook of National Accounting. Series F, No. 61. New York: United Nations, 1993.

International Covenant on Civil and Political Rights, 1966.

International Covenant on Economic, Social and Cultural Rights, 1966.

International Environmental Law (2nd ed.). Alexandre C. Kiss and Dinah Shelton, eds. Ardsley, NY: Transnational Publishers, 2000.

International Environmental Law and Policy (2nd ed.). David Hunter, James Salzman, and Durwood Zaelke, eds. New York: Foundation Press, 2002.

International Law and Sustainable Development: Past Achievements and Future Challenges. Alan Boyle and David Freestone, eds. New York: Oxford University Press, 1999.

International Law: Cases and Materials (4th ed.). Lori F. Damrosch, Louis Henkin, Richard C. Pugh, Oscar Schachter, and Hans Smit, eds. St. Paul, MN: West Group, 2001.

International Law: Classic and Contemporary Readings. Charlotte Ku and Paul F. Diehl, eds. Boulder, CO: Lynne Rienner Publishers, 1998.

Johannesburg Principles on the Role of Law and Sustainable Development. Adopted at the Global Judges Symposium held in Johannesburg, South Africa, 18–20 August 2002.

Judicial Independence Overview and Country-Level Summaries. The Asia Foundation, Asian Development Bank, Judicial Independence Project, Regional Technical Assistance No. 5987, October 2003.

Keohane, Robert O. and Joseph S. Nye, Jr. "Introduction." In *Governance in a Globalizing World.* Joseph S. Nye, Jr. and John D. Donahue, eds. Washington, D.C.: Brookings Institution Press, 2000.

Keyfitz, Nathan. "World Resources and the World Middle Class." *Scientific American,* 235(1), July 1976.

Khan, Herman. *The Next Two Hundred Years: A Scenario for America and the World.* New York: Morrow, 1976.

Kiss, Alexandre C. "Academy Lectures on Environmental Law." IUCN Academy of Environmental Law, 2003.

Kiss, Alexandre C. and Dinah Shelton. *International Environmental Law* (2nd ed.). Ardsley, NY: Transnational Publishers, 2000.

Kuznets, Simon. "Economic Growth and Income Inequality." *The American Economic Review*, 45(1), 1955.

Kyoto Protocol to the United Nations Framework Convention on Climate Change, 1998.

Lâm, Maivân Clech. *At the Edge of the State: Indigenous Peoples and Self Determination*. Ardsley, NY: Transnational Publishers, 2000.

Laszlo, Chris. *The Sustainable Company: How to Create Lasting Value Through Social and Environmental Performance*. Washington, D.C.: Island Press, 2003.

Legality of the Use by a State of Nuclear Weapons in Armed Conflict (1993–1996). International Court of Justice, Advisory Opinion of 8 July 1996.

Leontief, Wassily. "Environmental Repercussions and the Economic Structure: An Input-Output Approach." *The Review of Economics and Statistics*, 52(3), 1970.

_____. *Input-Output Economics* (2nd ed.). New York: Oxford University Press, 1986.

Leopold, Luna B., Frank E. Clarke, Bruce B. Hanshaw, and James R. Balsley. "A Procedure for Evaluating Environmental Impact." *U.S. Geological Survey Circular 645*. Washington, D.C.: U.S. Government Printing Office, 1971.

The Little Green Data Book 2000. Washington, D.C.: World Bank, 2000.

Lohani, Bindu N., J. Warren Evans, Robert R. Everitt, Harvey Ludwig, Richard A. Carpenter, and Shih-Liang Tu. *Environmental Impact Assessment for Developing Countries in Asia*, 2 Volumes. Manila: Asian Development Bank, 1997.

Lomborg, Bjørn. *The Skeptical Environmentalist: Measuring the Real State of the World*. New York: Cambridge University Press, 2001.

Lowe, Vaughan. "Sustainable Development and Unsustainable Arguments." In *International Law and Sustainable Development: Past Achievements and Future Challenges*. Alan Boyle and David Freestone, eds. New York: Oxford University Press, 1999.

Lutz, Ernst, ed. "Toward Improved Accounting for the Environment." An UNSTAT World Bank Symposium. Washington, D.C.: World Bank, 1993.

Malone, Linda A. *Emanuel Law Outlines: Environmental Law*. New York: Aspen Publishers, 2003.

Malthus, Thomas R. *An Essay on the Principle of Population*. London: J. Johnson, 1798.

_____. *An Essay on the Principle of Population (Great Minds Series)*. Amherst, NY: Prometheus Books, 1998.

_____. *An Essay on the Principle of Population; or, a View of its Past and Present Effects on Human Happiness; with an Inquiry into our Prospects Respecting the Future Removal or Mitigation of the Evils which it Occasions*. London: J. Johnson, 1803.

Malvicini, Cindy F. and Anne T. Sweetser. "Modes of Participation—Experiences from RETA 5894: Capacity Building and Participation Activities II." *Poverty and Social Development Paper No. 6*, Sections II and III. Manila: Asian Development Bank, 2003.

McBean, Edward A. and Frank A. Rovers. *Statistical Procedures for Analysis of Environmental Monitoring Data and Risk Assessment*. Englewood Cliffs, NJ: Prentice Hall, 1998.

Meadows, Donella H., Dennis L. Meadows, Jørgen Randers and William W. Behrens III. *Limits to Growth: A Report for the Club of Rome's Project on the Predicament of Mankind*. New York: Universe Books, 1972.

Meadows, Donella H., Dennis L. Meadows and Jørgen Randers. *Beyond the Limits: Confronting Global Collapse, Envisioning a Sustainable Future*. Post Mills, VT: Chelsea Green Publishing, 1992.

Meadows, Donella H., Jørgen Randers and Dennis L. Meadows. *Limits to Growth: The 30-Year Update*. Post Mills, VT: Chelsea Green Publishing, 2004.

"Millennium Development Goals: From Consensus to Momentum." *Global Monitoring Report 2005*. Washington, D.C.: World Bank, 2005.

"Minors Oposa v. Factoran." *International Legal Materials*, 33, 1994.

Monitoring Environmental Progress. Washington, D.C.: World Bank, 1995.

Morais, Herbert V. and Motoo Noguchi. *ADB Manual on Countering Money Laundering and the Financing of Terrorism*. Manila: Asian Development Bank, 2003.

Munasinghe, Mohan. "Environmental Economics and Sustainable Development." *World Bank Environment Paper No. 3*. Washington, D.C.: World Bank, 1993.

Munasinghe, Mohan and Ernst Lutz. "Environmental-Economic Evaluation of Projects and Policies for Sustainable Development." *World Bank Environment Working Paper 42*. Washington, D.C.: World Bank, 1991.

Nattrass, Brian and Mary Altomare. *The Natural Step for Business: Wealth, Ecology and the Evolutionary Corporation*. Gabriola Island, B.C.: New Society Publishers, 1999.

_____. *Dancing with the Tiger: Learning Sustainability Step by Natural Step*. Gabriola Island, B.C.: New Society Publishers, 2002.

"Natural Resource Accounts: Taking Stock in OECD Countries." *OECD Environment Monographs No. 84*. Paris: OECD, 1994.

Newell, Richard G. and William A. Pizer. "Discounting the Benefits of Climate Change Policies Using Uncertain Rates." *Resources*, 146, Winter 2002.

"New Facts on Globalization, Poverty and Income Distribution." *Issues Paper, Corporate Economists Advisory Group*. Paris: International Chamber of Commerce, 2003.

The New Yorker Collection, 2001.

Nordhaus, William D. "Lethal Model 2: The Limits to Growth Revisited." *Brookings Papers on Economic Activity*, 2, 1992.

OECD. *Towards Sustainable Development: Environmental Indicators*. Paris: Organization for Economic Co-operation and Development, 1998.

OECD. *The 2004 OECD List of High Production Volume Chemicals*. Paris: Organization for Economic Co-operation and Development, 2004.

Oposa, Antonio A., Jr. *A Legal Arsenal for the Philippine Environment*. Bantayan Island, Philippines: Batas Kalikasan Foundation, 2002.

_____. *The Laws of Nature and Other Stories*. Bantayan Island, Philippines: Batas Kalikasan Foundation, 2003.

Ott, Wayne. *Environmental Indices, Theory and Practice*. Ann Arbor, MI: Ann Arbor Science Publishers, 1978.

Our Common Future. Brundtland Commission (The World Commission on Environment and Development). New York: Oxford University Press, 1987.

Oxford English Reference Dictionary (2nd ed.). Judy Pearsall and Bill Trumble, eds. Oxford: Oxford University Press, 1996.

Pacyna, Jozef M. and Elisabeth G. Pacyna. "An Assessment of Global and Regional Emissions of Trace Metals to the Atmosphere from Anthropogenic Sources Worldwide." *Environmental Review*, 9, 2001.

Page, Talbot. "On the Problem of Achieving Efficiency and Equity, Intergenerationally." *Land Economics*, 73(4), 1997.

Pakistan: Access to Justice Program: Report and Recommendation of the President. Manila: Asian Development Bank, 2001.

Panayotou, Theodore. *Green Markets: The Economics of Sustainable Development*. San Francisco: ICS Press for the International Center for Economic Growth, 1992.

_____. *Instruments of Change: Motivating and Financing Sustainable Development*. London: Earthscan Publications, 1998.

Pant, Amber. E-mail message, September 2003.

Pearce, David W. "Optional Prices for Sustainable Development." In *Economics, Growth and Sustainable Environment*. David Collard, David W. Pearce and David Ulph, eds. London: MacMillan Press, 1988.

Pearce, David W. and Giles D. Atkinson. "Capital Theory and the Measurement of Sustainable Development: An Indicator of "Weak" Sustainability." *Ecological Economics*, 8(2), 1993.

Pearce, David W., Anil Markandya, and Edward B. Barbier. *Blueprint for a Green Economy*. London: Earthscan Publications, 1989.

Pezzey, John. "Sustainable Development Concepts: An Economic Analysis." *World Bank Environment Paper No. 2*. Washington, D.C.: World Bank, 1992.

Philippine Constitution, 1987.

Plant, Roger. *Indigenous Peoples/Ethnic Minorities and Poverty Reduction: Pacific Region*. Manila: Asian Development Bank, 2002.

Plato. *Great Books of the Western World*. Robert Maynard Hutchins, ed. Chicago: Encyclopaedia Britannica, 1952.

Policy on Cooperation Between ADB and NGOs. Manila: Asian Development Bank, 1998.

Population Reference Bureau. *1991 World Population Data Sheet*. Washington, D.C.: Population Reference Bureau, 1991.

Postel, Sandra L., Gretchen C. Daily and Paul R. Ehrlich. "Human Appropriation of Renewable Fresh Water." *Science*, 271(5250), 9 February 1996.

Poverty and the Environment. United Kingdom: Department for International Development, 2000.

Rao, Pinninti K. *Sustainable Development: Economics and Policy*. Oxford: Blackwell, 2000.

Redclift, Michael R. *Sustainable Development: Exploring the Contradictions*. London: Methuen, 1987.

Reducing Poverty: Major Findings and Implications. Manila: Asian Development Bank, 1999.

Rees, Sir Martin J. *Our Final Hour—A Scientist's Warning: How Terror, Error and Environmental Disaster Threaten Humankind's Future in this Century – on Earth and Beyond*. New York: Basic Books, 2003.

Repetto, Robert C. *World Enough and Time: Successful Strategies for Resource Management*. New Haven, CT: Yale University Press, 1986.

Report of the International Law Commission on the Work of its 29th Session. UN Doc. A/32/10, 1977.

Report of the UN General Assembly Session, 1997.

Research Studies: The Law of Energy for Sustainable Development. Adrian J. Bradbook, ed. Cambridge: Cambridge University Press, 2005.

Ricardo, David. *The Principles of Political Economy and Taxation* (1817). Reprint by Dover Publications, New York, 2004.

Rio Declaration on Environment and Development, adopted at the United Nations Conference on Environment and Development, 31 ILM 874, 1992.

Robinson, Nicholas A. "The 'Ascent of Man': Legal Systems and the Discovery of an Environmental Ethic." *Pace Environmental Law Review*, 15, 1998. Quoted in *Capacity Building for Environmental Law in the Asian and Pacific Region* (2nd ed.), Vol. I. Donna G. Craig, Nicholas A. Robinson, and Kheng-Lian Koh, eds. Manila: Asian Development Bank, 2003.

Rogers, Peter. "Natural Resources in the 21st Century: Crisis, Conflict, and Compromise." Presented at *Erdpolitik: Programm für das 21 Jahrhundert*, Rathaus, Zürich, October 1998.

_____. "Population and Environmental Deterioration: A Comparison of Conventional Models and a New Paradigm." In *Science with a Human Face: In Honor of Roger Randall Revelle*. Robert Dorfman and Peter Rogers, eds. Cambridge, MA: Harvard University Press, 1997.

_____. "Water Crisis in the Middle East and North Africa." *Encyclopaedia Britannica 1998 Book of the Year*. Chicago: Encyclopaedia Britannica, 1998.

Rogers, Peter and Imad Kordab. "Conflict Resolution in Water Resources Management: Ronald Coase Meets Vilfredo Pareto." Division of Engineering and Applied Sciences, Working Paper, Harvard University, October 2004.

Rogers, Peter, Kazi F. Jalal, Bindu N. Lohani, Gene M. Owens, Chang-Chung Yu, Christian M. Dufournaud, and Jun Bi. *Measuring Environmental Quality in Asia*. Cambridge, MA: Harvard University Press, 1997.

Rosegrant, Mark W. and Peter B. R. Hazell. *Rural Asia Transformed: The Quiet Revolution*. Washington, D.C.: Asian Development Bank, IFPRI, 1999.

Rotterdam Convention on the Prior Informed Consent Procedure for Certain Hazardous Chemicals and Pesticides in International Trade, 1998.

Sachs, Jeffrey D. "The End of Poverty." *Time Magazine*, March 6, 2005.

_____. *The End of Poverty: Economic Possibilities for Our Time*. New York: Penguin Press, 2005.

Saldanha, Cedric D. and John F. Whittle. *Using the Logical Framework for Sector Analysis and Project Design: A User's Guide*. Manila: Asian Development Bank, 1998.

Salim, Emil. "The Challenge of Sustainable Consumption as seen from the South." *Symposium on Sustainable Consumption*, Oslo, Norway, 19–20 January 1994.

Sands, Philippe. "International Law in the Field of Sustainable Development." *The British Year Book of International Law*, 65, 1994.

_____. *Principles of International Environmental Law* (2nd ed.). Cambridge: Cambridge University Press, 2003.

Schneider, Stephen H. "Abrupt Non-linear Climate Change, Irreversibility and Surprise." *Global Environmental Change*, 14, 2004.

Schneider, Stephen H., Armin Rosencranz, and John O. Niles. *Climate Change Policy. A Survey*. Washington, D.C.: Island Press, 2002.

Schwab, Klaus, Michael E. Porter and Jeffrey D. Sachs, eds. *The Global Competitiveness Report 2001– 2002*. World Economic Forum, Geneva, Switzerland, 2001. New York and Oxford: Oxford University Press, 2002.

Schwebel, Stephen M. "The Effect of Resolutions of the U.N. General Assembly on Customary International Law." *American Society of International Law Proceedings*, 73, 1979.

Selden, Mark and Alvin Y. So, eds. *War and State Terrorism: The United States, Japan, and the Asia-Pacific in the Long Twentieth Century*. Lanham, MD: Rowman and Littlefield, 2004.

Sen, Amartya. *Development as Freedom*. New York: Anchor Books, 2000.

_____. "Editorial: Human Capital and Human Capability." *World Development*, 25(12), 1997.

_____. *Social Exclusion: Concept, Application, and Scrutiny*. Manila: Asian Development Bank, 2000.

Shafik, Nemat and Sushenjit Bandyopadhyay. "Economic Growth and Environmental Quality: Time Series and Cross-Country Evidence." *Background Paper for the World Development Report, Policy Research Working Paper Series, No. 904*. Washington D.C.: World Bank, June 1992.

Simmons, Andrew. "Trade Investment and Sustainable Development." In *Earth Summit 2002: A New Deal*. Felix Dodds, ed. London: Earthscan Publications, 2000.

Simon, Julian L. *The Ultimate Resource*. Princeton, NJ: Princeton University Press, 1981.

Smith, Adam. *An Inquiry into the Nature and Causes of The Wealth of Nations* (originally published in 1776). Edwin Cannan, ed. Chicago: University of Chicago Press, 1976.

Smith, Douglas V. and Kazi F. Jalal. *Sustainable Development in Asia*. Manila: Asian Development Bank, 2000.

Smith, H. Jesse. "The Shape We're In: Introduction to Special Issue on the State of the Planet." *Science*, 302(5648), 14 November 2003.

Socolow, Robert H. "Can We Bury Global Warming?" *Scientific American*, 293(1), July 2005.

Solow, Robert M. "A Contribution to the Theory of Economic Growth." *Quarterly Journal of Economics*, 70(1), 1956.

_____. "Intergenerational Equity and Exhaustible Resources." *Review of Economic Studies*, 41, Symposium on the Economics of Exhaustible Resources, 1974.

_____. "Sustainability: An Economist's Perspective." The Eighteenth J. Seward Johnson Lecture, Marine Policy Center, Woods Hole Oceanographic Institution, 1991.

Speth, James Gustave. *Red Sky at Night: America and the Crisis of the Global Environment*. New Haven, CT: Yale University Press, 2004.

Status of Ratification of Selected Multilateral Environmental Agreements. Global Judges Symposium on Sustainable Development and the Role of Law, Johannesburg, South Africa, August 2002. Policy Series 6, August 2002.

Statute of the International Court of Justice, 26 June 1945.

Stavins, Robert N. "Comments on "Lethal Model 2: The Limits to Growth Revisited" by William D. Nordhaus." *Brookings Papers on Economic Activity*, 2, 1992.

Stiglitz, Joseph E. "Two Principles for the Next Round or, How to Bring Developing Countries in from the Cold." *The World Economy*, 23, 2000.

_____. *Globalization and Its Discontents*. London: Allen Lane, Penguin Press, 2002.

Stockholm Action Plan, 1972.

Stockholm Convention on Persistent Organic Pollutants, 2004.

Stockholm Declaration, 1972.

Strong, Maurice. "Required Global Changes: Close Linkages Between Environment and Development." In *Change: Threat or Opportunity*. Uner Kirdar, ed. New York: United Nations, 1992.

Stumbling Toward Sustainability. Dernbach, John C., ed. Washington, D.C.: Environmental Law Institute, 2002.

"Summary of Proposals in Reforming the United Nations." In *Our Global Neighborhood: The Report of the Commission on Global Governance*. Oxford: Oxford University Press, 1995.

Summers, Lawrence H. "A New Framework for Multilateral Development Policy." (Remarks to the Council on Foreign Relations, New York, NY.) *US Treasury News*, 20 March 1999.

Supporting Sustainable Development in Asia and the Pacific. CD ROM, Asian Development Bank, 2003.

A Survey of Sustainable Development: Social and Economic Dimensions. Jonathan M. Harris, Timothy A. Wise, Kevin P. Gallagher, and Neva R. Goodwin, eds. Washington, D.C.: Island Press, 2001.

Susskind, Lawrence, Sarah McKearnan, and Jennifer Thomas-Larmer. *The Consensus Building Handbook: A Comprehensive Guide to Reaching Agreement*. Thousand Oaks, CA: SAGE Publications, 1999.

Sustainable Development Reporting: Striking the Balance. Geneva, Switzerland: World Business Council for Sustainable Development, 2002.

Technological Trajectories and the Human Environment. Jesse H. Ausubel and H. Dale Langford, eds. Washington, D.C.: The National Academies Press, 1997.

Technology and Environment. Jesse H. Ausubel and Hedy E. Sladovich, eds. Washington, D.C.: The National Academies Press, 1989.

Technology Trends and National Policy. Washington, D.C.: National Research Council/U.S. Government Printing Office, 1937.

Thomas, William A. *Indicators of Environmental Quality.* New York: Plenum Press, 1972.

The Tobin Tax: Coping with Financial Volatility. Mahbub ul Haq, Inge Kaul, and Isabelle Grunberg, eds. Oxford and New York: Oxford University Press, 1996.

Townes, Charles. "On the Laser and the Fallability of Scientists." Washington D.C.: Cosmos Club Bulletin, October 1991.

Understanding Nonprofit Organizations: Governance, Leadership, and Management. J. Steven Ott, ed. Boulder, CO: Westview Press, 2001.

United Nations Charter, 1945.

United Nations Doc. A/CONE.151/26, Vol. I, 1992.

United Nations Population Division. *Population Challenges and Development Goals.* UN Department of Economic and Social Affairs, Population Studies Series No. 248, October, 2005.

United Nations Security Council Resolution 320, 1972.

United Nations Security Council Resolution 1373, adopted on September 28, 2001, concerning "terrorist attacks ... on 11 September 2001."

United States Constitution, 1787.

Universal Declaration of Human Rights, 1948.

Vienna Convention for the Protection of the Ozone Layer, 1985.

Vienna Convention on the Law of Treaties, 1969.

"Vital Signs." *World Water Institute Annual Report*, 2001.

von Weizsäcker, Ernst Ulrich, Amory B. Lovins, and L. Hunter Lovins. *Faktor Vier Doppelter Wohlstand, halbierter Naturverbrauch.* München: Droemer Knaur, 1995.

Vörösmarty, Charles J., Pamela Green, Joseph Salisbury, and Richard B. Lammers. "Global Water Resources: Vulnerability from Climate Change and Population Growth." *Science*, 289(5477), 2000.

Waggoner, Paul E. "How Much Land Can Ten Billion People Spare for Nature?" In *Technological Trajectories and the Human Environment.* Jesse H. Ausubel and H. Dale Langford, eds. Washington, D.C.: The National Academies Press, 1997.

Water in Crisis: A Guide to the World's Fresh Water Resouces. Peter H. Gleick, ed. New York: Oxford University Press, 1993.

Webster's II New Riverside University Dictionary. Boston: The Riverside Publishing Company, 1984.

Where Is the Wealth of Nations? Washington, D.C.: World Bank, 2006.

Whiteman, Marjorie M., ed. *Digest of International Law*, Vol. I. Washington, D.C.: U.S. Government Printing Office, 1963.

Wilkinson, Clive R., ed. *Status of Coral Reefs of the World: 2004*. Townsville, Australia: Australian Institute of Marine Science, 2004.

Willard, Bob. *The Sustainability Advantage: Seven Business Case Benefits of a Triple Bottom Line*. Gabriola Island, B.C.: New Society Publishers, 2002.

Wilson, Edward O. *The Diversity of Life*. Cambridge, MA: Belknap Press, 1992.

Womack, James P. and Daniel T. Jones. *Lean Thinking: Banish Waste and Create Wealth in Your Corporation*. New York: Simon & Schuster, 1996.

Women and the Environment. United Nations Environment Programme and Women's Environment and Development Organizations, 2004.

Women in the Republic of Maldives. Manila: Asian Development Bank, 2001.

"The World According to Corporate Social Responsibility." *The Economist*, January 2005.

World Bank. *Findings, Africa Region*. Washington, D.C.: World Bank, 1995.

World Bank. *World Development Report 2000/2001: Attacking Poverty*. Washington, D.C.: World Bank, 2001.

The World Conservation Strategy. Gland, Switzerland: IUCN, WWF and UNEP, 1980.

World Resources 1998-99. A Guide to the Global Environment: Environmental Change and Human Health. New York: Oxford University Press, 1998.

Yergin, Daniel and Martin Hillenbrand. *Global Insecurity: A Strategy for Energy and Economic Renewal*. Boston: Houghton Mifflin, 1982.

_____. *Global Insecurity: Beyond Energy Future: A Strategy for Political and Economic Survival in the 1980's*. New York: Penguin Books, 1983.

Yunus, Muhammad. *Banker to the Poor: Micro-Lending and the Battle Against World Poverty*. New York: PublicAffairs, 2003.

WEBSITES

Arriens, Wouter L., Jeremy Berkoff, Jeremy Bird, and Paul Mosley, eds. (1996). *Towards Effective Water Policy in the Asian and Pacific Region, Vol. I. Overview of Issues and Recommendations*. Asian Development Bank. Available at: http://www.adb.org/Publications/product.asp?sku=010796

Asian Development Bank. Available at: http://www.adb.org

Barbier, Edward B. (1987). "The Concept of Sustainable Economic Development." *Environmental Conservation*, 14. Excerpted definition of sustainable development available at: http://www.aocweb.org/em/Portals/2/ MIT%20Definitions.pdf

Brown, Lester (2004). "Data for Chapter 2: Stopping at Seven Billion." In *Outgrowing the Earth: The Food Security Challenge in an Age of Falling Water Tables and Rising Temperatures*. Earth Policy Institute. Available at: http://www.earth-policy.org/Books/Out/ch2data_index.htm

Cavanagh, John and Sarah Anderson (2004). "World's Billionaires Take a Hit, But Still Soar." Institute for Policy Studies. Available at: http://www.ips-dc.org/global_econ/billionaires.htm

Cobb, Clifford, Mark Glickman and Craig Cheslog (2001). "The Genuine Progress Indicator: 2000 Update." Available at: http://www.redefiningprogress.org/publications/2001/2000_gpi_update.pdf

Convention on Biological Diversity (2004). Special Issue on Alien Species. Available at: http://www. cbd.int/ programmes/cross-cutting/alien/default.asp

Dietz, Simon, Eric Neumayer, and Indra De Soysa (January 2006). "Corruption, the Resource Curse and Genuine Saving." Available at SSRN: http://ssrn.com/abstract=545502

The Earth Charter Initiative. Available at: http://www.earthcharter.org/

Ecological Footprint Quiz. Available at: http://www.myfootprint.org/

Economic Development Futures Web Journal (June 16, 2004). "The World's 7.7 Million Millionaires." Available at: http://don-iannone.com/edfutures/2004/06/worlds-77-million-millionaires.html

Emission Standards > European Union > Cars and Light Trucks. Available at: http://www.dieselnet. com/ standards/eu/ld.php

Environmental Data Science and Systems, Oak Ridge National Laboratory. Available at: http://www. esd.ornl. gov/research/environ_data_systems/index.shtml

Fajnzylber, Pablo, Daniel Lederman, and Norman Loayza (1998). *Determinants of Crime Rates in Latin America and the World: An Empirical Assessment.* The World Bank. Available at: http:// povlibrary.worldbank.org/ library/view/12879

FAO (1997). "FAOSTAT Statistical Database." Available at: http://faostat.fao.org/

FAO (2004). "Food Outlook No. 2." Available at: http://www.fao.org/docrep/006/j2518e/j2518e00.htm

Farm Subsidy Database, Environmental Working Group. Available at: http://www.ewg.org/farm/

Genuine Progess Indicator. Sustainability Indicators Program, Redefining Progress. Available at: http://www. redefiningprogress.org/projects/gpi/

Global Environment Facility. Available at: http://www.gefweb.org

Holdren, John (2006). Syllabus for ENR-100 course on "Environmental and Resource Science for Policy." Available at: http://ksgnotes1.harvard.edu/degreeprog/Syllabus.nsf/0/ 4D84012EB9D6C75E8525721E005 6716C/$FILE/enr100_syllabus_2006_9-12-06v3.pdf

Human Development Report 1990, UNDP. "Concept and Measurement of Human Development." Available at http://hdr.undp.org/reports/global/1990/en/

Human Development Report 1992, UNDP. "Global Dimensions of Human Development." Available at: http:// hdr.undp.org/reports/global/1992/en/

Human Development Report 1999, UNDP. "Globalization with a Human Face." Available at: http:// hdr.undp. org/reports/global/1999/en/

Human Development Report 2005, UNDP. "Economic Performance." Available at: http://hdr.undp. org/ statistics/data/indic/indic_137_1_1.html

Human Development Report 2006, UNDP. "Human Development Index." Available at: http://hdr. undp.org/ hdr2006/statistics/indicators/1.html

IGACtivities Newsletter, Issue No. 20, March 2000. Available at: http://www.igac.noaa.gov/newsletter/ igac20/ Mar_2000_IGAC_20.pdf

IISDnet (1995). "Sustainable Development Indicators ... Selected Sources." Marlene Roy, International Institute of Sustainable Development. Available at: http://www.iisd.org/ic/info/ss9504. htm

International Finance Corporation, World Bank Group. Available at: http://www.ifc.org

McFarquhar, Alister. "Environment Valuation, Project Appraisal and Political Consensus in the Third World." *Planning & Markets*. Available at: http://www-pam.usc.edu/volume4/v4i1a3s1.html

Merrill Lynch and Capgemini (2007). *World Wealth Report 2007*. 11th Annual World Wealth Report for 2006. Available at: http://www.ml.com/index.asp?id=7695_7696_8149_74412_79272_79918

Miller, George A. (1956) "The Magical Number Seven, Plus or Minus Two: Some Limits on Our Capacity for Processing Information." *Psychological Review*, 63(2). Available at: http://www.musanim.com/miller1956/

"The Most Deadly 100 Natural Disasters of the 20th Century." Available at: http://www.disastercenter.com/ disaster/TOP100K.html

Murcott, Susan (1997). "Sustainable Development: A Meta-Review of Definitions, Principles, Criteria Indicators, Conceptual Frameworks and Information Systems." AAAS Annual Conference, IIASA Symposium on Sustainability Indicators, Seattle, WA, Feb 13–18, 1997. Available at: http://www.aocweb. org/em/Portals/2/MIT%20Definitions.pdf

Murray, Christopher J. L. and Alan D. Lopez, eds. (1996). *The Global Burden of Disease: A Comprehensive Assessment of Mortality and Disability from Diseases, Injuries, and Risk Factors in 1990 and Projected to 2020*. Cambridge, MA: Harvard University Press. Published on behalf of the World Health Organization and the World Bank. Executive summary in seven sections available at: http://www.hsph.harvard.edu/ organizations/bdu/GBDseries.html

Negative Population Growth (2004). "Total Midyear World Population 1950–2050." Available at: http:// www.npg.org/facts/world_pop_year.htm

Ocean Technical Services, Inc. Available at: http://www.oceantech.com/

Salim, Emil (1994). "The Challenge of Sustainable Consumption as seen from the South." *Symposium on Sustainable Consumption*, Oslo, Norway, 19–20 January 1994. Excerpt available at: http://www.iisd.org/ susprod/principles.htm

Shah, Anup (2006). "Causes of Poverty: Poverty Facts and Stats." Available at: http://www.globalissues.org/ Traderelated/Facts.asp

Strong, Maurice (1992). "Required Global Changes: Close Linkages Between Environment and Development." In *Change: Threat or Opportunity*. Uner Kirdar, ed. New York: United Nations. Excerpt available at: http://www.aocweb.org/em/Portals/2/MIT%20Definitions.pdf

Sustainable Development Indicators. Available at: http://www.iisd.org/ic/info/ss9504.htm

Turn the Tide, New American Dream. Available at: http://www.newdream.org/cnad/user/turn_the_tide.php

United Nations (2005). *The Millennium Development Goals Report 2005*. Available at: http://www.un.org/docs/ summit2005/MDGBook.pdf

UN Charter. Available at: http://www.un.org/aboutun/charter/index.html

UN Millennium Development Goals. Available at: http://www.un.org/millenniumgoals/

UN Organizational Chart. Available at: http://www.un.org/aboutun/chart.html

UN Population Division (2005). "World Population Prospects: The 2004 Revision." Available at: http://www. un.org/esa/population/publications/WPP2004/wpp2004.htm

US Department of Commerce, Bureau of Economic Analysis (2005). Available at: http://www.bea. gov

Water For All: The Water Policy of ADB. Manila: Asian Development Bank, 2001. Available at: http:// adb.org/ Documents/Policies/Water/default.asp?p=wtrrefs

World Bank (2001). "Voices of the Poor." Available at: http://go.worldbank.org/HIN8746X10

World Bank (2004). *Beyond Economic Growth: An Introduction to Sustainable Development* (2nd ed.). Soubbotina, Tatyana P., World Bank. Available at: http://www.worldbank.org/depweb/english/ beyond/beyondco/ beg_all.pdf

World Bank (2007). "World Development Indicators 2007." Available at: http://go.worldbank.org/ 3JU2HA 60D0

World Bank Group's Energy Program (2002). "Poverty Reduction, Sustainability and Selectivity." Available at: http://siteresources.worldbank.org/INTENERGY/Publications/20269216/ energybrochure.pdf

World Conference on Human Rights (June 1993). "Vienna Declaration and Programme of Action." Available at: http://www.unhchr.ch/huridocda/huridoca.nsf/(Symbol)/A.CONF.157.23.En?Open Document

World Resources Institute (1998). "Population Growth: Stabilization." Available at: http://pubs.wri. org/pubs_ content_text.cfm?ContentID=2069

Zubair, Lareef (2005). "Scientific Background on the Indian Ocean Earthquake and Tsunami." Available at: http://iri.columbia.edu/~lareef/tsunami/

INDEX

Club of Rome, 20, 373, 386, 396
Coase, Ronald, 23–5, 277, 298, 391, 399
Coasian solution, 277–8
Cobb, Charles W., 31, 373, 391
Cobb, Clifford, 302–3, 391
Cobb-Douglas production function, 31, 391
Cobb, John B., Jr., 392
coefficient of variation, 137
Commission on Environmental Law of IUCN, 207,
210, 212
Commission on Sustainable Development, 192–3,
348–9
Community Development Carbon Fund, 334, 341
comprehensive indices of environmental quality, of
Inhaber, 120–1; of Rogers et al., 123–32
Conference of the International Law Association
(New Delhi, 2002), 196, 215
consensus building, 219, 230–4; handbook, 232, 400
consumer price index (CPI), 16, 292, 301
consumer surplus, 270, 272, 284
consumption patterns, 48, 65–71, 94, 342, 354, 379
consumption, per capita, 32, 67–9, 374
contingent valuation method, 283
Convention on Biological Diversity, 190, 204, 209–10,
391
Convention on Migratory Species (Bonn, 1979), 204,
208, 210, 391
Convention on Trade in Endangered Species
(Washington, DC, 1973), 208, 210, 212
cooking stove improvement project in the PRC, 80
COR. See cost of remediation
cornucopians, 20–1, 24, 32, 383
cost of remediation (COR), 16, 103, 116–7, 123–6,
130, 132
Costanza, Robert, 101–2, 306, 312, 392, 402
Council on Environmental Quality (CEQ), 16, 108,
140–5
CPI. See consumer price index
Craig, Donna G., 188, 207, 391, 398
cumulative impacts, 177

Daly and Cobb, 392
Daly, Herman E., 23, 27, 390, 392
Dalton, Robert E., 203–4, 392
D'Amato, Anthony, 186
Damrosch, Lori F., 208–9, 395
Davide, Hilario, Jr., 188
DDT (dichlorodiphenyltrichloroethane), 16, 55
death rates from infectious disease, 173–4
Declaration of the International Law Association
(New Delhi, 2002), 196–8, 201, 215, 392
Declaration of the United Nations Conference on
the Human Environment in 1972, 184
Declaration on the Establishment of a New
International Economic Order, 184, 190, 392

defensive expenditures, 23, 26–7
deforestation, causes of, 167–8
delayed impacts, 176
demand curves, 267–270, 272, 284
Department for International Development, UK
(DFID), 16, 52
depletion of resources, 50–1, 142, 208, 302–5,
310–12, 336–8
Depression of 1930, 261
Dernbach, John C., 193, 392, 400
desertification, 204, 238–9, 331, 356
developing countries, 48, 51, 53–4, 61–2, 67, 71–2,
75, 96, 98–9, 104, 108, 146, 159, 161, 176–7,
179, 182, 197, 205, 210, 219, 223, 226–9, 235–6,
240, 251, 289, 300, 314–5, 320–5, 328–34,
339–40, 343, 347, 350–5, 358, 364–7, 371,
377–8, 381–2, 391, 396, 404
development diamonds, 127–30, 251–2
development finance institution (DFI), 16, 228, 234,
241, 250–1, 346, 353, 366
DFI. See development finance institution
DFID. See Department for International
Development, UK
Diamond, Jared, 21, 392
Dickey-Lincoln Dam project, 146
Diehl, Paul F., 214, 393, 395
Digest of International Law, 401
Digest for U.S. Practice in International Law, 392
direct use values, 284
disaster management, 63–5, 227, 320, 329, 333, 353
disposable personal income, 300
distribution of resources, 65, 76–9, 103–4, 133–4
Dixon, John A., 13, 15, 260, 262, 265, 276, 281–2, 284,
300, 392
DNA (deoxyribonucleic acid), 16, 88
Do No Harm Policies, 316, 342
dose response curve, 112
Dower, Nigel, 185, 393
Dowling, J. Malcolm, 13, 393
Dufournaud, Christian M., 393
durability of wealth concept, 310

Earth Charter, 212–3, 367–8
Earth Summit (Rio de Janeiro, 1992), 7, 49, 159, 351,
364–5, 392, 399
ecological footprint, 70–1, 402
ecological threshold, 24, 176
economic benefits, as weighting indicator, 116–7
economic dimension, 10, 260 ff, 400
Economic Development Futures Web Journal, 48,
402
economic internal rate of return (EIRR), 16, 287–8,
292–3
economic sustainability, 162–3, 278, 292
economic value, 282 ff, 372–3

institutional safeguards, 162–3
Interagency Committee on Sustainable Development
    (IACSD), 346, 348
Inter-American Development Bank (IADB), 16, 21,
    146, 171, 314
intergenerational equity, 187–8, 211, 382, 400
International Atomic Energy Agency (IAEA), 348, 350
International Bank for Reconstruction and
    Development (IBRD), 16, 315, 334, 342, 350
International Centre for the Settlement of
    Investment Disputes, 342, 350
International Conference on Fresh Water (Bonn,
    2001), 161
International Conference on Financing for
    Development (Mexico, 2002), 161
International Court of Justice (ICJ), 16, 185–6, 189,
    193–6, 350
international custom, 186–7, 189, 194, 200, 399;
    articulation of, 189
International Development Association, 342, 350
international environmental law, 158, 184, 189, 196,
    202, 210
International Federation of Red Cross and Red
    Crescent, 63
International Finance Corporation, 342, 350
International Fund for Agricultural Development
    (IFAD), 314, 346, 348, 350
International Goals. See Millennium Development
    Goals (MDG)
International Labour Organization (ILO), 16, 242–3,
    346, 348, 350, 394
international law, 39, 184–96, 198, 200–1, 204–5, 207,
    213–5, 242–3, 391–6, 398–9, 401; role of judicial
    decisions in, 187–8; sources of, 186–8
International Monetary Fund (IMF), 16, 162, 226, 350
International Red Cross, 63–4
interquartile range, 135
interval scale, 111
investment loans, 314–15
involuntary resettlement, 10, 163, 219, 239–44, 257,
    316, 318
IPs. See indigenous peoples
irreversible damage, 98, 177
IUCN. See World Conservation Union, The
IUCN Academy of Environmental Law, 210, 395
Ivanova, Maria, 202–3, 393

Jalal, Kazi F., 23, 45, 51, 68–9, 73, 80–1, 90, 354, 358,
    399–400
Jefferson, Thomas, 210–1
Johannesburg Commitment on Sustainable
    Development, 162, 355–6
Johannesburg Principles on the Role of Law and
    Sustainable Development, 213, 395
Jones, Daniel T., 73

Kennedy, Scott, 13–5
Keohane, Robert O., 202, 395
Keyfitz hypothesis, 377–8
Keyfitz, Nathan, 374, 374–9, 395
Keynes, John Maynard, 261–2
Khan, Herman, 21, 395
Kile, Molly, 13–5
Kiss and Shelton, 158, 185–6, 189, 191–3, 201, 210,
    353, 395
Kiss, Alexandre, 158, 185–6, 189, 191–4, 196, 198,
    201, 210, 215, 353, 395
Kissinger, Henry, 92
Koh, Kheng-Lian, 13, 188, 207, 391, 398
Ku, Charlotte, 214, 393, 395
Kuznets Curve, 125, 176, 333–4, 374, 395
Kuznets, Simon, 23–4, 395
Kyoto Protocol, 94, 203, 330, 339–41, 377, 395

labor and capital, 260–1
Lake Superior, 141, 149–50
Lâm, Maivân Clech, 243, 395
Lammers, R. B., 401
land quality index, 120–1
land values, 282–3
land, labor and capital, 260
Laszlo, Chris, 347, 361–2, 395
Lederman, D., 78, 402
Lenoir, Rene, 245
Leontief, Wassily, 301, 396
Leopold, Aldo, 212
Leopold, Luna B., 147, 396
Leopold Matrix, 147–8
less developed countries, 109, 161
life cycle analysis, 32–9, 150
life expectancy at birth, 121–2, 127, 130, 174–5, 251
Loayza, N., 78, 402
Lohani, Bindu N., 150, 393, 396, 399
Lomborg, Bjørn, 21, 172–3, 175, 382–3, 396
Lorenz curve, 253, 256–7
Lovins, Amory, 394
Lovins, L. Hunter, 394
Lowe, Vaughn, 196, 396
Lutz, Ernst, 44, 301, 394, 396–7

macroeconomic policies, 303, 337–8
Malone, Linda A., 142, 144–6, 396
Malthus, Thomas Robert, 20–2, 28, 31, 262, 372–3,
    383, 386, 396
mangrove forests, 168–9, 227, 280–2
market failure, 47, 60–2, 278–80
Marx, Karl, 21, 260–2, 373
Marxism, 261–2
materials flow, 92–4, 371
maternal health, development goals for, 181
matrices, environmental baseline, 147–8

342–3, 358, 360–2, 368, 370, 381–3, 387–8, 390, 392–3, 398, 400–1; concept of, 42–6; life cycle analysis, examples of, 32–9; nine ways to achieve, 23–26; simple rule for, 27; weak and strong, 28

sustainability indicators, 103, 132

sustainable development, concept or principle?, 193–201; determinants of, 65–79; ecological, economic and socio-cultural approaches to, 43–4; environmental law and, 210–5; factors governing, 47–65; first formal treaty to refer to, 211; four principles of, 162; indicators for, 106 ff; legal status of, 195; links to environment and poverty, 50–2; operational criteria for, 45–6; see also environmental indicators, triple bottom line

Sustainable Development in Asia, 80–1, 400

sustainable economic growth, 43, 166, 317

sustainable environment, 278, 300

sustainable logging, 357

sustainable social net product (SSNP), 26–7

Sweetser, Anne, 13, 218, 396

tangible products, 282

Tangley, Laura, 100, 390

technology, per capita, 31–2, 38–9

Thomas, W. A., 106–7, 401

three "E's", the, 141, 260, 288. See also triple bottom line

tidal power, 95

Tobin tax, 62, 226, 364, 366, 401

top 10 lists, 326

total suspended particulates (TSP), 17, 117, 124, 153

traditional fuel, 326–7

traffic patterns, 149

Train, Russell, 141

transaction costs, 25, 72, 278–9

transport systems, latent, 150

treaty ratification, in US, 203–4; outside the US, 204–5

triple bottom line, 39, 42, 45, 71, 106, 260, 288, 297, 341, 358–9, 361, 401

trichloroethylene, 150

TSP. See total suspended particulates

Tuna/Dolphin dispute, 207–8, 353, 387

UN. See United Nations

UNCED. See UN Conference on Environment and Development

UN Charter, 198

UNCHE. See UN Conference on the Human Environment

UN Children's Fund (UNICEF), 348, 350

UN Commission for Sustainable Development (UNCSD), 346, 348–9

UN Conference on Environment and Development (UNCED), 17, 45, 98, 159, 184, 190, 210, 238, 328, 346–7, 365, 398; see also Earth Summit, Rio Conference

UN Conference on the Human Environment (UNCHE) (Stockholm, 1972), 7, 17, 42, 158–9, 162, 184, 190, 202–5, 351, 400; see also Stockholm Declaration

UN Conference on Trade and Development (UNCTAD), 348, 350–1

UNCSD. See UN Commission for Sustainable Development

UNCTAD. See UN Conference on Trade and Development

UN Department of Economic and Social Affairs (UN/DESA), 346, 348, 350

UN/DESA. See UN Department of Economic and Social Affairs

UN Development Programme (UNDP), 17, 47–9, 121, 219, 228, 251, 300, 307, 312, 332, 346, 348, 350, 364, 366, 394, 402–3

UN Disaster Relief Organization, 63

UNDP. See UN Development Programme

UN Economic and Social Commission for Asia and the Pacific (ESCAP), 16, 62, 350

UN Educational, Scientific and Cultural Organization (UNESCO), 21, 213, 346, 348, 350

UN Environment Programme (UNEP), 17, 44, 158, 175, 184, 202–3, 205, 207, 209–10, 215, 235, 237–8, 332, 346, 348–51, 356, 394, 402

UNEP. See UN Environment Programme

UNESCO. See UN Education Scientific and Cultural Organization

UNFPA. See UN Population Fund

UN Framework Convention on Climate Change, 190, 201, 204, 215

UN General Assembly, 22, 158–61, 177, 181, 184, 188–90, 244, 346, 348–51, 354, 356–7, 391–2, 394, 398–9

UNICEF. See UN Children's Fund

UN Industrial Development Organization (UNIDO), 21, 350

United Nations (UN), 16–7, 21, 30, 42, 44, 47, 53–4, 63, 89, 158, 184, 189–90, 203–4, 208, 236, 327, 332, 346, 348–51, 365, 391–5, 398, 400–2, 404

United States Agency for International Development (USAID), 17, 52, 146

UN Population Division, 54, 84, 404

UN Population Fund (UNFPA), 21, 53–4, 350

UN Report of the International Law Commission, 189, 398

UN Security Council, 190, 348–51, 353, 401

urbanization, 51, 84, 86–7, 218, 304, 381

urban statistical models, 148

USAID. See United States Agency for International Development

US Council on Environmental Quality, 16, 108